P9-EMQ-304

CLICK HERE TO KILL EVERYBODY

CLICK HERE TO KILL EVERYBODY

SECURITY AND SURVIVAL IN
A HYPER-CONNECTED WORLD

Bruce Schneier

W. W. NORTON & COMPANY
INDEPENDENT PUBLISHERS SINCE 1923
NEW YORK   LONDON

For information about permission to reproduce selections from this book, write to
Permissions, W. W. Norton & Company, Inc., 500 Fifth Avenue, New York, NY 10110

For information about special discounts for bulk purchases, please contact
W. W. Norton Special Sales at specialsales@wwnorton.com or 800-233-4830

Manufacturing by LSC Communications Harrisonburg
Book design by Daniel Lagin
Production manager: Julia Druskin

Library of Congress Cataloging-in-Publication Data

Names: Schneier, Bruce, 1963– author.
Title: Click here to kill everybody : security and survival in a
    hyper-connected world / Bruce Schneier.
Description: First edition. | New York : W.W. Norton & Company, [2018] |
    Includes bibliographical references and index.
Identifiers: LCCN 2018026844 | ISBN 9780393608885 (hardcover)
Subjects: LCSH: Internet—Security measures. | Internet—Safety measures. |
    Internet—Government policy. | Computer crimes.
Classification: LCC TK5105.8855 .S36 2018 | DDC 005.8—dc23
LC record available at https://lccn.loc.gov/2018026844

W. W. Norton & Company, Inc., 500 Fifth Avenue, New York, N.Y. 10110
www.wwnorton.com

W. W. Norton & Company Ltd., 15 Carlisle Street, London W1D 3BS

1 2 3 4 5 6 7 8 9 0

For Arlene, with best wishes

CONTENTS

CLICK HERE TO KILL EVERYBODY

INTRODUCTION

Everything Is Becoming a Computer

Consider these three incidents, and their implications.

Scenario one: In 2015, two security researchers took over the controls of a Jeep Cherokee. They did it from ten miles away through the vehicle's Internet-connected entertainment system. A video shows the driver's terrified expression as he's driving on a highway, powerless while the hackers turn on the air-conditioning, change the radio station, turn on the wipers, and eventually kill the engine. Since this was a demonstration and not a murder attempt, the researchers did not take control of the brakes or the steering, but they could have.

This isn't a one-off trick. Hackers have demonstrated vulnerabilities in several automobile models. They hacked in through the diagnostics port. They hacked in through the DVD player. They hacked in through the OnStar navigation system and the computers embedded in the tires.

Airplanes are vulnerable, too. There's been nothing as vivid as the Jeep demonstration, but security researchers have been making claims that the avionics of commercial airplanes are vulnerable via the entertainment system and through air-to-ground communications systems. For years, airplane manufacturers denied that hacking an airplane was possible. Finally, in 2017, the US Department of Homeland Security demonstrated a remote hack of a Boeing 757. No details were provided.

Scenario two: In 2016, hackers—presumably Russian—remotely detonated a cyberweapon named CrashOverride at the Pivnichna high-voltage power substation near Kiev in Ukraine, shutting it down.

The CrashOverride attack was different from the cyberattack that targeted the Prykarpattyaoblenergo control center in Western Ukraine the previous year. That attack also caused a blackout, but it was a more manual attack. There, the attackers—again, presumably Russian—gained access to the system via a malware backdoor, then remotely took control of the center's computers and turned the power off. (One of the station operators recorded a video of it happening.) CrashOverride, on the other hand, did it all automatically.

In the end, the people who received their power from the Pivnichna substation got lucky. Technicians there took the plant offline and manually restored power an hour or so later. It's unclear whether similar US plants have the same manual overrides, let alone staff with the skill to use them.

CrashOverride was a military weapon. It was modularly designed, and could easily be reconfigured for a variety of targets: gas pipelines, water treatment plants, and so on. It had a variety of other "payloads" that weren't even fired off in the Ukraine attack. It could have repeatedly cycled the substation power on and off, physically damaging the equipment and shutting down power for days or weeks. In the middle of a Ukrainian winter, this would be fatal for many people. And while this weapon was fired as part of a government operation, it was also a test of capability. In recent years, Russian hackers penetrated more than 20 US power stations, often accessing critical systems but without causing damage; these were also tests of capability.

Scenario three: Over a weekend in 2017, someone hacked 150,000 printers around the world. The hacker wrote a program that automatically detected common insecure printers and had them repeatedly print ASCII art and taunting messages. This kind of thing happens regularly, and it's basically vandalism. Earlier in the same year, printers at several US universities were hacked to print anti-Semitic flyers.

We haven't yet seen this kind of attack against 3D printers, but there's no reason to believe they are not similarly vulnerable. Hacking one would still only result in expense and annoyance, but the threat level changes dramatically when we consider bio-printers. These are still in their infancy, but the potential is that viruses customized to attack individual patients' cancers or other illnesses could be synthesized and assembled by automated equipment.

Imagine a future where those bio-printers are common in hospitals, pharmacies, and doctors' offices. A hacker with remote-access capabilities and the proper printing instructions could force a bio-printer to print a killer virus. He could force the printer to print lots of it, or force many printers to print smaller batches. If the virus could spread widely enough, infect enough people, and be persistent enough, we might have a worldwide pandemic on our hands.

"Click here to kill everybody," indeed.

Why are these scenarios possible? A 1998 car wasn't vulnerable to people miles away taking over its controls. Neither was a 1998 power substation. The current models are vulnerable, and the future bio-printer will be vulnerable, because at their core they are computers. Everything is becoming vulnerable in this way because everything is becoming a computer. More specifically, a computer on the Internet.

Your oven is a computer that makes things hot. Your refrigerator is a computer that keeps things cold. Your camera is a computer with a lens and a shutter. An ATM is a computer with money inside. And modern light bulbs are computers that shine brightly when someone—or some other computer—flips a power switch.

Your car used to be a mechanical device with some computers in it. Now, it is a 20- to 40-computer distributed system with four wheels and an engine. When you step on the brake, it might feel as if you're physically stopping the car, but in reality you're just sending an electronic signal to the brakes; there's no longer a mechanical connection between the pedal and the brake pads.

Your phone became a powerful computer in 2007, when the iPhone was introduced.

We carry those smartphones everywhere. And "smart" is the prefix we use for these newly computerized things that are on the Internet, meaning that they can collect, use, and communicate data to operate. A television is smart when it constantly collects data about your usage habits to optimize your experience.

Soon, smart devices will be embedded in our bodies. Modern pacemakers and insulin pumps are smart. Pills are becoming smart. Smart contact lenses will not only display information that is based on what you see, but monitor your glucose levels and diagnose your glaucoma. Fitness trackers are smart and increasingly capable of sensing our bodily states.

Objects are also getting smart. You can buy a smart collar for your dog and a smart toy for your cat. You can buy a smart pen, a smart toothbrush, a smart coffee cup, a smart sex toy, a smart Barbie doll, a smart tape measure, and a smart sensor for your plants. You can even buy a smart motorcycle helmet that will automatically call an ambulance and text your family if you have an accident.

We're already seeing the beginnings of smart homes. The virtual assistant Alexa and its cousins listen for your commands and respond. There are smart thermostats, smart power outlets, and smart appliances. You can buy a smart bathroom scale and a smart toilet. You can buy smart light bulbs and a smart hub to control them. You can buy a smart door lock that will allow you to give repair technicians and delivery people a onetime code to enter your home, and a smart bed that senses your sleeping patterns and diagnoses your sleep disorders.

In workplaces, many of those same smart devices are networked together with surveillance cameras, sensors that detect customer movements, and everything else. Smart systems in buildings will provide more efficient lighting, elevator operation, climate control, and other services.

Cities are starting to embed smart sensors in roads, streetlights, and sidewalk squares, as well as smart energy grids and smart transportation networks. Soon, cities will be able to control your appliances and other home devices to optimize energy use. Networks of smart driverless cars will automatically route themselves to where they're needed, minimizing energy use in the process. Sensors and controls in the streets will better regulate traffic, speed up both police and medical response times, and automatically report road flooding. Other sensors will improve the efficiency of public services, from dispatching police to optimizing garbage truck routes to repairing potholes. Smart billboards will recognize you as you walk by and display advertising tailored to you.

A power substation is really just a computer that distributes electricity, and—like everything else—it's on the Internet. CrashOverride didn't infect the Pivnichna substation directly; it was hiding in the computers of a control room miles away, which was connected to the station over the Internet.

This technological shift occurred during the last decade or so. It used to be that things had computers in them. Now they *are* computers with things attached to them. And as computers continue to get smaller and cheaper, they're being embedded into more things, and more things are turning into computers. You might not notice it, and you certainly don't shop for cars and refrigerators as computers; you buy them for their transportation and cooling functions. But they're computers, and that matters when it comes to security.

Our conception of the Internet is also shifting. We no longer go to a specific place in our homes or offices and log on to what appears to be a separate space. We no longer enter a chat room, download our e-mail, or—in many cases—surf the Internet. Those spatial metaphors don't make sense anymore, and in a few years, saying "I'm going on the Internet" will make about as much sense as plugging in a toaster and saying "I'm going on the power grid."

The name given to this ubiquitous connectivity is the "Internet of Things" (IoT). It's mostly a marketing term, but it is also very real. The tech analyst firm Gartner defines it as "the network of physical objects that contain embedded technology to communicate and sense or interact with their internal states or the external environment." It's about connecting all sorts of devices over the Internet, and letting them talk to us, each other, and different computer applications.

The magnitude of this change is staggering. In 2017, there were 8.4 billion things attached to the Internet—primarily computers and phones—an increase by a third over the previous year. By 2020, there are likely to be somewhere between 20 and 75 billion, depending on whose estimates you believe.

This explosive growth comes from vendors who are looking for a competitive edge, or who just want to keep up with the competition and decide that making their products "smart" will do the trick. As computers become smaller—and even cheaper—we will start seeing them in more places.

Your washing machine is already a computer that cleans clothes. When the newest, cheapest, and best embedded computers have Internet connectivity, it will be easier for your washing machine manufacturer to include that feature. And then it will become harder and harder for you to buy a new washing machine without Internet connectivity.

Two years ago, I tried and failed to buy a new car without an Internet connection. There were cars for sale without Internet connectivity, but it was standard in all of the cars I otherwise wanted. As the price of these technologies decreases, this will happen to everything. The Internet will become part of cheaper and less versatile devices, until it's a standard feature with everything.

Today, it might seem dumb that your washing machine has an Internet connection, and impossible that your T-shirt someday will. But in a few years, it will just be the normal state of things. Computers are still getting more powerful, smaller, and cheaper; all it will take for Internet-enabled clothing to become the norm is for the cost of a microprocessor to be lower than the benefit to the retailer of automatic inventory tracking pre-sale and of automatic use tracking post-sale. In another decade, you might not be able to buy a sensor-free T-shirt, and by then you'll take it for granted that your washing machine talks with the clothes it's washing and automatically determines the optimal cycle and detergent to use. Then the washing machine manufacturer will sell the information about what you're wearing—and no longer wearing—to the clothing manufacturers.

Whenever I talk about this kind of thing, there are people who ask, "Why?" They can understand reducing energy use but can't fathom why anyone would put their coffeepot or toothbrush on the Internet. "The 'Smart Everything' Trend Has Officially Turned Stupid," read one 2016 headline, about an early attempt at an Internet-connected refrigerator.

The answer is simple: market economics. As the cost of computerizing devices goes down, the marginal benefit—in either features provided or surveillance data collected—necessary to justify the computerization also goes down. This benefit could be to the user in terms of additional features, or to the manufacturer in terms of learning about and marketing to its user base. At the same time, chip suppliers are moving away from making specialty chips and towards making general-purpose, mass-produced, cheaper chips. As these embedded computers become standardized, it will be less expensive for manufacturers to include connectivity than to remove it. It will literally be cheaper to litter the city with sensors than to clean litter off the sidewalks.

There are advantages to computerizing everything—some that we can see today, and some that we'll realize only once these computers have reached critical mass. The Internet of Things will embed itself into our lives at every level, and I don't think we can predict the emergent properties of this trend. We're reaching a fundamental shift that is due to scale and scope; these differences in degree are causing a difference in kind. Everything is becoming one complex hyper-connected system in which, even if things don't interoperate, they're on the same network and affect each other.

There is more to this trend than the Internet of Things. Take the Internet of Things. Start with the IoT or, more generally, cyberphysical systems. Add the miniaturization of sensors, controllers, and transmitters. Then add autonomous algorithms, machine learning, and artificial intelligence. Toss in some cloud computing, with corresponding increases in capabilities for storage and processing. Don't forget to include Internet penetration, pervasive computing, and the widespread availability of high-speed wireless connectivity. And finally, mix in some robotics. What you get is a single global Internet that affects the world in a direct physical manner. It's an Internet that senses, thinks, and acts.

These are not distinct trends, but ones that converge with, build on, and reinforce each other. Robotics uses autonomous algorithms. Drones combine the IoT, autonomy, and mobile computing. Smart billboards combine personalization with the IoT. A system that automatically regulates water flowing over a dam combines cyberphysical systems, autonomous agents, and probably cloud computing.

And although we'd like to think otherwise, humans are just another component in many of these systems. We provide inputs to these computers and accept their outputs. We are the consumers of their automated functionality. We provide the connections and communications between systems that haven't quite become smart enough to cut us out of the loop. We move these systems around, at least the ones that aren't physically autonomous. We affect these systems, and we are affected by these systems. To a very real degree, we will become virtual cyborgs even if these devices remain distinct from our physiology.

We need a name for this new system of systems. It's more than the Internet, more than the Internet of Things. It's really the Internet + Things.

More accurately, the Internet + Things + us. Or, for short, the Internet+. Honestly, I wish I didn't have to coin a term, but I can't find an existing term that describes the apotheosis of all of those trends. So, "Internet+" it is, at least in this book.

Of course, words like "smart" and "thinks" are relative. At this point, they're more aspirational than anything else. Much of the IoT isn't very smart, and much of it will be stupid for a very long time. But it will continually grow smarter. And while it's very unlikely that we'll see conscious computers anytime soon, computers already behave intelligently on specific tasks. The Internet+ is becoming more powerful through all the interconnections we're building. It's also becoming less secure. This book tells the story of why that's true, and what we can do about it.

It's a complicated story, and I tell it in two parts. In Part I, I describe the current state of computer security—technically, politically, and economically—as well as the trends that got us here. Computers are becoming smaller and more adept at manipulating the physical world, but they're still basically the same computers we've been working with for decades. The technical security issues remain unchanged. The policy issues are the same ones we've been struggling with. And as computers and communications become embedded into everything, one industry after another will start looking like the computer industry. Computer security will become everything security, and the lessons of computer security will become applicable everywhere. And if there's one thing we know about computers, whether they're cars, power substations, or biological printers, it's that they're vulnerable to attack by hobbyists, activists, criminals, nation-states, and anyone else with technical capacity.

In Chapter 1, I briefly cover all the technical reasons why the Internet is so insecure. In Chapter 2, I discuss the primary way we maintain security in our systems—patching vulnerabilities when they're discovered—and why that will fail on the Internet+. Chapter 3 talks about how we prove who we are on the Internet, and how we can hide who we are. In Chapter 4, I explain the political and economic forces that favor insecurity: surveillance capitalism, cybercrime, cyberwar—and the more invasive corporate and government practices that feed off insecurity.

Finally, in Chapter 5, I describe why the risks are increasing, and how they will become catastrophic. "Click here to kill everybody" is hyperbole, but we're already living in a world where computer attacks can crash cars and disable power plants—both actions that can easily result in catastrophic deaths if done at scale. Add to that hacks against airplanes, medical devices, and pretty much all of our global critical infrastructure, and we've got some pretty scary scenarios to consider.

If you're a regular reader of my books, articles, and blog, a lot of Part I will be review. If you're new to all of this, the chapters are important groundwork for what's to come.

The thing about Internet+ security is that we're all used to it. Up to now, we've generally left computer and Internet security to the market. This approach has largely worked satisfactorily, because it mostly hasn't mattered. Security was largely about privacy, and entirely about bits. If your computer got hacked, you lost some important data or had your identity stolen. That sucked, and might have been expensive, but it wasn't catastrophic. Now that everything is a computer, the threats are about life and property. Hackers can crash your car, your pacemaker, or the city's power grid. That's catastrophic.

In Part II of this book, I discuss the policy changes necessary to secure the Internet+. Chapters 6, 7, and 8 deal with the what, the how, and then the who of improving Internet+ security. None of this is novel or complicated, but the devil is in the details. By the time you get through Chapter 8, I hope to have convinced you that the "who" is government. Although there is considerable risk in giving government this role, there isn't any viable alternative. The current sloppy state of Internet+ security is the result of poorly aligned business incentives, a government that prioritizes offensive uses of the Internet over defense, collective action problems, and market failures that require intervention to fix. One of the things I propose in Chapter 8 is a new government agency to coordinate with and advise other agencies on Internet+ security policy and technology. You might disagree with me. That's fine, but it's a debate we need to have.

Chapter 9 is more general. In order to be trusted, government needs to prioritize defense over offense. I describe how to do that.

Practically speaking, it's unlikely that many of the policy changes I propose in Chapters 6 through 9 will actually happen in the near term. So in Chapter 10, I try to be more realistic and discuss what is likely to happen and what we can do in response, both in the US and in other countries.

Chapter 11 talks about some current policy proposals that will actually damage Internet+ security. Chapter 12 is again general and discusses how we can create an Internet+ where trust, resilience, and peace are the norms—and what it might look like.

Fundamentally, I am making an argument for good government doing good. It can be a hard argument to make, especially in the strongly libertarian, small-government, anti-regulation computer industry, but it's an important one. We've all heard about the ways government makes mistakes, does its job badly, or simply gets in the way of technological progress. Less discussed are all the ways that government steers markets, protects individuals, and acts as a counterweight to corporate power. One of the major reasons the Internet+ is so insecure today is the absence of government oversight. As the risks become more catastrophic, we need government to get involved more than ever.

I end this book with a call to action—both to policy makers and to technologists. These policy discussions are inherently technical. We need policy makers who understand technology, and we need to get technologists involved in policy. We need to create and nurture the field of public-interest technologists. This need applies to more fields than Internet+ security. But I call for it in my particular area of technology, because it's the area I know.

Several additional themes weave throughout the book.

- *The security arms race.* It's often helpful to look at security as a technological arms race between attacker and defender. The attacker develops a new technology, and the defender develops some counter-technology in response. Or the defender develops some new defensive technology, forcing the attacker to adapt in some other way. How this arms race unfolds on the Internet+ is critical to understanding security.
- *Trust.* Although we often don't think about it, trust is critical to society's functioning at all levels. On the Internet, trust is everywhere. We trust the computers, software, and Internet services we use. We trust the parts of the network we can't see, and the manufacturing process of the devices we use. How we maintain this trust, and how it is undermined, are also critical to understanding security on the Internet+.

- *Complexity.* Everything about this problem is complex: the technology, the policy, the interaction of technology and policy. Also the politics, the economics, and the sociology. They're complex in many dimensions, and their complexity is increasing over time. Internet+ security is what is known as a "wicked problem"—which doesn't mean that it's evil, but rather that it's difficult or impossible to solve because it's so hard to even define the problem and requirements, let alone create a useful solution.

This book covers a lot of ground, which means that the book passes over much of it quickly and cursorily. The extensive endnotes are intended to be both references and invitations for further reading, and they were all verified at the end of April 2018. Those are on the book's website as well, where they are clickable links: https://www.schneier.com/ch2ke.html. If there are any updates to the book, that's where you'll find them. Schneier .com is also where you'll find my monthly e-mail newsletter and my daily-updated blog on these topics, as well as all my other writings.

I see these issues from a meta level. I'm a technologist at core, not a policy maker or even a policy analyst. I can describe the technological solutions to our security problems. I can even explain the sorts of new policies necessary to identify, generate, and implement those technological solutions. But I don't write about the politics of making those policy changes. I can't tell you how to garner support for or enact those policy changes, or even discuss feasibility. This is a gaping hole in the book, and I accept it.

I also write from a US perspective. Most of the examples are from the US, and most of the recommendations apply to the US. For one thing, it's what I know best. But I also believe that the US serves as a singular example of how things went wrong, and—because of its size and market position—the US is in a singular position to change things for the better. Although this is not a book about international issues and the geopolitics of Internet security, aspects of that are sprinkled around these chapters.

These issues are constantly evolving, and a book like this is necessarily a snapshot in time. I remember when I finished *Data and Goliath* in March 2014; I thought about its publication date six months in the future and hoped nothing would happen to change the book's narrative in the meantime. I'm feeling the same way right now, but more confident that a major event that would require a rewrite will not occur. Certainly, fresh stories and examples will arise, but the landscape I describe here is likely to be current for many years.

The future of Internet+ security—or cybersecurity, if you're of a military bent—is a huge topic, and most of the chapters in this book could easily be books in themselves. My hope is that by offering breadth rather than depth, I can familiarize readers with the lay of the land, provide a sense of the issues, and draft a road map towards improvement. My goals are to attract a larger audience to this important discussion, and to help educate people for a more informed discussion. We will be making significant decisions over the next few years, even if the decision we make is to do nothing.

These risks are not going away. They're not isolated to countries with less developed infrastructures or more totalitarian governments. They're not waning as we figure out the mess that is our dysfunctional political system in the US. And they're not going to magically solve themselves through market forces. To the extent that we solve them, it's going to be because we have deliberately decided to—and have accepted the political, economic, and social costs of our solutions.

The world is made of computers, and we need to secure them. To do that, we need to think differently. At a 2017 Internet security conference, former FCC chairman Tom Wheeler riffed off former secretary of state Madeleine Albright, quipping that "we're facing 21st-century issues, discussing them in 20th-century terms, and proposing 19th-century solutions." He's right, and we need to do better. Our future depends on it.

—Minneapolis, Minnesota, and Cambridge, Massachusetts, April 2018

PART I
THE TRENDS

A couple of years ago, I replaced my home thermostat. I travel a lot, and I wanted to be able to save energy on days I wasn't home. My new thermostat is an Internet-connected computer that I can control from my smartphone. I can set programs for when I am home and when I am away and monitor the temperature inside the house—all remotely. It's perfect.

Unfortunately, I also opened myself up to some potential problems. In 2017, a hacker bragged on the Internet that he was able to remotely hijack the Heatmiser smart thermostat—not the brand I have. Separately, a group of researchers demonstrated ransomware against two popular American thermostat brands—again, not mine—demanding payment in bitcoin to relinquish control. And if they could plant ransomware, they could also have recruited that thermostat into a bot network and used it to attack other sites on the Internet. This was a research project; no operational thermostats were harmed in the process, and no water pipes burst as a result. But next time might be my brand, and might not be so harmless.

The Internet+ means two things when it comes to security.

One: the security properties of our computers and smartphones will become the security properties of everything. So when you think about the insecurity of software, or the problems of log-in and authentication, or security vulnerabilities and software updates—all subjects we'll discuss in Part I of this book—they'll now apply not only to computers and phones, but to thermostats, cars, refrigerators, implanted hearing aids, coffeepots, streetlights, road signs, and everything else. Computer security will become everything security.

And two: all the lessons from computer security become applicable to everything. Those of us who have been in the field of computer security have learned a lot in the past few decades: about the arms race between attackers and defenders, the nature of computer failures, and the need for resilience—again, all subjects that we'll talk about later. These lessons used to be just about computers. Now they are lessons about everything.

There's one critical difference: the stakes are much higher.

The risks of an Internet that affects the world in a direct physical manner are increasingly catastrophic. Today's threats include the possibility of hackers remotely crashing airplanes, disabling cars, and tinkering with medical devices to murder people. We're worried about being GPS-hacked to misdirect global shipping and about counts from electronic voting booths being manipulated to throw elections. With smart homes, attacks can mean property damage. With banks, they can mean economic chaos. With power plants, they can mean blackouts. With waste treatment plants, they can mean toxic spills. With cars, planes, and medical devices, they can mean death. With terrorists and nation-states, the security of entire economies and nations could be at stake.

Security is an arms race between attacker and defender. Consider the battle between Internet advertisers and ad blockers. If you use an ad blocker—and about 600 million people in the world do—you'll notice that some sites now employ ad-blocker blockers to prevent you from viewing content until you disable your ad blocker. Spam is an arms race between the spammers developing new techniques and the anti-spam companies figuring out how to counter them. Click fraud is much the same: fraudsters employ various tricks to convince companies like Google that real people have clicked on web links and that Google owes the fraudsters money, while Google tries to detect them. Credit card fraud is a continuous arms race between attackers developing new techniques and the credit card companies countering with new ways to prevent and detect them. Modern ATMs are the result of a decades-old arms race between attackers and defenders, one that continues today with ever-smaller and more discreet "skimmers" to steal card information and PINs, and even remote attacks against ATMs over the Internet.

So, to understand Internet+ security, we need to start by understanding the current state of Internet security. We need to understand the technological, business, political, and criminal trends that have brought us to this state and continue to exert themselves, as well as the technological trends that define and constrain what's possible, and illustrate what's coming.

1

Computers Are Still Hard to Secure

Security is always a trade-off. Often it's security versus convenience, but sometimes it's security versus features or security versus performance. That we prefer all of those things over security is most of the reason why computers are insecure, but it's also true that securing computers is actually hard.

In 1989, Internet security expert Gene Spafford famously said: "The only truly secure system is one that is powered off, cast in a block of concrete and sealed in a lead-lined room with armed guards—and even then I have my doubts." Almost 30 years later, that's still true.

It's true for stand-alone computers, and it's true for the Internet-connected embedded computers that are everywhere. More recently, former National Cybersecurity Center director Rod Beckstrom summarized it this way: (1) anything connected to the Internet can be hacked; (2) everything is being connected to the Internet; (3) as a result, everything is becoming vulnerable.

Yes, computers are so hard to secure that every security researcher has his own pithy saying about it. Here's mine from 2000: "Security is a process, not a product."

There are many reasons why this is so.

MOST SOFTWARE IS POORLY WRITTEN AND INSECURE

I play Pokémon Go on my phone, and the game crashes all the time. Its instability is extreme, but not exceptional. We've all experienced this. Our computers and smartphones crash regularly. Websites don't load. Features don't work. We've all learned how to compensate. We compulsively save our data and back up our files, or use systems that do it for us automatically. We reboot our computers when things start behaving weirdly. We occasionally lose important data. And we don't expect our computers to work as well as the typical consumer products in our lives, even though we get continually frustrated when they don't.

Software is poorly written because, with only a few exceptions, the market doesn't reward good-quality software. "Good, fast, cheap—pick any two"; inexpensive and quick to market is more important than quality. For most of us most of the time, poorly written software has been good enough.

This philosophy has permeated the industry at all levels. Companies don't reward software quality in the same way they reward delivering products ahead of schedule and under budget. Universities focus more on code that barely works than on code that's reliable. And most of us consumers are unwilling to pay what doing better would cost.

Modern software is riddled with a myriad of bugs. Some of them are inherent in the complexity of the software—more on that later—but most are programming mistakes. These bugs were not fixed during the development process; they remain in the software after it has been finished and shipped. That any of this software functions at all is a testament to how well we can engineer around buggy software.

Of course, not all software development processes are created equal. Microsoft spent the decade after 2002 improving its software development process to minimize the number of security vulnerabilities in shipped software. Its products are by no means perfect—that's beyond the capabilities of the technologies right now—but they're a lot better than average. Apple is known for its quality software. So is Google. Some very small and critical pieces of software are high quality. Aircraft avionics software is written to a much more rigorous quality standard than just about everything else. And NASA had a famous quality control process for its space shuttle software.

The reasons why these are exceptions vary from industry to industry, company to company. Operating system companies spend a lot of money; small pieces of code are easy to get right; airplane software is highly regulated. NASA still has crazily conservative quality assurance standards. And even for relatively high-quality software systems like Windows, macOS, iOS, and Android, you're still installing patches all the time.

Some bugs are also security vulnerabilities, and some of those security vulnerabilities can be exploited by attackers. An example is something called a buffer overflow bug. It's a programming mistake that allows an attacker, in some cases, to force the program to run arbitrary commands and take control of the computer. There are lots of areas of potential mistakes like this, some easier to make than others.

Here, numbers are hard to pin down. We don't know what percentage of bugs are also vulnerabilities and what percentage of vulnerabilities are exploitable, and there is legitimate academic debate about whether these exploitable bugs are sparse or plentiful. I come down firmly on the side of plentiful: large software systems have thousands of exploitable vulnerabilities, and breaking into these systems is a matter—sometimes simple, sometimes not—of finding one of them.

But while vulnerabilities are plentiful, they're not uniformly distributed. There are easier-to-find ones, and harder-to-find ones. Tools that automatically find and fix entire classes of vulnerabilities, and coding practices that eliminate many easy-to-find ones, greatly improve software security. And when one person finds a vulnerability, it is more likely that another person soon will, or recently has, found the same vulnerability. Heartbleed is a vulnerability in web security. It remained undiscovered for two years, and then two independent researchers found it within days of each other. The Spectre and Meltdown vulnerabilities in computer chips existed for at least ten years before multiple researchers discovered them in 2017. I have seen no good explanation for this parallel discovery other than it just happens; but it will matter when we talk about governments stockpiling vulnerabilities for espionage and cyberweapons in Chapter 9.

The explosion of IoT devices means more software, more lines of code, and even more bugs and vulnerabilities. Keeping IoT devices cheap means less-skilled programmers, sloppier software development processes, and more code reuse—and hence a greater impact from a single vulnerability if it is widely replicated.

The software we depend on—that's running on our computers and phones, in our cars and medical devices, on the Internet, in systems controlling our critical infrastructure—is insecure in multiple ways. This isn't simply a matter of finding the few vulnerabilities and fixing them; there are too many for that. It's a software fact of life that we're going to have to live with for the foreseeable future.

THE INTERNET WAS NEVER DESIGNED WITH SECURITY IN MIND

In April 2010, for about 18 minutes, 15% of all Internet traffic suddenly passed through servers in China on the way to its destination. We don't know if this was the Chinese government testing an interception capability or it was an honest mistake, but we know how the attackers did it: they abused the Border Gateway Protocol.

The Border Gateway Protocol, or BGP, is how the Internet physically routes traffic through the various cables and other connections between service providers, countries, and continents. Because there's no authentication in the system and everyone implicitly trusts all information about speed and congestion, BGP can be manipulated. We know from documents disclosed by government-contractor-turned-leaker Edward Snowden that the NSA uses this inherent insecurity to make certain data streams easier to eavesdrop on. In 2013, one company reported 38 different instances where Internet traffic was diverted to routers at Belarusian or Icelandic service providers. In 2014, the Turkish government used this technique to censor parts of the Internet. In 2017, traffic to and from several major US ISPs was briefly routed to an obscure Russian Internet provider. And don't think this kind of attack is limited to nation-states; a 2008 talk at the DefCon hackers conference showed how anyone can do it.

When the Internet was developed, what security there was focused on physical attacks against the network. Its fault-tolerant architecture can handle servers and connections failing or being destroyed. What it can't handle is systemic attacks against the underlying protocols.

The base Internet protocols were developed without security in mind, and many of them remain insecure to this day. There's no security in the "From" line of an e-mail: anyone can pretend to be anyone. There's no security in the Domain Name Service that translates Internet addresses from human-readable names to computer-readable numeric addresses, or the Network Time Protocol that keeps everything in synch. There's no security in the original HTML protocols that underlie the World Wide Web, and the more secure "https" protocol still has lots of vulnerabilities. All of these protocols can be subverted by attackers.

These protocols were invented in the 1970s and early 1980s, when the Internet was limited to research institutions and not used for anything critical. David Clark, an MIT professor and one of the architects of the early Internet, recalls: "It's not that we didn't think about security. We knew that there were untrustworthy people out there, and we thought we could exclude them." Yes, they really thought they could limit Internet usage to people they knew.

As late as 1996, the predominant thinking was that security would be the responsibility of the endpoints—that's the computers in front of people—and not the network. Here's the Internet Engineering Task Force (IETF), the body that sets industry standards for the Internet, in 1996:

> It is highly desirable that Internet carriers protect the privacy and authenticity of all traffic, but this is not a requirement of the architecture. Confidentiality and authentication are the responsibility of end users and must be implemented in the protocols used by the end users. Endpoints should not depend on the confidentiality or integrity of the carriers. Carriers may choose to provide some level of protection, but this is secondary to the primary responsibility of the end users to protect themselves.

This is not obviously stupid. In Chapter 6, I'll talk about the end-to-end networking model, which means that the network shouldn't be responsible for security, as the IETF outlined. But people were too rigid about that for too long, and even aspects of security that only make sense to include inside the network were not being adopted.

Fixing this has been hard, and sometimes impossible. Since as far back as the 1990s, the IETF has offered proposals to add security to BGP to prevent attacks, but these proposals have always suffered from a collective action problem. Adopting the more secure system provides benefits only when enough networks do it; early adopters receive minimal benefit for their hard work. This situation results in a perverse incentive. It makes little sense for a service provider to be the first to adopt this technology, because it pays the cost and receives no benefit. It makes much more sense to wait and let others go first. The result, of course, is what we're seeing: 20 years after we first started talking about the problem, there's still no solution.

There are other examples like this. DNSSEC is an upgrade that would solve the security problems with the Domain Name Service protocol. As with BGP, there's no security in the existing protocol and all sorts of ways the system can be attacked. And as with BGP, it's been 20 years since the tech community developed a solution that still hasn't been implemented because it requires most sites to adopt it before anyone sees benefits.

THE EXTENSIBILITY OF COMPUTERS MEANS EVERYTHING CAN BE USED AGAINST US

Recall an old-style telephone, the kind your parents or grandparents would have had in their homes. That object was designed and manufactured as a telephone, and that's all it did and all it could do. Compare that to the telephone in your pocket right now. It's not really a telephone; it's a computer running a telephone app. And, as you know, it can do much, much more. It can be a telephone, a camera, a messaging system, a book reader, a navigation aid, and a million other things. "There's an app for that" makes no sense for an old-style telephone, but is obvious for a computer that makes phone calls.

Similarly, in the centuries after Johannes Gutenberg invented the printing press around 1440, the technology improved considerably, but it was still basically the same mechanical—and then electromechanical—device. Throughout those centuries, a printing press was only ever a printing press. No matter how hard its operator tried, it couldn't be made to perform calculus or play music or weigh fish. Your old thermostat was an electromechanical device that sensed the temperature, and turned a circuit on and off in response. That circuit was connected to your furnace, which gave the thermostat the ability to turn your heat on and off. That's all it could do. And your old camera could only take pictures.

These are now all computers, and as such, they can be programmed to do almost anything. Recently, hackers demonstrated this by programming a Canon Pixma printer, a Honeywell Prestige thermostat, and a Kodak digital camera to play the computer game Doom.

When I tell that anecdote from the stage at tech conferences, everyone laughs at these new IoT devices playing a 25-year-old computer game—but no one is surprised. They're computers; of course they can be programmed to play Doom.

It's different when I tell the anecdote to a nontechnical audience. Our mental model of machines is that they can only do one thing—and if they're broken, they don't do it. But general-purpose computers are more like people; they can do almost anything.

Computers are extensible. As everything becomes a computer, this extensibility property will apply to everything. This has three ramifications when it comes to security.

One: extensible systems are hard to secure, because designers can't anticipate every configuration, condition, application, use, and so on. This is really an argument about complexity, so we'll take it up again in a bit.

Two: extensible systems can't be externally limited. It's easy to build a mechanical music player that only plays music from magnetic tapes stored in a particular physical housing, or a coffee maker that only uses disposable pods shaped a certain way, but those physical constraints don't translate to the digital world. What this means is that copy protection—it's known as digital rights management, or DRM—is basically impossible. As we've learned from the experiences of the music and movie industries over the past two decades, we can't stop people from making and playing unauthorized copies of digital files.

More generally, a software system cannot be constrained, because the software used for constraining can be repurposed, rewritten, or revised. Just as it's impossible to create a music player that refuses to play pirated music files, it's impossible to create a 3D printer that refuses to print gun parts. Sure, it's easy to prevent the average person from doing any of these things, but it's impossible to stop an expert. And once that expert writes software to bypass whatever controls are in place, everyone else can do it, too. And this doesn't take much time. Even the best DRM systems don't last 24 hours. We'll talk about this again in Chapter 11.

Three: extensibility means that every computer can be upgraded with additional features in software. These can accidentally add insecurities, both because the new features will contain new vulnerabilities, and because the new features probably weren't anticipated in the original design. But, more importantly, new features can be added by attackers as well. When someone hacks your computer and installs malware, they're adding new features. They're features you didn't ask for and didn't want, and they're features acting against your interest, but they are features. And they can, at least in theory, be added to every single computer out there.

"Backdoors" are also additional features in a system. I'll be using this term a lot in the book, so it's worth pausing to define it. It's an old term from cryptography, and generally refers to any purposely designed access mechanism that bypasses a computer system's normal security measures. Backdoors are often secret—and added without your knowledge and consent—but they don't have to be. When the FBI demands that Apple provide a way to bypass the encryption in an iPhone, what the agency is demanding is a backdoor. When researchers spot a hard-coded extra password in Fortinet firewalls, they've found a backdoor. When the Chinese company Huawei inserts a secret access mechanism into its Internet routers, it has installed a backdoor. We'll talk more about these in Chapter 11.

All computers can be infected with malware. All computers can be commandeered with ransomware. All computers can be dragooned into a botnet—a network of malware-infected devices that is controlled remotely. All computers can be remotely wiped clean. The intended function of the embedded computer, or the IoT device into which the computer is built, makes no difference. Attackers can exploit IoT devices in all the ways they currently exploit desktop and laptop computers.

THE COMPLEXITY OF COMPUTERIZED SYSTEMS MEANS ATTACK IS EASIER THAN DEFENSE

Today, on the Internet, attackers have an advantage over defenders.

This is not inevitable. Historically, the advantage has seesawed between attack and defense over periods of decades and centuries. The history of warfare illustrates that nicely, as different technologies like machine guns and tanks shifted the advantage one way or another. But today, in computers and on the Internet, attack is easier than defense—and it's likely to remain that way for the foreseeable future.

There are many reasons for this, but the most important is the complexity of these systems. Complexity is the worst enemy of security. The more complex a system is, the less secure it is. And our billions of computers, each with their tens of millions of lines of code, connected into the Internet, with its trillions of webpages and unknown zettabytes of data—comprise the most complex machine humankind has ever built.

More complexity means more people involved, more parts, more interactions, more layers of abstraction, more mistakes in the design and development process, more difficulty in testing, more nooks and crannies in the code where insecurities can hide.

Computer security experts like to speak about the attack surface of a system: all the possible points that an attacker might target and that must be secured. A complex system means a large attack surface, and that means a huge advantage for a would-be attacker. The attacker just has to find one vulnerability—one unsecured avenue for attack—and gets to choose the time and method of attack. He can also attack constantly until successful. At the same time, the defender has to secure the entire attack surface from every possible attack all the time. And while the defender has to win every time, the attacker only has to get lucky once. It's simply not a fair battle—and the cost to attack a system is only a fraction of the cost to defend it.

Complexity goes a long way to explaining why computer security is still so hard, even as security technologies improve. Every year, there are new ideas, new research results, and new products and services. But at the same time, every year, increasing complexity results in new vulnerabilities and attacks. We're losing ground even as we improve.

Complexity also means that users often get security wrong. Complex systems often have lots of options, making them hard to use securely. Users regularly fail to change default passwords, or misconfigure access control on data in the cloud. In 2017, Stanford University blamed "misconfigured permissions" for exposing thousands of student and staff records. There are lots of these stories.

There are other reasons, aside from complexity, why attack is easier than defense. Attackers have a first-mover advantage, along with a natural agility that defenders often lack. They often don't have to worry about laws, or about conventional morals or ethics, and can more quickly make use of technical innovations. Because of the current disincentives to improve, we're terrible at proactive security. We rarely take preventive security measures until an attack happens. Attackers also have something to gain, while defense is typically a cost of doing business that companies are looking to minimize—and many executives still don't believe they could be a target. More advantages go to the attacker.

This doesn't mean that defense is futile, only that it's difficult and expensive. It's easier, of course, if the attacker is a lone criminal who can be persuaded to switch to an easier target. But a sufficiently skilled, funded, and motivated attacker will always get in. Talking about nation-state cyber operations, former NSA deputy director Chris Inglis was quoted as putting it this way: "If we were to score cyber the way we score soccer, the tally would be 462–456 twenty minutes into the game, i.e., all offense." That's about right.

Of course, just because attack is technically easy doesn't mean it's pervasive. Murder is easy, too, but few actually do it, because of all the social systems around identifying, condemning, and prosecuting murderers. On the Internet, prosecution is more difficult because attribution is difficult—a topic we'll discuss in Chapter 3—and because the international nature of Internet attacks results in difficult jurisdictional issues.

The Internet+ will make these trends worse. More computers, and especially more different kinds of computers, means more complexity.

THERE ARE NEW VULNERABILITIES IN THE INTERCONNECTIONS

The Internet is filled with emergent properties and unintended consequences. That is, even experts really don't understand how the different parts of the Internet interact with each other as well as we think we do, and we are regularly surprised by how things actually work. This is also true for vulnerabilities.

The more we network things together, the more vulnerabilities in one system will affect other systems. Three examples:

- In 2013, criminals hacked into Target Corporation's network, stealing data on 70 million customers and 40 million credit/debit cards. The criminals gained access into Target's network because they were first able to steal log-in credentials from one of the company's heating and air-conditioning vendors.

- In 2016, hackers collected millions of IoT computers—routers, DVRs, webcams, and so on—into a massive botnet called Mirai. Then they used that botnet to launch a distributed denial-of-service attack—a DDoS attack—against the domain name provider Dyn. Dyn provided a critical Internet function for many major Internet sites. So when Dyn went down, dozens of popular websites, like Reddit, BBC, Yelp, PayPal, and Etsy, were knocked offline.
- In 2017, hackers penetrated an unnamed casino's network through an Internet-connected fish tank, stealing data.

Systems can affect other systems in unforeseen, and potentially harmful, ways. What might seem benign to the designers of a particular system becomes harmful when it's combined with some other system. Vulnerabilities on one system cascade into other systems, and the result is a vulnerability that no one saw coming. This is how things like the Three Mile Island nuclear disaster, the *Challenger* space shuttle explosion, or the 2003 blackout in the US and Canada could happen.

Unintended effects like these have two ramifications. One: the interconnections make it harder for us to figure out which system is at fault. And two: it's possible that no single system is actually at fault. The cause might be the insecure interaction of two individually secure systems. In 2012, someone compromised reporter Mat Honan's Amazon account, which allowed them to gain access to his Apple account, which gave them access to his Gmail account, which allowed them to take over his Twitter account. The particular trajectory of the attack is important; some of the vulnerabilities weren't in the individual systems, but became exploitable only when used in conjunction with each other.

There are other examples. A vulnerability in Samsung smart refrigerators left users' Gmail accounts open to attack. The gyroscope on your iPhone, put there to detect motion and orientation, is sensitive enough to pick up acoustic vibrations and therefore can eavesdrop on conversations. The antivirus software sold by Kaspersky accidentally (or purposefully) steals US government secrets.

If 100 systems are all interacting with each other, that's about 5,000 interactions and 5,000 potential vulnerabilities resulting from those interactions. If 300 systems are all interacting with each other, that's 45,000 interactions. One thousand systems means half a million interactions. Most of them will be benign or uninteresting, but some of them will have very damaging consequences.

COMPUTERS FAIL DIFFERENTLY

Computers don't fail in the same way "normal" things do. They're vulnerable in three different and important ways.

One: distance doesn't matter. In the real world, we're concerned about security against the average attacker. We don't buy a door lock to keep out the world's best burglar. We buy one to keep out the average burglars that are likely to be wandering around our neighborhoods. I have a home in Cambridge, and if there's a super-skilled burglar in Canberra, I don't care. She's not going to fly around the world to rob my house. On the Internet, though, a Canberra hacker can just as easily hack my home network as she can hack a network across the street.

Two: the ability to attack computers is decoupled from the skill to attack them. Software encapsulates skill. That super-skilled hacker in Canberra can encapsulate her expertise into software. She can automate her attack and have it run while she sleeps. She can then give it to everyone else in the world. This is where the term "script kiddie" comes from: someone with minimal skill but powerful software. If the world's best burglar could freely distribute a tool that allowed the average burglar to break into your house, you would be more concerned about home security.

Free distribution of potentially dangerous hacking tools happens all the time on the Internet. The attacker who created the Mirai botnet released his code to the world, and within a week a dozen attack tools had incorporated it. This is an example of what we call malware: worms and viruses and rootkits that give even unskilled attackers enormous capabilities. Hackers can buy rootkits on the black market. They can hire ransomware-as-a-service. European companies like HackingTeam and Gamma Group sell attack tools to smaller governments around the globe. The Russian Federal Security Service had a 21-year-old Kazakh Canadian citizen, Karim Baratov, running the phishing attacks that led to the successful attack on the Democratic National Committee in 2016. The malware was created by the skilled hacker Alexsey Belan.

Three: computers fail all at once or not at all. "Class break" is a concept from computer security. It's a particular kind of security vulnerability that breaks not just one system, but an entire class of systems. Examples might be an operating system vulnerability that allows an attacker to take remote control of every computer that runs on that operating system. Or a vulnerability in Internet-enabled digital video recorders and webcams that allows an attacker to conscript those devices into a botnet.

The Estonian national ID card suffered a class break in 2017. A cryptographic flaw forced the government to suspend 760,000 cards used for all sorts of government services, some in high-security settings.

The risks are exacerbated by software and hardware monoculture. Nearly all of us use one of three computer operating systems and one of two mobile operating systems. More than half of us use the Chrome web browser; the other half use one of five others. Most of us use Microsoft Word for word processing and Excel for spreadsheets. Nearly all of us read PDFs, look at JPEGs, listen to MP3s, and watch AVI video files. Nearly every device in the world communicates using the same TCP/IP Internet protocols. And basic computer standards are not the only source of monocultures. According to a 2011 DHS study, GPS is essential to 11 out of 15 critical infrastructure sectors. Class breaks in these, and countless other common functions and protocols, can easily affect many millions of devices and people. Right now, the IoT is showing more diversity, but that won't last unless some pretty basic economic policies change. In the future, there will only be a few IoT processors, a few IoT operating systems, a few controllers, and a few communications protocols.

Class breaks lead to worms, viruses, and other malware. Think "attack once, impact many." We've conceived of voting fraud as unauthorized individuals trying to vote, not as the remote manipulation by a single person or organization of Internet-connected voting machines or online voter rolls. But this is how computer systems fail: someone hacks the machines.

Consider a pickpocket. Her skill took time to develop. Each victim is a new job, and success at one theft doesn't guarantee success with the next. Electronic door locks, like the ones you now find in hotel rooms, have different vulnerabilities. An attacker can find a flaw in the design that allows him to create a key card that opens every door. If he publishes his attack software, then it's not just the attacker, but anyone, who can now open every lock. And if those locks are connected to the Internet, attackers could potentially open door locks remotely—they could open every door lock remotely at the same time. That's a class break.

In 2012, this happened to Onity, a company that makes electronic locks fitted on over four million hotel rooms for chains like Marriott, Hilton, and InterContinental. A homemade device enabled hackers to open the locks in seconds. Someone figured that out, and instructions on how to build the device quickly spread. It took months for Onity to realize it had been hacked, and—because there was no way to patch the system (I'll talk about this in Chapter 2)—hotel rooms were vulnerable for months and even years afterwards.

Class breaks are not a new concept in risk management. It's the difference between home burglaries and house fires, which happen occasionally to different houses in a neighborhood over the course of the year, and floods and earthquakes, which either happen to everyone in the neighborhood or to no one. But computers have aspects of both at the same time, while also having aspects of a public health risk model.

This nature of computer failures changes the nature of security failures, and completely upends how we need to defend against them. We're not concerned about the threat posed by the average attacker. We're concerned about the most extreme individual who can ruin it for everyone.

ATTACKS ALWAYS GET BETTER, EASIER, AND FASTER

The Data Encryption Standard, or DES, is an encryption algorithm from the 1970s. Its security was deliberately designed to be strong enough to resist then-feasible attacks, but just barely. In 1976, cryptography experts estimated that building a machine to break DES would cost $20 million. In my 1995 book *Applied Cryptography*, I estimated that the cost had dropped to $1 million. In 1998, the Electronic Frontier Foundation built a custom machine for $250,000 that could break DES encryption in less than a day. Today, you can do it on your laptop.

In another realm, in the 1990s, cell phones were designed to automatically trust cell towers without any authentication systems. This was because authentication was hard, and it was hard to deploy fake cell phone towers. Fast-forward a half decade, and stingray fake cell towers became an FBI secret surveillance tool. Fast-forward another half decade, and setting up a fake cell phone tower became so easy that hackers demonstrate it onstage at conferences.

Similarly, the increasing speed of computers has made them exponentially faster at brute-force password guessing: trying every password until it finds the correct one. Meanwhile, the typical length and complexity of passwords that the average person is willing and able to remember has remained constant. The result is passwords that were secure ten years ago but are insecure today.

I first heard this aphorism from an NSA employee: "Attacks always get better; they never get worse." Attacks get faster, cheaper, and easier. What is theoretical today becomes practical tomorrow. And because our information systems stay around far longer than we plan for, we have to plan for attackers with future technology.

Attackers also learn and adapt. This is what makes security different from safety. Tornadoes are a safety issue, and we could talk about different defenses against them and their relative effectiveness, and wonder about how future technological advances might better protect us from their destructiveness. But whatever we choose to do or not do, we know that tornadoes will never adapt to our defenses and change their behavior. They're just tornadoes.

Human adversaries are different. They're creative and intelligent. They change tactics, invent new things, and adapt all the time. Attackers examine our systems, looking for class breaks. And once one of them finds one, they'll exploit it again and again until the vulnerability is fixed. A security measure that protects networks today might not work tomorrow because the attackers will have figured out how to get around it.

All this means that expertise flows downhill. Yesterday's top-secret military capabilities become today's PhD theses and tomorrow's hacking tools. Differential cryptanalysis was such a capability, discovered by the NSA sometime before 1970. In the 1970s, IBM mathematicians discovered it again when they designed DES. The NSA classified IBM's discovery, but the technique was rediscovered by academic cryptographers in the late 1980s.

Defense is always in flux. What worked yesterday might not work today and almost certainly won't work tomorrow.

2

Patching Is Failing as a Security Paradigm

There are two basic paradigms of security. The first comes from the real world of dangerous technologies: the world of automobiles, planes, pharmaceuticals, architecture and construction, and medical devices. It's the traditional way we do design, and can be best summed up as "Get it right the first time." This is the world of rigorous testing, of security certifications, and licensed engineers. At the extreme, it's a slow and expensive process: think of all the safety testing Boeing conducts on its new aircraft, or any pharmaceutical company conducts before releasing a new drug in the market. It's also the world of slow and expensive changes, because each change has to go through the same process.

We do this because the costs of getting it wrong are so great. We don't want buildings collapsing on us, planes falling out of the sky, or thousands of people dying from a pharmaceutical's side effects or drug interaction. And while we can't eliminate all those risks completely, we can mitigate them by doing a lot of up-front work.

The alternative security paradigm comes from the fast-moving, free-wheeling, highly complex, and heretofore largely benign world of software. Its motto is "Make sure your security is agile" or, in Facebook lingo, "Move fast and break things." In this model, we try to make sure we can update our systems quickly when security vulnerabilities are discovered. We try to build systems that are survivable, that can recover from attack, that actually mitigate attacks, and that adapt to changing threats. But mostly we build systems that we can quickly and efficiently patch. We can argue how well we achieve these goals, but we accept the problems because the cost of getting it wrong isn't that great.

In Internet+ security, these two paradigms are colliding. They're colliding in your cars. They're colliding in home appliances. They're colliding in computerized medical devices. They're colliding in home thermostats, computerized voting machines, and traffic control systems—and in our chemical plants, dams, and power plants. They're colliding again and again, and the stakes are getting higher because failures can affect life and property.

Patching is something we all do all the time with our software—we usually call it "updating"—and it's the primary mechanism we have to keep our systems secure. How it works (and doesn't), and how it will fare in the future, is important to understand in order to fully appreciate the security challenges we face.

There are undiscovered vulnerabilities in every piece of software. They lie dormant for months and years, and new ones are discovered all the time by everyone from companies to governments to independent researchers to cybercriminals. We maintain security through (1) discoverers disclosing a found vulnerability to the software vendor and the public, (2) vendors quickly issuing a security patch to fix the vulnerability, and (3) users installing that patch.

It took us a long time to get here. In the early 1990s, researchers would disclose vulnerabilities to the vendors only. Vendors would respond by basically not doing anything, maybe getting around to fixing the vulnerabilities years later. Researchers then started publicly announcing that they had found a vulnerability, in an effort to get vendors to do something about it—only to have the vendors belittle them, declare their attacks "theoretical" and not worth worrying about, threaten them with legal action, and continue to not fix anything. The only solution that spurred vendors into action was for researchers to publish details about the vulnerability. Today, researchers give software vendors advance warning when they find a vulnerability, but then they publish the details. Publication has become the stick that motivates vendors to quickly release security patches, as well as the means for researchers to learn from each other and get credit for their work; this publication further improves security by giving other researchers both knowledge and incentive. If you hear the term "responsible disclosure," it refers to this process.

Lots of researchers—from lone hackers to academic researchers to corporate engineers—find and responsibly disclose vulnerabilities. Companies offer bug bounties to hackers who bring vulnerabilities to them instead of publishing those vulnerabilities or using them to commit crimes. Google has an entire team, called Project Zero, devoted to finding vulnerabilities in commonly used software, both public-domain and proprietary. You can argue with the motivations of these researchers—many are in it for the publicity or competitive advantage—but not with the results. Despite the seemingly endless stream of vulnerabilities, any piece of software becomes more secure as they are found and patched.

It's not happily ever after, though. There are several problems with the find-and-patch system, many of which are being exacerbated by the Internet+. Let's look at the situation in terms of the entire ecosystem—researching vulnerabilities, disclosing vulnerabilities to the manufacturer, writing and publishing patches, and installing patches—in reverse chronological order.

Installing patches: I remember those early years when users, especially corporate networks, were hesitant to install patches. Patches were often poorly tested, and far too often they broke more than they fixed. This was true for everyone who released software: operating system vendors, large software vendors, and so on. Things have changed over the years. The big operating system organizations—Microsoft, Apple, and Linux in particular—have become much better about testing their patches before releasing them. As people have become more comfortable with patches, they have become better about installing them more quickly and more often. At the same time, vendors are now making patches easier to install.

Still, not everyone patches their systems. The industry rule of thumb is that a quarter of us install patches on the day they're issued, a quarter within the month, a quarter within the year, and a quarter never do. The patch rate is even lower for military, industrial, and healthcare systems because of how specialized the software is. It's more likely that a patch will break some critical functionality.

People who are using pirated copies of software often can't get updates. Some people just don't want to be bothered. Others forget. Some people don't patch because they're tired of vendors slipping unwanted features and software into updates. Some IoT systems are just harder to update. How often do you update the software in your router, refrigerator, or microwave? Never is my guess. And no, they don't update automatically.

Three 2017 examples illustrate the problem. Equifax was hacked because it didn't install a patch for its Apache web server that had been available two months previously. The WannaCry malware was a worldwide scourge, but it only affected unpatched Windows systems. The Amnesia IoT botnet made use of a vulnerability in digital video recorders that had been disclosed and fixed a year earlier, but existing machines couldn't be patched.

The situation is worse for the computers embedded in IoT devices. In a lot of systems—both low-cost and expensive—users have to manually download and install relevant patches. Often the patching process is tedious and complicated, and beyond the skill of the average user. Sometimes, ISPs have the ability to remotely patch things like routers and modems, but this is also rare. Even worse, many embedded devices don't have any way to be patched. Right now, the only way for you to update the firmware in your hackable DVR is to throw it away and buy a new one.

At the low end of the market, the result is hundreds of millions of devices that have been sitting on the Internet, unpatched and insecure, for the last five to ten years. In 2010, a security researcher analyzed 30 home routers and was able to break into half of them, including some of the most popular and common brands. Things haven't improved since then.

Hackers are starting to notice. The malware DNSChanger attacks home routers, as well as computers. In Brazil in 2012, 4.5 million DSL routers were compromised for purposes of financial fraud. In 2013, a Linux worm targeted routers, cameras, and other embedded devices. In 2016, the Mirai botnet used vulnerabilities in digital video recorders, webcams, and routers; it exploited such rookie security mistakes as devices having default passwords.

The difficulty of patching also plagues expensive IoT devices that you might expect to be better designed. In 2015, Chrysler recalled 1.4 million vehicles to patch the security vulnerability I opened this book with. The only way to patch them was for Chrysler to mail every car owner a USB drive to plug into a port on the vehicle's dashboard. In 2017, Abbott Labs told 465,000 pacemaker patients that they had to go to an authorized clinic for a critical security update. At least the patients didn't have to have their chests opened up.

This is likely to be a temporary problem, at least for more expensive devices. Industries that aren't used to patching will learn how to do it. Companies selling expensive equipment with embedded computers will learn how to design their systems to be patched automatically. Compare Tesla to Chrysler: Tesla pushes updates and patches to cars automatically, and updates the systems overnight. Kindle does the same thing: owners have no control over the patching process, and usually have no idea that their devices have even been patched.

Writing and publishing patches: Vendors can be slow to release security patches. One 2016 survey found that about 20% of all vulnerabilities—and 7% of vulnerabilities in the "top 50 applications"—did not have a patch available the same day the vulnerability was disclosed. (To be fair, this is an improvement over previous years. In 2011, a third of all vulnerabilities did not have a patch available on the day of disclosure.) Even worse, only an additional 1% were patched within a month after disclosure, indicating that if a vendor doesn't patch immediately, it's not likely to get to it anytime soon. Android users, for example, often have to wait months after Google issues a patch before their handset manufacturers make that patch available to users. The result is that about half of all Android phones haven't been patched in over a year.

Patches also aren't as reliable as we would like them to be; they still occasionally break the systems they're supposed to be fixing. In 2014, an iOS patch left some users unable to get a cell signal. In 2017, a flawed patch to Internet-enabled door locks by Lockstate bricked the devices, leaving users unable to lock or unlock their doors. In 2018, in response to the Spectre and Meltdown vulnerabilities in computer CPUs, Microsoft issued a patch to its operating system that bricked some computers. There are more examples.

If we turn to embedded systems and IoT devices, the situation is much more dire. Our computers and smartphones are as secure as they are because there are teams of security engineers dedicated to writing patches.

The companies that make these devices can support such big teams because they make a huge amount of money, either directly or indirectly, from their software—and, in part, compete on its security. This isn't true of embedded systems like digital video recorders or home routers. Those systems are sold at a much lower margin and in much smaller quantities, and are often designed by offshore third parties. Engineering teams assemble quickly to design the products, then disband or go build something else. Parts of the code might be old and out-of-date, reused again and again. There might not be any source code available, making it much harder to write patches. The companies involved simply don't have the budget to make their products secure, and there's no business case for them to do so.

Even worse, no one has the incentive to patch the software once it's been shipped. The chip manufacturer is busy shipping the next version of the chip, the device manufacturer is busy upgrading its product to work with this next chip, and the vendor with its name on the box is just a reseller. Maintaining the older chips and products isn't a priority for anyone.

Even when manufacturers have the incentive, there's a different problem. If there's a security vulnerability in Microsoft operating systems, the company has to write a patch for each version it supports. Maintaining lots of different operating systems gets expensive, which is why Microsoft and Apple—and everyone else—support only the few most recent versions. If you're using an older version of Windows or macOS, you won't get security patches, because the companies aren't creating them anymore.

This won't work with more durable goods. We might buy a new DVR every 5 or 10 years, and a refrigerator every 25 years. We drive a car we buy today for a decade, sell it to someone else who drives it for another decade, and that person sells it to someone who ships it to a Third World country, where it's resold yet again and driven for yet another decade or two. Go try to boot up a 1978 Commodore PET computer, or try to run that year's VisiCalc, and see what happens; we simply don't know how to maintain 40-year-old software.

Consider a car company. It might sell a dozen different types of cars with a dozen different software builds each year. Even assuming that the software gets updated only every two years and the company supports the cars for only two decades, the company needs to maintain the capability to update 20 to 30 different software versions. (For a company like Bosch that supplies automotive parts for many different manufacturers, the number would be more like 200.) The expense and warehouse size for the test vehicles and associated equipment would be enormous.

Alternatively, imagine if car companies announced that they would no longer support vehicles older than five, or ten, years. There would be serious environmental consequences.

We're already seeing the effects of systems so old that the vendors stopped patching them, or went out of business altogether. Some of the organizations affected by WannaCry were still using Windows XP, an unpatchable 17-year-old operating system that Microsoft stopped supporting in 2014. About 140 million computers worldwide still run that operating system, including most ATMs. A popular shipboard satellite communications system once sold by Inmarsat Group is no longer patched, even though it contains critical security vulnerabilities. This is a big problem for industrial-control systems, because many of them run outdated software and operating systems, and upgrading them is prohibitively expensive because they're very specialized. These systems can stay in operation for many years and often don't have big IT budgets associated with them.

Certification exacerbates the problem. Before everything became a computer, dangerous devices like cars, airplanes, and medical devices had to go through various levels of safety certification before they could be sold. A product, once certified, couldn't be changed without having to be recertified. For an airplane, it can cost upwards of a million dollars and take a year to change one line of code. This made sense in the analog world, where products didn't change much. But the whole point of patching is to enable products to change, and change quickly.

Disclosing vulnerabilities: Not everyone discloses security vulnerabilities when they find them; some hoard them for offensive purposes. Attackers use them to break into systems, and that's the first time we learn of them. These are called "zero-day vulnerabilities," and responsible vendors try to quickly patch them as well. Government agencies like the NSA, US Cyber Command, and their foreign equivalents also keep some vulnerabilities secret for their own present and future use. We'll talk about this much more in Chapter 9, but for now, understand that every discovered but undisclosed vulnerability—even if it is kept by someone you trust—can be independently discovered and used against you.

Even researchers who want to disclose the vulnerabilities they discover sometimes find a chilly reception from the device manufacturers. Those new industries getting into the computer business—the coffeepot manufacturers and their ilk—don't have experience with security researchers, responsible disclosure, and patching, and it shows. This lack of security expertise is critical. Software companies write software as their core competency. Refrigerator manufacturers, or refrigerator divisions of larger companies, have a different core competency—presumably, keeping food cold—and writing software is always going to be a sideline.

Just like the computer vendors of the 1990s, IoT manufacturers tout the unbreakability of their systems, deny any problems that are exposed, and threaten legal action against those who expose any problems. The 2017 Abbott Labs patch came a year after the company called the initial report of the security vulnerability—published without details of the attack—"false and misleading." That might be okay for computer games or word processors, but it is dangerous for cars, medical devices, and airplanes—devices that can kill people if bugs are exploited. But should the researchers have published the details anyway? No one knows what responsible disclosure looks like in this new environment.

Finally, researching vulnerabilities: In order for this ecosystem to work, we need security researchers to find vulnerabilities and improve security, and a law called the Digital Millennium Copyright Act (DMCA) is blocking those efforts. It's an anti-copying law that we will discuss in Chapter 4, and it includes a prohibition against security research. Technically, the prohibition is against circumventing product features intended to deter unauthorized reproduction of copyrighted works. But the effects are broader than that. Because of the DMCA, it's against the law to reverse engineer, locate, and publish vulnerabilities in software systems that protect copyright. Since software can be copyrighted, manufacturers have repeatedly used this law to harass and muzzle security researchers who might embarrass them.

One of the first examples of such harassment took place in 2001. The FBI arrested Dmitry Sklyarov at the DefCon hackers conference for giving a presentation describing how to bypass the encryption code in Adobe Acrobat that was designed to prevent people from copying electronic books. Also in 2001, HP used the law to threaten researchers who published security flaws in its Tru64 product. In 2011, Activision used it to shut down the public website of an engineer who had researched the security system in one of its video games. There are many examples like this.

In 2016, the Library of Congress—seriously, that's who's in charge of this—added an exemption to the DMCA for security researchers, but it's a narrow exemption that's temporary and still leaves a lot of room for harassment.

Other laws are also used to squelch research. In 2008, the Boston MBTA used the Computer Fraud and Abuse Act to block a conference presentation on flaws in its subway fare cards. In 2013, Volkswagen sued security researchers who had found vulnerabilities in its automobile software, preventing them from being disclosed for two years. And in 2016, the Internet security company FireEye obtained a court injunction against publication of the details of FireEye product vulnerabilities that had been discovered by third parties.

The chilling effects are substantial. Lots of security researchers don't work on finding vulnerabilities, because they might get sued and their results might remain unpublished. If you're a young academic concerned about tenure, publication, and avoiding lawsuits, it's just safer not to risk it.

For all of these reasons, the current system of patching is going to be increasingly inadequate as computers become embedded in more and more things. The problem is that we have nothing better to replace it with.

This gets us back to the two paradigms at the start of this chapter: getting it right the first time, and fixing things quickly when problems arise.

These have parallels in the software development industry. "Waterfall" is the term used for the traditional model for software development: first come the requirements; then the specifications; then the design; then the implementation, testing, and fielding. "Agile" describes the newer model for software development: build a prototype to meet basic customer needs; see how it fails; fix it quickly; update requirements and specifications; repeat again and again. The agile model seems to be a far better way of doing software design and development, and it can incorporate security design requirements, as well as functional design requirements.

You can see the difference in Microsoft Office versus the apps on your smartphone. A new version of Microsoft Office happens once every few years, and it is a major software development effort resulting in many design changes and new features. A new version of an iPhone app might be released every other week, each with minor incremental changes and occasionally a single new feature. Microsoft might use agile development processes internally, but its releases are definitely old-school.

We need to integrate the two paradigms. We don't have the requisite skill in security engineering to get it right the first time, so we have no choice but to patch quickly. But we also have to figure out how to mitigate the costs of the failures inherent in this paradigm. Because of the inherent complexity of the Internet+, we need both the long-term stability of the waterfall paradigm and the reactive capability of the agile paradigm.

3
Knowing Who's Who on the Internet Is Getting Harder

A famous *New Yorker* cartoon from 1993 showed two dogs talking to each other with this caption: "On the Internet, no one knows you're a dog." In 2015, a follow-up *New Yorker* cartoon showed two other dogs talking: "Remember when, on the Internet, nobody knew who you were?"

On the Internet, both of those things are true. We prove we are who we say we are all the time, usually by typing in a password that only we should know. At the same time, there are systems that allow both criminals and dissidents to secretly communicate without the authorities knowing who they are—and there are many instances of the authorities finding out anyway. There are also systems of anonymous communication, some as simple as creating a user account without associating it with a name. And finally, hackers can break into networks across the planet without being identified, and yet again, security firms and governments can sometimes identify them.

If it all sounds confusing and contradictory, that's because it is.

AUTHENTICATION IS GETTING HARDER, AND
CREDENTIAL STEALING IS GETTING EASIER

In 2016, Rob Joyce, then the head of the NSA's since-renamed Tailored Access Operations (TAO) group—basically, the country's chief hacker—gave a rare public talk. In a nutshell, he said that zero-day vulnerabilities are overrated, and credential stealing is how he gets into networks.

He's right. As bad as software vulnerabilities are, the most common way hackers break into networks is by abusing the authentication process. They steal passwords, set up man-in-the-middle attacks to piggyback on legitimate log-ins, or masquerade as authorized users. Credential stealing doesn't require finding a zero-day or an unpatched vulnerability, plus there's less chance of discovery, and it gives the attacker more flexibility in technique.

This isn't just true for the NSA; it's true for all attackers. It's how the Chinese hackers breached the Office of Personnel Management in 2015. The 2014 criminal attack against Target Corporation started with stolen log-in credentials. From 2011 to 2014, Iranian hackers stole log-in credentials of political and military leaders in the US, Israel, and other countries. The 2015 hacktivist who broke into the cyber arms manufacturer HackingTeam and published pretty much every proprietary document from that company used stolen credentials. And the 2016 Russian attacks against the Democratic National Committee used stolen credentials. One survey found that 80% of breaches are the result of abuse or misuse of credentials. Google looked at Gmail users from mid-2016 to mid-2017 and found 12 million successful phishing attacks every week.

Credential stealing is such an effective line of attack because authentication is so prevalent. Everything personal or proprietary is protected by it, in one form or another, so there are plenty of opportunities to crack it. Getting authentication to be both usable and secure is hard; in many cases, it's impossible. And most of our systems are designed such that once someone is authenticated, they can do pretty much everything.

The most common authentication mechanism is username and password. You're intimately familiar with it. With far too many passwords to remember, you've probably exhibited all the behaviors that help make this system so insecure: choosing weak passwords, reusing important passwords, writing passwords down and leaving them in public places.

Attackers leverage these behaviors. They guess passwords. They steal passwords from your computers and distant servers. They steal them from one system and try them on another system. They guess the answers to the "secret questions" used for backup authentication. They trick users into revealing them.

On March 19, 2016, John Podesta, then-chair of Hillary Clinton's presidential campaign, received an e-mail from a Russian intelligence unit code-named Fancy Bear, purporting to be a Google security alert. After receiving bad advice from the IT department, Podesta clicked on the link and entered his password into a fake Google log-in page—giving Russian intelligence access to a decade of his e-mails.

Podesta was the victim of a phishing attack. It's easy to poke fun at him, but I am more sympathetic. It can be very hard for the victim, especially if he's not technically savvy, to recognize a carefully crafted phishing message. And if he'd resisted the March 19 e-mail, the Fancy Bear hackers would have tried again. And again. And they only needed to get lucky once.

Phishing can be either targeted or mass. In one mass phishing attack, discovered in 2017, fraudsters used hacked accounts to send e-mails to those hacked users' contacts, with a worm posing as a Google Docs file that harvested the victim's Google credentials when they logged in to Google, and then forwarded itself to all of the victim's contacts. Google found and disabled the worm, but estimates are that it affected a million Gmail users.

If there's a moral to all of this, it's that passwords provide terrible security. They're okay for low-security applications, but not for anything more.

There are three basic ways to authenticate you: something you know, something you are, and something you have. Passwords are something you know. They authenticate you because supposedly only you know them.

An example of something you are is biometrics. Fingerprints, facial scans, iris scans, hand geometry—there are lots of different ways. Both the iPhone and the Google Pixel, for example, allow users to log in using their fingerprint or face as identification.

Something you have is a token of some sort. These are things you carry with you that can be used to authenticate you. They used to be physical objects with a screen that displayed an ever-changing number, a card or dongle you would plug into your computer, or a physical key that would unlock a system. Today, they are more likely apps or text messages on your phone.

There are ways to hack all of these systems. Biometrics can be fooled with photographs, fake fingers, and the like. Phones can be hijacked to give the attacker access to the apps or text messages stored on them. In general, replacing passwords with one of these doesn't improve things much.

Using two of them together—that's two-factor authentication—does improve security. Both Google and Facebook offer two-factor authentication via a text message on your smartphone. (This, of course, isn't perfect, either. Some versions have been hacked.) Sprint, T-Mobile, Verizon, and AT&T are working together to come up with a similar system. In 2017, Google introduced its Advanced Protection Program for high-risk users. Among other security protections, it requires an authentication device that you have to carry with you. My network at Harvard uses one of these systems: the combination of my password (something I know) and an interaction with my smartphone (something I have).

Another option we're starting to see is differential authentication. Facebook might let you authenticate with a simple password from your own computer, but require more extensive authentication if you are using a new or strange computer. Your bank might let you use your normal authentication procedure for routine transactions, but require more authentication if you want to transfer a large amount, or transfer money to an account in another country. There's also research into continuous authentication based on your biometric characteristics. That is, if a system knows how you tend to type or swipe, it can flag your account if you suddenly start behaving differently.

Authentication is always a trade-off between security and usability. An annoying system, no matter how secure, will be bypassed by annoyed users. For example, we'll write our passwords on a sticky note and stick it on our monitors. (Sticky-note passwords regularly show up in the backgrounds of press photos and videos.) One of the biggest advantages biometrics have over passwords is that they're easier to use. A friend of mine used to keep her smartphone unlocked, because typing in a password was just too annoying. Then she got a Google Pixel with a fingerprint reader, and because it was so easy to use she started locking her phone. We might argue whether she'd be more secure with a complex password, but there's no argument that she's more secure than she was when she disabled authentication entirely.

Running an authentication system is difficult. Both Google and Facebook offer authentication services for third parties, and many retailers, blogs, and games allow people to log in with their Google or Facebook account, effectively outsourcing identification and authentication to those companies. Some countries do this, too. Estonia's national identification system, the one with the security vulnerability I mentioned in Chapter 1, enables citizens and foreign residents to access a variety of government services, including voting. India has established a biometric national ID system that will be used by both government agencies and companies. Even the US has Login.gov, a centralized identity and authentication provider for use by the public sector.

On the one hand, these systems are good because many services can be built on a single strong authentication and identity system. On the other hand, these systems create a single point of failure, and therefore carry considerable risk.

Your smartphone has evolved into a centralized security hub for pretty much everything. It's where you can access all of your accounts: your e-mail, your chat clients, your social networking sites, your banking and credit card sites. It's also a central controller hub for the Internet of Things. If you have an IoT something, chances are you control it via your smartphone, from your Tesla to your thermostat to your Internet-connected toys. And all of these systems rely on the phone's authentication. You don't have to log in separately to your e-mail, Facebook, Tesla, or thermostat. The companies all assume that if you have access to your phone, you're you.

This is a major single point of failure. A hacker can convince a cell provider like Verizon or AT&T to transfer control of a victim's phone number to a device under the hacker's own control. Once they succeed—and it's surprisingly easy to do—they can reset all of the victim's accounts that use the phone number for backup: Google, Twitter, Facebook, Apple. They'll reset bank accounts and then steal all the money. In the future, we're going to have to authenticate to everything—our cars, our appliances, our environment—which will make the effects of compromise considerable.

Other attacks attempt to piggyback on a valid authentication. A hacker who is monitoring a user's computer can wait for the user to log in to a real banking website, and then manipulate what the user sees on the screen and sends to the bank in order to change, for example, the destination of bank transfers. This is called a man-in-the-middle attack, and it works even if the bank has instituted two-factor authentication.

To defend against such attacks, one can monitor the system looking for signs of hacked accounts, and then use differential authentication. This would be your bank noticing that you just tried to wire $50,000 to an account in Romania that you've never had any financial transactions with before, and calling you to double-check before letting the transfer go through. A credit card issuer might flag and hold for verification big-ticket purchases where the card is not physically present, or any purchases of gift cards. Some banking apps monitor a user's location via a smartphone app, and block credit card purchases made from somewhere else. For corporate networks, there's an entire industry of products that monitor the network, looking for signs of successful hacking. Their quality is mixed, and it's yet another arms race between attacker and defender.

We need authentication to be both easy to use and highly secure. Those are contradictory requirements, and we're going to need some clever thinking to make progress here. Even so, authentication will become even less convenient than it is right now—there's no way around it.

This situation always reminds me of people from my grandparents' generation who never got used to house keys. They would always keep their doors unlocked, and they resented the inconvenience of having to lock their doors: they had to remember, they had to always carry a key with them, their friends couldn't get in without a key, and on and on and on. For me, it's an inconvenience that I have been used to all my life. Sure, I've locked myself out of my home and had to call my wife to help me out, or pay for the occasional locksmith. But for me, it's a small inconvenience for the trade-off of a more burglar-resistant home. Seat belts are the same. When I was a child, no one wore one. Today, children won't let people drive unless they're wearing one. Similarly, I've adapted to two-factor authentication systems. It's a small inconvenience for the trade-off of a more hacker-resistant account.

Authentication is central to the Internet+. Pretty much every computerized thing will use some authentication system to know who it should talk to, who it should listen to, and who is allowed to control it. This will be true for big things like your car and nuclear power plants, and little things like toys and smart light bulbs. We'll be authenticating ourselves to things all the time, and they'll be authenticating themselves to us.

So much of the Internet+ will rely on identification and authentication—and the reliable, scalable systems to do this that don't exist yet. Your thermostat will want to talk to your furnace. Your appliances will want to talk to your electric meter. Your toys will want to talk to each other.

Updates need to be authenticated, to prevent attackers from tricking you into installing a malicious update. This was one of the techniques that the computer worm Stuxnet used. For years, though, hackers have been using valid signing authorities to create valid authentication signatures for bad updates. Many of the supply-chain vulnerabilities I'll talk about in Chapter 5 are the result of faulty authentication.

Some of these communications will be critical. Cars will communicate with each other—both what they're seeing from their sensors and what their intentions are. Medical devices will communicate with each other and with doctors, and will change their behavior accordingly. The local power company will communicate with all major appliances in the community. Different building systems will communicate with each other. As we learned in Chapter 2, every device will need to receive authenticated security patches. All of this will have to happen automatically. And it will happen constantly, millions of times a day.

We don't know how to scale that. The protocol we use to authenticate nearby devices to each other is Bluetooth, and that only works because we are involved in the process during setup. When we pair phones with cars, for example, we are authenticating each to the other and enabling the devices to communicate without our involvement after that. But that is only feasible if there are only a few devices that need to pair. When we have thousands of devices that need to communicate with each other, it will be impossible for us to manually pair all of them. And while the hub-and-spoke model of having all authentication going through central authorities—like our smartphones—will solve some of this, it won't solve all of it.

Attacks will have serious consequences. If I can impersonate you to your devices, I can take advantage of you. This is the identity theft of the future, and it's scary. If I can feed your devices faulty information, I can manipulate those devices in a harmful way. If I can fool your devices into thinking I'm more trusted than I am, I can give commands in your name. We don't fully understand the consequences of these attacks, because we don't fully understand the scope of the systems.

This brings us to identification. We identify ourselves when we set up accounts in person or on the Internet. How solid that identification is depends on the account. With a bank, it is a solid identification based on a face-to-face interaction in a branch office. With a credit card purchase, it's a weaker authentication based on a person knowing a bunch of personal information. Sometimes identification is tied to a phone number, an address, a national ID card, or a driver's license. Facebook has a "real name" policy: people are supposed to use their real names, but there isn't any verification unless there's a dispute of some sort. Google requires a phone number to set up a Gmail account—although people can use an anonymous "burner" phone. Other times, identification isn't based on anything. My Reddit account is nothing more than a unique username; the only identification is to itself and all the posts I've made under that username. That makes it pseudonymous.

Tying something to your identity means you have a reliable way to prove that you are you, and that nobody else is you. It includes authentication, but it's stronger than that. You can authenticate an anonymous bank account, which proves that you're the same person who deposited the money last week. Identifying a bank account proves that the money belongs to you by name.

Identification is never foolproof. When I first got a passport, I had to physically visit a government office. To impersonate someone else, I would have to be able to forge the "breeder documents"—the identification documents people need to obtain a new identification document—that the passport office demands. Hard, but not impossible. People have obtained real driver's licenses in fake names using forged breeder documents. It's harder when the government tracks its citizens from birth, but that has its own problems.

Impersonation is always going to be easier to pull off when it's done remotely. Again, it's a security versus convenience trade-off. The big companies that want our attention are always going to prefer convenience. We do, too. Eventually, both will need a push towards security.

ATTRIBUTION IS GETTING BOTH HARDER
AND EASIER, DEPENDING

Attribution is the identification of someone who does not want to be identified. But while he wants to remain anonymous, the authorities want to
identify him. Maybe he's committing fraud, or maybe he's trying to gain
unauthorized access to a nuclear power plant. In some countries, he might
be publishing material criticizing the government, or trying to download
porn. In all of these cases, law enforcement agents want to attribute the
actions to some identifiable person or group.

Much of the time, attribution is easy. If the person is using an account
associated with his credit card number, or his real name, or his phone number, attribution is simply a matter of getting that information from whatever
service provider has it. There might be legal hurdles—law enforcement might
have to get a warrant, or might be stymied by jurisdictional issues because
the information is in another country—but there are no technical hurdles.

Sometimes, attribution is difficult but still possible. Even people who
deliberately take pains to hide their identity find that they slip up.

Ross Ulbricht was "Dread Pirate Roberts," the American man behind
the Silk Road e-commerce site for illegal goods and services. He was found
by a dogged FBI agent who pieced together a years-old chat room post, an
old e-mail address, and a chance interview with FBI agents investigating
something else.

Pedophiles have been arrested after being identified from back-
ground details in photos: a camping spot in Minnesota, a blurry logo
on a sweatshirt, or a package of potato chips. A Belarusian who ran the
massive Andromeda botnet was identified and arrested because he accidentally reused an instant-messaging account number associated with
his real name. The Texas hacker Higinio O. Ochoa III was identified and
arrested because location metadata in a photograph led investigators to
his girlfriend.

This kind of attribution can be expensive and time-consuming.
Whether someone can have a presence on the Internet and hide themselves
from the police depends both on that person's skill and care and the skill
and funding of the police who are trying to unmask them. Most of the time,
it's simply not worth it to attribute individual actions on the Internet.

Things are very different when we consider national intelligence organizations, like the NSA, that can surveil broad swaths of the Internet. For them, attribution is much easier.

In 2012, then–US secretary of defense Leon Panetta said publicly that the US—presumably the NSA—has "made significant advances in . . . identifying the origins" of cyberattacks. Other US government officials have privately said that they've solved the so-called attribution problem. We don't know how much of this is posturing, but I believe there's a lot of truth to these statements.

In the 2016 talk I mentioned early in this chapter, the NSA's Rob Joyce said:

> It's amazing the amount of lawyers that DHS, FBI and NSA have, so if the government is saying that we have positive attribution too, you ought to book it. Attribution is really really hard, so when the government's saying it, we're using the totality of the sources and methods we have to help inform that. [But] because those advanced persistent threats aren't going away, . . . we can't bring all that information to the fore and be fully transparent about everything we know and how we know it.

This is attribution at the national level. And while the NSA can sometimes identify individual people—the US indicted 5 Chinese for hacking into US corporations in 2014, and 13 Russians for interfering with the 2016 US election—it's easier to attribute attacks to a particular nation.

Basically, the NSA has eliminated anonymity through massive surveillance. If you can watch everything, you're better able to piece together disparate clues and figure out what's going on and who's who. You can probably even do that automatically. That's what countries like China and Russia are trying to do with the wide-reaching surveillance of the Internet in their countries.

Don't assume that a lack of public attribution means no attribution. Unless attribution is followed by an effective response, it makes a country look weak, and it often makes sense for a nation not to publicly attribute a cyberattack unless it can respond.

Additionally, much of the evidence the NSA collects is classified. And while it might be okay to release the information, the details of the information often reveal how it was collected—that's the "sources and methods" Joyce was referring to—which is also classified. This means that the US government often can't explain why it attributes an attack to a particular country or group, which means there is no way to independently verify its attribution. This, if you're someone who tends to distrust the government, is bad. And while it's obvious that the NSA needs to keep its sources and methods secret, government officials will need to expose them if they expect the general public to believe their attribution claims and support any retaliatory actions they're going to take.

The main points are these: (1) Attribution can be difficult, especially for countries that don't do broad Internet surveillance or have forensics expertise within their own organizations. (2) Attribution takes time; it can be weeks or months before the victim country knows who attacked it. (3) The virtual nature of the attacks and ease of hiding their origins means that the attacking country can always deny its involvement. (4) Attribution can rely on classified evidence that may make it hard to refute those denials. (5) Non-nation-state actors have many of the same capabilities as countries, making it even harder to figure out whether the country's leadership is actually responsible.

The 2014 hack of Sony Pictures by the North Koreans, who published both proprietary company information and unreleased movies, is a good example of the attribution problem. In the days after the attack, there was a legitimate debate as to whether the attacks were perpetrated by a nation-state with a $20 billion military budget, or a couple of guys in a basement somewhere. (I was on the wrong side of this debate; I was betting on the couple of guys.) It was three weeks before the US definitively attributed the attacks to North Korea. And because much of the attribution evidence was secret, many computer security experts simply didn't believe it. It wasn't until the *New York Times* reported on some of the intelligence evidence from the NSA that I believed the government's attribution.

There's an attribution gap right now between countries that are good at it and countries that are not. Countries like China are concerned that the US will be able to publicly attribute attacks to them, but that they won't be able to name and shame other countries in the same way. And smaller countries like Estonia and Georgia have much less hope of figuring out who attacked them in cyberspace. It's not impossible—antivirus companies regularly attribute attacks—but it's difficult and takes even more time. And no one else is at the level of the NSA.

At the country level, this disparity will result in an arms race: detection versus detection evasion. I think evading detection will get easier in the future, at least when it comes to the most capable attackers. Right now, Russia doesn't do much to hide its tracks, because there's not much retaliation and it has stopped caring if it's called out. As attribution technologies get more sophisticated, and if we start retaliating, then countries will spend more effort hiding themselves—or falsely casting blame on some third party.

A different sort of arms race will play out at the individual level. People will continue to make mistakes, and law enforcement will get better at attributing attacks. But there will always be people who are skilled, lucky, or just unimportant enough to remain anonymous.

4

Everyone Favors Insecurity

Flaws in the technology are not the only reason we have such an insecure Internet. Another important reason, maybe even the main reason, is that the Internet's most powerful architects—governments and corporations—have manipulated the network to make it serve their own interests.

Everyone wants you to have security, except from them. Google is willing to give you security, as long as it can surveil you and use the information it collects to sell ads. Facebook offers you a similar deal: a secure social network, as long as it can monitor everything you do for marketing purposes. The FBI wants you to have security, as long as it can break that security if it wants to. The NSA is just the same, as are its equivalents in the UK, France, Germany, China, Israel, and elsewhere.

The reasons differ—and the parties involved will never admit this plainly—but basically, insecurity is in the interests of both corporations and governments. They both benefit from loopholes in security and work to maintain them. Corporations want insecurity for reasons of profit. Governments want it for reasons of law enforcement, social control, international espionage, and cyberattack. The dynamics of all of this are complicated, so we'll take it a step at a time.

SURVEILLANCE CAPITALISM CONTINUES TO DRIVE THE INTERNET

Corporations want your data. The websites you visit are trying to figure out who you are and what you want, and they're selling that information. The apps on your smartphone are collecting and selling your data. The social networking sites you frequent are either selling your data, or selling access to you based on your data. Harvard Business School professor Shoshana Zuboff calls this "surveillance capitalism," and it's the business model of the Internet. Companies build systems that spy on people in exchange for services.

This surveillance is easy because computers do it naturally. Data is a by-product of computer processes. Everything we do that involves a computer creates a transaction record. This includes browsing the Internet, using—and even just carrying—a cell phone, making a purchase online or with a credit card, walking past a computerized sensor, or saying something in the same room as Amazon's Alexa. Data is also a by-product of any socializing we do using computers. Phone calls, e-mails, text messages, and Facebook chatter all create transaction records. As I've previously written, we're all leaving digital exhaust as we go through our lives.

Our data used to be thrown away because the value of it was so marginal and using it was so difficult. Those days are over. Today, data storage is so cheap that all of this data can be saved. This is the raw material that has become "big data." It is fundamentally surveillance data, and it's being collected and used by corporations, primarily to support the advertising model that underpins much of the Internet.

If you look at lists of the world's most valuable companies over the past decade, you'll find the ones that engage in surveillance capitalism: Alphabet (Google's parent company), Facebook, Amazon, and Microsoft. Apple is the exception; it makes its money only by selling hardware, and that's why its prices are higher than the competition's.

The advertising model of the Internet is getting more personal. Companies are trying to figure out your emotions. They're trying to determine what you're paying attention to and how you react. They're trying to learn what images you respond to, and exactly how to flatter you. They're doing all of this so as to more precisely and effectively advertise to you, and sell things to you.

No one knows how many online data brokers and tracking companies operate in the US; I've read estimates from 2,500 to 4,000. These corporations know an amazing amount about us from the devices we use and carry. Our cell phones reveal where we are at all times: where we live, where we work, who we spend time with. They know when we wake up and when we go to sleep—because checking our phones is often the first and last thing we do in a day. And because everyone has a cell phone, they know who we sleep with.

Take a moment to consider who else knows where your smartphone is, and therefore where you are. That list would include any apps that you've given the permission to track your location—and some that track your location by other means. There are obvious ones: Google Maps and Apple Maps. There are also less obvious ones. In 2013, researchers discovered that apps like Angry Birds, Pandora Internet Radio, and the Brightest Flashlight—yes, a flashlight app—also tracked their users' locations.

Smartphones now contain many different sensors. Any Wi-Fi networks your phone connects to can pinpoint your location, even if your phone is just trying to associate with Wi-Fi networks as you walk around. Your phone's Bluetooth can notify nearby computers that you're around. The company Alphonso provides apps with the ability to use the phone's microphone to collect data on what people are watching on television. Facebook has a patent on using accelerometer and gyroscope readings from multiple phones to detect when people are facing each other or walking together. And on and on and on.

There are other ways to determine your location. Did you use your credit card at a store? Did you use an ATM? Maybe you passed by one of the thousands of security cameras in a city. (And while the camera probably didn't identify you, soon automatic face recognition will become common enough that it will.) Did an automatic license plate scanner register your car?

Surveillance companies know a lot about us. Google is probably the best example. Internet search is incredibly intimate. We never lie to our search engines. Our interests and curiosities, hopes and fears, desires and sexual proclivities, are all collected and saved by the companies that search the Internet in our name.

To be clear: when I say "Google knows" or "Facebook knows," I am not implying that the companies are sentient or even conscious. Rather, I mean two very specific things. One: Google's computers contain data that would allow a person who has access to it—either authorized or unauthorized—to learn the facts, if they chose to do so. Two: Google's automatic algorithms can use this data to make inferences about us and perform automated tasks based on them.

In the future, our devices will be able to reconstruct a startlingly intimate model of who we are, what we think about, where we go, and what we do. Refrigerators will monitor our food consumption and, by extension, our health. Our cars will know when and how often we violate traffic laws, and might tell the police or our insurance companies. Fitness trackers will try to figure out our moods. Our beds will know how well we've slept. Already, all new Toyota cars track speed, steering, acceleration, and braking—even whether a driver has her hands on the wheel.

The twin enticements of surveillance capitalism are "free and convenient." It has shaped the commercial Internet for over two decades. Soon it will drive much, much more. And it requires insecurity to operate at peak efficiency. As long as companies are free to gather as much data about us as they possibly can, they will not sufficiently secure our systems. As long as they buy, sell, trade, and store that data, it's at risk of being stolen. And as long as they use it, we risk its being used against us.

CORPORATE CONTROL OF CUSTOMERS AND USERS IS NEXT

Computers don't just allow us to be surveilled to a degree never before possible; they also allow us to be controlled. It's a new business model: forcing us to pay for features individually, use only particular accessories, or subscribe to products and services that we previously purchased. This kind of control relies on Internet insecurity.

If you're a farmer who just bought a tractor from John Deere, you might think that tractor is yours. That might be the way it used to be, but things are different today. Because tractors contain software—because they're in essence just computers with an engine, wheels, and a tiller attached—John Deere has been able to move from an ownership model to a licensing model. In 2015, John Deere told the copyright office that farmers receive "an implied license for the life of the vehicle to operate the vehicle." And that license comes with all sorts of rules and caveats. For one, farmers now have no right to repair or modify their tractors; instead, they have to use authorized diagnostic equipment, parts, and repair facilities that John Deere has monopoly control over.

Apple maintains strict control over which apps are available in its store. Before an app can be sold or given away to iPhone customers, it has to be approved by Apple. And the company has some strict rules about what it will and won't allow. No porn, of course, and no games about child labor or human trafficking—but also no political apps. This latter rule meant that Apple censored apps that tracked US drone strikes and apps containing "content that ridicules public figures." Such restrictions put Apple in a position to be able to implement government censorship demands. And it has done so: in 2017, Apple removed security apps from its China store.

Apple is an extreme example, but it's not the only company that censors your Internet. Facebook regularly censors posts, images, and entire websites. YouTube censors videos. Google censors search results. Google has also banned an app that randomly clicks on ads from its Chrome browser because the app messes with its advertising business model.

Normally, we wouldn't have a problem with a company making decisions about which products it chooses to carry. If Walmart won't sell music CDs with a parental warning advisory label, we are all free to buy those albums elsewhere. But many Internet companies can be very powerful, more so than predominantly brick-and-mortar stores, even chains as enormous as Walmart, because they benefit from what is called the network effect. That is, they become more useful as more people use them. One telephone is useless, and two are marginally useful, but an entire network of telephones is very useful. The same thing is true for fax machines, e-mail, the web, text messages, Snapchat, Facebook, Instagram, PayPal, and everything else. The more people use them, the more useful they are. And the more powerful the companies that control them become, the more control those companies can exert over you.

Unless you know how to jailbreak your phone to remove its restrictions, sideload apps, and live with a warranty-free device that can't receive updates without a lot of effort, the iTunes store is the only place you can go for iPhone apps. So if Apple decides not to carry an app, there is no way for ordinary customers to get it.

In most cases, control equals profits. Facebook controls how people get their news, taking power—and ad revenue—away from traditional newspapers and magazines. Amazon controls how people buy their stuff, taking power away from traditional retailers. Google controls how people find information, taking power away from all sorts of more traditional information systems. The battle over net neutrality is all about the telecommunications providers wanting to control your Internet experience.

In older writings, I have described the situation on the Internet as feudal. We give up control of our data and capabilities in exchange for services. I wrote:

> Some of us have pledged our allegiance to Google: we have Gmail accounts, we use Google Calendar and Google Docs, and we have Android—probably Pixel—phones. Others have pledged allegiance to Apple: we have Macintosh laptops, iPhones, and iPads; and we let iCloud automatically synchronize and back up everything. Still others of us let Microsoft do it all. Or we buy our music and e-books from Amazon, which keeps records of what we own and allows downloading to a Kindle, computer, or phone. Some of us have pretty much abandoned e-mail altogether . . . for Facebook.

These companies are like feudal lords in that they protect us from outside threats, and also in that they have surprisingly complete control over what we're allowed to see and do.

Companies are eyeing the Internet+ in the same way. Philips wants its controller to be the central hub for your light bulbs and other electronics. Amazon wants Alexa to be the central hub for your entire smart home. Both Apple and Google want their phones to be the singular device through which you control all your IoT devices. Everyone wants to be central, essential, and in control of your world.

And companies will give away services for free to get that access. Just as Google and Facebook give away services in exchange for the ability to spy on their users, companies will do the same thing with the IoT. Companies will offer free IoT stuff in exchange for the data they receive from monitoring the people using it. Companies owning fleets of autonomous cars might offer free rides in exchange for the ability to show ads to the passengers, mine their contacts, or route them past or make an intermediate stop at particular stores and restaurants.

Battles for control of customers and users are going to heat up in the coming years. And while the monopolistic positions of companies like Amazon, Google, Facebook, and Comcast allow them to exert significant control over their users, smaller, less obviously tech-based companies—like John Deere—are attempting to do the same.

This corporate power grab is all predicated on abusing the DMCA—the same law I discussed back in Chapter 2, that stymies the patching of software vulnerabilities. The DMCA was designed by the entertainment industry to protect copyright. It's a pernicious law that has given corporations the ability to enforce their commercial preferences with the rule of law. Because software is subject to copyright, protecting it with DRM copy protection software invokes the DMCA. The law makes it a crime to analyze and remove the copy protection, and hence to analyze and modify the software. John Deere enforces its prohibitions against farmers maintaining their own tractors by copy-protecting the tractors' embedded computers.

Keurig coffee makers are designed to use K-cup pods to make single servings of coffee. Because the machines use software to verify the codes printed on the K-cups, Keurig can enforce exclusivity, so only companies who pay Keurig can produce pods for its coffee machines. HP printers no longer allow you to use unauthorized ink cartridges. Tomorrow, the company might require you to use only authorized paper—or refuse to print copyrighted words you haven't paid for. Similarly, tomorrow's dishwasher could enforce which brands of detergent you use.

As the Internet+ turns everything into computers, all that software will be covered by the DMCA. This same legal trick is used to tie peripherals to products, to force consumers to only buy authorized compatible components, or only buy repair services from authorized dealers. This affects smartphones, thermostats, smart light bulbs, automobiles, and medical implants. And while some companies have overreached their DMCA claims and have lost in court, such power grabs are still a common tactic.

Often, user control goes hand in hand with surveillance. In order to ensure compliance with whatever restrictions they demand from their customers and users, companies often closely monitor what those customers and users are doing. Then they deny the customers access to that data. Customers are rebelling.

People are increasingly trying to hack their own medical devices. Hugo Campos is one of them. For years, he has had an implanted cardioverter defibrillator, which controls his heart condition but also continuously collects data about his heart. Think of it as something like a Fitbit with electro-shock capabilities. But unlike a Fitbit, his implanted device is proprietary, and Campos has been unable to access this data. He has resorted—so far, unsuccessfully—to suing the manufacturer. None of the companies that make implantable devices—Medtronic, Boston Scientific, Abbott Labs, and Biotronik—will allow patients access to their own data, and there's nothing anyone can do about it. The data is owned by the companies.

Similarly, people have been hacking their Toyota Priuses since 2004 to improve fuel efficiency, disable annoying warnings, get better diagnostic information out of the engine, modify engine performance, and access options available in European and Japanese versions of the car but not in the US version. These hacks may void the warranty, but the car manufacturers can't stop them. There are hacks and cheat codes for many other car models, too.

It's no different with automobile black-box data. Police and insurance companies use the data post-crash, but users don't have access to it. (A California law allowing individuals to access their car's data stalled because of opposition from car manufacturers.) And John Deere tractor owners have resorted to buying pirated firmware from Ukraine in order to repair their own tractors.

This isn't a black-and-white issue. We don't want people to have unfettered ability to hack their own consumer devices. For example, thermostats deliberately have wide control limits. Changing the software to maintain the temperature can damage the heating system by forcing it to turn on and off too frequently. Similarly, that pirated tractor software from Ukraine might remove—either accidentally or on purpose—a piece of the software that protects the transmission, causing it to fail more often. If John Deere is responsible for transmission repairs, that's a problem.

Similarly, we don't want people to hack their cars in ways that break emission control laws, or their medical devices in ways that evade legal restrictions surrounding the use of those devices. For example, some people are hacking their insulin pumps to create an artificial pancreas—a device that will measure their blood sugar levels and automatically deliver the proper doses of insulin on a continuous basis. Do we want to give them the ability to do that, or do we want to make sure that only regulated manufacturers produce and sell those devices? I'm not sure where the proper balance lies.

As the Internet+ permeates more of our lives, this kind of conflict will play out everywhere. People will want access to data from their fitness trackers, appliances, home sensors, and vehicles. They'll want that data on their own terms, in formats they can use for their own purposes. They'll want to be able to modify those devices to add functionality. Device manufacturers and governments will try to prevent such enhanced capability— sometimes for profit or anticompetitive reasons, sometimes for regulatory reasons, and sometimes just because vendors didn't bother making the data or controls accessible.

All of this reduces security. In order for companies to control us in the ways they want, they will build systems that allow for remote control. More importantly, they will build systems that assume the customer is the attacker and needs to be contained. This is a design requirement that runs counter to good security, because it gives outside attackers an avenue to gain access. At the same time, hackers can add insecurities through customers' back-room modifications to take control.

GOVERNMENTS ALSO USE THE INTERNET FOR SURVEILLANCE AND CONTROL

Governments want to surveil and control us for their own purposes, and they use the same insecure systems that corporations have given us to do it.

In 2017, the University of Toronto's research center Citizen Lab reported on the Mexican government's surveillance of what it considered political threats. The country had purchased surveillance software—spyware—from the cyberweapons manufacturer NSO Group, and had used it to spy on journalists, dissidents, political opponents, international investigators, lawyers, anti-corruption groups, and people who supported a tax on soft drinks.

Many other countries use Internet spyware to surveil their residents. The products of FinFisher, another commercial spyware company, were found in 2015 to be used by Bosnia, Egypt, Indonesia, Jordan, Kazakhstan,

Lebanon, Malaysia, Mongolia, Morocco, Nigeria, Oman, Paraguay, Saudi Arabia, Serbia, Slovenia, South Africa, Turkey, and Venezuela. This software was being deployed against dissidents, activists, journalists, and other individuals these governments wanted to arrest, intimidate, or just monitor.

Government surveillance for political and social control is normal on today's Internet. The same technologies that gave us surveillance capitalism also enable governments to conduct their own surveillance. The degree to which this has been occurring has come to light only in the past few years, and it shows no signs of slowing down. In fact, the Internet+ will almost certainly bring with it more government surveillance—some of it for good, but a lot of it for ill.

Modern government surveillance piggybacks on existing corporate surveillance. It isn't that the NSA woke up one morning and said: "Let's spy on everyone." It said: "Corporate America is spying on everyone. Let's get ourselves a copy." And it does—through bribery, coercion, threats, legal compulsion, and outright theft—collecting cell phone location data, Internet cookies, e-mails and text messages, log-in credentials, and so on. Other countries operate in a similar fashion.

Internet surveillance often involves the cooperation of telecommunications providers, who give the intelligence agencies copies of everything that goes through their switches. The NSA is a master of this, collecting the data that flows across US borders and internationally through its agreements with partner countries. We know that the NSA installs surveillance equipment at AT&T switches inside the US, and has collected cell phone metadata from Verizon and others. Similarly, Russia gets bulk access to data from ISPs inside its borders.

Most countries don't have either the budget or the expertise to develop this caliber of surveillance and hacking tools. Instead, they buy surveillance and hacking tools from cyberweapons manufacturers. These are companies like FinFisher's seller Gamma Group (Germany and the UK), HackingTeam (Italy), VASTech (South Africa), Cyberbit (Israel), and NSO Group (also Israel). They sell to countries like the ones I listed in the beginning of this section, allowing them to hack into computers, phones, and other devices. They even have a conference, called ISS World and nicknamed the "Wiretappers' Ball," and they explicitly market their products to repressive regimes for this purpose.

Internet surveillance has also been used for the purposes of foreign espionage for as long as the Internet has been around. The NSA might have led the way, but other countries weren't far behind. Early espionage operations against the US included Moonlight Maze in 1999 (probably Russia), Titan Rain in the early 2000s (almost certainly China), and Buckshot Yankee in 2008 (no idea who was behind this one).

The Chinese have been conducting cyberespionage operations against the US government for decades. Over the years, China has stolen the blueprints and design documents for several weapons systems, including the F-35 fighter plane. In 2010, China hacked into Google to get at the Gmail accounts of Taiwanese activists. In 2015, we learned that China was accessing the e-mail accounts of top US government officials. Also in 2015, the Chinese hacked into the Office of Personnel Management (OPM) and stole detailed personnel files of, among others, every US citizen with a security clearance.

Over the past decade, antivirus companies have exposed sophisticated hacking and surveillance tools from Russia, China, the US, the US and Israel together, Spain, and several unidentified countries. In 2017, North Korea hacked the South Korean military, stealing classified wartime contingency plans.

This isn't just political or military intelligence, but the widespread theft of intellectual property from corporations by other governments. China, for example, has stolen so much commercial intellectual property from the US that Chinese espionage was one of the key items of discussion between President Obama and Chinese president Xi Jinping in 2015, when the two countries reached an agreement to desist. (China does seem to have toned down its economic cyberespionage as a result.)

All of this is considered normal. Spying is a legitimate peacetime activity, and normally, countries can do whatever they can get away with. Just as the NSA spied on German chancellor Angela Merkel's smartphone, someone else spied on White House chief of staff John Kelly's smartphone. Even though the OPM breach affected 21.5 million Americans, we couldn't really condemn China, because we do the same thing. Indeed, Director of National Intelligence James Clapper said at the time: "You have to kind of salute the Chinese for what they did."

The country whose activities we know the most about is the US. The

NSA is in a class by itself for several reasons. One: its budget is significantly larger than that of any comparable agency on the planet. Two: most of the world's large tech companies are located inside the US—or in one of its partner countries—giving it greater access to their data. Three: the physical location of the planet's major Internet cables results in much of the world's communications going through the US at some point. And four: the NSA has secret agreements with other countries for even greater access to the raw communications networks of the planet.

US law enforcement conducts surveillance as well, but it's fundamentally different from what the NSA does. Law enforcement officers are governed by a different and more restrictive set of laws, and have to follow due-process laws concerning search and seizure. We can argue about whether those laws are well crafted, and how diligently the police follow them, but they do have important consequences. Law enforcement has to target its surveillance on individual suspects; the NSA does not. Law enforcement needs the evidence it collects to be admissible in court; the NSA does not. Law enforcement usually jumps in after a crime has occurred; the NSA conducts espionage on ongoing activities.

Some countries take surveillance to an extreme, using the Internet to spy on their entire population. China leads the way: the country's social media platforms are all monitored by the government, and offending statements can be censored. (The government's goal is not so much to limit speech as it is to limit the ability to create social movements, organize protests, and the like.)

Aside from surveillance, many countries use the Internet for censorship and control of their citizens. Authoritarian governments saw the Arab Spring and the "color revolutions" of the early 2000s as an existential threat, and believe that this kind of control is essential to the regime's survival. Countries like Russia, China, and Iran directly prosecute people who publish certain material, force companies to do their censorship for them, or steer online discussions in innocuous directions. Here, too, China takes the lead. It has the most extensive censorship regime of any country. The Great Firewall of China is a comprehensive system designed to limit access to the global Internet from inside China. And in 2020, the Chinese government plans to enact a "social credit" system. Each citizen will be given a score based on all their surveilled activities, and that score will be used as a gateway to various rights and privileges. And China exports its expertise in social control to other totalitarian countries.

Not all censorship is nefarious. France and Germany censor Nazi speech. Lots of countries censor speech that is considered to be copyright violation. And pretty much everyone censors child pornography.

To accomplish all this espionage, surveillance, and control, nation-states are making use of the Internet's insecurities, as I'll talk about more in Chapter 9. This isn't going away anytime soon, and will continue to be one of the driving forces behind nations' Internet+ security policies.

CYBERWAR IS THE NEW NORMAL

Some say cyberwar is coming. Some say cyberwar is here. Some say cyberwar is everywhere. In truth, "cyberwar" is a term that everyone uses, that no one agrees on, and that has no agreed-upon definition. But whatever we're calling it, countries are using the inherent insecurity of the Internet to attack each other. They're prioritizing the ability to attack over the ability to defend, which helps perpetuate an insecure Internet for all of us.

Stuxnet, discovered in 2010, was a sophisticated weapon developed by the US and Israel to attack the Natanz nuclear weapons plant in Iran. It specifically targeted a Siemens brand of programmable logic controllers that automate factory equipment like the centrifuges used to enrich weapons-grade uranium. It spread through Windows computers, looking for specific Siemens centrifuge controllers. When it found them, it repeatedly sped up and slowed down the centrifuges, causing them to tear themselves apart—while at the same time hiding what they were doing from the operators.

Militaries and national intelligence agencies all over the Internet are breaking into foreign computers, and in some cases causing both virtual and physical damage. International rules and norms about what's allowed and what's a just and proportional response remain mostly undefined. This environment favors attack over defense, just as Internet security technology makes attack easier than defense. And the dynamics are much different from those of conventional warfare.

Targets are not limited to military sites and systems, but extend to industrial sites for things like oil production, chemical processing, manufacturing, and power generation, all of which are now controlled via the Internet.

A cyberattack can be part of a larger operation. In 2007, Israel attacked a Syrian nuclear plant. This wasn't a cyberattack; conventional warplanes bombed the place. But there was a cyber component. Before the planes took off, Israeli hackers conducted a cyberattack to disable radar and anti-aircraft systems in Syria and neighboring countries. In 2008, Russia coordinated conventional and cyber operations in an attack against Georgia. The US conducted a series of cyber operations during the Iraqi war in 1990–1991. In 2016, President Obama acknowledged that the US is conducting cyber operations as part of its larger offensive against ISIS.

Sometimes attacks are exploratory or preparatory. In 2017, we learned about a group of Russian hackers who broke into at least 20 power company networks in the US and Europe, in some cases gaining the ability to disable the system. In 2016, the Iranians did the same thing to a dam in upstate New York. Experts surmise that these operations were reconnaissance for potential future action. This is something known as "preparing the battlefield," and many countries appear to be doing it to each other.

The risks have increased as our world has become more computerized, more networked, and more standardized. During the Cold War, most military computers and communications systems were distinct from their civilian counterparts, but no more. Millions of Department of Defense computers run Windows, including the computers that control weapons systems. The same computers and networks you have in your home and office control the critical infrastructure of pretty much every country. This makes the Internet itself a potential target.

It's not just the stronger powers attacking the weaker, as with Russia attacking the networks of Estonia in 2007, Georgia in 2008, and Ukraine repeatedly. A smaller nation-state can inflict disproportionate damage on its target in cyberspace for many of the reasons discussed in Chapter 1. For example, the Syrian Electronic Army attacked US news sites in 2013, and Iran attacked Las Vegas's Sands Hotel in 2014.

Countries vary widely in their capabilities. On the high end are countries with fully developed military cyber commands and intelligence agencies that can create their own custom attack tools. These include the US, the UK, Russia, China, France, Germany, and Israel. They are well funded, very skilled, and not easily dissuaded. They are the elite few, although most of their cyber operations are not sophisticated, because security is generally so bad that they don't have to be. One tier lower than the high end are countries that buy commercial tools and services from the cyberweapons manufacturers mentioned earlier. And even lower are the countries that simply use criminal hacking software they've downloaded off the Internet. Both of these tiers of countries can also hire cyber mercenaries. Increasing capabilities seems to require little more than making it a priority. If an isolated and heavily sanctioned country like North Korea can go from a nonentity in cyberspace to a significant threat in less than a decade, anyone can do it.

The risks of nation-state cyberattack are increasing, and governments are taking notice. Every year, the US director of national intelligence submits a Worldwide Threat Assessment document to the Senate and House select committees on intelligence. It's a good guide to what we're concerned about. The 2007 document didn't mention cyber threats at all. Even in the 2009 report, "the growing cyber and organized crime threat" was discussed only at the end of the document, where it felt like an afterthought. By 2010, cyber threats were the first threat listed in the annual report; and since then, they've been painted in increasingly dire terms. From the 2017 report:

> Our adversaries are becoming more adept at using cyberspace to threaten our interests and advance their own, and despite improving cyber defenses, nearly all information, communication networks, and systems will be at risk for years.
>
> Cyber threats are already challenging public trust and confidence in global institutions, governance, and norms, while imposing costs on the US and global economies. Cyber threats also pose an increasing risk to public health, safety, and prosperity as cyber technologies are integrated with critical infrastructure in key sectors. These threats are amplified by our ongoing delegation of decisionmaking, sensing, and authentication roles to potentially vulnerable automated systems. This delegation increases the likely physical, economic, and psychological consequences of cyber attack and exploitation events when they do occur.

Similarly, the Munich Security Conference—the most important international security policy conference in the world—didn't have a panel on cybersecurity until 2011. Now, cybersecurity has its own separate event.

We're all within the blast radius. Even a well-targeted cyberweapon like Stuxnet damaged networks far away from the Iranian Natanz nuclear plant. In 2017, the global shipping giant Maersk had its operations brought to a halt by NotPetya, a Russian cyberweapon used against Ukraine. The company was a bystander caught in the cross fire of an international cyberattack.

So far, most cyberattacks haven't happened in wartime. There was no war when the US and Israel attacked Iran with Stuxnet in 2010, or when Iran attacked the Saudi national oil company in 2012. There was no war when North Korea used WannaCry to lock up computer systems around the world in 2017, or in the years prior when the US conducted cyber operations against North Korea in an attempt to sabotage its nuclear program. In 2012, a senior Russian general published a paper articulating what became known as the Gerasimov Doctrine, calling for "the use of special-operations forces and internal opposition to create a permanently operating front," including engagement in "long-distance, contactless actions against the enemy" via "informational actions, devices, and means." That sounds a lot like the Russian hacking of the 2016 US election process. In today's world, the lines between war and peace are blurred, and covert tactics—such as the cyber operations discussed in this chapter—have become more important. Other countries seem to agree. This is why some people are saying that we're already involved in cyberwar.

There are cyberattacks that will be considered acts of war. And the US has stated that any response to such attacks won't necessarily be constrained to cyberspace. Still, most offensive actions in cyberspace have been conducted in a grey zone between peace and war—a state that political scientist Lucas Kello calls "unpeace"—and no one is sure how to respond. The US responded to the North Korean attack against Sony with some minor sanctions. The US responded to Russian hacking of the 2016 elections by closing consulates and expelling diplomats. Most countries respond to attacks with strong words, if that.

There are several reasons for the limited response. The first is that there isn't a clearly defined line between what is considered an act of war and what is not. International espionage is generally considered to be a valid peacetime activity; killing large numbers of people is generally considered to be an act of war. Everything else is in the middle.

As I described in Chapter 3, attribution can be difficult. In particular, there is a continuum of government involvement in cyberattack. Cyber policy expert Jason Healey developed an entire spectrum, from state-encouraged to state-coordinated to state-executed attacks, with many other shades of involvement in between. So, even if you can attribute an attack to a geographical location, it can be hard to figure out whether and to what degree a government is responsible.

The final reason why responses to attacks tend to be muted is that it can be hard to tell the difference between cyberespionage and cyberattack until it is too late—because until the last second, when an unauthorized intruder either copies everything or fires off a destructive payload, they look exactly the same.

Military cyberattacks have largely been ineffective over the long term. Espionage is easy. And short-term harmful but fleeting effects, like a power blackout in Ukraine, are easy. But anything more seems to be hard. Although Stuxnet was successful, at best it slowed Iran down by a couple of years, and had minimal effect on any international negotiations. The US also used cyberattacks to thwart North Korea in its attempts to build an atomic weapon and delivery system. Here again, the operations had very little long-term effect. Cyberweapons were used in the recent armed conflict in Ukraine, as well as in Syria's civil war; again, the effects were minimal.

A few more issues emphasize the importance and prevalence of attack over defense in modern cyberwarcraft. Cyberweapons are unique among weapons in that they are inherently unstable. That is, if you have a cyber-weapon that uses a certain vulnerability to deliver its payload, I can disable that weapon by locating and patching the vulnerability. This means that a nation finding itself at a temporary advantage will have to weigh the risks of launching a preemptive attack against the risks of having its arsenal depleted by ongoing defensive research. This instability makes cyberweapons more attractive to use, and to use now, before they are independently discovered.

And cyberweapons can be stolen and put to use in a way that conventional weapons cannot. In 2009, China exfiltrated the blueprints and other data for the US F-35 fighter aircraft from Lockheed Martin and a number of subcontractors. While that intellectual-property theft undoubtedly saved the Chinese government some of the $50 billion the US spent on development, as well as many years of effort, the Chinese military still had to design and build the planes. By contrast, the attackers who stole cyber-weapons from both the NSA and the CIA were able to use them with minimal additional time and cost. And when those hacking tools were leaked to the public, both foreign governments and criminals immediately deployed them for their own purposes.

Countries are also getting more brazen in their attacks. The continuing attacks against the US by Russia, China, and North Korea—and the occasional attacks by Iran, Syria, and others—demonstrate that other countries can attack us with impunity.

Honestly, the US has only itself to blame. We prioritized offense over defense. We were the ones who first used the Internet for both espionage and attack. Via the NSA, we undermined confidence in American technology companies. We pushed the envelope of what's acceptable. And because we felt we had an advantage over other countries, we didn't try to negotiate any treaties or establish any norms. At the same time, we developed the Internet as a commercial space where security was an afterthought, if that. Our actions were shortsighted, and now our actions are coming back to bite us.

The result is what foreign-policy scholars call a "security dilemma." Attack is not only easier than defense; it's cheaper than defense. So if a country wants to become more powerful in cyberspace, it's smarter to invest in offense—which means using the Internet's inherent insecurities. But if everyone does that, the world becomes less stable and the Internet becomes even less secure. This is the cyberwar arms race that nations find themselves in right now.

Western democracies are both the most vulnerable countries on the planet and the most unprepared for cyberattack. This is not to say that other countries aren't also worried. Sir John Sawers, the former head of the UK's MI6, said this in 2017: "I think both China and the United States—and probably Russia too—feels more vulnerable to being attacked than they feel the power of being able to attack themselves."

As national-security reporter Fred Kaplan wrote about the US: "We have better cyber rocks to throw at other nations' houses, but our house is glassier than theirs." I'll talk much more about this in Chapter 9.

The upshot is that countries have found themselves in this new state of perpetual unpeace, where the rules of engagement are still unwritten and everything is off-balance and unfamiliar. The major powers, all perceiving their own vulnerability, are naturally loath to lay down their cyber arms, all of which rely on vulnerabilities in the Internet. To preserve and enhance their offensive capabilities in this unfamiliar theater of war, they work diligently to perpetuate insecurity. In Chapters 9 and 10, I'll talk more about how they do this, why their logic is exactly wrong, and what they need to do to reverse course.

CRIMINALS BENEFIT FROM INSECURITY

Of course criminals prefer an insecure Internet; it's more profitable for them.

Willie Sutton famously robbed banks because "that's where the money is." Today, the money is online, and increasingly, criminals are, too. Criminals steal money from our bank accounts. They steal our credit card data and use it to commit fraud, or they steal our identity information and use that. They also lock up our data and then try to coerce us into paying for its return—that's ransomware.

In early 2018, the Indiana hospital Hancock Health was the victim of a cyberattack. Criminals—we have no idea who—encrypted its computers and demanded $55,000 in bitcoin to unlock them. Medical staff had no access to computerized medical records. Even though they had backups, they feared that the time required to restore the data would put patients at risk. They paid up.

Ransomware is increasingly common and lucrative. Victims range from organizations, as in the preceding story, to individuals. Kaspersky Lab reported that attacks on business tripled, and the number of different ransomware variants increased 11-fold, during nine months in 2016. Symantec found that average ransom amounts jumped from $294 in 2015 to $679 in 2016 to over $1,077 in 2017. Carbon Black reported that total sales of ransomware software on the black market increased 25 times from 2016 to 2017, to $6.5 million. Ransomware now comes with detailed instructions on how to pay, and some of the criminals behind the ransomware even have telephone help lines to assist victims. (If you're thinking that a help line is risky for the criminals, remember the international nature of this. The criminals don't fear prosecution in their home countries.) All in all, it's a billion-dollar business.

Cybercrime is a global big business, netting anywhere from $500 billion to $3 trillion annually, depending on whose analysis you trust. Additional losses due to intellectual-property theft are thought to cost another $225 to $600 billion per year.

Much of cybercrime involves impersonation: subverting the authentication systems discussed in Chapter 3. Walking into a bank pretending to be someone else is a dangerous way to make money, but doing the same thing on a bank's website is much easier and less risky. Often, all the criminal needs is the victim's username and password. It's no different with credit cards: if a criminal has the victim's card number and other information—name, address, whatever—he can use the card for whatever he wants. This is identity theft. It has many variants, all based on stolen credentials and impersonation.

CEO fraud, or "business e-mail compromise," is a specific form of identity theft. A thief pretends to be a company's CEO or other executive officer and sends an e-mail to accounts payable, telling them to send a check to the criminal. Or to send a copy of every employee's W-2 tax form, as a precursor to filing a fake tax return. Or to divert the proceeds of a real estate sale. This ploy can be very effective if the criminal does his research; we are all used to treating e-mails from the boss as legitimate and important.

There's more. A lot of cybercrime follows from this question: I've hacked into all of these computers; now what can I do with them? Turns out that the answer is: plenty. Criminals have harnessed large numbers of hacked computers into bot, or zombie, networks. Botnets can be used for all sorts of things: sending spam at high rates, solving CAPTCHAs, and mining bitcoin. Hackers use bots to commit click fraud: repeatedly clicking on ads on sites they control and collecting revenue from the third parties that place them, or clicking on ads placed by competitors and forcing them to pay. They use massive botnets to launch DDoS attacks against other victims.

If you control millions of bots, you can use them to overwhelm the Internet connections of individuals and even companies, and kick them off the Internet. These attacks can be hard to defend against, and it really is a contest of size: whether the defender's data pipe is large enough to handle all the incoming traffic. Sometimes the attackers extort money from companies with a threat.

International criminal organizations exploit legal and jurisdictional loopholes around the globe. They sell attack tools and even offer crimeware-as-a-service, also known as CaaS. According to Interpol:

> The CaaS model provides easy access to tools and services across the entire spectrum of criminality, from entry-level to top-tier players, including those with other motivations such as hacktivists or even terrorists. This allows even entry-level cybercriminals to carry out attacks of a scale disproportionate to their technical capability.

Individual criminals specialize in such things as credential stealing, payment fraud, and money laundering. They sell hacking tools and offer botnet services. There are even governments that engage in criminal activities, and governments that turn a blind eye to criminals in their countries who operate internationally. North Korea is particularly egregious. It employs hackers to raise money for government coffers, and in 2016 it stole $81 million from Bangladesh Bank.

Of course, profit isn't the only criminal motivation. People commit crimes out of hate, fear, revenge, politics, and so on. It's hard to find data on what percentage of total crime is not financial. We do know that people commit such crimes regularly. And, increasingly, they're committing them on the Internet—cyberstalking, stealing and publishing personal information for political gain or out of personal spite, and otherwise causing harm.

Every day, there are more computers to hack and control, and more data to steal. We're already seeing this. We've seen webcams, DVRs, and home routers hacked, made part of bot networks, and used to launch DDoS attacks. We've seen home appliances like refrigerators used to send spam e-mails. Attackers have bricked IoT devices, rendering them permanently nonfunctional.

We haven't yet experienced murder committed over the Internet, but the capability exists. Back in 2007, then–vice president Dick Cheney's heart defibrillator was specially modified to make it harder for him to be assassinated. In 2017, a man sent a tweet designed to cause a seizure in an epileptic recipient. Also in 2017, WikiLeaks published information about the CIA's work on hacking cars remotely.

Ransomware is also coming to the Internet of Things. Our embedded computers are no more resistant to ransomware than your laptop is, and criminals already understand that one obvious defense against computer ransomware—restoring the data from backup—won't work when lives are at immediate risk. Hackers have demonstrated ransomware against smart thermostats. In 2017, an Austrian hotel had its electronic door locks hacked and held for ransom. Cars, medical devices, home appliances, and everything else hackers can get into are next. The potential for additional criminal revenue is enormous.

And so is the potential for serious harm. A bricked car displaying a demand for $200 worth of bitcoin is an expensive inconvenience; a similar demand at speed is life-threatening. It's the same with medical devices. In 2017, the NotPetya ransomware shut down hospitals across the US and the UK. In some cases, UK hospitals were so incapacitated that they had to delay surgeries, route incoming emergency patients elsewhere, and replace damaged medical equipment. Over the next few years, we'll watch the attacks shift mostly to IoT devices and other embedded computers. We saw the harbinger of this trend in the Mirai botnet in 2016. It corralled a wide variety of IoT devices into the world's largest botnet, and while it was not used to spread ransomware, it could easily have done so.

5

Risks Are Becoming Catastrophic

The trends in the previous four chapters are not new—not the technical realities, not the political and economic trends, nothing. What's changing is how computers are being used in society: the magnitude of their decisions, the autonomy of their actions, and their interactions with the physical world. This increases the threat over several dimensions.

INTEGRITY AND AVAILABILITY ATTACKS ARE INCREASING

Information security is traditionally described as a triad consisting of confidentiality, integrity, and availability. You'll see it called the "CIA triad," which admittedly is confusing in the context of national security. But basically, the three things I can do with your data are steal a copy of it, modify it, or delete it.

Until now, threats have largely been about confidentiality. These attacks can be expensive, as when the North Koreans hacked Sony in 2014. They can be embarrassing, as in the theft of celebrity photos from Apple's iCloud in 2014 or the breach of the Ashley Madison adultery site in 2015. They can be damaging, as when the Russians hacked the Democratic National Committee in 2016, or when unnamed hackers stole 150 million personal records from Equifax in 2017. They can even be a threat to national security, as in the case of the Office of Personnel Management data breach of 2015. These are all confidentiality breaches.

Once you give computers the ability to affect the world, though, the integrity and availability threats matter more. Information manipulation is an increasing threat as systems become more capable and autonomous. Denial of service is an increasing threat as systems become more essential. Hacking is an increasing threat as systems have implications to life and property. My car has an Internet connection. And while I am worried that someone will hack into the car and eavesdrop on my conversations through the Bluetooth connection (a confidentiality threat), I am much more worried that they will disable the brakes (an availability threat) or modify the parameters of the automatic lane-centering and following-distance systems (an integrity threat). The confidentiality threat affects my privacy; the availability and integrity threats can kill me.

It's the same with databases. I am concerned about the privacy of my medical records, but I am even more concerned that someone could change my blood type or list of allergies (an integrity threat) or shut down lifesaving equipment (an availability threat). One way of thinking about this is that confidentiality threats are about privacy, but integrity and availability threats are really about safety.

Larger systems are vulnerable as well. In 2007, the Idaho National Laboratory demonstrated a cyberattack against an industrial turbine, causing it to spin out of control and eventually self-destruct. In 2010, Stuxnet basically did the same thing to Iranian nuclear centrifuges. In 2015, someone hacked into an unnamed steel mill in Germany and disrupted control systems such that a blast furnace could not be properly shut down, resulting in massive damage. And in 2016, the Department of Justice indicted an Iranian hacker who had gained access to the Bowman Dam in Rye, New York. According to the charges, he had the ability to remotely operate the dam's sluice gates. He didn't do anything with this access, but he could have.

These are the industrial-control systems known as SCADA. Our dams, power plants, oil refineries, chemical plants, and everything else are on the Internet—and vulnerable. And because all of them affect the world directly and physically, the risks increase dramatically as they come under computer control.

These systems will fail, and sometimes they'll fail badly. They'll fail by accident, and they'll fail under attack. Sociologist Charles Perrow studies complexity and accidents, and presciently wrote in 1984:

> Accidents and, thus, potential catastrophes are inevitable in complex, tightly coupled systems with lethal possibilities. We should try harder to reduce failures—and that will help a great deal—but for some systems it will not be enough.... We must live and die with their risks, shut them down, or radically redesign them.

In 2015, an 18-year-old outfitted a drone with a handgun for a science project and posted a YouTube video of that handgun being fired remotely.

That's just one way someone could use the Internet+ to commit murder. Someone could also take control of a victim's car at speed, hack a hospital drug pump to send the victim a fatal dose of something, or compromise electrical systems during a heat wave. These are not theoretical concerns. They've all been demonstrated by security researchers.

Cars are vulnerable. So are airplanes, commercial ships, electronic road signs, and tornado sirens. Nuclear weapons systems are almost certainly vulnerable to cyberattacks, as are the electronic systems that warn people of them. Satellites, too.

For society to work, we need to trust the computer processes that affect our lives. Attacks against the integrity of data undermine this trust. There are many examples. In 2016, Russian government hackers broke into the World Anti-Doping Agency and altered data from athletes' drug tests. In 2017, hackers—possibly hired by the government of the United Arab Emirates—hacked into a news agency in Qatar and planted inflammatory quotes falsely attributed to the country's emir, praising Iran and Hamas, and precipitating a diplomatic crisis between Qatar and its neighbors.

There is evidence that the Russians accessed voter databases in 21 US states on the eve of the 2016 election. The effects were minimal, but a more extensive integrity or availability attack would be devastating.

This is how it was phrased in the US director of national intelligence's 2015 Worldwide Threat Assessment:

Most of the public discussion regarding cyber threats has focused on the confidentiality and availability of information; cyber espionage undermines confidentiality, whereas denial-of-service operations and data-deletion attacks undermine availability. In the future, however, we might also see more cyber operations that will change or manipulate electronic information in order to compromise its integrity (i.e. accuracy and reliability) instead of deleting it or disrupting access to it. Decision-making by senior government officials (civilian and military), corporate executives, investors, or others will be impaired if they cannot trust the information they are receiving.

In separate testimonies before multiple House and Senate committees in 2015, then–director of national intelligence James Clapper and then–NSA director Mike Rogers spoke about these sorts of threats. They consider them far more serious than the confidentiality threat, and believe that the US is vulnerable.

The 2016 Worldwide Threat Assessment describes the threat this way:

> Future cyber operations will almost certainly include an increased emphasis on changing or manipulating data to compromise its integrity (i.e., accuracy and reliability) to affect decisionmaking, reduce trust in systems, or cause adverse physical effects. . . . Russian cyber actors, who post disinformation on commercial websites, might seek to alter online media as a means to influence public discourse and create confusion. Chinese military doctrine outlines the use of cyber deception operations to conceal intentions, modify stored data, transmit false data, manipulate the flow of information, or influence public sentiments—all to induce errors and miscalculation in decisionmaking.

We're also worried about criminals. Between 2014 and 2016, the US Treasury Department ran a series of exercises to help banks plan for data manipulation attacks related to transactions and trades, and then established a program to help banks restore customer accounts after a widespread attack. Someone inserting fake data into the financial system could wreak havoc; no one would know which transactions were real, and sorting it out manually could easily take weeks.

This all makes security critical in a way it hasn't been before. There is a fundamental difference between crashing your computer and losing your spreadsheet data, and crashing your pacemaker and losing your life, even though they might involve the same computer chips, the same operating system, the same software, the same vulnerability, and the same attack software.

ALGORITHMS ARE BECOMING AUTONOMOUS AND MORE POWERFUL

At their core, computers run software algorithms. In Chapter 1, I talked about the bugs and vulnerabilities and the increased vulnerability from complexity, but there's a new aspect that makes the problem even worse.

Machine learning is a particular class of software algorithm. It's basically a way of instructing a computer to learn by feeding it an enormous amount of data and telling it when it's doing better or worse. The machine-learning algorithm modifies itself to do better more often.

Machine-learning algorithms are popping up everywhere because they do things faster and better than humans, especially when large amounts of data are involved. They give us our search results, determine what's on our social network news feeds, score our creditworthiness, and determine which government services we're eligible for. They already know what we've watched and read, and they use that information to recommend books and movies we might like. They categorize photographs and translate text from one language to another. They play Go as well as a master; read X-rays and diagnose cancers; and inform bail, sentencing, and parole decisions. They analyze speech to assess suicide risk and analyze faces to predict homosexuality. They're better than we are at predicting the quality of fine Bordeaux wine, hiring blue-collar employees, and deciding whether to punt in football. Machine learning is used to detect spam and phishing e-mails, and also to make phishing e-mails more individual and believable, and therefore more effective.

Because these algorithms essentially program themselves, it can be impossible for humans to understand what they do. For example, Deep

Patient is a machine-learning system that has surprising success at predicting schizophrenia, diabetes, and some cancers—in many cases performing better than expert humans. But although the system works, no one knows how, even after analyzing the machine-learning algorithm and its results.

On the whole, we like this. We prefer the more accurate machine-learning diagnostic system over the human technician, even though it can't explain itself. For this reason, machine-learning systems are becoming more pervasive in many areas of society.

For the same reasons, we're allowing algorithms to become more autonomous. Autonomy is the ability of systems to act independently, without human supervision or control. Autonomous systems will soon be everywhere. A 2014 book, *Autonomous Technologies*, has chapters on autonomous vehicles in farming, autonomous landscaping applications, and autonomous environmental monitors. Cars now have autonomous features such as staying within lane markers, following a fixed distance behind another car, and braking without human intervention to avert a collision. Agents—software programs that do things on your behalf, like buying a stock if the price drops below a certain point—are already common.

We're also allowing algorithms to have physical agency. This is what I was thinking about when I described the Internet+ as an Internet that can affect the world in a direct physical manner. When you look around, computers with physical agency are everywhere, from embedded medical devices to cars to nuclear power plants.

Some algorithms that might not seem autonomous actually are. While it might be technically true that human judges make bail decisions, if they all do what the algorithm recommends because they believe the algorithm is less biased, then the algorithm is as good as autonomous. Similarly, if a doctor never contradicts an algorithm that makes decisions about cancer surgery—possibly out of fear of a malpractice suit—or if an army officer never contradicts an algorithm that makes decisions about where to target a drone strike, then those algorithms are as good as autonomous. Inserting a human into the loop doesn't count unless that human actually makes the call.

The risks in all of these cases are considerable.

Algorithms can be hacked. Algorithms are executed using software, and—as I discussed in Chapter 1—software can be hacked. All the examples in the previous chapters are the result of hacking software.

Algorithms require accurate inputs. Algorithms need data—often data about the real world—in order to function properly. We need to ensure that the data is available when those algorithms need it, and that the data is accurate. Sometimes the data is naturally biased. And one of the ways of attacking algorithms is to manipulate their input data. Basically, if we let computers think for us and the underlying input data is corrupt, they'll do the thinking badly and we might not ever know it.

In situations of what's called adversarial machine-learning, the attacker tries to figure out how to feed the system specific data that causes it to fail in a specific manner. One research project focused on image-classifying algorithms and found they were able to create images that were totally unrecognizable by humans and yet classified with high confidence by machine-learning networks. A related research project was able to fool visual sensors on cars with fake road signs in ways that wouldn't fool human eyes and brains. Yet another project tricked an algorithm into classifying rifles as helicopters, without knowing anything about the algorithm's design. (It's now a standard assignment in university computer science classes: fool the image classifier.)

Like the Microsoft chatbot Tay, which became racist and misogynistic because of deliberately fed data, hackers can train all sorts of machine-learning algorithms to do unexpected things. Spammers could similarly figure out how to fool anti-spam machine-learning algorithms. As machine algorithms become more prevalent and more powerful, we should expect more of these kinds of attacks.

There are also new risks in algorithms' speed. Computers make decisions and do things much faster than people. They can make stock trades in milliseconds, or shut power off for millions of homes at the same time. Algorithms can be replicated repeatedly in different computers, with each instance of an algorithm making millions of decisions per second. On the one hand, this is great because algorithms can scale in ways people can't—or at least can't easily, cheaply, and consistently. But speed can also make it harder to put meaningful checks on an algorithm's behavior.

Often, the only thing that slows algorithms down is interaction with people. When algorithms interact with each other at computer speeds, the combined results can quickly spiral out of control. What makes an autonomous system more dangerous is that it can do serious damage before a human intervenes.

In 2017, Dow Jones accidentally published a story about Google buying Apple. It was obviously a hoax, and any human reading it would have immediately realized it, but automated stock-trading bots were fooled—and stock prices were affected for two minutes until the story was retracted.

That was just a minor problem. In 2010, autonomous high-speed financial trading systems unexpectedly caused a "flash crash." Within minutes, a trillion dollars of stock market value was wiped out by unintended machine interactions, and the incident ended up bankrupting the company that caused the problem. And in 2013, hackers broke into the Associated Press's Twitter account and falsely reported an attack on the White House. This sent the stock markets down 1% within seconds.

We should also expect autonomous machine-learning systems to be used by attackers: to invent new attack techniques, to mine personal data for purposes of fraud, to create more believable phishing e-mails. They will only get more sophisticated and capable in the coming years.

At the DefCon conference in 2016, the US Defense Advanced Research Projects Agency (DARPA) sponsored a new kind of hacking contest. "Capture the Flag" is a popular hacking sport: organizers create a network filled with bugs and vulnerabilities, and teams defend their own part of the network while attacking other teams' parts. The Cyber Grand Challenge was similar, except teams submitted programs that tried to do the same automatically. The results were impressive. One program found a previously undetected vulnerability in the network, patched itself against the bug, and then proceeded to exploit it to attack other teams. In a later contest that had both human and computer teams, some computer teams outperformed some human teams.

These algorithms will only get more sophisticated and more capable. Attackers will use software to analyze defenses, develop new attack techniques, and then launch those attacks. Most security experts expect offensive autonomous attack software to become common in the near future. And then it's just a matter of the technology improving. Expect the computer attackers to get better at a much faster rate than the human attackers; in another five years, autonomous programs might routinely beat all human teams.

As Mike Rogers, the commander of US Cyber Command and the director of the NSA, said in 2016: "Artificial intelligence and machine learning . . . is foundational to the future of cybersecurity. . . . We have got to work our way through how we're going to deal with this. It is not the if, it's only the when to me."

Robots offer the most evocative example of software autonomy combined with physical agency. Researchers have already exploited vulnerabilities in robots to remotely take control of them, and have found vulnerabilities in teleoperated surgical robots and industrial robots.

Autonomous military systems deserve special mention. The US Department of Defense defines an autonomous weapon as one that selects a target and fires without intervention from a human operator. All weapons systems are lethal, and they are all prone to accidents. Adding autonomy increases the risk of accidental death significantly. As weapons become computerized—well before they're actual robot soldiers—they, too, will be vulnerable to hacking. Weapons can be disabled or otherwise caused to malfunction. If they are autonomous, they might be hacked to turn on each other or their human allies in large numbers. Weapons that can't be recalled or turned off—and also operate at computer speeds—could cause all sorts of lethal problems for friend and foe alike.

All of this comes together in artificial intelligence. Over the past few years, we've read some dire predictions about the dangers of AI. Technologists Bill Gates, Elon Musk, and Stephen Hawking, and philosopher Nick Bostrom, have all warned of a future where artificial intelligence—either as intelligent robots or as something less personified—becomes so powerful that it takes over the world and enslaves, exterminates, or ignores humanity. The risks might be remote, they argue, but they're so serious that it would be foolish to ignore them.

I am less worried about AI; I regard fear of AI more as a mirror of our own society than as a harbinger of the future. AI and intelligent robotics are the culmination of several precursor technologies, like machine-learning algorithms, automation, and autonomy. The security risks from those precursor technologies are already with us, and they're increasing as the technologies become more powerful and more prevalent. So, while I am worried about intelligent and even driverless cars, most of the risks are already prevalent in Internet-connected drivered cars. And while I am worried about robot soldiers, most of the risks are already prevalent in autonomous weapons systems.

Also, as roboticist Rodney Brooks pointed out, "Long before we see such machines arising there will be the somewhat less intelligent and belligerent machines. Before that there will be the really grumpy machines. Before that the quite annoying machines. And before them the arrogant unpleasant machines." I think we'll see any new security risks coming long before they get here.

OUR SUPPLY CHAINS ARE INCREASINGLY VULNERABLE

There's another class of attacks that we have addressed only peripherally, and that's supply-chain attacks. These are attacks that target the production, distribution, and maintenance of computers, software, networking equipment, and so on—everything that makes up the Internet+, which means everything.

For example, there is widespread suspicion that networking products made by the Chinese company Huawei contain government-controlled backdoors, and that computer security products from Kaspersky Lab are compromised by the Russian government. In 2018, US intelligence officials warned against buying smartphones from the Chinese companies Huawei and ZTE. Back in 1997, the Israeli company Check Point was dogged by rumors that the Israeli government added backdoors into its products. In the US, the NSA secretly installed eavesdropping equipment in AT&T facilities and collected information on cell phone calls from mobile providers.

All of these hacks target the underlying products and services we use on the Internet and the trust we have in them. They demonstrate the vulnerability of our very international supply chain for technological products.

These risks were never considered in the course of the Internet's evolution, and they're largely an accidental outcome of its unexpected growth and success. Our hardware is made in Asia where production costs are low. Our programmers come from all over the world, and more and more programming is done in countries like India and the Philippines, where labor costs less than in the US. The result is a supply-chain mess. A product's computer chips might be manufactured in one country and assembled in another, run software written in a third, and be integrated into a final system in a fourth before it is quality tested in a fifth and sold to a customer in a sixth. At any of those steps, the security of the final system can be subverted by those in the supply chain. All of those countries have their own local governments with their own incentives, and any one of them can coerce their own citizens into doing their bidding. Adding a backdoor onto a computer chip during the fabrication process is straightforward, and resistant to most detection techniques.

One of the ways governments try to defend against some of these attacks is to demand to see the source code for the software they buy. China demands to see source code. So does the US. Kaspersky offered to let any government see its source code after it was accused of having backdoors inserted by the Russian government. Of course, this cuts both ways: countries can use offered source code to find vulnerabilities to exploit. In 2017, HP Enterprise faced criticism because it had given Russia the source code to its ArcSight line of network security products.

Governments aren't just compromising products and services in their own countries during the design and production process. They're interdicting the distribution process as well, either individually or in bulk. According to NSA documents from Edward Snowden, the NSA was looking to put its own backdoor in Huawei's equipment. We know from the Snowden documents that NSA employees would routinely intercept Cisco networking equipment being shipped to foreign customers and install eavesdropping equipment. That was done without Cisco's knowledge—and the company was livid when it found out—but I'm sure there are other American companies that are more cooperative. Backdoors have been discovered in Juniper firewalls and D-Link routers—and there's no way to tell who placed them there.

Hackers have introduced fake apps into the Google Play store. They look and act like real apps—and have similar enough names to fool people—but they collect your personal information for malicious purposes. One report said that 4.2 million fake apps were downloaded by unsuspecting people in 2017. This included a fake WhatsApp app. Users got lucky here; it was just designed to steal advertising revenue, not to eavesdrop on people's conversations.

Here are more examples from 2017. Hackers linked to China compromised the legitimate download site for a popular Windows tool called CCleaner, resulting in millions of users unsuspectingly downloading a malware-infected version of the software. Unknown hackers corrupted the legitimate software update mechanism for a piece of Ukrainian accounting software to spread NotPetya malware throughout the country. Another group used fake antivirus updates to spread malware. Researchers demonstrated how to hack an iPhone by infecting a third-party replacement screen. And there are enough similar attacks that some people are warning not to buy any used IoT devices from sites like eBay.

Larger systems are vulnerable to these attacks, too. In 2012, China funded, and Chinese companies built, the new headquarters for the African Union in Addis Ababa, Ethiopia—including the building's telecommunications systems. In 2018, the African Union discovered that China was using that infrastructure to spy on the organization's computers. I am reminded of the US embassy that Russian contractors built in Moscow during the Cold War; it was riddled with listening devices.

Supply-chain vulnerabilities are an enormous security issue, and one we are largely ignoring. Commerce is so global that it just isn't feasible for any country to keep its entire supply chain within its borders. Pretty much every US technology company makes its hardware in countries like Malaysia, Indonesia, China, and Taiwan. And while the US government occasionally touches on this issue by blocking the occasional merger or acquisition, or by banning the occasional hardware or software product, those are minor interventions in what is a much larger problem.

IT'S ONLY GETTING WORSE

Our critical dependence on the Internet is, well, becoming critical. In a 2012 speech, then–secretary of defense Leon Panetta warned:

> An aggressor nation or extremist group could use these kinds of cyber tools to gain control of critical switches. They could derail passenger trains, or even more dangerous, derail trains loaded with lethal chemicals. They could contaminate the water supply in major cities, or shut down the power grid across large parts of the country.

This is from the 2017 Worldwide Threat Assessment:

Cyber threats also pose an increasing risk to public health, safety, and prosperity as cyber technologies are integrated with critical infrastructure in key sectors. These threats are amplified by our ongoing delegation of decisionmaking, sensing, and authentication roles to potentially vulnerable automated systems.

This is from the 2018 version:

The potential for surprise in the cyber realm will increase in the next year and beyond as billions more digital devices are connected—with relatively little built-in security—and both nation states and malign actors become more emboldened and better equipped in the use of increasingly widespread cyber toolkits. The risk is growing that some adversaries will conduct cyber attacks—such as data deletion or localized and temporary disruptions of critical infrastructure—against the United States in a crisis short of war.

To be sure, some of this is hyperbole. But much of it is not.

In 2015, Lloyd's of London developed a hypothetical scenario of a large-scale cyberattack on the US power grid. Its attack scenario was realistic, not any more sophisticated than what Russia did to Ukraine in December 2015 and June 2017, combined with the Idaho National Lab demonstration attack against power generators. Lloyd's researchers envisioned a blackout that affected 95 million people across 15 states and lasted anywhere from 24 hours to several weeks, costing between $250 billion and $1 trillion—depending on the details of the scenario.

The admittedly clickbait title of this book refers to the still-science-fictional scenario of a world so interconnected, with computers and networks so deeply embedded in our most important technical infrastructures, that someone could potentially destroy civilization with a few mouse clicks. We're nowhere near that future, and I'm not convinced we'll ever get there. But the risks are becoming increasingly catastrophic.

There's a general principle at work. Advances in technology allow attacks to scale, and better technology means that fewer attackers can do more damage. Someone with a gun can do more damage than someone with a sword, and that same person armed with a machine gun can do more damage still. Someone armed with plastic explosives can do more damage than someone with a stick of dynamite, and someone with a dirty nuke can do more damage still. That gun-carrying drone will become cheaper and easier to make; maybe someday it will be possible to easily make one on a 3D printer; there's already a kludgy demo on YouTube.

We've already seen this scaling on the Internet. Cybercriminals can steal more money from more bank accounts faster than criminals on foot. Digital pirates can copy more movies faster to cloud servers than when people had to use VHS tapes. The governments of the world have learned that the Internet allows them to eavesdrop more efficiently than the old telephone networks ever did. The Internet allows attacks to scale to a degree impossible without computers and networks.

Remember in Chapter 1 where I talked about distance not mattering, class breaks, and the ability to encapsulate skill into software? These trends become even more dangerous as our computer systems become more critical to our infrastructure. Risks include someone crashing *all* the cars—to be fair, it's more likely crashing all the cars of a particular make and model year that share the same software—or shutting down *all* the power plants. We're worried about someone robbing *all* the banks at once. We're worried about someone committing mass murder by seizing control of *all* the insulin pumps of the same manufacturer. These catastrophic risks have simply never been possible before the interconnection, automation, and autonomy afforded by the Internet.

As we move into the world of the Internet+, where computers permeate our lives at every level, class breaks will become increasingly perilous. The combination of automation and action at a distance will give attackers more power and leverage than they have ever had before. The US has always seen itself as a risk-taking society, and we prefer to act first and clean up afterwards. But if the risks are too great, can we continue in this vein?

This is the risk that keeps me up at night. It's not a "Cyber Pearl Harbor," where one nation launches a surprise attack against another. It's a criminal attack that escalates out of control.

Additionally, there's an asymmetry between different nations. Liberal democracies are more vulnerable than totalitarian countries, partly because we rely on the Internet+ more and for more critical things, and partly because we don't engage in heavy-handed centralized control. At a 2016 press conference, President Obama admitted as much: "Our economy is more digitalized, it is more vulnerable, partly because . . . we have a more open society, and engage in less control and censorship over what happens over the Internet."

This asymmetry makes deterrence more difficult. It makes preventing escalation more difficult. And it puts us in a more dangerous position with respect to other countries in the world.

An interesting thing happens when increasingly powerful attackers interact with society. As technology makes each individual attacker more powerful, the number of them we can tolerate decreases. Think of it basically as a numbers game. Thanks to the way humans behave as a species and as a society, every society is going to have a certain percentage of bad actors—which means a certain crime rate. At the same time, there's a particular crime rate that society is willing to tolerate. As the effectiveness of each criminal increases, the total number of criminals a society can tolerate decreases.

As a thought experiment, assume the average burglar can reasonably rob a house a week, and a city of 100,000 houses might be willing to live with a 1% burglary rate. That means the city can tolerate 20 burglars. But if technology suddenly increases each burglar's efficiency so that he can rob five houses a week, the city can only tolerate four burglars. It has to lock up the other 16 in order to maintain that same 1% burglary rate.

Society actually does this. People don't calculate the equation explicitly, but it's no less real. If the crime rate gets too high, we start complaining that there aren't enough police. If the crime rate gets too low, we start complaining that we're spending too much money on police. In the past, with inefficient criminals, we were willing to live with a given percentage of criminals in our society. As technology makes each individual criminal more efficient, the percentage we can tolerate decreases.

This is the real risk of terrorism in the future. Because terrorists can potentially do so much more damage with modern technology, we have to ensure that there are proportionally fewer of them. This is why there has been so much talk about terrorists with weapons of mass destruction. The technologies that we most feared after 9/11 were nuclear, chemical, and biological. Later, radiological weapons were added to those three. Cyberweapons have been invoked in the same breath as the others, mostly because of the high uncertainty as to how bad they can be. Electromagnetic pulse weapons are specifically designed to disable electronic systems. I'm sure that future technological developments will result in still-unimagined technologies of mass destruction, but these are the ones we fear today.

Internet terrorism is still a few years away. Even the 2017 Worldwide Threat Assessment limits concerns about terrorism and the Internet to coordination and control:

> Terrorists—to include the Islamic State of Iraq and ash-Sham (ISIS)—will also continue to use the Internet to organize, recruit, spread propaganda, raise funds, collect intelligence, inspire action by followers, and coordinate operations. Hizballah and HAMAS will continue to build on their cyber accomplishments inside and outside the Middle East. ISIS will continue to seek opportunities to target and release sensitive information about US citizens, similar to their operations in 2015 disclosing information about US military personnel, in an effort to inspire attacks.

My guess is that we're not going to see Internet terrorism until the Internet can kill people in a graphic manner. Shutting off the electricity of a million people doesn't terrorize in the same way. It happens regularly by accident, and even if some people die, it will only be a footnote to the event. Driving a truck into a crowd of people guarantees top billing on the nightly news, even if it's low-tech. But Internet attackers are getting more aggressive, ingenious, and tenacious every year, and someday Internet terrorism involving planes or cars will be possible.

What makes these attacks so different from conventional ones is the damage they can cause. The potential consequences are so great that we believe we cannot afford to have even one serious incident. To return to that thought experiment, we fear that technological advances will render each attacker so powerful that we cannot tolerate even one successful attack.

In November 2001, then–vice president Dick Cheney articulated the "One Percent Doctrine," described by journalist Ron Suskind thus: "If there was even a 1 percent chance of terrorists getting a weapon of mass destruction—and there has been a small probability of such an occurrence for some time—the United States must now act as if it were a certainty." In essence, I have just supplied a rationale for Cheney's doctrine.

Some of these new risks have nothing to do with attacks by hostile nations or terrorists. Rather, they arise from the very nature of the Internet+, which encompasses and connects almost everything, making it all vulnerable *at the same time*. Like large utilities and financial systems, the Internet+ is a system that's too big to fail. Or, at least, the security is too important to fail because the attackers are too powerful to succeed and their results would be too catastrophic to consider.

These failures could come from smaller attacks, or even accidents, that cascade badly. I have long thought that the 2003 blackout that covered most of the northeastern US and southeastern Canada was the result of a cyberattack. It wasn't deliberate by any stretch of the imagination, but the attack happened on a day that a Windows worm—Blaster—was spreading virulently and causing computers to crash. The official report on the blackout specifically said that none of the computers directly controlling the power grid were running Windows, but the computers that were monitoring those computers were, and the report said that some of them were offline. I blame the virus for hiding the small initial power outage long enough for it to have catastrophic effects, although the authors of the virus had no idea this would happen and couldn't have deliberately done it on a bet.

Similarly, the authors of the Mirai botnet didn't realize that their attack against Dyn would result in so many popular websites being knocked offline. I don't think they even knew what companies used Dyn's DNS services, and that they were a single point of failure without any backup. In fact, three college students wrote the botnet to gain an advantage in the video game Minecraft.

Damage to computers controlling physical systems radiates outwards. A 2012 attack against the Saudi Arabian national oil company only affected the company's IT network. But it erased all data on over 30,000 hard drives, crippling the company for weeks and affecting oil production for months—which had an effect on global availability. The shipping giant Maersk was hit so badly by NotPetya that it had to halt operations at 76 port terminals around the world.

Devices not normally associated with critical infrastructure can also cause catastrophes. I've already mentioned class breaks against systems like automobiles, especially driverless cars, and medical devices. To this we can add mass murder by swarms of weaponized drones, the disruption of critical systems by ever-more-massive botnets, using biological printers to produce lethal pathogens, malicious AIs enslaving humanity, malicious code received from space aliens hacking the planet, and all the things we haven't thought of yet.

Okay; let's pause to catch our collective breath. We tend to panic unduly about the future. Think of all the doomsday scenarios throughout history that never happened. During the Cold War, many were sure that humans would kill themselves in a thermonuclear war. They put less money into long-term savings. Some people decided not to have children, because what was the point? In hindsight, there are a lot of reasons why neither the US nor the USSR started World War III, but none of them were obvious at the time. Partly, it turned out our world's leaders weren't as fanatical as we thought they were. Over the years, there were plenty of technical glitches in both the US's and the USSR's missile detection systems—instances where the equipment clearly showed that the country was under nuclear attack—and in neither instance did the country retaliate. The Cuban Missile Crisis is probably the closest we came politically to a nuclear war, although the 1983 false alarm is a good close second. Yet it didn't happen.

Our collective fears after the 9/11 terrorist attacks were similar. That singular event, with its 3,000-person death toll and $10 billion cost in property and infrastructure damage, was way out of proportion to every other terrorist attack we have experienced in the history of our planet (although much less damaging than the annual death toll from automobiles, heart disease, or malaria). But instead of regarding it as a singular event unlikely to be repeated anytime soon, people decided it was the new normal. The truth is that the typical terrorist attack looks more like the Boston Marathon bombings: 3 people dead, 264 people injured, and not a lot of ancillary damage. Bathtubs, home appliances, and deer combined kill many more Americans per year on average than do terrorists. But while we seem to be coming out of our collective PTSD reaction to 9/11, we're still much more fearful of terrorist threats than makes sense, given the actual risk. In general, people are very bad at assessing risk.

For years, I have been writing about what I call "movie-plot threats": security threats so outlandish that, while they make great movie plots, are so unlikely that we shouldn't waste time worrying about them. I coined the term in 2005 to poke fun at all the scary, overly specific terrorism stories the media was peddling: terrorists with scuba gear, terrorists dispersing anthrax from crop dusters, terrorists contaminating the milk supply. My point was twofold. One: we are a species of storytellers, and detailed stories evoke a fear in us that general discussions of terrorism don't. And two: it makes no sense to defend against specific plots; instead, we should focus more on general security measures that work against any plot. With respect to terrorism, that's intelligence, investigation, and emergency response. Smart security measures will be different for other threats.

It's easy to discount the more extreme scenarios in this chapter as movie-plot threats. Individually, some of them probably are. But collectively, these are classes of threat that have precursors in the past and will become more common in the future. Some of them are happening now, to a varying degree of frequency. And while I certainly have the details wrong, the broad outlines are correct. As with fighting terrorism, our goal isn't to play whack-a-mole and stop a few particularly salient threats, but to design systems from the start that are less likely to be successfully attacked.

PART II
THE SOLUTIONS

nternet+ security looks pretty bleak. The threats are increasing, the attackers are more brazen, and the defenses are increasingly inadequate.

All the blame shouldn't fall on the technology. Engineers already know how to secure some of the problems I've mentioned. Hundreds of companies, and even more academic researchers, are working on new and better security technologies against the emerging threats. The challenges are hard, but they're "send a man to the moon" hard and not "travel faster than light" hard. And while nothing is a panacea, there really isn't any limit to engineers' creativity in coming up with novel solutions to hard problems.

Still, I don't think it will get better anytime soon. My pessimism stems primarily from the policy challenges. The current state of Internet security is a direct result of business decisions made by corporations and military/espionage decisions made by governments—everything I wrote about in Chapter 4. What we've learned from the past few decades is that computer security is more a human problem than a technical problem. What's important is the law and economics, and the psychology and sociology—and what's critical is the politics and governance.

Consider spam. For years, spam was a problem you had to deal with on your computer, or maybe with help from your ISP if it provided local anti-spam services. The most efficient way to identify and delete spam was in the network, but none of the Internet backbone companies bothered, because they didn't really care and had no way to bill the user for their effort. The situation only changed when the economics of e-mail changed. Once most users had accounts at one of only a few large e-mail providers and most e-mail passed between them, it suddenly made sense for them to provide anti-spam services to all of their users automatically. The result was a slew of technologies that detect and quarantine spam. Today, spam still constitutes just over half of all e-mail, but 99.99% of it is blocked. It's one of computer security's success stories.

Consider credit card fraud. In the early days of credit cards, banks passed most of the costs of fraud on to consumers. The result was that banks did little to prevent fraud. That changed in 1974, when the US enacted the Fair Credit Billing Act, limiting consumer liability to the first $50. By forcing banks to pay the costs of fraud, Congress provided a fraud reduction incentive. The result was all the anti-fraud measures that are now in place: real-time card verification, back-end expert systems that search transaction streams for signs of fraud, manual card-activation requirements, chip cards, and so on. These measures all reduced overall fraud and—more importantly—they weren't anything that customers could possibly have implemented.

UK banks were more able to pass the costs of fraud on to consumers, so they were slower to adopt these measures. The EU's Payment Services Directives have sought to align consumer protection more with US standards, but have left wiggle room for banks to claim that customers must have been grossly negligent. (Amazingly, the UK may make this even worse.) And similarly, in the US, debit cards weren't secured until another law forced banks to pay the costs of fraud, just as they did for credit cards.

In both of those examples, once we got the incentives for security right, the technologies came along to make it happen. With spam, it took a change in the e-mail ecosystem to shift the incentives of e-mail providers. With credit cards, it took a law to shift the incentives of banks. Similarly, Internet+ security is primarily a problem of incentives—and of policy.

Until now, we have left both the market and the government largely alone and able to operate in secret, and they have settled on the situation I described in Part I. That's the unsatisfactory state of security with the current policies we have in place. The market won't improve things as long as there's more near-term profit to be had in spying on us and selling our data, keeping security details secret from consumers and users, and ignoring security and hoping for the best. Governments won't improve things as long as they're largely controlled by corporate lobbyists, and by organizations, like the NSA and Justice Department, that prefer spying to security.

If we want to change the balance of losses due to poor security and expenses due to security improvements, we're going to have to change the incentives. It will be our representative governments, working transparently, that will change things for the better. Government is the missing piece in Internet+ security today. Although there will certainly be all sorts of problems getting it done, I don't see any other way it will work. Government involvement, whether in the form of regulation, liabilities, or direct funding, isn't a panacea, but neither is its absence. At its best, government enables us all to overcome collective action problems, to finance efforts that don't emphasize near-term payoffs, and to establish baselines of what is acceptable behavior. At its worst, government is captured by private interests or becomes an entrenched bureaucracy more concerned with its own survival than with governing. The reality is likely to be somewhere between the two.

In my book on trust, *Liars and Outliers*, I wrote that "security is a tax on the honest." I mean that very generally: the additional costs we all incur because some of us are dishonest. We pay for it in higher store prices because the owners have hired guards and installed security cameras to deal with shoplifting.

Security spending is a kind of dead weight. It doesn't do anything productive; instead, it reduces the bad things that happen. If banks didn't need to spend money on security, their services could be cheaper. If governments didn't need to spend money on police or military, they could lower taxes. If you and I didn't have to worry about burglary, we could save money by not buying door locks, burglar alarms, and window bars. In some countries, something like a quarter of all labor can be defined as "guard labor."

Internet+ security is no different. The tech analyst firm Gartner estimates 2018 worldwide Internet security spending at $93 billion. If we want more security, we're going to have to spend money to get it. We're going to have to pay higher prices for our computers, phones, IoT devices, Internet services, and everything else. There is simply no other option. The policy questions involve how we're going to pay for it.

Sometimes it makes sense for us to pay for security individually. Home security works that way. We each buy our own door locks, and some of us also purchase burglar alarm systems. Some of us spend our money on guns in our homes. Maybe the wealthiest among us pay for bodyguards, panic rooms, or, if you're a James Bond villain, henchmen. These are all expenses, but they're personal. Whatever you do doesn't affect me, and whatever I do doesn't affect you.

Sometimes it makes sense for us to pay for security collectively. Policing works that way. We don't say: "If you want some policing, then pay for it yourself." Instead, a portion of the taxes we all pay goes towards community police services. We do this because common benefits are most effectively provided through collective decision-making and funding. The police protect society in general (at least theoretically), regardless of whether specific individuals want protection.

In the end, our improved security for the Internet+ will likely be a mixture of individual and collective expenditures, all of which I will talk about in Part II. Individual expenditures will include security programs for our computers and firewalls for our networks. Collective expenditures will include police investigations of cybercrime, military cyberwarfare units, and investments in Internet infrastructure. Companies will build security into their products, either because the market demands it or because government forces them to. There will be lawsuits where there's insecurity, insurance to protect against losses, and the resultant security increase to prevent the lawsuits and reduce the insurance premiums. It won't be one thing; it will be a patchwork of many things—just like security in the real world.

It'll be expensive. But here's the thing: we're paying it anyway. It's hard to get good numbers on how much Internet insecurity costs, but we have a range. A 2017 Ponemon Institute report concluded that one in four companies will be hacked at an average cost of $3.6 million each. A Symantec report estimated that 978 million people in 20 countries were affected by cybercrime in 2017, at a cost of $172 billion. A 2018 study by RAND provided the most comprehensive analysis I've seen, and the results are all over the map.

We found that resulting values are highly sensitive to input parameters; for instance, using three reasonable sets of parameters from existing research and our own data analysis, we found that cyber crime has a direct gross domestic product (GDP) cost of $275 billion to $6.6 trillion globally and total GDP costs (direct plus systemic) of $799 billion to $22.5 trillion (1.1 to 32.4 percent of GDP).

Regardless of which estimate you use, it's a lot of money. And that cost will be a drag on the economy, whether we pay it all in losses, or pay some of it in security measures designed to minimize those losses. Anything we pay in losses is wasted. But anything we pay in improved security results in better security technologies, fewer criminals, more secure corporate practices, and so on—all things that will continue to pay off year after year.

There's a joke that says technologists look to the law to solve their problems, while lawyers look to technology to solve their problems. In truth, to make any of this work, technology and law have to work together. This is the most important lesson of the Edward Snowden documents. We always knew that technology could subvert law. Snowden showed us that law—especially secret law—can also subvert technology. Both must work together, or neither can work.

Part II describes how we can do that.

6

What a Secure Internet+ Looks Like

I n 2016, the Norwegian Consumer Council evaluated three Internet-connected dolls. The group found that the companies' terms of use and privacy policies showed a "disconcerting lack of regard for basic consumer and privacy rights," and were "generally vague about data retention," and that two of the toys "transfer personal information to a commercial third party, who reserves the right to use this information for practically any purpose, unrelated to the functionality of the toys themselves." It gets worse:

> It was discovered that two of the toys have practically no embedded security. This means that anyone may gain access to the microphone and speakers within the toys, without requiring physical access to the products. . . .
>
> Furthermore, the tests found evidence that voice data is being transferred to a company in the US, who also specialize in collecting biometric data such as voice-fingerprinting. Finally, it was revealed that two of the toys are embedded with pre-programmed phrases endorsing different commercial products, which practically constitutes product-placement within the toys themselves.

I use one of the dolls, My Friend Cayla, as a demonstration in the Internet security policy class I teach at Harvard Kennedy School. It's ridiculously easy for even my nontechnical students to hack. All they need to do is open up their phone's Bluetooth control panel and connect to the doll from their seats. They can then eavesdrop on what the toy hears, and send messages through the toy's speakers. It's a super-creepy demonstration of how bad the security of a commercial product can get. Germany banned My Friend Cayla because it's effectively an eavesdropping device that leaves the audio it records unprotected on the Internet, although it's still for sale in other countries. And it's not just one-off dolls; Mattel's Hello Barbie had similar problems.

In 2017, the consumer credit-reporting agency Equifax announced that 150 million Americans, just under half of the population, had had their personal data stolen. The attackers gained access to full names, Social Security numbers, birth dates, addresses, and driver's license numbers—exactly the information needed to commit the identity theft frauds I talked about in Chapter 4. This was not a sophisticated attack, and we still have no idea who did it. The attackers used a critical vulnerability in the Apache website software that had been patched two months earlier. Equifax had been notified by Apache, US-CERT, and the Department of Homeland Security about the vulnerability, but didn't get around to installing the patch until months after the attackers used it to breach the network. The company's insecurity was incredible. When I testified about it to the House Energy and Commerce Committee, I called it "laughably bad." And it wasn't an isolated incident; Equifax had a history of security failures.

I wish these were exceptional stories, but they're not. It really is that bad out there. And without some serious intervention, it won't get any better.

In a nutshell, what we need to do is to engineer "security by design." For the engineering reasons discussed in Chapter 1 and the political/market reasons discussed in Chapter 4, security often takes a back seat to speed of development and additional features. Even for larger companies that should know better, computer security is traditionally regarded as a compliance exercise that both slows and adds cost to development. It's been shoehorned in at the end of a development process, hastily and not very effectively. This has to change. Security needs to be engineered into every system, and every component of every system, from the beginning and throughout the development process.

I admit this sounds obvious, but you have to remember that security isn't something that was designed into the Internet from the beginning, and it's not something that the market generally rewards. It's a bit like the slow process by which we all convinced automobile companies, through regulation and market pressure, to embrace "fuel efficiency by design."

Highly regulated industries like avionics and medical devices already employ security by design. We also see it in banking applications, and from operating system companies like Apple and Microsoft. But the practice needs to spread beyond those isolated cases.

We need to secure the Internet+. We need to secure our software, data, and algorithms. We need to secure our critical infrastructure and our computing supply chain. We need to do it comprehensively, and we need to do it now. This chapter is an attempt to work out some broad outlines of what that might look like. I'm focusing on the *what*, saving the *how* and the *who* for the following two chapters.

To be fair, these are only the basics, and there are many subtleties to the threats discussed in Part I that I won't address at all. The recommendations in this chapter aren't meant to be definitive; they're a starting place for discussion. All the principles proposed here need to be expanded, and eventually make their way into voluntary or mandatory industry standards.

But if we don't start somewhere, we'll never get to the hard stuff.

SECURE OUR DEVICES

When the Internet was nascent, it made some sense to let anything connect to it, but that's no longer tenable. We need to establish security standards for computers, software, and devices. That might sound easy, but it's not. Because software is now embedded into everything, this quickly turns into security standards that encompass everything—which is simply too broad to be sensible.

But if everything is a computer, we need to think about holistic design principles. All devices need to be secure without much intervention by users. And while it is fine to have different levels of security in response to different threats, everything should start from a common base.

To that end, I offer ten high-level design principles to improve both the security and the privacy of our devices. While these are not specific enough to be standards, they are a basis from which standards can be developed.

1. *Be transparent.* Vendors should clearly state how their security works, which threats they secure against and which they don't, and so on. If a vendor will no longer support a device after a certain date, it should tell customers far enough in advance to allow adequate upgrade planning.

2. *Make the software patchable.* All devices must have the ability to accept software and firmware updates, and a way to authenticate them as valid. Vendors also need to patch quickly once vulnerabilities are discovered, and products should be able to regularly check for patches. This is vital; even with all the problems of patching that I discussed in Chapter 2, unpatchable software is even worse.

3. *Test pre-production.* All software should be tested for security before it is released.

4. *Enable secure default operation.* Devices should be secure out of the box, without requiring users to configure them. They should not have weak or default passwords. Two-factor authentication should be used whenever possible. Remote administration features should be disabled unless necessary.

5. *Fail predictably and safely.* If a device loses its Internet connection, it should fail gracefully, in a way that does not cause any harm.

6. *Use standard protocols and implementations.* Standard protocols are generally more secure and better tested, and custom protocols are the opposite. Devices should use standard communications protocols and implementations, and should be interoperable with other applications and devices. Vendors should not create their own protocols unless there's no other option.

7. *Avoid known vulnerabilities.* Vendors should not ship products that contain known vulnerabilities.

8. *Preserve offline functionality.* Users should be able to turn off all

incoming and outgoing network connections while still being able to use the device. For example, an Internet-connected refrigerator should keep things cold even when not connected to the Internet.

9. *Encrypt and authenticate data.* Data should be encrypted on the devices, and communications to and from them should be both encrypted and authenticated.

10. *Support responsible security research.* Vendors should allow research on their products and welcome vulnerability reports, not harass researchers.

Those principles, and some of the items in the next section, are from a working group on national security—of which I am a member—organized by the Berkman Klein Center for Internet and Society and funded by the Hewlett Foundation.

None of these principles is new or radical. While researching for this book, I collected 19 different security and privacy guidelines for the IoT, created by the IoT Security Foundation, the Online Trust Alliance, the state of New York, and other organizations. They're all similar, which makes them a good indication of what security professionals think should be done. But they're all voluntary, so no one actually follows them.

SECURE OUR DATA

Just as we need security design principles for computers, we need them for data. It used to be that the two were basically the same, but today they are separate. We no longer store our most personal data on computers that are physically close to us; we store them in the cloud, on massive servers owned by others—possibly in other countries.

Often our data, too, is owned by others—collected without our knowledge or consent. These databases are tempting targets for attackers of all stripes. We need security principles surrounding data and databases that would apply to all organizations that keep personal databases:

1. *Minimize data collection.* Companies should only collect the data they need and no more.

2. *Store and transfer data securely.* This data should be secured, both in transit and in storage.

3. *Minimize data use.* Data should only be used when it is essential.

4. *Be transparent in data collection, use, storage, and deletion.* Companies should clearly state which user data is being collected, how it is stored and used, and when it is deleted.

5. *Anonymize data wherever possible.* If it is not necessary to identify the individuals in the data, it should be anonymous.

6. *Allow users to access, inspect, correct, and delete their data.* Companies should not keep the data they have secret from the people the data is about.

7. *Delete data when it is no longer needed.* Data should only be stored as long as necessary.

Critical to any rules covering personal information will be a definition of what personal information is. Traditionally, we've defined it very narrowly. "PII"—personally identifiable information—has been the term used. That's not sufficient. We now know that all sorts of information can be combined to identify individuals, and that anonymizing data is much harder than it seems. We need very broad definitions of what counts as personal information—for example, data from apps on your phone, and even the list of add-ons installed in your browser—and thus needs to be protected as such.

These criteria appear in my 2015 book *Data and Goliath*. Most of them are part of the EU's General Data Protection Regulation, which I'll talk about in Chapter 10. Again, they are general design principles. And they are probably the hardest sell in this chapter. Companies will fight being forced to secure their devices, but it will benefit them in the long run. Rules about securing data have the potential to threaten surveillance capitalism. Companies will argue that they need to collect everything for possible future analysis, to train machine-learning systems, and because it might be valuable someday. But we'll need such rules as databases of personal information become larger and ever more personal.

Much of this data will be in the cloud. This trend is a matter of simple economics and will be the model of computing for the foreseeable future. In many ways, this is a good thing. In fact, I think that people moving their data and processing into the cloud is our most fruitful avenue for security improvements. Already, Google does a better job of securing our data than most individuals or small businesses can do themselves. Cloud providers have both the security expertise and economies of scale that individuals and small businesses lack, and anything that gives people security without their having to become security experts is a win.

Still, there are risks: having multiple different users on the same network increases the opportunities for internal hacking, and large cloud providers—like large databases of personal data—are enticing targets for powerful attackers. We need significantly more research in cloud security. While most of the principles I listed in this section are germane to the amassers of personal databases, some also apply to cloud computing providers.

SECURE OUR ALGORITHMS

We expect a lot from our algorithms. And as they continue to replace human beings in decision processes, we're going to need to trust them absolutely. At a high level, we expect accuracy, fairness, reproducibility, respectfulness of human and other rights, and so on. I'm focusing on security.

The threat is basically that an algorithm will behave in an unintended manner, either because it was programmed badly or because its data or software was hacked. Transparency is an obvious solution. The more transparent an algorithm is, the more it can be inspected and audited—for security or any other property we want our algorithms to have.

The problem is that transparency isn't always achievable in algorithms, or even desirable. Companies have legitimate trade secrets that they need to keep confidential. Transparency can represent a security risk, because it gives attackers information that can help them game the system. For example, knowing Google's algorithm for page ranking can help people optimize websites for the algorithm, and knowing the military's algorithm for identifying people by drone can help individuals hide.

Additionally, transparency is not always sufficient. Modern algorithms are so complex that it's not even feasible to determine if they're accurate, let alone fair or secure. Some machine-learning algorithms have models that are simply beyond human comprehension.

That last point is important. Sometimes transparency is impossible. No one knows how some machine-learning algorithms work, including their designers. The algorithms are fundamentally incomprehensible to humans. Think of them as black boxes: data goes in, decisions come out, and what happens in between remains something of a mystery.

Even if an algorithm can't be made public, or if there is no way to understand how it works, we can demand explainability. That is, we can demand that algorithms explain their reasoning. So, for example, when an algorithm makes a medical diagnosis or scores a job candidate for suitability, it can also be required to provide reasons for its decisions.

This isn't a panacea. Because of the way machine learning works, explanations might not be possible or understandable by humans, and requiring them often reduces the accuracy of the underlying algorithms because it forces them to be simpler than they would otherwise be.

So maybe what we really want is accountability. Or contestability. Perhaps we need the ability to inspect an algorithm, or interrogate it with sample data and examine the results. Maybe all we need is auditability.

If nothing else, we can treat algorithms like humans. Humans are terrible at explaining their reasoning, and their decisions are filled with unconscious biases. Too often, an explanation—a logical series of steps taken to reach a decision—is really nothing more than a justification. Our subconscious brain makes the decision, and the conscious brain justifies it with an explanation. The psychological literature is filled with studies that demonstrate this.

Still, we are able to judge humans' biases by looking at their decisions. Similarly, we can judge algorithms by looking at their outputs. After all, what we want to know is if an algorithm used to score job candidates is sexist, or if an algorithm used to make parole decisions is racist. And we might decide that, for some applications, machine-learning algorithms are simply not appropriate, because we want more control over how a decision is made.

I don't have any concrete recommendations for how we can secure our algorithms, because this is all too new. We are just getting started figuring out what is possible and feasible. Right now, our goals should be as much transparency, explainability, and auditability as possible.

SECURE OUR NETWORK CONNECTIONS

Most of us connect to the Internet through one or more ISPs. These are large companies like AT&T, Comcast, BT, and China Telecom, and they are very powerful. A 2011 report calculated that the top 25 telecommunications companies in the world connect 80% of all Internet traffic. This centralization might be bad for consumer choice, but it affords us a potential security benefit. Because ISPs sit between our homes and the rest of the Internet, they are in a unique position to provide security—especially for home users. We need some security principles for ISPs:

1. *Provide a secure connection to consumers.* ISPs need to do more than give consumers an Internet connection; they need to secure that connection as well. To some extent, they can provide a firewall between the user and the rest of the Internet. And to the extent that users' connections are not encrypted, they can scan for malware. (Some ISPs are already blocking child porn in this manner.)
2. *Help configure users' Internet devices.* Certainly, ISPs are in the best position to ensure that consumers' routers are configured securely, but they can also help manage the security of all Internet devices connected to that router.
3. *Educate consumers about threats.* Because ISPs are the companies that connect consumers to the Internet, they are in the best position to educate consumers about Internet threats.
4. *Inform consumers of infections in their infrastructure.* Because ISPs connect consumers to the Internet, they can monitor that connection for signs of malware and other infections. They should inform the consumer whenever they discover a threat. In the future, ISPs may have the responsibility for blocking insecure consumer devices from connecting to the Internet.
5. *Publicly report security incident statistics.* ISPs already know things like the amount of spam, the number of compromised computers, details of denial-of-service attacks, and so on. They should publish that information in aggregate to preserve the anonymity of their individual customers.
6. *Work with other ISPs to share information about imminent threats and*

during emergencies. Again, ISPs can learn about attacks and help
each other to mitigate their effects.

This list draws from a paper by cybersecurity consultant Melissa
Hathaway, who was a senior policy advisor to former presidents George W.
Bush and Barack Obama.

These principles would grant ISPs considerable power, and that comes
with considerable danger. If ISPs can configure users' security, they can
configure it to allow government access. And if they can discriminate
between different types of traffic, they can violate net neutrality for all
sorts of economic or ideological reasons. These are real concerns, and we
need better policies to alleviate them. But users shouldn't have to be security experts to use the Internet safely, and ISPs will have to step up as a first
line of defense.

SECURE THE INTERNET

Heartbleed is the cool name that researchers gave to a serious vulnerability in OpenSSL, the encryption system that protects your web browsing.
If the connection between your web browser and the website you're reading is encrypted, the encryption is likely done by OpenSSL. The protocol
is public, and the code is open-source. Heartbleed was discovered in 2014,
two years after it was accidentally introduced in the software. It was a
huge vulnerability—at the time I called it "catastrophic"—affecting an estimated 17% of the Internet's web servers, as well as end-user devices, from
servers to firewalls to power strips.

The vulnerability allowed attackers to find usernames and passwords,
account numbers, and more. Fixing Heartbleed was a massive undertak-
ing, requiring coordination among websites, certificate authorities, and
web browser companies around the world.

Two factors precipitated Heartbleed. One: OpenSSL, a critical piece
of software, was maintained by one person and a few helpers, all working
for free in their spare time. Two: no one had subjected OpenSSL to a good
security analysis. It's a classic collective action problem. The code is open-
source, so anyone can evaluate it. But everyone thought that someone else

would evaluate it, so no one took the effort to actually do it. The result was that the vulnerability remained undetected for over two years.

In response to Heartbleed, industry created something called the Core Infrastructure Initiative. Basically, the big tech companies all got together and established a testing program for open-source software that we all rely on. It's a good idea that should have been done a decade earlier, but it's not enough.

In Chapter 1, I explained that the Internet was never designed with security in mind. That was okay when the Internet was primarily at research institutions and used primarily for academic communication. That's less okay today, when the Internet supports much of the world's critical infrastructure.

ISPs do more than connect consumers to the Internet. "Tier 1" ISPs manage the Internet backbone, running the large, high-capacity networks around the world. These are companies you have likely never heard of— Level 3, Cogent, GTT Communications—because end users aren't their customers. These companies can also do more to secure the Internet:

1. *Provide authentic and authoritative routing information.* Remember in Chapter 1 where I talked about the Border Gateway Protocol, and how countries can maliciously route Internet traffic to aid in eavesdropping? ISPs are the ones to prevent this.
2. *Provide authentic and authoritative naming information to reduce domain name hijacking.* Similarly, ISPs are the ones who can prevent malicious attacks against the Domain Name Service.
3. *Commit to treating all traffic equally, and not differentiating service based on data content.*

There are other things Tier 1 ISPs could do that involve monitoring traffic and interdicting attacks. For instance, they could block all sorts of things: spam, child pornography, Internet attacks, and so on. All of these things, however, currently require ISPs to engage in bulk surveillance of Internet traffic, and they won't work if the traffic is encrypted. And given the choice, we are much more secure if Internet traffic is end-to-end encrypted. I'll talk more about that in Chapter 9.

SECURE OUR CRITICAL INFRASTRUCTURE

In 2008, unidentified hackers broke into the Baku-Tbilisi-Ceyhan oil pipeline in Turkey. They gained access to the pipeline's control system and increased the pressure of the crude oil flowing inside, causing the pipe to explode. They also hacked the sensors and video feeds that monitored the pipeline, preventing operators from learning about the explosion until 40 minutes after it happened. (Remember what I said in Chapter 1 about new vulnerabilities in the interconnections? The attackers got into the pipeline control systems through a vulnerability in the communications software of those video cameras.)

In 2013, we learned that the NSA had hacked into the Brazilian national oil company's network. The NSA's purpose was almost certainly to gather intelligence and not attack. I've already mentioned Iran's 2012 cyberattack against Saudi Aramco, the Saudi national oil company, and Russia's 2015 and 2016 cyberattacks against the Ukrainian power grid. In 2017, someone was able to spoof the GPS that ships use to navigate, fooling them as to their location.

I wrote in Chapter 4 that we're in the middle of an increasingly asymmetrical cyber arms race. I wrote about the increasing asymmetry in this regard. With nonstate actors like terrorists, the asymmetry is even greater. We need to better secure our critical infrastructure in cyberspace.

Before we can do that, though, we'll need to decide what counts as "critical infrastructure." The term is complex and ambiguous, and what counts varies with shifts in technological and social developments. In the US, a series of documents from the White House and the Department of Homeland Security outlines what the government counts as critical infrastructure. A 2013 presidential directive identified 16 "critical infrastructure sectors." Much of what's included is obvious, like air transportation, oil production and storage, and food distribution. Some of it makes less sense, like retail centers and large sports stadiums. Yes, those are places where large numbers of people gather, and it would be a national tragedy if a bomb killed hundreds or thousands in any of those places, but they hardly seem critical in the same way that the power grid does.

If everything is a priority, then nothing is a priority. We need to make some hard choices, designating certain sectors as more vital than others.

The 2017 US National Security Strategy identified six key areas: "national security, energy and power, banking and finance, health and safety, communications, and transportation." Some people add election systems. I think that energy, finance, and telecommunications are the first three to focus on, because they underpin everything else. If we're looking for where to find most of the near-term catastrophic risks discussed in Chapter 5, it's there. And it's where we'll get the most security for our money.

Why aren't we doing more to secure critical infrastructure today? There are several reasons:

One: it's expensive. The threat model we need to defend against is often a sophisticated foreign military unit fielding highly skilled professional attackers. This isn't easy, and it isn't cheap.

Two: it's easy for both the public and policy makers to discount future hypothetical risks. Until US citizens experience an actual cyberattack against critical infrastructure in the US—neither the North Korean attack against Sony or attacks against other countries like Saudi Arabia and Estonia count here—it's not going to be a priority.

Three: the political process is complicated. President Obama designated 16 broad sectors as part of our critical infrastructure in order to ensure that every industry felt properly recognized. Any attempt to prioritize will be met with resistance from industries that feel slighted by a lower ranking. So, while it might be easy for me to say that our power grid and telecommunications infrastructure should be secured first because everything else is built on top of them, it's harder for the government to say that.

Four: the government doesn't have direct control over most of our critical infrastructure. You'll often hear that 85% of the US critical infrastructure is in corporate hands. That statistic comes from a 2002 document issued by the Office of Homeland Security, and seems to be a rough guess. Certainly, it depends on which industry we're talking about. As I explained earlier, private owners are more likely to underspend on security because it's more profitable to save money every year and take the risk.

And five: spending money on infrastructure isn't sexy. Even when a country touts its infrastructure investments, it usually means building shiny new bridges rather than repairing rickety old ones. Despite both Presidents Obama and Trump touting their infrastructure investments, spending to maintain what already exists isn't a priority; just look at our crumbling national infrastructure in so many areas. This problem can be even worse when it comes to security. These expenditures have a long time horizon, and it's hard to take credit for nothing going wrong. By the time it is obvious that the spending was justified, the politician who approved it might no longer be in office.

That we need to secure our critical infrastructure from cyberattack isn't a new or controversial idea, and governments, industry groups, and academia have conducted many studies of the issue. The challenges are considerable, though. I'm not discussing specifics, because this book is meant to be general, but any defense will necessarily need to be dynamic, integrating a disparate array of people, organizations, data, and technical capabilities. And our infrastructure is made up of complex systems, with gazillions of subsystems and subcomponents—some of which have been around for decades. Fixing any of this will be expensive, but it's doable.

DISCONNECT SYSTEMS

One of the top-secret NSA documents disclosed by Edward Snowden was a presentation that contained a slide with then–NSA director Keith Alexander's motto: "Collect it all." A similar motto for the Internet+ today might be "Connect it all." Maybe that's not such a good idea.

We need to start disconnecting systems. If we cannot secure complex systems to the extent required by their real-world capabilities, then we must not build a world where everything is computerized and interconnected. It's part of what I meant when I talked about engineering security by design at the beginning of this chapter: if we're building a system and the only way to secure it is by not connecting it, that should be considered a valid option.

This might be regarded as heresy in today's race to network everything, but large, centralized systems are not inevitable. Technical and corporate elites may be pushing us in that direction, but they really don't have any good supporting arguments other than profit maximization.

Disconnecting can happen in several ways. It can mean creating separate "air gapped" networks. (These have vulnerabilities as well, and are not a security panacea.) It can mean going back to non-interoperable systems. And it can mean not building connectivity into systems in the first place.

There are also incremental ways to do this. We can enable local communications only. We can design dedicated devices, reversing the current trend of turning everything into a general-purpose computer. We can move towards less centralization and more-distributed systems, which is how the Internet was first envisioned.

This is worth explaining. Before the Internet, the telephone network was smart. Complex call-routing algorithms resided inside the network, whereas the telephones that connected to it were dumb. Before the Internet, this was also the model for other computerized networks. The Internet turned that model on its head. Most of the smarts were pushed to computers at the edge of the network, and the network became as dumb as possible—a change that made the Internet a hotbed of innovation. Anyone could invent something new—a new piece of software, a new mode of communication, a new hardware device—and as long as it conformed to the basic Internet protocols, it could connect. There was no certification process, no centralized approval system—nothing. Smart devices, dumb network. For students of Internet architecture, this is called the "end-to-end principle." And by the way, it's what everyone in favor of network neutrality wants to preserve.

I anticipate that we will eventually reach a high-water mark of computerization and connectivity. There will be a backlash. It won't be driven by the market, but by norms and laws and policy decisions that put the safety and welfare of society above individual corporations and industries. It will require a major social shift, and a hard one for many to swallow, but our safety will depend on it.

Henceforth, we will make conscious decisions about what and how we interconnect. We can draw an analogy with nuclear power. The early 1980s saw a dramatic rise in the use of nuclear power, before we recognized that it was just too difficult and dangerous to secure nuclear waste. Today, we still have nuclear power, but there's somewhat more consideration about when and where to build nuclear plants, and when to choose one of the many alternatives. Someday, computerization is going to be like that.

But not today. We're still in the honeymoon phase of connectivity. Governments and corporations are punch-drunk on our data, and the rush to connect everything is driven by an even greater desire for power and market share.

7

How We Can Secure the Internet+

By and large, technologies already exist to satisfy all of the principles in the previous chapter. Yes, there are vulnerabilities remaining. Yes, there are usability issues with some of the solutions. But for the most part, these are commonsense security principles that could be put in place today—if there were only some incentive for companies to do so.

We need to create that incentive by crafting strong public policies. There are basically four places policy can exert its influence on society. The first is *ex ante*: rules that attempt to prevent bad things from happening. These include regulations on products and product categories, licensing of professionals and products, testing and certification requirements, and industry best practices. They also include subsidies or tax breaks for doing things right. The second is *ex post*: rules that punish bad behavior after it's already happened. This includes fines for insecurity and liabilities when things go wrong. The third is by mandating disclosure: product-labeling laws and other transparency measures, testing and rating agencies, information sharing between government and industry, and breach disclosure laws. (Some of these disclosures are *ex ante* and others are *ex post*.) And the fourth is what I would broadly categorize as measures that affect the environment. These include deliberate market design, funding for research and education, and using the procurement process as a means to drive product improvement more broadly. That's the toolbox. It's what we have to work with.

The goal of these kinds of policies isn't to require that everything be made safe, but to create incentives for safe behavior. It's to put our fingers on the scales by raising the cost of insecurity or (less commonly) lowering the cost of security.

Critical to any policy is the enforcement process. Standards can be enforced by government, by professional organizations, by industry groups, or by other third parties through either coercive or market pressure. There are four basic ways that Internet+ security policies can be enforced. One: through norms such as best practices. Norms provide a reference point that consumer advocacy groups, the media, and corporate shareholders can use to hold companies to account. Two: voluntarily, through self-regulation. Sometimes industry and professional bodies have an interest in creating and enforcing voluntary standards. These serve to increase consumer trust, and form a protective barrier to entry for new competitors. Three: through litigation. If customers or businesses can sue when they suffer damage, companies increase their security to avoid those lawsuits. Four: through regulatory bodies. Government agencies with the power to issue fines, demand recalls, or force companies to redress defects can enforce standards.

Political considerations may push us towards a particular set of policy solutions as a default. I, for example, hope to demonstrate that government needs to play a major role in all of these policy initiatives. Others prefer more market-led initiatives. Additional options include non-binding government guidelines, voluntary best-practice standards, and multi-stakeholder international agreements. But that's for Chapter 8; in this chapter, I will focus on the *how* without worrying about who will do it.

On their own, none of the measures I propose in this chapter are sufficient. Minimum security standards won't solve everything. Liabilities won't solve everything. That's okay, though, because none of them will work in isolation. All of the suggestions in this chapter will interact with each other, sometimes complementarily and sometimes contradictorily. If we're going to secure the Internet+, it'll be through a series of mutually reinforcing policies—just like everything else in society.

CREATE STANDARDS

First and foremost, we need to create actual standards for many of the principles I listed in Chapter 6.

I use the term "standard" deliberately and in the policy sense. There's a distinction in law about prescriptive rules, which are rigid, and more flexible, principle-based standards. Standards afford choice or discretion, can provide a framework for balancing several different factors, and can adapt to changing circumstance. So, while a rule might be "The speed limit in snow is 35 mph," a standard might be "Exercise caution when it's snowing." In Internet+ security, rigid rules might include "Consumers must have the ability to inspect their personal data" and "Enable secure default operation." A standard requiring the owner of a database to "Take due care" to protect personal information leaves a lot of room for interpretation, and that meaning can change as technology changes.

Another Internet+ standard might include the principle that IoT vendors need to "Take best efforts not to sell insecure products." This might sound wishy-washy, but it's a real legal standard. If an IoT device gets hacked and regulators can show that the manufacturers used insecure protocols, didn't encrypt their data, and enabled default passwords, then they obviously did not take best efforts. If they did all of those things and more, and a hacker found a vulnerability that couldn't reasonably be predicted or prevented, then they might not be considered at fault.

We're likely to need both rules and standards. How either of those things is carried out, however, will be subject to a more flexible standard. My guess is that in the dynamic world of Internet+ security, most regulations will be in the form of principle-based standards and not rigid rules.

There will necessarily be different standards for different types of things. For example, we're not going to treat large, costly stuff like a refrigerator the same way we treat low-cost, disposable stuff like a light bulb. If the latter has a vulnerability, the right thing to do is to throw it away and buy a new one—possibly forcing the manufacturer to pay for the swap. Refrigerators are different, but they're also likely to have fewer producers. It will be easier to impose standards on those few producers.

In general, it's much more effective to focus on outcomes than on procedures. It's called "outcomes-based regulation," and it's increasingly common in most areas—from building codes, to food safety, and emissions reductions. For example, a standard should not prescribe the patching methodology that a product should have. That's too detailed, and something the government isn't good at doing, especially in a rapidly evolving technological environment. Better to require a specific result—that IoT products should have a secure way of being patched—and let the industry figure out how to achieve it. This approach to regulation can stimulate innovation rather than inhibiting it. Think of the difference between requiring that appliances be x% more efficient next year and specifying a particular engineering design.

We also need to standardize the safety protocols that businesses using Internet+ devices should follow. The National Institute of Standards and Technology's "Framework for Improving Critical Infrastructure Cybersecurity" is a great example of this type of standard. It's a comprehensive guide for private-sector organizations to proactively assess and minimize their cybersecurity risk.

Standards regulating business processes, like how to prevent, detect, and respond to cyberattacks, are also important. If done right, these can motivate businesses to improve their overall Internet security and make better decisions about which technologies to buy and how to use them. Less obviously, standardizing these types of business processes also makes it easier for business executives to share ideas, impose requirements on third-party partners, and tie security standards to insurance. They also serve as a model for best practices in litigation, and courts can refer to them when making decisions.

Unfortunately, the NIST Cybersecurity Framework is only voluntary at this stage, but it's gaining traction. In 2017, it became mandatory for federal agencies. Making it compulsory for everyone would be an easy regulatory win.

Along the same lines, the US government has something called FedRAMP, which is a security assessment and authorization process for cloud services. It also uses a NIST standard, and federal agencies are supposed to buy from certified vendors.

Certainly, any standards will evolve over time—as the threats change, as we learn more about what's effective and what's not, and as technologies change and Internet-connected devices become more powerful and pervasive.

CORRECT MISALIGNED INCENTIVES

Imagine a CEO with the following choice: spend an additional 5% on the cybersecurity budget to make the corporate network, products, or customer databases more secure, or save that money and take the chance that nothing will go wrong. A rational CEO will choose to save the money, or spend it on new features to compete in the market. And if the worst happens—think of Yahoo in 2016 or Equifax in 2017—most of the costs of the insecurity will be borne by other parties. Equifax's CEO didn't get his $5.2 million severance pay, because he resigned, but he did keep his $18.4 million pension and probably his stock options. His failed bet cost the company somewhere between $130 million and $210 million, but that wasn't relevant to him at the time. Neither was the fact that it was the wrong long-term decision for the company.

This is a classic Prisoner's Dilemma. If every company spent the extra money on security, Wall Street would just accept the expense as normal, but with everyone choosing their own short-term self-interest, any company that thinks long-term and spends more is immediately penalized, either by shareholders when its profits are lower or by customers when its prices are higher. We need some way to coordinate companies and convince them all to improve security together.

The economic considerations go further. Even after deciding to prioritize security over near-term profits, a CEO will only spend enough money to secure the system up to the value of the company. This is important. Disaster recovery models will be built around losses to the company, and not losses to the country or to individual citizens. And while the maximum loss to the company is everything the company is worth, the true costs of a disaster can be much greater. The *Deepwater Horizon* disaster cost BP about $60 billion, but the environmental, health, and economic costs were much greater. Had that company been smaller, it would have gone out of business long before it paid out all that money. All of those extra costs that a company avoids paying are externalities, and borne by society.

Some of this is psychology as well. We are biased towards preferring sure smaller gains over risky larger gains, and risky larger losses over sure smaller losses. Spending on preventive security is a sure small loss: the cost of more security. Reducing spending is a sure small gain. Having an insecure network, or service, or product, is risking a large loss. This doesn't mean that no one ever spends money on security, only that it's an uphill battle to overcome this cognitive bias—and it explains why so often CEOs are willing to take the chance. Of course, this is assuming that the CEOs are knowledgeable on the threats, which they almost certainly are not.

This willingness to assume the risks of having an insecure network results partly from the lack of clear legal liabilities for producing insecure products, which I'll talk about more in the next section. Years ago, I joked that if a software product maimed one of your children, and the software manufacturer knew that it would but decided not to tell you because it might hurt its sales, it still would not be liable. That joke only worked because back then, software couldn't possibly maim one of your children.

There are other reasons security incentives aren't aligned properly. Big companies with few competitors don't have much incentive to improve the security of their products, because users have no alternative; they either buy a product—security warts and all—or go without. Small companies don't have much incentive either, because improving security will slow down product development and constrain their products' features, and they won't be rewarded for it by the market.

Worse, companies have strong incentives to treat security problems as PR issues, and keep knowledge about security vulnerabilities and data compromises to themselves. Equifax learned about its 2017 hack in July, but managed to keep the fact secret until September. When Yahoo was hacked in 2014, it kept the fact secret for two years. Uber, for a year.

When this information does become public, it's still not enough. Despite the bad press, congressional inquiries, and social media outrage, companies generally don't get punished in the market for bad security. One study found that stock prices of breached companies are unaffected in the long term.

We've seen the consequences of badly aligned incentives before. In the years leading up to the 2008 financial crisis, bankers were effectively gambling with other people's money. It was in their interest to make as much profit as they could in the short run, but they had no incentive to think about the consequences for families who put all their savings into risky products. Most consumers had no choice but to trust their bankers' advice, because they were not financial experts and could not evaluate their risks.

After the crisis, Congress introduced the Dodd-Frank Act to realign incentives. Bankers now face higher statutory duties (for example, they must first consider whether a consumer could reasonably repay a loan before writing one) and increased penalties for misconduct.

Something like 90% of the Internet's infrastructure is privately owned. Among other things, this means that it is managed to optimize the short-term financial interests of the corporations that can affect it, not the interests of users or the overall security of the network.

We need to change the incentives so that companies are forced to care about the security implications of their products.

One way to do this is by fining companies—and their directors—when they get things wrong. These fines have to be big enough to change the company's risk equation. The cost of insecurity is generally calculated as threat multiplied by vulnerability multiplied by consequences. If that's less than the cost to mitigate the risk, a rational company accepts the risk. Fines, assessed either after an incident or as a penalty for insecure practices, raise the cost of insecurity and make paying for security that much more financially attractive.

In some cases, the fines might drive companies into bankruptcy. This is severe, but it's the only way to demonstrate to the rest of the industry that we're serious about cybersecurity. If a person kills your spouse, they will get sent to jail and might even be subjected to the death penalty. If a corporation kills your spouse, it should face the same end. Author John Greer proposes sending convicted corporations to "pseudo-jail": they would be taken over by the government, have all investors wiped out, and then be sold off at some later date. If we're afraid to impose the death penalty on corporations, then corporations will realize they can skimp on security and count on the public's mercy.

Another way of thinking about this is that if a company can only stay in business by externalizing the cost of security, maybe it shouldn't stay in business. Those companies don't ask the public to pay their employees' salaries, so why should we have to pay for their security failures? It's like a factory that can only stay in business by illegally polluting; we'd all be better off if we closed it down.

Consider regulated professions like law and accountancy. Firms specializing in these professional services take their legal responsibilities seriously—in part because the consequences can be dire. You'd be hard-pressed to find a partner in an auditing firm for whom the collapse of Arthur Andersen does not loom large. Arthur Andersen was a "Big Five" global accounting firm, with 85,000+ employees, that more or less disappeared overnight after accusations that it had inappropriately audited Enron's financial accounts—a serious regulatory offense.

And this failure of Arthur Andersen illustrates another point. The Arthur Andersen employees did fine, as pieces of the company were acquired by other companies. A similar company driven out of business because of negligent security practices would also have its departments acquired by other, hopefully more diligent, companies.

But even this isn't enough. In particular, startup companies would rationally ignore security and risk fines or even pseudo-jail. They're already risking much more on much less, and know that success depends on luck at least as much as on business skill. It's smart for them to use their limited time and budget to grow bigger faster, take the chance, and worry about security later. Their investors and board members would counsel that as well.

In 2015, Volkswagen was caught cheating on its emissions control tests. Because software controls engine operation, programmers were able to create an algorithm that detected when an emissions test was being conducted and modified the engine's behavior in response. The result? From 2009 to 2015, 11 million cars worldwide—500,000 in the US—emitted up to 40 times more pollutants than local laws allowed. The company was hit with fines and penalties totaling almost $30 billion, and that's significant. But my fear is that the big lesson of the Volkswagen case won't be that companies that cheat will get caught; it'll be that companies can get away with cheating for six years. That's longer than the tenure of most CEOs, who would expect to cash out long before the big fines kicked in. (Note: one VW manager and one engineer received prison sentences for their actions.)

To be sure, this is just one aspect of a much larger problem of incentives inside corporations. The only way to motivate companies is to hold company executives and board members (including venture capitalists, who routinely sit on the boards of companies they invest in) personally responsible for security failures. This will raise the personal costs of insecurity, and make it less likely that those individuals will cut corners out of self-interest.

Such accountability may be coming soon. Under current law in the US and the GDPR (General Data Protection Regulation) in the EU, executives and board members could face liability for data breaches. And the force of public expectation is moving in this direction, too. Equifax's CEO, CIO, and CSO were all forced into early retirement in the wake of that hack. In the UK, the CEO of TalkTalk resigned after that company was fined £400,000 because it leaked customer data.

There is precedent for holding these people accountable. The Sarbanes-Oxley Act regulates corporate financial conduct and misconduct. It was passed in 2002 as a response to the crimes and abuses of Enron in order to rectify the many conflicts of interest that undermined the effectiveness of a lot of corporate law. According to Sarbanes-Oxley, directors can be held personally responsible for their companies' behavior, which makes them highly motivated not to let the companies do anything illegal. The law's reality might be much less than its aspirations, but it's definitely the right idea. We need to think about doing the same kind of thing with software security.

I'm not going to pretend that changing liability responsibilities won't be a huge battle. It's hard to add liabilities where they're not already required, because it's a radical change for the affected industries—and they will fight it every step of the way. But not doing it will be worse for society.

Finally, correcting incentives doesn't have to be just about imposing penalties for getting things wrong. Companies might be more likely to publicly disclose information about security breaches if they received some level of liability exemption. They might also be more inclined to share vulnerability information with competitors or with the government if they receive assurances that their sensitive intellectual property will be protected. And tax credits have their place, too.

CLARIFY LIABILITIES

Fines by government agencies are not the only way to tilt the Internet+ towards security. The government can change the law to make it easier for users to sue companies when their security fails.

SmartThings is a centralized hub that works with compatible light bulbs, locks, thermostats, cameras, doorbells, and more, controlled by a free phone app. In 2016, a group of researchers found a boatload of security vulnerabilities in the system. They were able to steal the codes that would unlock the door, trigger a fake fire alarm, and disable some security settings.

If one of these vulnerabilities enabled a thief to break into your home, whose problem would this be? Yours, of course. If you read SmartThings Inc.'s terms of service, you use SmartThings products entirely at your own risk, under no circumstances is SmartThings liable for any damages whatsoever in the case of any failure or malfunction, and you agree to hold SmartThings harmless for any and every possible claim.

Since the beginning of personal computers, both hardware and software manufacturers have disclaimed liability when things go wrong. This made some sense in the early years of computing. The reason we have the Internet is that companies were able to market buggy products. If computers were subject to the same product liability regulations as stepladders, they probably wouldn't be available on the market yet.

Some of this inequity is enforced by the terms of service that govern the liability relationship between you and the company whose software you use. These are the "terms of service" that you must confirm you've read, even though no one reads through them. Not that it would matter if you did; the companies reserve the right to modify terms at will without telling you.

Companies aren't liable if their programs lose your data, or expose it to criminals, or result in harm. Neither are cloud services. Terms of service more or less force you to assume all the risk when you use companies' products and services, and they protect the companies from lawsuits when problems arise.

Suing software vendors is also expensive. Most users can't go it alone; they need class-action lawsuits. To forestall this, many terms of service include binding arbitration agreements. Such agreements force unhappy users to go into arbitration, which is generally much friendlier to the companies than court is. Preventing class-action suits also greatly favors the companies.

All of this is made worse by the exemption of software from normal product liability law. By international standards, the US has pretty tough product liability laws, but only when it comes to tangible products. Users of defective tangible products can sue anyone in the chain of distribution, from the manufacturer who made it to the retailer who sold it. Software manages to evade all of this, both because it's often licensed rather than purchased, and because code is legally categorized as a service rather than a product. And even when it is a product, the manufacturer can disclaim liability in the end-user license agreement—something the courts have upheld.

There are two other big problems.

First, where defective software has resulted in losses, courts have been reluctant to accept that software companies *caused* that harm. Judges have tended to blame hackers for exploiting vulnerabilities, not companies for creating the opportunity in the first place. The need for evidence complicates this further. If you live in the US, you were almost certainly a victim of the Equifax breach. But if your information is used for fraud and identity theft, you won't be able to prove that the Equifax hack was to blame. Your information has probably been stolen on multiple occasions from multiple databases. This is why it is so hard to sue companies like Equifax when they lose your personal data: all of the data Equifax failed to secure is already available on the black market, so one more breach caused no new harm.

After the Mirai botnet caused the biggest DDoS attack in US history, the FTC tried and failed to hold D-Link router manufacturers accountable. But it could not prove that any individual routers were used as part of the Mirai botnet—only that D-Link routers were insecure and that some of them were used.

Second, users consistently struggle to prove that they have suffered "harm," as the law defines that term. Courts will only hear cases of this type where there are allegations of monetary harm, which is very hard to demonstrate for privacy violations.

In 2016, the FTC issued a finding that LabMD had engaged in "unfair practices" by failing to protect its customers' sensitive information. The FTC found that LabMD had not implemented even basic data security measures, and had left sensitive medical and financial information exposed for almost a year. LabMD challenged the FTC's ruling in the US Court of Appeals. It argued that since there were no known instances of the exposed data being used for illicit purposes, its customers had not been "harmed" by its lax security and the FTC had no authority to sanction it.

The signs are that the court will rule in LabMD's favor—a ruling that will hamper the agency's future ability to penalize organizations that breach customer privacy.

In Chapter 1, I mentioned the electronic-lock company Onity, whose hotel locks in major hotel chains were hacked to enable burglaries. The hotel chains' 2014 class-action lawsuit was thrown out because the locks still functioned, and the plaintiffs couldn't point to actual burglaries as a result of the security vulnerability.

Liability law doesn't have to work this way. We need only look at the history of product liability for manufactured goods. After the Industrial Revolution, the law at first continued the harsh principle of *caveat emptor*: "Let the buyer beware." However, as manufacturing became industrialized, and products more complex, courts and legislators slowly recognized that it was unreasonable to expect consumers to assess the safety of products they bought. From the late 1800s, product liability laws gradually emerged. Then, from the mid-20th century, most industrial economies moved to "strict liability" standards. If their product causes physical harm, manufacturers are liable, even if they were not negligent in making that product defective. In the 1940s, the California Supreme Court famously explained why strict liability for manufactured goods makes sense: "Public policy demands that responsibility be fixed wherever it will most effectively reduce the hazards to life and health inherent in defective products that reach the market." This argument also applies to the Internet+.

Additionally, people shouldn't have to demonstrate that they suffered monetary harm in order to hold software vendors liable for preventably faulty products. The law could provide for statutory damages in the event that companies have ineffective security for the devices they sell, the services they provide, or the data they keep. Statutory damages would be triggered once poor security was proved, without any further requirements for monetary harm. This is the way wiretap law works; if a police department is proved to have wiretapped someone illegally, that police department has to pay statutory damages. This is also the way copyright law works; an infringer has to pay damages to the copyright holder, even if there was no economic harm at all. It obviously won't work for all areas of Internet+ security liability, but it will for some.

I believe all these types of arguments will gain traction in relation to the Internet+. Already, regulatory agencies are considering issues of data privacy and computer security. Also, many of the products that are becoming computerized and connected—cars, medical devices, appliances, toys, and so on—are already subject to liability laws. When connected versions of these things start killing people, the courts will take action and the public will demand legislative change.

However, today's software is still more or less in the dark ages of product liability. When things go wrong, the loss generally must be borne by the user—companies more or less get off scot-free.

Liability won't necessarily stifle innovation. Liabilities aren't meant to be a black-and-white, all-or-nothing means of government intervention. Regularly, the law establishes carve-outs from liability in some circumstances. This happened in the 1980s, when the small-aircraft industry was almost bankrupted because of excessive liability judgments. There could also be caps on damages, as there are for some medical malpractice claims, although we need to be careful that any caps don't undermine the desired incentives of liabilities. And while it's clear that software manufacturers don't deserve 100% of the liability for a security incident, it is equally clear that they don't deserve 0%. Courts can figure this out.

Where there is risk of liability, the insurance industry follows. A properly functioning insurance market will protect companies from being forced out of business by liability claims. It makes them factor in the risk that their products will cause users' harm as a normal cost of doing business.

Insurance is also a self-reinforcing mechanism for improving security and safety, while still allowing companies room to innovate. The insurance industry imposes costs on bad security. A company whose products and services prove to be insecure will face higher premiums, motivating it to spend money to improve security and reduce those premiums. On the other side, a company that adheres to reasonable standards and is hacked anyway will be protected from a large court judgment because its insurance company will pay it.

Insurance also works on the individual level. If we require people who purchase dangerous technologies to also purchase insurance, then we are effectively privatizing the regulation of these technologies. The market will determine what that insurance will cost, depending on the security of the technologies. Manufacturers could make their products cheap to insure by adding more security. In either case, consumers will pay for the risk inherent in what they buy.

There are challenges to creating these new insurance products. There are two basic models for insurance. One: the fire model, where individual houses catch on fire at a fairly steady rate, and the insurance industry can calculate premiums based on the predicted rate. Two: the flood model, where infrequent, large-scale events affect large numbers of people—but again at a fairly steady rate. Internet+ insurance is complicated because it follows neither of those models but instead has aspects of both: individuals are hacked at a steady (albeit increasing) rate, while class breaks and massive data breaches affect lots of people at once. Also, the constantly changing technology landscape makes it difficult to gather and analyze the historical data necessary to calculate premiums.

Perhaps it would be more accurate to use a health-insurance model: sickness is inevitable, and contagions can spread widely, so insurers should focus on risk prevention and incident response rather than straight reimbursement. Insurance companies are starting to figure out how to price premiums for cybersecurity insurance, though—in some cases scoring companies according to their security practices. More will happen once we better clarify liabilities.

CORRECT INFORMATION ASYMMETRIES

Recently, I had occasion to research baby monitors. They're surveillance devices by design, and can pick up a lot more than a baby's cries. Of course, I had a lot of security questions. How is the audio and video transmission secured? What's the encryption algorithm? How are encryption keys generated, and who has copies of them? If data is stored on the cloud, how long is it stored and how is it secured? How does the smartphone app, if the monitor uses one, authenticate to the cloud server? Many brands are hackable, and I wanted to buy a secure one.

Uniformly, the product marketing materials are minimally informative. The analog monitors say nothing about security. The digital ones make vague statements like: "[Our] technology transmits a secure, encrypted signal so you can rest assured you're the only one who can hear your baby." Some claim to follow various wireless standards, and pair sender and receiver via some sort of encryption. Others rely entirely on transmission power and channel switching for security. All toss around the word "secure" without explaining what it means. Basically, comparison shopping is impossible. I couldn't tell the good from the bad, which means the average consumer has no chance.

Security is complex and largely opaque, and right now there is no way for users to distinguish secure products from insecure ones. Baby monitors are pretty simple. The problem of IoT devices will get even more complicated as devices—and the interconnections between them—become more complex. The lack of information combined with the complexity of the systems is disempowering to consumers, and almost certainly lulls them into thinking that devices are more secure than they are.

In economics, this is known as a "lemons market." Vendors only compete on features that buyers can perceive, and ignore features—like security—that they can't. So, vague, pacifying claims about security are more likely to lead to a sale than detailed explanations of security features.

The result is that insecure products drive secure products out of the market, because there's no return on investment for security. We've seen this over and over again in computer and Internet security, and we're going to see it in the Internet+ as well. Security must be made meaningful, vivid, and obvious to the consumer; once consumers know more, they will be empowered to make better choices.

Many industries have labeling requirements. Think of nutrition and ingredient labels on food, all the fine print that accompanies pharmaceuticals, fuel efficiency stickers on new cars, and so on. Such labeling enables consumers to make better buying decisions. There is nothing like this today in computer security.

One helpful labeling requirement for computerized products would be a discussion of the threat model that the device is designed to be secure against. Looking again at that baby monitor—random channel switching might thwart a casual eavesdropper, but not a more sophisticated attacker. Other security measures would be stronger than channel switching. If the manufacturer explains the security in a simple manner, consumers can do more comparison shopping. I'm thinking of statements like: "This baby monitor uniquely pairs the transmitters and receivers to each other"; "Transmissions are encrypted between transmitter and receiver, which secures against neighborhood eavesdroppers"; "Transmissions on your wireless network are encrypted, which secures against network eavesdroppers"; or "This product encrypts audio and video sent to the cloud, which secures against Internet eavesdroppers." And while a lot of that may be gobbledygook to the average consumer, product review sites can use the information to make better recommendations.

Samsung did something like this with its smart television, but it was buried in the fine print of its policy:

> Please be aware that if your spoken words include personal or other sensitive information, that information will be among the data captured and transmitted to a third party through your use of Voice Recognition.

Product labels should also explain the user's security responsibilities. Baby monitors are routinely put in bedrooms. It's much easier to leave a monitor on all the time than to switch it on and off, which means that it's very likely going to capture and transmit activity that the user doesn't want broadcast. I want the product label to put the user on notice that this will happen. "When the transmitter is on, it relays every sound it captures to our headquarters in San Jose." Or: "This product will need to be updated regularly; registered users will receive updates for at least the next five years." The general idea is that users need to be informed where the product's security features start and end, how security needs to be maintained, and when users are on their own.

Perhaps the most useful way to give customers information on product labels is a rating system. Secure products and services could get a higher rating, a seal of security, or some other simple marking that could guide customers' buying decisions. It's an interesting idea, and lots of government agencies are thinking about this—in the UK, the EU, Australia, and elsewhere.

We need more transparency in cloud services. Right now, you have no idea how Google secures your e-mail. My hope is that liabilities will change this. If a retail company is liable for securing its customers' data, then it will have to hold its cloud service providers liable. And those service providers will, in turn, have to hold their cloud infrastructure providers liable.

This sort of cascading liability will force everyone to be more transparent, if for no other reason than to satisfy demands from insurance companies.

If there were security standards, a government agency or an independent organization could test products and services against them to assign the ratings. Self-reporting could also work. In 2017, two senators introduced the Cyber Shield Act, which would have directed the Department of Commerce to develop security standards for IoT devices. Companies could display a label on their products touting their adherence to the standards. The bill went nowhere, but an industry consortium or another third party could easily do the same. The standards could even be tied to insurance.

Alternatively, companies might be rated according to their processes and practices, perhaps using the design principles from Chapter 6. That's something like what Underwriters Laboratories does. The group was created by the insurance industry in 1894 to test the safety of electrical equipment. It doesn't demonstrate that a product is safe, but uses a checklist to confirm that the manufacturer followed a set of safety rules.

Consumers Union—the organization behind *Consumer Reports*—has been looking into doing some kind of security testing of IoT products for years. It may even have a viable rating system by the time this book is published. But while it may be able to rate automobiles and major appliances, the sheer number—and the rapid change—of cheaper consumer devices will be too much for any general-purpose organization to deal with.

In the computer security field, two existing rating programs are worth mentioning. The Electronic Frontier Foundation's Who Has Your Back? project evaluates companies' commitments to protecting users when the government seeks private data. And the Open Technology Institute's Ranking Digital Rights initiative evaluates companies on how they respect freedom of expression and privacy.

When it comes to products, though, there will be some pitfalls in setting up a security rating system. One is that there are no simple tests with simple results. We can't extensively test a piece of software and pronounce it secure. And any security rating changes with time; what was verifiably secure last year might be demonstrably insecure this year. This is more than a matter of time and expense. We're butting up against some technological limits of computer science theory: our inability to declare something "secure" in any meaningful way.

Still, there's a lot we can do. We can test a product against a known suite of attack techniques and declare it resistant. We can test it for behaviors indicative of security failures and demonstrate a corner-cutting development process. We can test against many of the design principles from Chapter 6. And we can do much of this without the consent of the companies developing and selling the software.

We'll have to find the right balance of manageable testing requirements and security. For instance, the FDA requires testing of computerized medical devices. Initially, its rules required complete retesting if there was any software change, including patches to fix vulnerabilities, but it has since revised those rules so that updates that don't change functionality don't require retesting. This is not the most secure way to do things, but it is probably the most reasonable compromise.

We'll also have to figure out how to educate customers to understand the meaning of the ratings, rankings, descriptions, or seals of approval. How do we explain that a logo stating that an IoT toy says "Meets A-1 industry security standards" doesn't actually mean that the toy is guaranteed to be secure—only that it meets some minimal security standards that may be good enough today against certain threats? In the food world, there are a zillion competing ratings and scales; we don't want that to happen with Internet+ security.

Despite these problems, some sort of security rating will be essential. I have trouble imagining any market-based security improvements without it.

Beyond product labeling and security ratings, there are two other good ways to give consumers more information. The first is breach disclosure laws, which require companies to notify individuals when their personal information is stolen. Such notifications not only alert people that their data has been stolen, but give all of us information about the security practices of the companies that store personal data. In the US, 48 states have these sorts of laws. They're all different: what information counts as personal, how long the companies have to disclose, when they can delay disclosure, and so on.

There have been several failed attempts at a national law. In theory, I am in favor of this, but I worry that it will be less comprehensive than the laws of some states—notably Massachusetts, California, and New York—and that it will preempt all the existing state laws. Right now, the state laws are de facto national laws, because every successful company has users in all 50 states.

These state laws need to be expanded. Incident reporting where there's no loss of personal information remains voluntary, and participation is generally low because companies fear bad press or litigation. Breach disclosure laws need to encompass other sorts of breaches as well. If a piece of critical infrastructure is breached, for example, there should be a requirement for the owner to report it.

The second way to give consumers more information is to improve vulnerability disclosure. In Chapter 2, I talked about how security researchers find vulnerabilities in computer software, and how publishing those research results is critical to motivating software vendors to fix them. Vendors hate the process because it makes them look bad, and in some cases they've successfully sued researchers under the DMCA and other laws. This situation needs to be reversed; instead, we need laws protecting researchers who find vulnerabilities, responsibly disclose them to the software vendor, and publish their results after a reasonable time. Not only will improved vulnerability disclosure nudge companies to increase their security to avoid unflattering publicity, but it will also give consumers important information about the security of different products.

INCREASE PUBLIC EDUCATION

Public education is vital for Internet+ security. Citizens need to understand their role in cybersecurity; like every other aspect of personal or public safety, our individual actions matter. Additionally, an educated public will be able to pressure companies to improve their security, either by refusing to use insecure products or services, or by pressuring government to take action where appropriate.

There have been attempts at public-awareness campaigns for Internet security. The Department of Homeland Security unveiled a "Stop. Think.Connect." campaign in 2016. That you almost certainly aren't familiar with it demonstrates how effective it has been. Perhaps other campaigns can do better.

Education is hard. We need to educate people that security matters and how to make security choices, without necessarily turning them into security engineers. These are technical issues, yet we don't want to create a world where only technical experts are guaranteed security. That's where we are right now with our laptops and home networks. The complexity of these systems is beyond the understanding of average consumers. You have to be an expert to configure them, so most people don't bother. We have to do better.

Today, a lot of security advice we give to users just covers for bad security design. We tell people not to click on strange links. But it's the Internet; clicking is what links are for. We also tell them not to insert strange USB drives into their computers. Again, what else would you possibly do with a USB drive? We have to do better: we need systems that remain secure regardless of which links people click on, and regardless of which USB drives they stick into their computers.

Compare this to the automobile. When cars were first introduced, they were sold with a repair manual and a tool kit; you needed to know how to fix one to drive one. As cars became easier to use and service stations more common, even the mechanically disinclined were able to buy one. We've reached this place with computers, but not with computer security.

There are areas where public education won't help. For low-cost devices, there is no market fix, because the threat is primarily botnets, and neither the buyer nor the seller knows enough about them to care (except for people like me, and maybe some of my readers). The owners of the webcams and DVRs used in the denial-of-service attacks can't tell, and mostly don't care: their devices were cheap to buy, they still work, and the owners don't know any victims. The sellers of those devices don't care: they're now selling newer and better models, and their customers only care about price and features. Think of it as a kind of invisible pollution.

For more expensive devices, and as safety risks increase, the market works better. Automobile drivers and airline passengers want their modes of transport to be secure. Education might actually help people make better choices about the security of their products, just as they do today about the safety of their automobiles.

We can teach users specific behaviors, as long as they're simple, actionable, and make obvious sense. In public health, we've taught people that they should wash their hands, sneeze into the crook of their arm, and get an annual flu vaccine. Fewer people do those things than we might like, but most know they should.

RAISE PROFESSIONAL STANDARDS

There are many rules you have to follow if you want to build a building. You need to hire an architect to design it. That architect has to be state certified. Any complicated engineering needs to be approved by a certified engineer. The construction company you hire needs to be licensed. The electricians and apprentices that the construction company hires all need to be licensed by state boards. To navigate the complexities of all this, you'll certainly need to hire an attorney and accountant. Both will be certified and licensed through tests administered by state professional certification boards. Of course, the real estate agent who helped you buy the land was licensed as well.

Professional certification is a higher standard than occupational licensing, but right now there is no system for either certifying or licensing software designers, software architects, computer engineers, or coders of any kind. Creating one is not a new idea; it has been promoted in the industry for decades. Existing organizations for software professionals, like the Association for Computing Machinery and the IEEE Computer Society, have studied this issue at length and have proposed several different licensing schemes and professional development criteria for software engineers. The International Organization for Standardization (ISO) has some relevant standards as well. There has always been fierce pushback from developers, both for personal reasons and because software engineering is not engineering in the traditional sense. It isn't a discipline where the engineer applies known principles based on science to create something new. This makes it hard to figure out what a professional software engineer is, let alone what competencies they require.

Even so, I believe this will change. There will be some level of software engineer that will be licensed—either by the government or by some professional association with the government's approval—and that engineer will be required to sign off on a software design in the same way that a certified architect signs off on building plans.

It will take a lot of work to get there, though. You can't just create a licensed profession out of thin air; an entire educational infrastructure needs to be in place. So before it happens, we'll need to be able to consistently train software engineers in reliability, safety, security, and other responsibilities. We'll need a curriculum in colleges and universities, and continuing education for engineers in the middle of their careers. We'll need professional organizations to step up and define what accreditation looks like, and what sort of recertification is needed in this fast-changing environment. We'll also need to figure out how to account for the international nature of software development.

None of this will be easy, and it will likely take decades to get it all working. It took three centuries for medicine to become a profession in post-Renaissance Europe; we can't wait anywhere near that long. Today, anything we can do to move towards increased professionalism will benefit the field in the long run.

CLOSE THE SKILLS GAP

Along with raising professional standards, we need to drastically increase the number of cybersecurity professionals.

The lack of trained people is called the cybersecurity skills gap, and it's been a major topic of conversation at almost every IT security event I have attended in recent years. Basically, there aren't enough security engineers to meet the demand. This is true at every level: network administrators, programmers, security architects, managers, and chief information security officers.

The numbers are scary. Various reports forecast 1.5 million, 2 million, 3.5 million, or 6 million cybersecurity jobs going unfilled globally in the next few years because demand is exceeding supply. Whichever estimate is correct—and my prediction is towards the higher side—this could be a disaster. All of the technical security solutions discussed in this book require people, and if we don't have the people, the solutions won't get implemented.

Jon Oltsik, an industry analyst who has been following this issue, writes: "The cybersecurity skills shortage represents an existential threat to our national security." Given current trends, it's hard to argue with that assessment.

The solution is both obvious and difficult to implement. On the supply side, we need to expose students to cybersecurity as children, graduate more software engineers with a cybersecurity specialty, and create mid-career retraining programs to shift practicing engineers over to cyberse-curity. We need to attract more women and minorities to cybersecurity careers. We need to pour money into all of this, and quickly.

On the demand side, we need to automate away those jobs wher-ever possible. We're already starting to see the benefits of automation for security, and the situation will improve significantly once the benefits of machine learning and artificial intelligence start to kick in. This leads directly into my next recommendation.

INCREASE RESEARCH

We have some serious technical security problems to solve. And while there is already a lot of research and development under way, we need more strategic long-term, high-risk/high-reward research into technologies that can dramatically alter the balance between attacker and defender. Today, there are far too few resources devoted to this type of R&D.

Most business organizations won't engage in this sort of research because any payoff is distant and nebulous. The majority of substantive improvements in the coming decades will result from government-funded academic research.

We need smaller-scale, near-term applied research as well. Academic institutions can't do it all; companies must also step in. A research tax credit could provide the proper incentive for development of secure prod-ucts and services.

Research has the potential to change some of the fundamental assumptions about Internet+ security discussed in Chapter 1. I've seen calls for a cyber Manhattan Project, a cyber moonshot, and other similar buzz-phrases. I don't know if we're ready for anything like that, though. Those sorts of projects need specific tangible goals. A generic goal of "improving cybersecurity" just doesn't cut it.

Whatever the mechanism, we need a concerted and sustained research and development project for new technologies that can secure us against the wide variety of threats we're facing now and in the coming years and decades. It's ambitious, yes, but I don't think we have any alternative. The primary thing holding us back is the severe lack of trust of government by the tech industry.

Again, nothing new here. This call has been made for climate change, food and overpopulation, space exploration, and many other problems we collectively face.

FUND MAINTENANCE AND UPKEEP

There's a lot of talk in the US about our failing national infrastructure—roads, bridges, water systems, schools and other public buildings—and the need for a massive investment to modernize them all. We also need to be talking about a massive investment in our Internet infrastructure. It's not as old as our physical infrastructure, but in some ways it's just as decrepit.

Computers degrade faster than conventional physical infrastructure. You know this is true; you are much more likely to upgrade your laptop and phone because the older models don't work as well than to upgrade your automobile or refrigerator. Companies like Microsoft and Apple maintain only the most recent few versions of their operating systems. After a decade, it can actually be risky to keep using old computer hardware and software.

We're not going to replace the Internet with something else; the current technologies are too pervasive for that to work. Instead, we'll have to upgrade pieces of it, one at a time, all while maintaining backwards compatibility. Someone needs to coordinate that. Someone also needs to fund development and maintenance of the critical pieces of Internet infrastructure. Someone needs to work with technology companies to help secure shared pieces of infrastructure, and respond quickly to vulnerabilities when they occur. In the next chapter, I argue that government is that "someone."

After we're done upgrading our critical Internet infrastructure, we'll need to keep upgrading it. The era where you can build a system and have it work for decades is over (if it ever existed); computer systems need to be upgraded continuously. We need to accept this new, minimalist life span; we need to figure out how to keep our systems current; and we need to get ready to pay for it. This will be expensive.

8

Government Is Who Enables Security

Airplanes should be incredibly dangerous. You're inside what's basically a rocket, hurtling through the air at 600 miles per hour. A modern airplane has upwards of six million parts, many of which have to work perfectly. Something fails, and the plane crashes. Common sense says that it's super risky.

Airlines compete with each other on all sorts of attributes. They compete on price and routes. They compete on seat pitch and legroom. They compete on amenities in their premium cabins. They compete on nebulous "feel good" emotions with evocative branding. But they don't compete on safety. Safety—and security—is set by the government. Airlines and airplane manufacturers are required to comply with all sorts of regulations. And it's all invisible to the consumer. No airline ever touts its safety or security records in advertisements. But every time I board a plane—182 times in 2017—I know that the flight will be safe.

It wasn't always like this. Airplanes used to be incredibly dangerous, and fatal accidents were common. What changed was airplane safety regulation. Over the decades, government has forced improvement after improvement in airplane design, flight procedures, pilot training, and so on. The result is that today, commercial airplanes are the safest way to travel, ever.

We need to do the same for Internet security. There are several models to consider for setting and enforcing the security standards described in Chapter 6. An independent testing agency could judge manufacturers on adherence to the standards. Consumers Union—a not-for-profit company funded by magazine subscriptions and grants—could be a model for that. We could rely on the market—that means customers—to demand more security by favoring more-secure products and services.

I'm not optimistic about any of those ideas, for all the reasons discussed in the previous chapter. Government is by far the most common way we improve our collective security, and it is almost certainly the most efficient. It's how we change business incentives. It's how we pay for common defense. It's how we solve collective action problems and prevent free riding.

I can think of no industry in the past 100 years that has improved its safety and security without being compelled to do so by government. This is true for buildings and pharmaceuticals. It's true for food and workplaces. It's true for automobiles, airplanes, nuclear power plants, consumer products, restaurants, and—more recently in the US—financial instruments. In every one of those cases, before government regulation, sellers simply kept producing dangerous or harmful products and selling them into a naive market. Even when there was popular outrage, it took government to change the behavior of business owners. From the manufacturers' point of view, it's simply rational to hope for the best, rather than spend money up front to make their products safer. After all, the buying public often can't tell the difference until something goes wrong, and producers are biased to prefer an immediate benefit—cost savings—over a longer-term safety or security benefit.

Whenever industry groups write about this, they stress that any standards should be voluntary. This is their own self-interest talking. If we want a standard enforced, it needs to be mandatory. Anything else is not going to work, because the incentives aren't aligned properly.

A NEW GOVERNMENT AGENCY

Governments operate in silos. The Food and Drug Administration has jurisdiction over medical devices. The Department of Transportation has jurisdiction over ground vehicles. The Federal Aviation Administration has jurisdiction over aircraft, but doesn't consider the privacy implications of drones to be part of its mandate. The Federal Trade Commission oversees privacy to a degree, but only in the case of unfair or deceptive trade practices. The Department of Justice gets involved if a federal crime is committed.

For data, jurisdiction can change depending on use. If data is used to influence a consumer, the FTC has jurisdiction. If that data is used to influence a voter, that's the Federal Election Commission's jurisdiction. If the same data is used in the same way to influence a student in a school, the Department of Education gets involved. In the US, there's no authority for harms due to information leakage or privacy violations—unless the company involved made false promises to the consumer. Each agency has its own approach and its own rules. Congressional committees fight over jurisdiction; the federal departments and commissions all have their own separate domains: everything from agriculture to defense to transportation to energy. Sometimes states have concurrent regulatory authority— California, for example, has long been a leader in Internet privacy issues—and sometimes the federal government preempts state actions.

This is not how the Internet works. The Internet, and now the Internet+, is a freewheeling integrated system of computers, algorithms, and networks. It's the opposite of a silo. It grows horizontally, destroying traditional barriers so that people and systems that never previously communicated are now able to do so. Whether it's large personal databases or algorithmic decision-making or the Internet of Things or cloud storage or robotics, these are all technologies that interrelate with each other in very profound ways. Right now on my smartphone, there are apps that log my health information, control my energy use, and interact with my car. That phone has entered the jurisdiction of four different US federal agencies— the FDA, DOE, DOT, and FCC—and it's barely gotten started.

These electronic platforms are general and need a holistic approach to policy. They all use computers, and any solutions we come up with will have to be general. I'm not saying there will be one set of regulations that covers every computer in every application, but there needs to be a single framework, applicable to all computers, whether they're in your car, plane, phone, thermostat, or pacemaker.

I am proposing a new federal agency: a National Cyber Office (NCO). My model is the Office of the Director of National Intelligence (ODNI), created by Congress in the wake of the 9/11 terrorist attacks as a single entity to coordinate intelligence across the US government. The ODNI's job is to set priorities, coordinate activities, allocate funds, and cross-pollinate ideas. It's not a perfect model, and the ODNI has been criticized for how ineffective its cross-agency coordination has been. But this sounds like the model we need for the Internet+.

The initial purpose of this new agency would not be to regulate, but instead to advise other areas of government on issues that touch on the Internet+. Such advice is badly needed by other federal agencies, and by lawmakers at all government levels. The agency could also direct research where needed, convene meetings of stakeholders on different issues, and file *amicus curiae* briefs in court cases where its expertise would be valued. Instead of an enforcement agency like the FTC or the FDA, think of this agency as more like the Office of Management and Budget or the Department of Commerce: a repository of expertise.

The NCO would recognize that Internet+ policy necessarily spans multiple agencies, and that those agencies need to retain their existing scopes of responsibility. But many solutions need to be centrally coordinated, and someone needs to hold individual agencies accountable. So much of Internet+ hardware, software, protocols, and systems overlaps between wildly different applications.

This new agency could also manage other government-wide security initiatives, such as updating the NIST Cybersecurity Framework, and developing the other types of security standards I listed in Chapter 6, the academic grant-making and research tax credit I mentioned in Chapter 7, the security requirements that should be part of the government's own procurement process, and government-wide best practices. It could manage partnerships between government and industry, and help develop strategies that encompass both. It would also serve as a counterweight to the military and national-security government organizations that are already setting policy in this space. Some of this is being done by NIST today, and some by the National Science Foundation, but neither NIST nor the NSF could easily be modified into this new role. It would make sense to move these functions into the new dedicated agency.

Finally, this agency would be a place for the government to consolidate its expertise. A dedicated Internet+ agency could attract (and pay competitive salaries to) talented individuals to help craft and advise on policy matters. This means that the agency would consist of engineers and computer scientists working closely with experts in law and policy. This is a theme I will return to in the Conclusion: the importance of technologists and policy makers working closely together.

Once the NCO was established, other "centers of excellence" could be created under its umbrella. Again, the ODNI is a good model, with its National Counterterrorism Center and National Counterproliferation Center. I imagine that the NCO might need a National Artificial Intelligence Center and a National Robotics Center, and perhaps even a National Algorithms Center. We might create a National Cyberdefense Academy—an interagency facility with a variety of classes, certifications, and tracks that all agencies could send staff to for training. It would also have to coordinate closely with the Department of Homeland Security, and probably the Department of Justice.

Eventually, in some way, regulation will have to cut across multiple Internet+ domains. Maybe this new agency will be the regulatory body, but more likely the existing agencies that already regulate various industries will continue to do so, adding Internet+ security regulations to their portfolios. Their broad mandates make them more nimble than Congress. They can respond to changes in technology or markets. They can motivate companies to change their behavior.

A model based on the FTC might be useful. The FTC doesn't have specific rules. Instead, it has vague rules and prescribed outcomes, and it pursues the most flagrant violators. Everyone else watches the FTC's actions and fines, and tries to be slightly better than the companies that get penalized. The FTC also issues guidance and works with the industry to promote compliance. And although it is sometimes described as toothless, the result is public awareness of norms of acceptable business conduct, accountability for those found to have violated them, and continuous improvement across the board.

Here's one example: in 2006, Netflix published 100 million anonymous movie reviews and ratings as part of a contest. Researchers were able to de-anonymize some of that data, which surprised pretty much everyone. The FTC took action against Netflix only when the company took no better care with customer data when it ran a second contest the following year.

Today, both the FCC and the SEC have the authority to require publicly traded companies to audit and then certify their own cybersecurity. Those agencies could take an existing security framework and use it, or create one of their own.

I'm not the first to suggest this. A research group advising the European Commission proposed the formation of the European Safety and Security Engineering Agency. Ashkan Soltani, former chief technologist at the FTC, proposed a new "federal technology commission." University of Washington law professor Ryan Calo proposed a Federal Robotics Commission. And Matthew Scherer of George Mason University proposed an agency to regulate artificial intelligence.

Some other countries are thinking along these lines. Israel created its National Cyber Bureau in 2011 to both increase the country's defenses in cyberspace and advise the rest of the government on cyber-related issues. The UK created the National Cyber Security Centre in 2016 to "help protect our critical services from cyber attacks, manage major incidents, and improve the underlying security of the UK Internet through technological improvement and advice to citizens and organisations." To my mind, both of these organizations are too closely tied to the military and therefore to the part of the government that relies on Internet insecurity, but they're a start.

There is significant historical precedent in the US for this idea. New technologies regularly lead to the formulation of new government agencies. Trains did. Cars did. Airplanes did. The invention of radio led to the formation of the Federal Radio Commission, which became the Federal Communications Commission. The invention of nuclear power led to the formation of the Atomic Energy Commission, which became the Department of Energy.

We can debate the specifics, and the appropriate limits of this new agency. We can debate the organizational structure. But whatever the format, we need some government agency to be in charge of this.

I do think that Internet+-era regulation will look different from industrial-era regulation. The Internet is already governed on a multistakeholder model, whereby governments, industry, technologists, and civil society come together to resolve issues pertaining to its functioning. My guess is that this model is much more suited to Internet+ regulation than the other models we're used to.

There are reasonable objections to this proposal. Government agencies are inefficient. They often lack needed expertise. They are bureaucracies, and lack vision and foresight. There are problems in speed, scope, efficacy, and the potential of regulatory capture. And—of course—there's the pervasive opinion that government should just get out of the way.

But those worries exist, regardless of whether there is a single new government agency or the authority is delegated among a dozen or so existing government agencies. The value of a single agency is considerable. The alternative is to craft Internet+ policy ad hoc and piecemeal, in a way that adds complexity and doesn't counter emerging threats.

Of course, the devil is in the details, and I don't have any of them. My NCO idea might not work, and I'm okay with that. My hope is that, at a minimum, it can start a discussion.

GOVERNMENT REGULATIONS

The computer industry has largely been regulation-free. That's partly the result of the nascence of the industry. It's partly the result of the industry's relative initial harmlessness, and an unwillingness on the part of its leaders to recognize how much things have changed. And it's largely the result of governmental reluctance to risk disrupting the enormous wealth generator that the industry has become. I think these days are coming to an end and Internet+ regulation is inevitable. There are several reasons.

One: governments tend to regulate industries that are choke points for the overall economy, like telecommunications and transportation. The Internet+ is definitely one of these, and it's increasingly more of an economic linchpin. Two: governments regulate consumer products and services that can kill people, and the Internet+ is rapidly joining the club. Three: many existing industries being permeated by computers—from toys to appliances to automobiles to nuclear power plants—are already regulated.

It's important to realize that regulation is more than a list of things either required or forbidden. That's regulation at its most blunt, but most of the time it's far more nuanced. Regulation can create responsibilities and leave the details up to the market. It can push in one direction or the other. It can change incentives. It can nudge instead of force. It can be flexible enough to adapt to changes in both technology's and society's expectations.

The goal isn't to be perfectionistic. We don't demand that automobile manufacturers produce the safest car possible. We mandate safety standards like seat belts and air bags, require crash tests, and leave the rest to the market. This approach is essential in an environment as dynamic as the Internet+.

Europe is already significantly increasing its Internet regulations— we'll talk about the EU's General Data Protection Regulation in Chapter 10—and some US states are moving in a similar direction. While there's little appetite in Washington for any sort of regulation, that appetite could increase quickly if a disaster occurs that takes a significant number of lives or destroys a certain portion of our economy.

The US has started to regulate at the federal level, but in fits and starts, and only on an industry-specific basis. For example, the FDA has issued guidance to medical-device manufacturers on regulatory requirements for Internet-connected devices. The agency doesn't conduct the testing itself; developers test their products and services against the standards and submit their documentation to the FDA for approval. This is serious business. The FDA is not shy about denying approval to products that fail or demanding the recall of products that cause harm.

Rules for privacy of patients' medical data are substantially different from those governing privacy of consumer data. As you'd expect, medical-data rules are much more stringent. Many developers of new health-related products and services are trying to position their wares as consumer devices, so they don't require FDA approval. This sometimes works, as with health trackers like Fitbit. And sometimes the FDA fights back, as it did with genetic data collected by 23andMe.

For cars, the Department of Transportation has only issued voluntary security standards. Voluntary standards are never as effective as mandatory standards, but they can help. For example, in a lawsuit the court will often assess voluntary compliance with DOT guidance to help determine whether a manufacturer was negligent.

The FAA has taken a different approach with drone regulation. It does not require design certification for each new drone that enters the market; instead, it indirectly regulates consumer drones through policies that restrict how and where they can be used.

There have been some successes. In 2015, the FTC sued Wyndham

Hotels over its computer security. Wyndham had terrible security practices that allowed hackers to repeatedly break into its networks and steal data about Wyndham customers. The FTC argued that because Wyndham had a privacy policy that made promises the company did not keep, it was deceiving the customer.

The court battle was complicated, and largely hinged on matters of authority that aren't relevant here. But what's interesting is that one of Wyndham's defenses was that the FTC couldn't fine it for not being secure enough, because the FTC never told Wyndham what "secure enough" meant in the first place. The Federal Court of Appeals sided with the FTC, basically saying that it was Wyndham's job to figure out what "secure enough" meant and that it had screwed up by not doing so.

CHALLENGES OF REGULATION

The Internet is the most dynamic environment there is. Regulation, especially wrongheaded or excessive regulation, can retard new technologies and new innovations. In security, it can inhibit the flexibility and agility required to keep up with changing threats.

When it comes to regulating the Internet+, I see four problems: speed, scope, efficacy, and the potential of stifling the industries being regulated.

Speed first: government policy change is slow compared to the speed of technological innovation. It used to be the other way around; it was almost 40 years after Alexander Graham Bell first commercialized the telephone that it became a commonplace item. For the television, it took over 30 years. Those days are over. E-mail, cell phones, Facebook, Twitter—these penetrated society much faster than technologies of the previous decades. (It took 13 years for Facebook to amass two billion regular users worldwide.) We're at the point where law will always lag behind technology. By the time regulations are issued, they're often laughably out-of-date. A good example is the EU's regulations requiring notices about cookies on websites; this would have made sense in 1995, but by the time the regulation came into force in 2011, web tracking was much more complex. Similarly, courts will always be trying to apply outdated laws to more modern situations, and—even worse—technological changes will result in laws having all sorts of unintended consequences.

Next, scope: laws tend to be written narrowly, focused on specific technologies. These laws can fail when technologies change. Most of our privacy laws were written in the 1970s, and while the concerns haven't changed, the technology has. Here's an example: the Electronic Communications Privacy Act was passed in 1986. One of the things the law did was regulate the privacy of e-mail, giving different privacy protections for two types of e-mail. To access newly received e-mail, the government needs a warrant. To access e-mail that's been sitting on the server for more than 180 days, the government may search without any restrictions. In 1986, that made sense. Storage was expensive. People accessed their e-mail by having their e-mail client bring the mail from the server to their computer. Anything left on the server for more than six months was considered abandoned, and we have no privacy rights in abandoned property. Today, everybody leaves their e-mail on the server for six months and even six years. That's how Gmail, Hotmail, and every other web-based e-mail system works. The law makes an important distinction between services that provide communication and services that process and store data—a distinction that no longer makes sense. The logic behind that old law has been completely reversed by technology, but it's still in force.

This will happen repeatedly until we start writing laws that are technology neutral. If we focus on the human aspects of the law rather than the technological aspects, we can protect laws against both speed and scope problems. For example, we could write laws that address "communication," regardless of whether it's by voice, video, e-mail, text, private message, or whatever technology comes next. Our technological future is filled with emergent properties of new technologies, and regularly we'll be surprised.

There's another, and completely different, scope problem with regulations: How general should we make them? On the one hand, it's obvious that we need different standards for cars and airplanes than we do for toys and other household objects, and different regulations for financial databases than we do for anonymous traffic data. On the other hand, the interconnectedness of everything makes things like toys and pothole data less innocuous than they might appear.

Additionally, it's hard to know exactly where regulations should stop. Yes, we're going to regulate things that affect the world in a direct physical manner, but because everything is interconnected and the threats are interlocking, it's impossible to carve out any portion of the Internet+ and definitively say that it doesn't matter. Someone might suggest not bothering to regulate low-cost Internet devices, but vulnerabilities in these can affect critical infrastructure. Someone else might suggest exempting pure software systems because they don't have physical agency, but they can still have real-world effects: think of software that decides who gets released on bail or parole. Regulations should probably cover these systems as well.

The third problem with regulating the Internet+ is efficacy. Large corporations are very effective at evading regulation. The big tech companies are spending record amounts of money lobbying in Washington, to the point that they're now spending twice what the banking industry does, and many times more than oil companies, defense contractors, and everyone else. Google alone spent $6 million on lobbying in just three months of 2017. And even without such lobbying, these companies are enormous wealth generators for the US, and Congress is loath to risk disrupting that.

We're already seeing examples. One is the way developers of fitness devices worked to persuade the FDA that their products are not medical devices and therefore not subject to FDA rules. Data brokers have performed similar lobbying maneuvers with respect to personal information held in their databases. As privacy law professor Julie Cohen has said: "Power interprets regulation as damage and routes around it."

We need to regulate fairly, and we need to regulate well. Both goals are hard to achieve in practice. Lots of regulations don't work. We've already seen examples of these in Internet security: the CAN-SPAM Act that didn't stop spam, the Child Online Protection Act that didn't protect children, and the DMCA that didn't prevent the making of unauthorized copies. We'll see more ineffective and counterproductive legislative proposals in Chapter 11.

And regulation is only as effective as the enforcement. In the US, the FTC has taken legal action against robocallers, "do not call" list violators, deceptive telco advertisers, and excessive data collection by toys and televisions. FTC fines range from a few hundred thousand dollars to millions. But the agency is hamstrung by limited resources to investigate and bring cases, which allows the more clever companies to evade FTC regulations—potentially indefinitely. The chances of getting caught and successfully sued are so low that any rational company would simply take the chance.

Regulations are consistently co-opted. Instead of promoting the common good, they're aimed at promoting some private agenda. This happens all the time, but the example closest to my field is the copyright office. It's not a voice of the people, and its regulations aren't designed to promote fairness. It's a voice of the copyright holders—large companies like Disney—and its regulations are largely designed to promote the interests of those companies. I could say the same thing about many industries and the agencies that are supposed to regulate them. This is regulatory capture, and I could spend an entire chapter on it. It's very common and happens for a lot of reasons, and I see no reason why Internet regulation will be immune from the same forces. If regulators become an enforcement arm of an entrenched industry group, the results can be worse than doing nothing at all.

The fourth and last problem with regulations is that they can stifle innovation. I think we just have to accept that, and in certain rare cases we may even want to do so deliberately. Unfettered innovation is only acceptable for benign technologies. We regularly put limits on technologies that can kill us, because we believe the safety and security are worth it. The precautionary principle dictates that when the potential of harm is great, we should err on the side of not deploying a new technology without proof of security. This way of thinking will become more important in a world where an attacker can open all of the door locks or hack all of the power plants. We don't want to—and can't—stop technological progress, but we can make deliberate choices between technological futures, or speed up or delay certain technologies with respect to the others.

We won't get new features for our computers and devices at the same furious pace we're used to, and that will be a benefit when the features could potentially kill you. But, as I've mentioned a couple of times, regulations can encourage innovation as well. By providing incentives to private industry to solve security problems, we're likely to get more security.

We will need to work carefully through this. Regulations might disproportionally burden small companies where technological innovation tends to happen. They often benefit large incumbents who have the money to satisfy them, and end up serving as a protectionist barrier against new entrants into the industry rather than fostering competition. I don't want to minimize these problems, but we've dealt with them in other industries and I'm confident that we can find the right middle ground here as well.

NORMS, TREATIES, AND INTERNATIONAL REGULATORY BODIES

Okay. I admit it. I've palmed a card throughout this chapter by ignoring the international nature of the problem. How can I propose that US citizens enact domestic regulations to solve what is inherently an international problem? Even if the US and the EU both pass strict regulations on IoT security, what's to stop cheap, insecure products from coming over the borders from Asia or elsewhere?

It's a fair criticism. Countries can regulate what is manufactured or sold within their borders. Many countries already do that for pretty much all consumer products. We can create a blacklist of products or manufacturers, and force companies like Amazon and Apple to remove them from their online stores. But that'll only go so far. Unless we allow ourselves to be subjected to pervasive and invasive searches, we can't regulate what crosses the border in suitcases, mail-order packages, or Internet downloads. We can't regulate software services purchased from foreign websites; censoring them is simply not an option. This is nothing new, and something we'll have to deal with.

Even so, domestic regulations can have a powerful effect worldwide. Unlike car manufacturers, which sell different products in different countries based on things like emissions control laws, software is more of a write-once-sell-everywhere kind of business. If a large enough market regulates a software product or service, it is likely that the manufacturer will simply make that change worldwide, rather than having to maintain multiple products. Because the Internet is global, regulating cybersecurity is a bit like imposing emissions standards: if a country regulates on its own, it bears all the costs, while the rest of the world shares in the benefits.

International cooperation is coming. It is often in governments' interests to harmonize laws. Most countries are concerned about protecting their economies and infrastructure from interruption. States also have an interest in cooperating to fight cybercrime. Smart, organized crime groups engage in what I call jurisdictional arbitrage: specifically basing their criminal activities in countries that have lax cybercrime laws, easily bribable police forces, and no extradition treaties. We know that both Russia and China turn a blind eye to crime that is directed abroad. There are hacker havens in Nigeria, Vietnam, Romania, and Brazil as well. For poor countries, organized cybercrime can actually be a source of wealth and prosperity. Some states, like North Korea, actively engage in state-sponsored cybercrime to boost the regime's coffers.

There are some promising developments in this area. There are hundreds of national response teams—CERTs or CSIRTs—around the world. These groups often cooperate across borders and provide a way for incident responders to share information. The Budapest Convention on Cybercrime has now been ratified by 52 countries, although notably not by some of the significant players, such as Russia, Brazil, China, and India. The treaty provides a framework for international police and judicial cooperation on cybercrime.

We don't want governments managing the Internet. Much of the Internet's innovation stemmed from the US government's benign neglect. Today, countries worldwide want to be much more involved in how their domestic Internet is managed. At the extreme, large and powerful countries like Russia and China want to control their domestic Internet in ways that increase their surveillance, censorship, and control over their citizens.

The current governance model for the Internet is multi-stakeholder, consisting of governments, companies, civil society, and interested technologists. As dysfunctional as it might feel sometimes, such a model is our best defense against an insecure Internet. It also prevents a splintering—called balkanization—of the Internet that might result from totalitarian countries enforcing their own demands.

Norms—informal rules for individuals, corporations, and nations for what is acceptable behavior—regulate far more of our society than most people realize. However, we currently don't have established international norms regulating the use of cyberweapons. And the current norm regarding cyberespionage is that it's okay. As we saw in Chapter 4, countries are in the middle of a cyber arms race. And every country is pretty much making it up as it goes along.

Political scientist Joseph Nye believes that countries can develop norms limiting cyberattacks. For a variety of reasons, it's in the self-interest of nations to agree on things like not attacking each other's infrastructure in peacetime, or not using cyberweapons against civilians first in wartime. These norms will eventually find their way into treaties and other more formal agreements.

One roadblock to consensus is that many countries don't think of cybersecurity simply in terms of preventing attacks from hostile attackers. It's also about ensuring that dissenting ideas don't influence domestic politics. Viral dissident content can represent just as much of a threat as viral code. This makes multilateral bargaining hard, but not impossible.

The UN had its GGE—Group of Governmental Experts on Developments in the Field of Information and Telecommunications in the Context of International Security—which came up with a good list of internationally agreed-upon norms in 2013. These were immediately blocked by countries like China that didn't agree with them, and in 2017, the group disbanded in deadlock.

Still, there is probably some common ground. If states can't agree not to stockpile cyberweapons, for instance, it's nevertheless plausible that they could agree to some nonproliferation standards for cyberweapons. The Proliferation Security Initiative (PSI) has been relatively successful at addressing illegal trafficking in WMD. Over a hundred countries, including the usually nonconformist Russia, have agreed to become involved. The idea is to prevent weapons proliferation by having better safety standards and export controls, by interdicting WMD materials, and through information-sharing and capacity-building exercises.

With any agreements there will be compliance problems. Cyberweapons are easy to hide from treaty inspectors, and offensive capabilities look a lot like defensive capabilities. But the early nuclear treaties signed in the 1960s had problems, too, yet they started what in retrospect was a successful process that made the world much safer.

Some ideas for how to get started on the path towards an international cybersecurity agreement are already on the table. In a 2014 report, cyber policy expert Jason Healey recommended creating an international regulatory regime similar to what was established after the 2008 global financial crisis. In the same year, Matt Thomlinson of Microsoft proposed a "G20+20 group" of 20 governments and 20 global information and communications technology firms to draft a set of principles for acceptable behavior in cyberspace. Microsoft's president and chief legal officer Brad Smith proposed a "Geneva convention" for cyberspace, setting parts of it off limits from intergovernmental meddling. Google has its own proposal. At this point, these ideas are clearly aspirational.

Setting norms is a long process. We are likely to get further with incremental cooperation, and agreements, than we are with striving for a perfect grand bargain straight away. And even so, there will be countries that won't comply with any rules, standards, guidelines, or whatever else we come up with. We will deal with this the same way we do in any other area of international law. It won't be perfect, but we'll work with it and improve it over time.

Unfortunately, we in the US are setting norms with our own behavior. By using the Internet for both surveillance and attack, we are telling the world that those things are okay. By prioritizing offense over defense, we are making everyone less safe.

9

How Governments Can Prioritize Defense over Offense

I f governments are going to take on this central role in improving Internet+ security, as I've been arguing they must, they need to shift their priorities. Right now, they prioritize maintaining the ability to use the Internet for offensive purposes, as I described in Chapter 4. But if we are ever going to make any progress on security, they need to switch their thinking and start prioritizing defense. Governments should support what Jason Healey calls a "defense dominant" strategy.

Yes, offense is essential to defense. Intelligence and law enforcement agencies in liberal democracies have legitimate needs to monitor hostile governments, surveil terrorist organizations, and investigate criminals. They use the insecurities in the Internet to do all of those things, and they make legitimate claims about the security benefits that result. They don't characterize themselves as being anti-security. In fact, their rhetoric is very pro-security. But their actions undermine the security of the Internet.

The NSA has two missions: surveilling the communications of other countries' governments, and protecting the US government's communications from surveillance. In the bygone world of point-to-point circuits, these missions were complementary, because the systems didn't overlap. The NSA could figure out how to monitor a naval communications link between Moscow and Vladivostok and use that expertise to protect the naval communications link between Washington, DC, and Norfolk, VA. Eavesdropping on Soviet and Warsaw Pact communications systems didn't affect American communications, because the radio systems were different. Subverting Chinese military computers didn't affect American computers, because the computers were different. In a world where computers were rare, networks were rarer still, and interoperability was bespoke, the NSA's actions abroad had no effect inside the US.

This is no longer true. With few exceptions, we all use the same computers and phones, the same operating systems, and the same applications. We all use the same Internet hardware and software. There is simply no way to secure US networks while at the same time leaving foreign networks open to eavesdropping and attack. There's no way to secure our phones and computers from criminals and terrorists without also securing the phones and computers of those criminals and terrorists. On the generalized worldwide network that is the Internet, anything we do to secure its hardware and software secures it everywhere in the world. And everything we do to keep it insecure similarly affects the entire world.

This leaves us with a choice: either we secure our stuff, and as a side effect also secure their stuff; or we keep their stuff vulnerable, and as a side effect keep our own stuff vulnerable. It's actually not a hard choice. An analogy might bring this point home. Imagine that every house could be opened with a master key, and this was known to the criminals. Fixing those locks would also mean that criminals' safe houses would be more secure, but it's pretty clear that this downside would be worth the trade-off of protecting everyone's house. With the Internet+ increasing the risks from insecurity dramatically, the choice is even more obvious. We must secure the information systems used by our elected officials, our critical infrastructure providers, and our businesses.

Yes, increasing our security will make it harder for us to eavesdrop, and attack, our enemies in cyberspace. (It won't make it impossible for law enforcement to solve crimes; I'll get to that later in this chapter.) Regardless, it's worth it. If we are ever going to secure the Internet+, we need to prioritize defense over offense in all of its aspects. We've got more to lose through our Internet+ vulnerabilities than our adversaries do, and more to gain through Internet+ security. We need to recognize that the security benefits of a secure Internet+ greatly outweigh the security benefits of a vulnerable one.

Here's what I propose the US and other democratic governments should do to emphasize defense over offense. Taking these actions will go a long way towards securing the Internet+. Even more importantly, the shift in priorities from offense to defense will allow governments to fulfill the badly needed role of Internet+ security enablers.

DISCLOSE AND FIX VULNERABILITIES

Recall Chapter 2, where I talked about software vulnerabilities. They have both offensive and defensive uses, and when someone discovers one, there's a choice. Choosing defense means alerting the vendor and getting it patched. Choosing offense means keeping the vulnerability secret and using it to attack others.

If an offensive military cyber unit—or a cyberweapons manufacturer—discovers a vulnerability, it keeps that vulnerability secret so that it can be exploited. If it is used stealthily, it might remain secret for a long time. If unused, it will remain secret until someone else discovers it. This is true for the vulnerabilities the NSA exploits to eavesdrop, and the vulnerabilities US Cyber Command exploits for its offensive weaponry. Eventually, the affected software's vendor finds out about the vulnerability—the timing depends on when and how extensively the vulnerability is used—and issues a patch to fix it.

Discoverers can sell vulnerabilities. There's a rich market in zero-days for attack purposes: to criminals on the black market and to governments. Companies like Azimuth sell vulnerabilities and hacking tools only to democracies; many others are much less discerning. And while vendors offer bounties for vulnerabilities to motivate disclosure, they can't match the rewards offered by criminals, governments, and cyberweapons manufacturers. One example: the not-for-profit Tor Project offers a bug bounty of $4,000 for vulnerabilities in its anonymous browser, while the cyberweapons manufacturer Zerodium will pay up to $250,000 for an exploitable Tor vulnerability.

Back to the NSA's dual mission: it can play either defense or offense. If the NSA finds a vulnerability, it can alert the vendor and get it fixed while it's still secret, or hold on to it and use it to surveil foreign computer systems. Fixing the vulnerability strengthens the security of the Internet against all attackers: other countries, criminals, hackers. Leaving the vulnerability open makes the agency better able to attack others. But each use runs the risk that the target government will learn of the vulnerability and use it—or that the vulnerability will become public and criminals will start using it. As Harvard law professor Jack Goldsmith wrote, "Every offensive weapon is a (potential) chink in our defense—and vice versa."

Many people have weighed in on this debate. Activist and author Cory Doctorow calls it a public health problem. I have said similar things. Computer security expert Dan Geer recommends that the US government corner the vulnerabilities market and fix them all. Both Microsoft's Brad Smith and Mozilla have commented on this, demanding more vulnerability disclosure by governments.

President Obama's Review Group on Intelligence and Communications Technologies, convened post-Snowden, concluded that vulnerabilities should only be hoarded in rare instances and for short times.

> We recommend that the National Security Council staff should manage an interagency process to review on a regular basis the activities of the US Government regarding attacks that exploit a previously unknown vulnerability in a computer application or system. . . . US policy should generally move to ensure that Zero Days are quickly blocked, so that the underlying vulnerabilities are patched on US Government and other networks. In rare instances, US policy may briefly authorize using a Zero Day for high priority intelligence collection, following senior, interagency review involving all appropriate departments.

The reason these arguments aren't obviously convincing is the cyberwar arms race I talked about in Chapter 4. If we give up our own offensive capabilities in order to make the Internet safer, that would amount to unilateral disarmament. Here's former NSA deputy director Rick Ledgett in 2017:

> The idea that these problems would be solved by the U.S. government disclosing any vulnerabilities in its possession is at best naive

and at worst dangerous. Such disclosure would be tantamount to unilateral disarmament in an area where the U.S. cannot afford to be unarmed. . . . And this is not an area in which American leadership would cause other countries to change what they do. Neither our allies nor our adversaries would give away the vulnerabilities in their possession.

Moreover, not all vulnerabilities are created equal. Some are what the NSA calls "NOBUS." That stands for "nobody but us" and is meant to designate a vulnerability that the US has found and can exploit, but that no one else can exploit—because it requires more resources than anyone else has, or its discovery is based on some specialized knowledge that no one else has, or its use requires some unique technology that no one else has. If a vulnerability is NOBUS, the argument goes, then the US can safely reserve it for offense because no one else can use it against us.

This approach seems sensible on the surface, but the details quickly become a morass. In the US, the decision about whether to disclose or use a vulnerability takes place during what's called the "vulnerabilities equities process" (VEP), a secret interagency process that considers the various "equities"; that is, the reasons for keeping the vulnerability secret. In 2014, then–White House cybersecurity coordinator Michael Daniel wrote a public explanation of the VEP that lacked any real details. In 2016, the official, heavily redacted White House document establishing the policy was released to the public. In 2017, new cybersecurity coordinator Rob Joyce published a revised VEP policy with some more details. So we have some clues, but still not enough information to adequately judge the policy.

We don't know how the government decides what to disclose and what to hoard. We do know that only organizations with different equities in a particular vulnerability have a say in whether that vulnerability is kept secret; and that no one in the VEP seems to be specifically charged with arguing for increased security through disclosure; and that private citizens concerned with securing data at risk from a given vulnerability are not represented.

It is inevitable that the VEP will result in the nondisclosure of vulnerabilities with powerful offensive potential—no matter how much risk they impose. For example, ETERNALBLUE—the critical Windows vulnerability that the Russians stole from the NSA and then published in 2017—was deemed suitable for hoarding and not for disclosing. That seems crazy. Any process that allows such a serious vulnerability in such a widely used system to remain unpatched for over five years isn't serving security very well.

This raises the concern that the VEP is leading to much more vulnerability hoarding than is wise. Vulnerabilities are independently discovered far more often than random chance alone would suggest. The reason seems to be that certain types of research fall in and out of vogue, and multiple research groups are often investigating the same areas. This implies that if the US government discovers a vulnerability, there is a reasonable chance someone else will independently discover it. Plus, NOBUS doesn't take into account countries stealing vulnerabilities from each other, like ETERNALBLUE. Both the NSA and the CIA have had cyberattack tools, including zero-day vulnerabilities, stolen and published. These included some pretty nasty Windows vulnerabilities that the NSA had been exploiting for years. Maybe nobody else could have independently discovered them, but that didn't matter once they were stolen and published.

We also don't know how many vulnerabilities go through the process. In 2015, we learned that the US government discloses 91% of the vulnerabilities it discovers, although it is unclear whether this figure refers to exploitable vulnerabilities, or whether the percentage is padded by the much larger number of total vulnerabilities. Without knowing the denominator, the statistic is meaningless.

My guess is similar to what Jason Healey writes:

> Every year the government only keeps a very small number of zero days, probably only single digits. Further, we estimate that the government probably retains a small arsenal of dozens of such zero days, far fewer than the hundreds or thousands that many experts have estimated. It appears the U.S. government adds to that arsenal only by drips and drabs, perhaps by single digits every year.

Finally, we don't even know which classes of vulnerabilities go through the process and which don't. It seems as if all vulnerabilities discovered by the government—probably almost entirely by the NSA—go through the process, but not vulnerabilities purchased from third parties, or based on bad design decisions like having a default password. What about vulnerabilities that the NSA finds after infiltrating foreign networks and stealing their cyberweapons? We don't know.

We do know that vulnerabilities are reassessed annually; that's a good thing. And as much as I want the US VEP to improve, at least the US has a process. No other country has anything similar—at least, nothing that's public. Many countries would never disclose vulnerabilities in order to improve the world's cybersecurity. We don't know anything about European countries, although I know Germany is working on some sort of disclosure policy.

There are more wrinkles that affect the VEP. Cyberweapons are a combination of a payload (the damage the weapon does) and a delivery mechanism (the vulnerability used to get the payload into the enemy network). Imagine that China knows about a vulnerability and is using it in a still-unfired cyberweapon, and that the NSA learns about it through espionage. Should the NSA disclose and patch the vulnerability, or hoard it for attack? If it discloses, it disables China's weapon, but China could find a replacement vulnerability that the NSA won't know about. If it hoards, it's deliberately leaving the US vulnerable to cyberattack. Maybe someday we can get to the point where we can patch vulnerabilities faster than the enemy can use them in an attack, but we're nowhere near that point today.

An unpatched vulnerability puts everyone at risk, but not uniformly. The US and other Western countries are at high risk because of our critical electronic infrastructure, intellectual property, and personal wealth. Countries like North Korea are at much less risk, so they have less incentive to fix vulnerabilities. Fixing vulnerabilities isn't disarmament; it's making our own countries much safer. We also regain the moral authority to negotiate any broad international reductions in cyberweapons, and we can decide not to use them even if others do.

It's clear to many observers that the VEP is badly broken. Despite Joyce's attempt at transparency, there's really no way for the public to judge its efficacy. From what we can tell of the results, the secret process isn't resulting in a balance between the various equities. Instead, it's making us much less secure.

Rick Ledgett is correct that our enemies will continue to stockpile vulnerabilities regardless of what we choose to do. But if we do choose disclosure, four things will happen. One: the vulnerabilities we disclose will eventually get fixed, depriving everyone of them. Two: security will improve as we all learn from vulnerabilities that are found and disclosed. Three: we will set an example for other countries and can then begin to change the global norm. And four: once organizations like the NSA and the CIA willingly relinquish these attack tools, we will be able to get these agencies firmly on the side of defense over offense. And once those four things happen, we can actually make progress on securing the Internet+ for everyone.

DESIGN FOR SECURITY AND NOT FOR SURVEILLANCE

It's not just necessary to find security vulnerabilities in existing software systems. Far too often, governments intervene in security standards—not to ensure that they're strong, but to weaken them. That is, they prioritize offense over defense.

For example, IPsec is an encryption and authentication standard for Internet data packets. I was around in the 1990s when the Internet Engineering Task Force—that's the public, multi-stakeholder standards group for the Internet—debated these standards, designed to defend against a broad spectrum of attacks. The NSA participated in the process, and deliberately worked to make the protocol less secure. Specifically, it tried to make minor changes that weakened the security, pushed for a then-weak encryption standard, demanded a no-encryption option, delayed the process in a variety of ways, and generally made the standard so complex that any implementation would be both difficult and insecure. I evaluated the standard in 1999 and concluded that its unnecessary complexity had a "devastating effect" on security. Today, end-to-end encryption still isn't ubiquitous on the Internet, although it's getting better.

A second example: in the secret government-only standards process for digital cellular encryption, many believe that the NSA ensured that algorithms used to encrypt voice traffic between the handset and the tower are easily breakable, and that there is no end-to-end encryption between the two communicating parties. The result is that your cell phone conversations can easily be monitored.

Both of these were probably part of NSA's BULLRUN program, whose aim was to weaken public security standards. (The UK's analogous program was called Edgehill.) And in both of these cases, the resulting insecure communications protocols have been used by both foreign governments and criminals to spy on private citizens' communications.

Sometimes the government weakens security by law. CALEA, the Communications Assistance for Law Enforcement Act, is a 1994 law that required telephone companies to build wiretapping capabilities into their phone switches so that the FBI could spy on phone users. Fast-forward to today, and the FBI—and its equivalents in many other countries—are demanding similar backdoors into computers, phones, and communications systems. (More about this in Chapter 11.)

And sometimes, the US government doesn't have to deliberately weaken security standards. Sometimes, the standards are designed insecurely for other reasons and the government takes advantage of that insecurity—while at the same time hiding the fact and delaying attempts to secure those systems.

"Stingray" is now a generic name for an IMSI-catcher, which is basically a fake cell phone tower originally sold by Harris Corporation (as StingRay) to various law enforcement agencies. (It's actually just one of a series of devices with fish names—AmberJack is another—but it's the name used in the media.) Basically, a stingray tricks nearby cell phones into connecting to it. The technology works because the phone in your pocket automatically trusts any cell tower within range. There's no authentication in the connection protocols between the phones and the towers. When a new tower appears, your phone automatically transmits its international mobile subscriber identity (IMSI), a unique serial number that enables the cellular system to know where you are. This enables collection of identification and location information of the phones in the vicinity and, in some cases, eavesdropping on phone conversations, text messages, and web browsing.

The use of IMSI-catchers by the FBI and other law enforcement agencies in the US was once a massive secret. Only a few years ago, the FBI was so scared of explaining this capability in public that the agency made local police departments sign nondisclosure agreements before using the technique, and instructed them to lie about their use of it in court. When it seemed possible that local police in Sarasota, Florida, might release documents about IMSI-catchers to plaintiffs in civil rights litigation against them, federal marshals seized the documents. Even after the technology became common knowledge, and a key plot point on television shows like *The Wire*, the FBI continued to pretend it was a big secret. As recently as 2015, St. Louis police dropped a case rather than talk about the technology in court.

Cellular companies could add encryption and authentication to their standards, but as long as most people don't understand their phone's insecurities, and cellular standards are still set by government-only committees, it's unlikely.

It's basically the NOBUS argument. When the cell phone network was designed, putting up a cell tower was an incredibly difficult technical exercise, and it was reasonable to assume that only legitimate cell providers would do it. With time, the technology became cheaper and easier. What was once a secret NSA interception program and a secretive FBI investigative tool became usable by less-capable governments, cybercriminals, and even hobbyists. In 2010, hackers were demonstrating their home-built IMSI-catchers at conferences. By 2014, dozens of IMSI-catchers had been discovered in the Washington, DC, area, collecting information on who knows whom, and run by who knows which government or criminal organization. Now, you can browse the Chinese e-commerce website Alibaba .com and buy your own IMSI-catcher for under $2,000. You can also download public-domain software that will turn your laptop into one with the right peripherals.

Another example: IP intercept systems are used to eavesdrop on what people do on the Internet. Unlike the surveillance by companies like Facebook and Google that happens at the sites you visit, or surveillance that happens on the Internet backbone, this surveillance happens near the point at which your computer connects to the Internet. Here, someone can eavesdrop on everything you do.

IP intercept systems also exploit existing vulnerabilities in the underlying Internet communications protocols. Most of the traffic between your computer and the Internet is unencrypted, and what is encrypted is often vulnerable to man-in-the-middle attacks because of insecurities in both the Internet protocols and the encryption protocols that protect it.

We know from the Snowden documents that the NSA conducts extensive data collection operations in the Internet backbone, and directly benefits from the lack of encryption on the Internet. But so do other countries, cybercriminals, and hackers.

Similarly, when the Internet protocols were first designed, adding encryption would have slowed down those early computers considerably; then, it felt like a waste of resources. Now, computers are cheap and software is fast, and what was difficult to impossible only a few decades ago is now easy. At the same time, the Internet surveillance capabilities once unique to the NSA have become so accessible that criminals, hackers, and the intelligence services of any country can employ them.

It's no different with cell phone encryption or CALEA-mandated wiretapping systems. That same phone-switch wiretapping capability was used by unknown attackers to wiretap more than a hundred senior members of the Greek government over the course of ten months in the early 2000s. CALEA inadvertently caused vulnerabilities in Cisco Internet switches. And, according to Richard George, the former NSA technical director for information assurance, "when the NSA tested CALEA-compliant switches that had been submitted prior to use in DoD systems, the NSA found security problems in every single switch submitted for testing."

In each of these stories, the lesson is the same: NOBUS doesn't last. Even former NSA and CIA director Michael Hayden, who popularized the term in the public press, wrote in 2017 that "the NOBUS comfort zone is considerably smaller than it once was." In a world where everyone uses the same computers and communications systems, any insecurity we deliberately insert—or even that we find and conveniently use—can and will be used against us. And just like fixing vulnerabilities, we are much safer if our systems are designed to be secure in the first place.

ENCRYPT AS MUCH AS POSSIBLE

Governments should have the goal of encrypting as much of the Internet+ as possible. There are many facets to this.

One: we need end-to-end encryption for communications. This means that all communications should be encrypted from the sender's device to the receiver's device, and that no one in the middle should be able to read that communication. This is the encryption used by many messaging apps, like iMessage, WhatsApp, and Signal. This is how encryption in your browser works. In some cases, true end-to-end encryption isn't desirable. Most of us want Google to be able to read our e-mail, because that's how it sorts it into folders and deletes spam. In those cases, we should encrypt communications up to the point of our designated (and presumably trusted) communications processor.

Two: we need to encrypt our devices. Encryption greatly increases the security of any end-user device, but is especially important for general-purpose devices like computers and phones. These are often central nodes in our Internet+ life, and they must be as secure as possible.

Three: we need to encrypt the Internet. Data should be encrypted whenever possible as it moves around the Internet. Unfortunately, we've all become accustomed to an unencrypted Internet, and there are many protocols that demonstrate that fact. When you log on to a strange Wi-Fi network, what usually happens is that your surfing is intercepted by the router and the page you want is replaced with a log-in screen. That happens because your data isn't being encrypted. Even though this feature takes advantage of unencrypted communications, we need to encrypt anyway and develop other ways to log in.

And four: we need to encrypt the large databases of personal information that are out there.

Encryption isn't a panacea. Attacks against authentication often bypass encryption by stealing the password of an authorized user. And encryption won't prevent government-on-government espionage. All the lessons of Chapter 1 still hold: computers are very hard to secure. We know that the NSA is able to circumvent most encryption by attacking the underlying software. But those attacks are more targeted.

An encrypted communications system or computer isn't impenetrably secure, and one without encryption isn't irrevocably insecure. But encryption is a core security technology. It protects our information and devices from hackers, criminals, and foreign governments. It protects us from surveillance overreach of our own governments. It protects our elected officials from eavesdropping, and our IoT devices from being subverted. Increasingly, it protects our critical infrastructure. Combined with authentication, it's probably the single most essential security feature for the Internet+. Many security failures can be traced to a lack of encryption.

Ubiquitous encryption forces the attacker to specifically target its attacks. It makes bulk surveillance impossible in many cases. This affects government-on-population surveillance much more than government-on-government espionage. And it hurts repressive governments much more than it hurts democracies. Encryption is beneficial to society, even though the evildoers can use it to secure their communications and devices as well as anyone else.

This is not a universally held position. There is strong pressure to weaken encryption, not only from totalitarian governments that want to spy on their citizens but from politicians and law enforcement officials in democracies, who see encryption as a tool used by criminals, terrorists, and—with the advent of cryptocurrencies—people who want to buy drugs and launder money.

I, and many security technologists, have argued that the FBI's demands for backdoors are just too dangerous. Of course, criminals and terrorists have used, are using, and will continue to use, encryption to hide their plots from the authorities, just as they will use many other aspects of society's capabilities and infrastructure. In general, we recognize that cars, restaurants, and telecommunications can be used by both honest and dishonest people. Society thrives nonetheless because the honest so greatly outnumber the dishonest. As a thought experiment, compare the idea of mandating backdoors with the tactic of adding a governor to every car engine to ensure that no one ever speeds. Yes, that would help prevent criminals from using cars as getaway vehicles, but we would never accept the burden on honest citizens. Weakening encryption for everyone is harmful in exactly the same way, even if the effects aren't as obvious. I'll talk more about this in Chapter 11.

SEPARATE SECURITY FROM SPYING

Not only is the NSA's dual mission at odds with itself; it also doesn't make sense organizationally. Offense gets the money, attention, and priority. As long as the NSA has responsibility for both offense and defense, it'll never be fully trusted to secure the Internet+. This means the organization as currently constituted is harmful to cybersecurity.

We need strong government agencies on the side of security, and that means splitting apart the NSA and significantly funding defensive initiatives. In *Data and Goliath*, I recommended splitting the NSA into three organizations: one to conduct international electronic espionage, one to provide security in cyberspace, and a third—rolled into the FBI—to conduct legal domestic surveillance. If the security organization could work closely, or even become a part of, the Internet+ regulatory agency I described in Chapter 8, it would go a long way to making the world safer.

It's the same in other countries. As long as the UK's National Cyber Security Centre is subservient to GCHQ (that's the Government Communications Headquarters, the country's surveillance agency), it can never be fully trusted. A better model is Germany. The German Federal Office for Information Security (BSI) reports to the chancellor via a different minister than does the Federal Intelligence Service (BND), its offensive agency.

Separating security from spying (and also attack) has other benefits as well. Disclosing vulnerabilities is very hard for an organization that also wants to use them offensively. Sure, the two agencies might be allocated different amounts of funding, but at least that process is public and subject to some scrutiny. In general, the separation will reduce the secrecy that's currently surrounding everything that is government security in cyberspace. That secrecy primarily comes from the offensive capabilities and mission.

Less secrecy also means more oversight, and that's a key issue with agencies like the NSA. The more their authorities, capabilities, and programs can be debated in public, the less likely they are to be abused.

Unfortunately, in 2016, the NSA underwent a major reorganization where it combined its offensive and defensive directorates into a single operational directorate. While that makes a lot of sense technically—the same skills and expertise are required for both—it's the exact opposite of what we need politically. If the NSA is ever to be trusted to secure the Internet+ rather than attack it, defense can't be commingled with offense. Just as the intelligence and attack capabilities are now separate organizations (the NSA and US Cyber Command, respectively), even though the skills and expertise are the same, defense and offense need to be separate organizations.

MAKE LAW ENFORCEMENT SMARTER

If we're going to prioritize defense over offense, we're going to have to recognize the challenges this creates for law enforcement. The FBI needs investigative capabilities suitable for the 21st century.

In 2016, the FBI demanded that Apple unlock an iPhone belonging to the dead San Bernardino terrorist Syed Rizwan Farook. Apple has implemented encryption on phones by default, and the FBI couldn't access the data. Because it was an iPhone 5C, Apple had access to the data. (Apple improved the security of later iPhone models.) Apple resisted the FBI's demand, primarily because it recognized it as a test case for the agency's ability to force it—and any tech company—to bypass the security of its systems and devices.

It's the same backdoor demand we've heard from the FBI for decades, and I'll talk about it more in Chapter 11. For the FBI, this was a good test case, and it thought it would easily prevail in court. Apple, along with pretty much every cybersecurity professional, fought back hard. Eventually, the FBI got some unidentified "third party"—probably the Israeli company Cellebrite—to break into the phone without Apple's help. No court decided anything.

After it was all over, I and a group of colleagues wrote a paper about this issue with the title "Don't Panic." We meant that title literally; the FBI and others should stop panicking about encryption. Crimes won't suddenly become unsolvable just because the FBI can't extract data from computers or can't eavesdrop on digital communications, any more than crime was unsolvable before any of us used computers or communicated digitally. We gave three main reasons not to panic:

1. Metadata can't be encrypted, because it needs to remain in a usable form while inside the network. Law enforcement can always learn who is talking to whom—and where, and when—even if they don't know exactly what's being said.

2. When people use third parties for data storage and processing, that data can't be encrypted. Even companies that provide encrypted data storage often allow for files to be recovered, because that's what most users demand. All of that data will always be available with a warrant, and in some cases without one.

3. If everything is becoming a computer, then everything is becoming a potential surveillance device. Specifically, all of the new sensors that power the Internet of Things will give law enforcement vast

new data streams that won't be end-to-end encrypted, allowing for both real-time surveillance and after-the-fact access and recovery.

The truth is that the FBI has lost a lot of its technical expertise. Before there were cell phones, when people's conversations would irretrievably evaporate as soon as the words were spoken, the FBI had all sorts of investigative techniques it could bring to bear on an unsolved crime. Starting in the mid-1990s, its work became easier: get data off the cell phone. Now it's more than 20 years later and that era is coming to a close, but all the FBI agents who remember the old days have retired. All the agency's current employees are people who only know that there's important data on smartphones.

This has to change. If we're going to do the right thing and field ubiquitous security systems without any backdoors, the FBI needs new expertise in how to conduct investigations in the Internet+ era. In her testimony to the House Judiciary Committee, mathematician and cybersecurity policy expert Susan Landau described this:

The FBI will need an investigative center with agents with a deep technical understanding of modern telecommunications technologies; this means from the physical layer to the virtual one, and all the pieces in between. Since all phones are computers these days, this center will need to have the same level of deep expertise in computer science. In addition, there will need to be teams of researchers who understand various types of fielded devices. This will include not only where technology is and will be in six months, but where it may be in two to five years. This center will need to conduct research as to what new surveillance technologies will need to be developed as a result of the directions of new technologies. I am talking deep expertise here and strong capabilities, not light.

There are many pieces to this. In addition to better computer forensics, the FBI needs lawful hacking capabilities that it can use in exceptional circumstances. The FBI also needs to provide technical assistance to state and local law enforcement agencies, which are facing the same problems with technological forensics and evidence gathering. This problem is not going away, and it's going to change with time. The FBI needs to continuously adapt.

To make this happen, the FBI must establish a viable career path for technical investigators. Right now there is none, and you'd be hard-pressed to find a top computer science undergrad thinking about a career in law enforcement. This is why the FBI's computer forensic experts tend to come from outside the field. If the FBI is going to attract and retain the best talent, it will need to successfully compete with the private sector.

This won't be cheap. Landau estimates that it will cost hundreds of millions of dollars per year. But that's much less than the billions of dollars Internet+ insecurity will cost society, and really the only solution that will work.

RETHINK THE RELATIONSHIP BETWEEN GOVERNMENT AND INDUSTRY

The government can't do this alone. The private sector can't do this alone. Any real solutions require government and industry to work closely together.

Many of the recommendations in the previous chapters try to delineate the contours of that partnership. Whether they are software vendors, Internet companies, IoT manufacturers, or critical infrastructure providers, businesses need to understand their responsibilities.

This means more information sharing between government and the private sector. This isn't a new idea, and the past four US presidents have made attempts at this. Most critical-industry sectors have their own information-sharing and analysis centers, where government and businesses can share intelligence information. Some other countries have similar organizations: the UK's Centre for the Protection of National Infrastructure, the EU's European Energy–Information Sharing and Analysis Centre (EE-ISAC), Spain's Grupo Trabalho Seguridad, and Australia's Trusted Information Sharing Network for Critical Infrastructure Resilience.

The reality always falls short, because both government and industry tend to value receiving information more than giving it. This is rational; the existing costs and barriers often outweigh the advantages.

Much of what the NSA and FBI know is classified, and the agencies haven't figured out how to share their data with companies that lack staff with security clearances. Much industry data is proprietary or embarrassing, and won't be shared without assurances that it won't go any further. Reducing the amount of secrecy in government cybersecurity will go a long way to making information sharing easier, as will providing some assurances of confidentiality, and perhaps indemnification, to companies that share information.

This is easier for critical infrastructure. Governments have long been involved in regulating these industries, and they have experience dealing with threats against these industries. However, information sharing needs to extend past what is traditionally critical infrastructure.

One option is to create a national cyber incident data repository, which would allow businesses to anonymously report breach information to a database. The FAA maintains an anonymous database of airplane near misses. Reporting is voluntary but expected, and engineers can search the database for trends that help them build safer planes, safer airport runways, and safer procedures.

Another idea is to create a "National Cybersecurity Safety Board" for Internet-related disasters, modeled on the National Transportation Safety Board, the independent transport accident investigation bureau. This NCSB would investigate the most serious incidents, issue findings about fault, and publish information about which security measures actually work (and which don't). It could also issue something like the NTSB's annual "Most Wanted List" of the most critical changes needed to prevent future accidents.

Whatever we do, it will have to scale for the Internet+. For example, whenever a car crashes, everyone will want the data: the traffic police, the affected insurance agencies, the automobile manufacturer, the local safety agency, and so on.

Nongovernmental networks like the Cyber Threat Alliance have emerged to fill the huge gap for trusted information sharing. Created in 2014 by five US-based security vendors, the Cyber Threat Alliance has rapidly expanded globally. The idea is to help defenders get ahead of attackers (addressing some of the asymmetries we spoke about in Chapter 1) by sharing intelligence about attack methods and motives. While vital, this informal information sharing is no substitute for models that also include information on documented security failures. Companies are reluctant to share this information with each other, which speaks to the need for a government role in facilitating—or even mandating—more information sharing.

We also need to recognize the limits of any public–private partnership, and figure out what to do when civilians are attacked by governments on the Internet. Imagine that the North Korean military physically attacked a US media company. Or that the Iranian military stormed a US casino. We wouldn't expect those companies to defend themselves. We would expect the US military to defend those companies, as we expect them to defend all US citizens against foreign attack.

What happens if those two countries attack US companies, as indeed they did, in cyberspace? Regardless of how much information the government shared with those companies, can we really expect Sony to defend itself against North Korea, or the Sands Casino to defend itself against Iran? Do we even want private companies to respond to foreign military attack? I don't think so.

We also can't expect corporations like Westinghouse Electric and US Steel to defend themselves against Chinese military hacking. We shouldn't expect the Democratic and Republican national committees—and certainly not state and local political organizations—to defend themselves against Russian government hacking. In none of these cases is it a fair fight.

One of the core arguments of this book is that businesses need to do more to secure their devices, data, and networks. That would go a long way to defend against incursions by foreign governments, and it would make successful attacks harder. It's no longer good enough to pretend the threat doesn't exist. But in the end, militaries will always have better skill and more funds than civilian defenders. There will always be attacks that are beyond the ability of civilian defenders to resist. And government should remain the only institution with the authority and capability to respond to large-scale nation-state attacks in cyberspace. Such response might require coordination with and assistance from the private sector, but it should not be the private sector's responsibility.

So what's the model here? Is it a Cyber National Guard? Is it a Cyber Corps of Engineers? Do we expect US Cyber Command to defend civilian networks inside the US? Or should that be the charge of the Department of Homeland Security? Estonia has a volunteer Cyber Defence Unit made up of nongovernment experts that can be called on in times of national emergency. I don't know if that's what we need here, but we need something.

Any such organized governmental defense against nation-state attacks on private entities is a long way off, though. Until then, individuals and organizations must take more responsibility for their own security than they have at any time since the closing of the American frontier in 1890.

10

Plan B: What's Likely to Happen

Story one: In the aftermath of the 2017 Equifax hack, there was bipartisan outrage in Congress and a lot of talk about regulating data brokers—and those who collect and sell our personal data in general. Despite some very strong words, a flurry of congressional hearings, and several proposals, nothing came of any of it. Even a bill imposing the tiniest of regulation specifically on credit bureaus went nowhere. The only thing Congress did was pass a law preventing consumers from suing Equifax.

Story two: The 2017 Internet of Things Cybersecurity Improvement Act was a modest piece of legislation. It didn't prescribe, regulate, or otherwise force any company to do anything. It imposed minimum security standards on IoT devices purchased by the US government. Those standards were reasonable and not very onerous, along the lines of the things I discussed in Chapter 6. The bill went nowhere. There were no hearings. It was never voted on by any committee. It barely made the papers after it was introduced.

Story three: In 2016, President Obama established the Commission on Enhancing National Cybersecurity. Its mandate was broad:

The Commission will make detailed recommendations to strengthen cybersecurity in both the public and private sectors while protecting privacy, ensuring public safety and economic and national security, fostering discovery and development of new technical solutions, and bolstering partnerships between Federal, State, and local government and the private sector in the development, promotion, and use of cybersecurity technologies, policies, and best practices. The Commission's recommendations should address actions that can be taken over the next decade to accomplish these goals.

At the end of that year, the bipartisan group issued its report. It's a good document based on solid research; it contains 16 recommendations with 53 specific action items that the administration could do to improve Internet security. While there are things I quibbled with, it wasn't a bad road map for both immediate action and long-term policy planning. It's almost two years later, and only one of the recommendations has been turned into policy: making the NIST Cybersecurity Framework mandatory for government agencies. No agency has yet followed that policy. The rest of the report has been ignored.

THE US WILL DO NOTHING SOON

As you read the previous four chapters, you might have found it easy to accuse me of painting a nightmare and responding with daydreams—that while my recommendations might be a good list of what we should do, they bear no resemblance to what we actually will do.

Partly, I agree. I don't foresee Congress taking on the powerful computer and Internet industries and imposing enforceable security standards. I don't foresee any increase in spending on our cyberspace infrastructure. I don't foresee the creation of any new federal regulatory agencies. And I don't foresee either the military or the police forgoing the offensive uses of cyberspace in order to improve the defensive.

Let me talk about the psychology of this for a minute. Just as the CEOs of companies tend to underspend on security, politicians tend to underplay threats that aren't immediately salient. Imagine a politician looking at a large budget allocation for mitigating a hypothetical, long-term, strategic risk. She could designate funds for that purpose, or for more immediate political priorities. If she does the latter, she's a hero with her constituents, or at least the constituents from her party. If she sticks with spending on security, she risks being criticized by her opponents for wasting money or ignoring those immediate priorities. This is worse if the threat doesn't materialize (even if it's the spending that causes that). It's even worse if the threat materializes when the other party is in power: they'll take the credit for keeping people secure.

In all the years I've been writing about these issues, I have seen very little serious policy progress. I have seen the ever-more-powerful IT industry digging in its heels and opposing any governmental limits on its behavior, and legislators without the stomach to take it on. I have seen law enforcement groups in multiple countries propose technical changes that weaken security, painting anyone who opposes them as weak on crime and terrorism. I have seen government get accused of over- and under-regulating *at the same time.* And I have seen new technologies become mainstream without any thought about security or regulation.

Meanwhile, the risks have grown more dire, the consequences more catastrophic, and the policy issues more intractable. The Internet has become critical infrastructure; now it's becoming physical. Our data has moved onto computers managed by other companies. Our networks have become global.

Governments regulate things that kill people, and when the Internet starts killing people it will be regulated. It's true that fear is a powerful motivator, and can overcome the psychological bias towards doing nothing and the political bias towards smaller government.

What would such an event look like?

That depends on the time frame. Some observers have noted parallels between today's Internet+ and the pre-1970s automobile industry. Free from regulation, manufacturers were building and selling unsafe cars, and people were dying. It was the 1965 publication of Ralph Nader's *Unsafe at Any Speed* that spurred the government into action, resulting in a slew of safety laws covering seat belts, headrests, and so on. A slew of Internet+ related fatalities could cause a similar regulatory flurry.

On the other hand, companies have been killing people via the environment for decades. Rachel Carson published *Silent Spring* in 1962, before the EPA was formed in 1970—and almost 50 years later, the EPA's regulations are still insufficient to combat the threats. Never underestimate the power of industry lobbying groups to push their own agendas, even at the expense of everyone else.

The difference between events that prompt immediate versus sluggish reactions might lie in the ability to connect a fatality to the underlying insecurity. Environmental fatalities are much harder to pin on a specific cause than is an automobile fatality. This is also true on the Internet. When you're the victim of identity theft, it's very hard to point to the specific instance of hacking that precipitated it. Even when a power plant is hacked and a city is plunged into darkness, it can be hard to know exactly which vulnerability was to blame.

I'm not optimistic in the near term. As a society, we haven't even agreed about any of the big ideas. We understand the symptoms of insecurity better than the actual problems, which makes it hard to discuss solutions. We can't figure out what the policies should be because we don't know where we want to go. Even worse, we're not having any of these big conversations. Aside from forcing tech companies to break encryption to satisfy law enforcement, Internet+ security isn't an issue that most policy makers are concerned about—apart from the occasional strong words. It's not debated in the media. It's not a campaign issue in any country I can think of. We don't even have a commonly agreed-upon vocabulary for talking about these issues.

Compare this to money laundering, child porn, or bribery. Those are all big international problems with complex geopolitical implications and nuanced policy solutions. But for those issues, at least we all agree about the direction we want the world to head in. With Internet+ security, we're nowhere close to there yet.

Plus, the threats are all jumbled together. "Cyber" is an umbrella term that encompasses everything from cyberbullying to cyberterrorism. That might make sense from a technological perspective—the Internet+ is the common aspect—but it makes no sense from a policy perspective. Cyberbullying, cybercrime, cyberterrorism, and cyberwar are not the same, and they're different from cyberespionage and surveillance capitalism. Some threats are properly countered by the police, and some by the military. Other threats are not the government's business at all, and are properly countered by the affected party. Some need to be countered through legislation. Just as we don't think about road rage and car bombs in the same way, even though they both involve cars, we can't treat all cyber threats in the same way. I don't think US policy makers understand that yet, but they'll need to if we want them to act reasonably and responsibly.

My prediction is continued legislative inaction in the US in the near term. The regulatory agencies, especially the FTC, will continue to investigate and fine the most egregious violators. And there will be no changes in regulating either government surveillance or surveillance capitalism. Any fatalities will be blamed on specific individuals and products, and not on the system that enables them. Despite the imminent threats, I think it will take the younger generation coming into power before any real change in the US takes place.

OTHERS WILL REGULATE

There's more hope in Europe. The EU is the world's single largest market and is turning into a regulatory superpower. And it has been regulating data, computers, and the Internet. The GDPR—General Data Protection Regulation—is a sea change in privacy law. It's a sweeping EU-wide regulation that affects any company in the world that handles personal data about EU citizens. The complex law primarily focuses on data and privacy, but also contains requirements for computer and network security. Moreover, it's a reasonable blueprint for what the EU might eventually do with respect to Internet+ security and safety.

For example, the GDPR mandates that personal data can only be collected and saved for "specific, explicit, and legitimate purposes," and only with explicit consent of the user. Consent can't be buried in the terms and conditions, nor can it be assumed unless the user opts in. Users have the right to access their personal data, correct false information, and object to particular uses of their data. Users also have the right to download their data and use it elsewhere, and demand that it be erased. The provisions go on and on.

The GDPR's regulations only affect European users and customers, but will have repercussions worldwide. For example, pretty much all Internet companies have European users, and if they suffered a data breach they would invariably have to quickly publicize it. If companies have to explain their data collection and use practices to Europeans, we'll all learn what they are. Additionally, legislatures worldwide—from Argentina to Colombia to South Korea—are reviewing their privacy laws to ensure they are adequate by the new EU standards, since the EU now links free-trade agreements to the partner nation's privacy regulations.

The GDPR was passed in 2016 and took effect in May 2018, with enforcement expected sometime in 2019. Organizations are already doing things to comply with the law, but in many cases they're waiting to see what implementation and enforcement will look like.

I think EU enforcement will be harsh. Fines can be as high as 4% of a company's global revenue. And in 2017, we saw several demonstrations that the EU isn't afraid to go after the biggest Internet companies. The EU fined Google 2.4 billion euros (and threatened to further fine the company 5% of its daily revenue) for the manner in which it presented search results for shopping services. Separately, the EU fined Facebook 110 million euros for misleading regulators about its ability to link Facebook and WhatsApp accounts.

Compare potential fines for digital insecurity in the US and the EU. In 2017, the state of New York fined Hilton Hotels $700,000 for two 2015 breaches involving personal information—including credit card numbers—of 350,000 customers. That's $2 per person and, for a company with $410 billion in revenue, basically a rounding error. Under the GDPR, the fine would have been $420 million.

The EU is regulating computer security in other ways, too. If you look at product packaging in Europe—and often in the rest of the world—you'll notice a lowercase "ce" on the label somewhere. This means that the product conforms to all applicable European standards, including one for responsible vulnerability disclosure. Like the GDPR, the "ce" mark only affects products sold in Europe. Nonetheless, these standards will get incorporated into international trade agreements like GATT, and they will affect products everywhere.

My guess is that the EU will turn its attention to security and the Internet of Things and, more generally, cyberphysical systems. As Cambridge University professor Ross Anderson and his colleagues wrote, referring to security from the sorts of damaging attacks I talked about in Chapter 5 as "safety": "The EU is already the world's main privacy regulator, as Washington doesn't care and no one else is big enough to matter; it should aim to become the main safety regulator too—or risk compromising the safety mission it already has." If the EU starts flexing its regulatory muscle in this way on safety and security, companies will take notice.

The question is how this will affect the rest of the world. There are several possibilities.

Automobiles are often designed for local markets. A car sold in the US is different from the same model sold in Mexico, because the environmental laws are different and manufacturers optimize engines to comply with local laws. The economics of building and selling a vehicle easily allows for this differentiation. Software is different. It's much easier to maintain one version of a piece of software and sell it everywhere, especially when embedded in a product. If European regulations force minimum security standards on routers or Internet-connected thermostats, those are likely to be sold throughout the world. (California fuel emissions standards affect cars sold all over the US.) And if companies have to meet those standards anyway, they're likely to boast about it on their packaging.

This could go either way for products and services that make their money on surveillance. In April 2018, Facebook announced that it would change its data collection, use, and retention practices for its users worldwide as a result of the GDPR. It remains to be seen what other companies will do.

I don't think there are any other markets large enough to matter. Singapore has the Personal Data Protection Act, South Korea has the Personal Information Protection Act, and Hong Kong has the Personal Data (Privacy) Ordinance, but it's hard to tell whether these laws have any teeth. If enforced, the affected companies would probably just pull out of those countries rather than change their business practices worldwide. There might be exceptions for larger markets—and maybe Korea falls in that category—and for expensive Internet-enabled devices, but there might not. I could easily imagine major car manufacturers ignoring the regulations and daring the governments to ban their products, and the governments backing down.

Some other countries are starting to regulate, too. In 2017, India's Supreme Court recognized a right to privacy for the first time in the nation's history. Eventually, this might result in some stronger laws in that country. Singapore passed a new Cybersecurity Act in 2018, formalizing minimum standards and reporting obligations for critical infrastructure providers, and establishing a Commissioner for Cybersecurity position with broad investigation and enforcement powers. New Israeli security regulations affecting organizations that run databases came into effect in 2018; they include requirements for encryption, staff security training, security testing, and backup and recovery procedures.

Even the UN is starting to regulate. The United Nations Economic Commission for Europe sets standards for cars. Its regulations affect not only the EU, but also other countries in Europe, Africa, and Asia that make cars. Its regulations will certainly affect any future autonomous computers in cars.

In the US, some states are trying to fill the regulatory gap left by the federal government by prosecuting companies with weak security. New York, California, and Massachusetts lead the way here. In 2016, New York fined Trump Hotels for data breaches, and California investigated companies that abuse student data. In 2017, Massachusetts sued Equifax, and Missouri began investigating Google's data-handling practices. Thirty-two state attorneys general joined the FTC to penalize computer manufacturer Lenovo for installing spyware on its laptops. Even the city of San Diego is suing Experian over a 2013 data breach.

In 2017, New York State's Department of Financial Services issued security regulations affecting banks, insurers, and other financial services companies. The rules required these corporations to have a chief information security officer, conduct regular security testing, provide security awareness training to employees, and implement two-factor authentication on their systems. In 2019, these standards will also apply to their vendors and third-party contractors.

In 2017, California temporarily tabled a bill requiring IoT manufacturers to disclose the data they were collecting on customers and users. Ten other states debated legislation on IoT privacy in the absence of any federal movement on this issue. I expect more of this sort of thing in 2018 and beyond.

In January 2018, California's Senate passed the "Teddy Bears and Toasters" bill that would require manufacturers to equip all Internet-connected devices sold in California with security features appropriate to the device.

As this book went to press, the bill was before the legislature. California's legislature is also considering a proposal to create a "California Data Protection Authority" inspired by the GDPR.

WHAT WE CAN DO

So there is some progress. But in the absence of meaningful regulation, what do we do?

We can try to comparison shop for security, but that's difficult. Corporations don't make their security practices public, precisely because they don't want them to factor into consumers' buying decisions or future lawsuits. If you want to buy a DVR with better security because you don't want it to become part of a botnet, you can't. If you want to buy a thermostat or a doorbell with better security because you don't want anyone hacking it, you can't. You can't study Facebook's or Google's privacy and security practices—only their vague promises. As long as corporations don't use security and privacy as a market differentiator, you cannot base your buying decisions on them. And while an organization like Consumers Union might be able to help, it'll just be a part of a larger solution.

There are some things concerned consumers can do. We can research different IoT products, try to determine which ones take security seriously, and refuse to purchase products that don't. We can see what sorts of smartphone permissions an app demands, try to research what data is being collected and what is being done with it, and refuse to install apps that seek irrelevant and invasive access. I admit that this is a tall order, and most people won't bother.

In some cases, we can opt out, but that option is going to become increasingly rare. Soon, just as it is now effectively impossible to live a normal modern life without an e-mail address, a credit rating, or a credit card, it will be impossible not to be connected to the Internet of Things. These are the tools for living a normal life in the early 21st century.

We can—and should—shore up our own personal cybersecurity. There's plenty of good advice on the Internet, mostly related to data privacy. But in the end, a significant portion of our cybersecurity is out of our hands, because our data is in others' hands.

Organizations have more options because of their size and budget.

Out of pure self-interest—both economic and reputational—they need to make cybersecurity a board-level concern. Yes, these are technical risks, but attacks already can grievously damage a company. I am the CTO of IBM Resilient and a special advisor to IBM Security, and have repeatedly seen that companies make smarter security decisions when senior management is involved.

Organizations need to know about the security of the devices and services they're using, both on their network and in the cloud. They should make any decisions about the Internet+ deliberately, and ensure that new equipment acquisitions don't unintentionally affect their network. This is going to be an uphill battle. My prediction is that organizations will find the Internet+ creeping into their networks in ways they don't expect or even know about. Someone will buy a coffee machine or refrigerator with an Internet connection. The smart lighting system, or elevators, or overall building control system will connect to the internal corporate network.

Organizations need to know where their data is. Already it can be a battle to keep your data under your control on your network. The cloud is enticing; it's easy to park your data on other people's computers without really understanding the ramifications. An instructive story from Sweden came to light in 2017. Two years previously, the Swedish Transport Agency moved all of its data to the cloud, including classified information that should have never left the government's internal networks. My guess is that the person who made the decision never considered the security ramifications.

Organizations need to use their buying power to make the Internet+ a more secure place, both for themselves and for everyone else. They should apply pressure on manufacturers to improve security, both through their own purchasing decisions and through industry associations. They should engage with policy makers, and lobby their governments for regulations to improve security. Although corporations are almost pathologically anti-regulation, this is one area where smart regulations can create new incentives that actually lower the overall cost of security, and the cost of security failures.

We have to accept that we're stuck with the government we have, and not the government we wish we had. And if we can't rely on government as the first mover here, our only hope is that some companies step up and make the Internet+ secure anyway. It's not much, but it's what we have.

What I will say about trust in Chapter 12 is probably the most important thing to remember. We are forced to trust everyone whose products and services we use. Try to understand who you are trusting and to what degree, and make those trust decisions as intelligently as possible. Make your decisions about the cloud, the Internet of Things, and everything else with as much knowledge and forethought as you can.

This can mean making some hard choices. Who will you allow to violate your privacy and security in exchange for a service? Would you prefer to give Google or Apple access to your e-mail? Would you prefer to give Flickr (owned by Yahoo) or Facebook your photos? Do you prefer Apple's iMessage or Facebook's WhatsApp—or the independent Signal or Telegram—for your text messages?

It also means deciding on the countries to which you prefer to make yourself vulnerable. US companies are subject to US law, and will almost certainly relinquish data in response to court orders. Storing your data in another country might insulate you from US law, but will subject you to that country's laws. And while the NSA's global surveillance is unmatched in the world, US law constrains the NSA far more than similar agencies are constrained elsewhere—and you have more legal protection of your data when it's stored in the US than when it's stored elsewhere.

Making these decisions can be impossible and—honestly—most people won't bother. Facebook might be headquartered in California, but it maintains data centers all over the world; your data will likely be stored in several of them. Many companies you deal with use cloud services with data scattered around the world. Whatever service provider you decide to patronize, you're not likely to know for sure which countries' laws will apply to your data. But some companies push back against data requests, depending on the customer's location—for example, Microsoft's ongoing battle with the Department of Justice about turning over data from an Irish customer stored in Ireland to the FBI.

I see two ways to think about this. The first is that you are already subject to the laws of your home country, and the most prudent course is to minimize the number of additional countries whose laws your data is subject to. Conversely, any incriminating data is more likely to get you in trouble in your home country, so making it harder for your domestic law enforcement agency to access it is the more prudent course. For myself, I choose the first option. Elsewhere I have argued that, given the choice, I would rather have my data under the jurisdiction of the US government than under pretty much any other government on the planet. I've taken a lot of flak for that opinion, but I still stand by it.

11

Where Policy Can Go Wrong

I n the previous chapter, I said that governments regulate things that kill people. The Internet+ is about to fall into this category. When policy makers wake up to this, we will no longer have a choice between government regulation and no government regulation. Our choice will be between smart government regulation and stupid government regulation.

It's the stupid that worries me. Nothing motivates a government like fear: both fear of attack and fear of looking weak. Remember the months after the 9/11 terrorist attacks? The PATRIOT Act was passed almost unanimously and with little debate, and a small-government Republican administration created and funded an entire new government agency that has since mushroomed to nearly a quarter-million employees to protect the "homeland." Both of these actions were poorly thought out, and we'll be living with the consequences for years or decades to come.

Whatever Congress does in the wake of an Internet+ security disaster might make headlines, but it probably won't improve security. Congress could enact laws and policies that inadequately address the underlying threats, while actually exacerbating the problems.

One example of inadequate legislation is the Child Online Protection Act, passed in 1998. Its purpose was to protect minors from Internet porn.

Its provisions were not only sweeping and unworkable, but also would have embedded a pervasive surveillance architecture into even the remotest corners of the Internet. Luckily, the courts prevented the law from taking effect. Another example is the DMCA, first discussed in Chapter 2. Not only does it not prevent digital piracy, it harms all of our security.

This chapter is also about what might happen in the near term, and outlines some of the bad policy ideas currently being debated. Any of them could become law quickly after a disaster.

DEMANDING BACKDOORS

In Chapter 9, I talked about the need to put security ahead of surveillance, and how governments often work against that principle. The NSA does it surreptitiously, by weakening encryption. The FBI wants to do it publicly, by forcing companies to insert backdoors into their encryption systems.

This isn't a new demand. Pretty much continuously since the 1990s, US law enforcement agencies have claimed that encryption has become an insurmountable barrier to criminal investigation. In the 1990s, alarm was raised about encrypted phone calls. In the 2000s, FBI representatives, in their discussions of encryption, began to refer to the perils of "going dark," and turned their concern to encrypted messaging apps. In the 2010s, encrypted smartphones have become the new peril.

The rhetoric is uniformly dire.

Here's then–FBI director Louis Freeh, scaring the House Permanent Select Committee on Intelligence in 1997: "The widespread use of robust unbreakable encryption ultimately will devastate our ability to fight crime and prevent terrorism."

Here's then–FBI general counsel Valerie Caproni, scaring the House Judiciary Committee in 2011: "As the gap between authority and capability widens, the government is increasingly unable to collect valuable evidence in cases ranging from child exploitation and pornography to organized crime and drug trafficking to terrorism and espionage—evidence that a court has authorized the government to collect. This gap poses a growing threat to public safety."

Here's then-FBI director James Comey, scaring the Senate Judiciary Committee in 2015: "We may not be able to identify and stop terrorists who are using social media to recruit, plan, and execute an attack in our country. We may not be able to root out the child predators hiding in the shadows of the Internet, or find and arrest violent criminals who are targeting our neighborhoods. We may not be able to recover critical information from a device that belongs to a victim who cannot provide us with the password, especially when time is of the essence."

And here's Deputy Attorney General Rod Rosenstein, trying to scare me personally—I was in the audience at the Cambridge Cyber Summit—in 2017: "But the advent of 'warrant-proof' encryption is a serious problem. It threatens to destabilize the constitutional balance between privacy and security that has existed for over two centuries. Our society has never had a system where evidence of criminal wrongdoing was totally impervious to detection, even when officers obtain a court-authorized warrant. But that is the world that technology companies are creating."

The Four Horsemen of the Internet Apocalypse—terrorists, drug dealers, pedophiles, and organized crime—always scare people. "Warrant-proof" is a particularly scary phrase, but it just means that a warrant won't get the information. Papers burned in a fireplace are also "warrant-proof."

The notion that the world has never seen a technology that is impervious to detection is complete nonsense. Before the Internet, many communications were permanently unavailable to the FBI. Every voice conversation irrevocably disappeared after the words were spoken. Nobody, regardless of legal authority, could go backwards in time and retrieve a conversation or track someone's movements. Two people could go for a walk in a secluded area, look around and see no one, and have a confidence of privacy that is now forever lost. Today, we're living in the golden age of surveillance. As I said in Chapter 9, what the FBI needs is technical expertise, not backdoors.

Over the decades, the government has proposed a variety of backdoors. In the 1990s, the FBI suggested that software developers provide copies of every encryption key. The idea was called "key escrow," akin to everyone having to give the police a copy of their house key. In the early 2000s, the FBI argued that software vendors should deliberately insert vulnerabilities into computer systems, to be exploited by law enforcement when necessary. A decade later, demands devolved to a more general "Figure out how to do this." More recently, the FBI has suggested that tech companies use their update process to push fake updates to specific users and install backdoors into individual software packages on demand. Rosenstein has given this security-hostile proposal the friendly-sounding name of "responsible encryption." By the time you read this, there might be a different preferred solution.

This isn't just playing out in the US. UK policy makers are already implying that the 2016 Investigatory Powers Act gives them the power to force companies to sabotage their own encryption. In 2016, Croatia, France, Germany, Hungary, Italy, Latvia, and Poland called on the EU to demand that companies add backdoors. Separately, the EU is considering legislation that bans backdoors. Australia is also trying to mandate access. In Brazil, courts temporarily shut down WhatsApp three times in 2016 because local police couldn't access encrypted messages. Egypt blocked the encrypted messaging app Signal. Many countries banned BlackBerry devices until the company allowed governments to eavesdrop on communications. And both Russia and China routinely block apps they can't monitor.

No matter what it's called or how it's done, adding backdoors for law enforcement in computers and communications systems is a terrible idea. Backdoors go against our need to put security before surveillance. While in theory it would be great for police to be able to eavesdrop on criminal suspects, gather forensic evidence, or otherwise investigate crimes—assuming proper policies and warrants were in place—there's no way to design this securely. It's impossible to build a backdoor mechanism that only works in the presence of a legal warrant, or when a law enforcement officer tries to use it for legitimate purposes. Either the backdoor works for everyone or it doesn't work for anyone.

This means that any backdoor will make us all less secure. It'll be used by foreign governments and criminals, against our political leaders, against our critical infrastructure, against our corporations—against everybody. It'll be used against our diplomats and spies overseas, and our law enforcement agents at home. It'll be used to commit crimes, facilitate government espionage, and enable cyberattacks. It's an incredibly stupid idea that keeps being proposed.

If the US successfully imposes backdoor requirements on US companies, there's nothing to stop other governments from making the same demands. All sorts of repressive countries, from Russia and China to Kazakhstan and Saudi Arabia will demand the same level of "lawful access," even though their laws are designed to punish political dissidents.

Rosenstein's idea to use the update process is particularly damaging. There are already vulnerabilities in the update process. We are all more secure when everybody installs updates as quickly as possible. One security measure we're starting to see is more transparency in updates, so individual systems can be sure that the update they're receiving is both authorized by the company and applicable to every user. This is important for security; recall in Chapter 5 when I talked about attackers co-opting the update process to deliver malware. The FBI's requirements would prevent companies from adding such transparency and other security measures to the update process.

If the update mechanism is a known method for the police to hack into someone's computers and devices, all sorts of people will turn automatic update off. This loss of trust will take years to regain, and the overall effect on security will be devastating. This is akin to hiding combat troops in Red Cross vehicles. We don't do it, even if it is an effective tactic.

Finally, using the update process to enable the delivery of malware would make it much less secure. If an update occurs infrequently, a company can build strong security around the authentication process. If a company like Apple received multiple requests per day to unlock phones—the FBI claimed in 2017 that it had 7,000 phones it couldn't unlock—the routine procedures it would have to put in place to respond to those requests would be much more vulnerable to attack.

Those who understand security know backdoors are dangerous. A 2016 congressional working group concluded: "Any measure that weakens encryption works against the national interest." Lord John Evans, who ran the UK's MI5, said: "My personal view is that we should not be undermining the strength of cryptography across the whole of the cyber market because I think the cost of doing that would be very considerable."

More important than all of this, giving the FBI what it wants won't solve its problem.

Even if the FBI succeeds in forcing large US companies like Apple, Google, and Facebook to make their devices and communications systems insecure, many smaller competitors offer secure products. If Facebook adds a backdoor to WhatsApp, the bad guys will move to Signal. If Apple adds a backdoor to its iPhone encryption, the bad guys will move to one of the many encrypted voice apps.

Even the FBI is less demanding in private. Conversations I and others have had with FBI officials suggest they are generally okay with optional encryption, since most bad guys don't bother turning it on. What they object to is encryption by default.

And that's precisely the reason we need it. Defaults are powerful; most of us don't know enough, or otherwise don't bother, to turn on optional security features on our computers, phones, web services, IoT devices, or anything else. And while the FBI is correct that the average criminal won't turn on optional encryption, the average criminal will make other mistakes that will leave them vulnerable to investigation—especially if the FBI improves its digital investigative techniques. It's the smart criminals that the FBI should be worried about, and those criminals will use the more secure alternatives.

Backdoors harm the average Internet user, both good and bad. The FBI myopically and histrionically focuses on the bad guys. But once we realize there are far more good guys on the Internet than bad ones, it's obvious that the benefits of ubiquitous strong encryption outweigh the disadvantages of giving criminals access to strong encryption.

LIMITING ENCRYPTION

In the US, prior to the mid-1990s, encryption was regulated as a munition. Software and hardware products using encryption were export controlled, just like grenades or rifles. Strong encryption couldn't be exported, and any product for export had to be weak enough for the NSA to easily break. These controls ended when the Internet—and the international tech community—rendered them obsolete because the notion of "export" of software no longer made sense.

There's talk of bringing encryption controls back. In 2015, then–UK prime minister David Cameron proposed banning strong encryption in the country entirely. Current prime minister Theresa May echoed this after the 2017 London Bridge terrorist attack.

This is a step beyond mandating backdoors in popular encryption systems like WhatsApp and the iPhone. This is making any computer system, software, or service featuring strong encryption illegal. The problem, of course, is that national laws are domestic and software is international. In 2016, I surveyed the market for encryption products. Out of 865 software products from 55 different countries, 811 would be immune from a UK ban because they were created outside the UK. If the US passed a similar ban, 546 products would be immune.

Keeping those foreign products out of a country would be impossible. It would require blocking search engines from finding foreign encryption products. It would require monitoring all communications to ensure that no one downloaded a foreign encryption product from a website. It would require scanning every computer, phone, and IoT device entering the country, whether carried by a person at the border or sent through the mail. It would require banning open-source software and online code repositories. It would require banning, and interdicting at the border, books that contained encryption algorithms and code. In short, it's simply crazy.

If attempted, the result of such a ban would be even worse than mandating backdoors. It would force all of us to be much less secure against all threats. It would put domestic companies that had to comply at a competitive disadvantage against those that didn't. And it would give criminals and foreign governments an enormous advantage.

I don't think this is likely to happen, but it is possible. In the past year, I have seen a change in rhetoric around encryption. In their attempts to demand backdoors, Justice Department officials are quick to paint encryption as a criminal tool, with evocative references to those Four Horsemen of the Internet Apocalypse and anonymity services like Tor. On a completely different front, "crypto" is starting to be used as a shorthand for cryptocurrencies like bitcoin, and painted as a tool for those who want to buy illegal goods on the scarily named Darknet. The result is that the positive uses for cryptography and the ways it protects all of our security are being crowded out of the conversation. If this trend continues, we might see serious proposals to ban strong encryption.

In 2015, Mike McConnell, Michael Chertoff, and William Lynn, three former senior government officials with extensive experience in these matters, wrote about the importance of computer and Internet security to national security:

We believe that the greater public good is a secure communications infrastructure protected by ubiquitous encryption at the device, server and enterprise level without building in means for government monitoring.

These sentiments run counter to the official position of their former employers, but safely retired and widely respected, the three felt free to speak out. We need to change the official position of government, so that everyone works towards more security for everyone.

BANNING ANONYMITY

There are regular calls to ban anonymity on the Internet. They come from those who want to control hateful and harassing speech, under the assumption that if you can find the trolls, you can banish them—or, better yet, they would be too ashamed to be trollish. They come from those who want to prevent cybercrime, assuming that being able to identify someone makes it easier to apprehend them. They come from those who want to arrest spammers, stalkers, drug dealers, and terrorists.

Banning anonymity takes various forms, but you can basically think of it as giving everyone the Internet equivalent of a driver's license. We would all use that license to configure our computers and sign up for various Internet services like e-mail accounts, and no one without one would have any access.

This won't work, for four reasons.

First, we don't have the real-world infrastructure to provide Internet user credentials based on other identification systems: passports, national identity cards, driver's licenses, or whatever. Remember what I wrote in Chapter 3 about identification and breeder documents. Second, a system like this might make identity theft rarer, but would also make it much more profitable.

These two reasons alone explain why mandatory identification for Internet usage is a bad idea. Right now, there are plenty of adequate identification and authentication systems. Banks manage well enough to let you transfer money online, and companies like Google and Facebook manage well enough that they allow others to use their systems. There are several competing smartphone payment apps. Your cell phone number is turning into a unique identifier that's good enough for purposes such as two-factor authentication.

However, when we build a mandatory identification system, we need to catch precisely those people who want to subvert the system. Every existing identification system is already subverted by teenagers trying to buy alcohol in face-to-face transactions. Securing a mandatory identification system for the Internet would be much more difficult.

Third, any such system would have to work globally. But consider that anyone from any country can pretend to be from anywhere else. If the US were to outlaw anonymity and mandate that its citizens use driver's licenses to register in person for an e-mail address, any American could simply get an anonymous e-mail account from another country without an ID requirement. So, either we acknowledge that anyone can obtain an anonymous e-mail address, or we prohibit communicating with the rest of the world. Neither option will work.

Fourth, and most importantly, it is always possible to set up an anonymous communications system on top of an identified communications system. Tor is a system for anonymous web browsing, used by both political dissidents and criminals around the world. I'm not going to cover how it works here, but it can provide anonymity even if everyone on the system is positively identified.

Those are the reasons why banning anonymity won't work. It's terrible because it's bad for society. Anonymous speech is valuable—and in some countries, lifesaving. The ability for individuals to maintain multiple personas for different aspects of their lives is valuable. Banning anonymity would sacrifice an essential liberty in exchange for the illusion of temporary safety.

This doesn't mean everyone deserves anonymity in all things. Society already bans anonymity in many areas. You are not permitted to drive an anonymous car on public roads; all cars must have license plates. Similar rules are coming for drones. The US has imposed know-your-customer rules on banks around the world. The boundary between spaces where anonymity is permitted and where it is forbidden seems to be the point where someone can cause significant physical or economic damage. As the Internet+ crosses that boundary, expect more spaces with less anonymity.

MASS SURVEILLANCE

Mass surveillance isn't limited to totalitarian countries. The US government collected phone call metadata on most Americans until 2015, and still has access to this information on demand. Many local governments keep comprehensive data about people's movements, collected from license plate scanners mounted on street poles and mobile vans. And, of course, many corporations have us all under surveillance through a variety of mechanisms. Governments regularly demand access to that data in ways that don't require a warrant, such as subpoenas and national security letters.

I worry that some of the catastrophic risks I wrote about in Chapter 5 will lead policy makers to go beyond backdoors and weakened cryptography, to authorize ubiquitous domestic surveillance. Leaving out the *1984*-like ramifications that make it a terrible idea on the face of it, the effectiveness of ubiquitous surveillance is very limited. It's only useful between the moment a new capability becomes possible and the moment it becomes easy.

To understand how this might happen, consider the development curve of any particular destructive technology. In the early days of a technology's development, super-damaging scenarios just aren't possible. Right now, for example, despite what television and movies like to portray, we do not have the technical knowledge required to concoct a super-germ that can kill millions of people.

As biological science develops, catastrophic scenarios become possible but extremely expensive. Making them a reality would require concerted effort on the scale of the World War II Manhattan Project, or similar military efforts to develop and build biological weapons.

As technology continues to improve, damaging capabilities become cheaper and available to increasingly smaller and less organized groups. At some point, it becomes possible for a conspiracy to implement a catastrophe. Both money and expertise would be required, but both can be readily acquired. One could envision a large-scale effort to disrupt the global economy by coordinated attacks on stock exchange IT systems or on critical infrastructure, such as power plants or airline navigational systems.

This is the point at which ubiquitous surveillance might possibly provide security. The hope would be to detect the conspiracy in its planning stages, and collect enough evidence to connect the dots and disrupt the plot before it happens. This is the primary justification of the current NSA's ubiquitous anti-terrorism surveillance efforts.

But while ubiquitous surveillance could succeed in the majority of those cases, primarily against less technically savvy attackers, it would fail against the most motivated, most skilled, and best-funded attackers. As technology improves, the number of conspirators and the amount of planning required to unleash havoc shrinks further, making surveillance-based detection even less effective. Think of Timothy McVeigh's fertilizer bomb, and the handful of accomplices who helped him attack the Alfred P. Murrah Federal Building. Maybe ubiquitous surveillance could have detected the plot in the planning and purchasing stages, but probably not. Targeted surveillance, based on old-fashioned follow-the-lead police work, might more effectively identify those who advocate violent overthrow of the US government and go about assembling bomb-making materials.

As technology continues to improve, and catastrophic scenarios might be effected by only one or two people, ubiquitous surveillance becomes useless. We already know of incidents like this. No amount of surveillance can stop mass shootings like the ones at Fort Hood (2009), San Bernardino (2015), or Las Vegas (2017). No amount of surveillance could have stopped the DDoS attacks against Dyn. The failure to anticipate the Boston Marathon bombing was less a failure of mass surveillance than a failure to follow investigative leads, if indeed it can be considered a failure at all.

At best, mass surveillance can only ever buy society time. Even then, it wouldn't be very effective. Surveillance is more effective at social control than at crime prevention, which is why it's such a popular tool among authoritarian governments.

This doesn't mean we won't see domestic mass surveillance, especially in the wake of another catastrophic terrorist attack. As bad as we are at defending against what we perceive to be catastrophic threats, we are very good about panicking over specific scenarios involving these threats. And historically, the panic is much more dangerous to freedom and liberty than the actual threats themselves. Furthermore, there will always be new technological threats at different points along that development curve, each potentially justifying mass surveillance.

HACKING BACK

Hacking back is another terrible idea, one that frequently rears its ugly head. Basically, it's private counterattack. It's an organization going on the offensive to retaliate against its attackers—in the pursuit of a criminal, to acquire evidence, or to recover stolen data. Sometimes it goes by the euphemism "active cyber defense," but that just serves to hide what it really is: server-to-server combat. It's illegal today in every country, but there's constant talk about making it legal.

Proponents like to talk about two specific scenarios that might justify hacking back. The first is when victims know the location of their stolen data; they could hack into that computer and delete the data. The second scenario is an ongoing attack; they could hack into their attacker's computer and stop the attack in real time.

On the surface this might seem reasonable, but it could quickly result in disaster. First, there are the difficulties of attribution I wrote about in Chapter 3. How can an organization be sure who is attacking it, and what happens if it erroneously penetrates an innocent network while retaliating? It's easy to disguise the source of an attack, or route an attack through an innocent middleman.

Second, what happens if a "hackbacker" penetrates a network in a foreign country? Or worse, that country's military? It would almost certainly be considered a crime, and might create an international incident. So many countries use surrogates, front companies, and criminals to do their dirty work on the Internet that the chances of a mistake, miscalculation, or misinterpretation are already high. Authorized hacking back would add to the mess, and we don't want some company to accidentally start a cyberwar.

Third, hacking back is ripe for abuse. Any organization could go after a competitor by staging an attack against its own servers, or by planting sensitive files in its competitor's network—and then go hacking back.

Fourth, it would be easy for hostilities to escalate. An enterprising schemer could start a battle between two organizations by spoofing hacks by each against the other.

Fifth and finally, it's unclear whether this is even an effective tactic. Vengeance is satisfying, but there's no evidence that hacking back either improves security or has a deterrent effect.

The real reason this is a terrible idea, though, is that it sanctions vigilantism. There are reasons why you are not allowed to break into your neighbor's house to retrieve an item, even if you know they stole it from you. There's a reason we no longer issue letters of marque, which authorized private merchant ships to attack and capture other vessels. These sorts of capabilities are rightly the sole purview of governments.

Almost everybody agrees with this. Both the FBI and the Justice Department caution against hacking back. A 2017 bill legitimizing some hackback tactics died with minimal support. The main exception seems to be Stewart Baker—attorney and former NSA and DHS senior official—who regularly recommends hacking back. And some cybersecurity companies around the world are pushing for legal authorization, because they want to offer hackback services to corporate customers. Israel seems to want to be a home country for this industry.

Despite its illegality, hacking back is already happening. Companies that offer hackback services don't advertise openly, and they're likely hired through intermediary companies and with deniable contracts. Like corporate bribery, it exists, and some companies break international law by engaging in the practice.

My guess is that this will always be the case. Regardless of what the US and like-minded countries do, others will be safe havens for this practice. This means we need to treat hacking back like bribery: we need to declare it illegal everywhere in the world, and prosecute US companies that engage in it. We need to push for international treaties and norms against hacking back. And we need to do our best to marginalize the outliers. Right now, there is no official US stance on hacking back, but I believe there will be one soon.

RESTRICTING THE AVAILABILITY OF SOFTWARE

Historically, we have often relied on scarcity for security. That is, we secure ourselves from the malicious uses of a thing by making that thing hard to obtain. This has worked well for some things—polonium-210, the smallpox virus, and anti-tank missiles come to mind—and less well for others: alcohol, drugs, handguns. The Internet+ destroys that model.

The radio spectrum is tightly regulated, and numerous rules govern who can transmit on which frequencies. Some are reserved for the military, others for the police, and still others for communications between aircraft and ground control. There are frequencies you can only broadcast on if you have a license, and others you can only broadcast on if you have a specific communications device.

Before computers, this was all enforced by limiting what sorts of radios were commercially available. A normal off-the-shelf radio would only tune to the legal frequencies. This solution wasn't perfect—it was always possible to buy or build a radio that could transmit or receive on other channels—but that was a complicated solution that required specialized knowledge (or at least access to specialized equipment). It wasn't a perfect security solution, but it was good enough for most purposes. Today, radios are just computers with antennas attached, and you can buy a software-defined radio card for your PC that will allow you to broadcast on any frequency.

In Chapter 4, I talked about the risks from people hacking their own computers to evade common and reasonable laws. I've also talked about the potential for people to modify their automobile software in violation of emissions control laws, their 3D printers to make objects in violation of copyright laws, and their biological printers in violation of laws about killing large numbers of people.

In each of these new technologies, we're going to have levelheaded calls to restrict what users can do with their devices. For example, what Mattel, Disney, censors, and gun-control advocates are going to want is a 3D printer that will let the customer make any object except those on a list of prohibited objects.

This is exactly the same issue as the copyright problem. Digital rights management was the technical solution that failed, and the DMCA was the law that came after. It has only been effective at preventing hobbyists from making copies of digital music and movies. It hasn't prevented professionals from doing the same thing, and it hasn't prevented the spread of copyrighted works with the DRM protections removed.

The fear of hacked autonomous-car software or printed killer viruses will be much greater than the fear of illegally copied songs. The industries that will be affected are much more powerful than the entertainment industry. Both government and the private sector will look at the entertainment industry's experience with DRM and correctly conclude that the problem is that computers are, by nature, extensible. They will look at the DMCA and conclude that the law wasn't sufficiently onerous and restrictive. I worry that analogous laws for 3D printers, bio-printers, cars, and so on will be supported by government and private interests working together against users.

Laws restricting access to software that allows people to modify their IoT computers might work against most people for a while, but in the end, they would be ineffective because the Internet allows the free flow of software and information worldwide, and because a domestic-only law would never keep computers out of a country. This isn't simply a matter of accepting a mostly effective solution and living with the exceptions. With songs and other digital content, the cost of failure is minimal. With these new technologies, the cost of failure will be much higher.

We need to solve these problems directly: not with laws limiting the use of technology or computer capabilities, but by developing counteracting capabilities.

With respect to radios, one solution would be to enable all the radios to police themselves. Radios could be transformed into a detection grid that located malicious or improperly configured transmitters, and then forwarded that information to the police, who could then investigate alleged violations. Radio systems could be designed to withstand attempts at eavesdropping and jamming so that rogue transmitters couldn't interfere with their operation. There would, of course, be details to be worked out. My goal here isn't to solve the technical problem—only to demonstrate that solutions can be found.

This is a general lesson that will apply to many aspects of the Internet+, from 3D and bio-printers to autonomous algorithms and artificial intelligence. If we're going to live in a world where individuals can cause widespread damage, we're eventually going to have to figure out how to engineer around the threats inherent in each system. DMCA-like restrictions will buy us some time, but they won't solve our security problems.

12

Towards a Trusted, Resilient, and Peaceful Internet+

Human beings operate on trust. No other species trusts at anywhere near the scale we do. Society would collapse without trust; indeed, society would have never formed without it. We trust continually, throughout our days, without even a second thought. And it's not as if we have any choice. We trust the food in our supermarkets not to make us sick. We trust the people we pass on the street not to attack us. We trust banks not to steal our money. We trust other drivers not to hit us. Of course, as you read this you're thinking about caveats and exceptions, but the reason you're thinking about them is that they're so rare. Unless you're living in a lawless part of the planet, every day you're blindly trusting millions of people, organizations, and institutions. That we hardly think about it is testament to how well the system actually works.

Think about your computer and all of the companies you are forced to trust, simply by using it. You trust the designers and manufacturers of the chips inside it, and the company that assembled it. In fact, you trust the entire supply chain, from the manufacturer to the company that sold it to you. You trust the company that wrote your operating system—likely Microsoft or Apple—and the companies that wrote the software you're using. That includes applications like your browser and word processor, and security software like your antivirus program. You trust the Internet services you're using: your e-mail provider, your social networking platforms, and any cloud services handling your data. You trust your Internet service provider, and the companies that designed, built, and installed your home router. There are easily dozens of companies you have no choice but to trust, along with the governments of the countries those companies are from. Any one of them has the capability to subvert your security and take advantage of you. Any one of them can have insecure processes that allow others to do the same.

You trust all of those entities because you have to, not because you think any of them are trustworthy. On the Internet, the universe of trustworthy actors is shrinking considerably. A 2017 survey illustrated that 70% of Americans believe it is at least somewhat likely that their phone calls and e-mails are being monitored by the government. People all over the world mistrust the NSA and the US in general.

That 2016 Obama cybersecurity report I talked about in Chapter 10 put it this way:

> The success of the digital economy ultimately relies on individuals and organizations trusting computing technology and trusting the organizations that provide products and services that collect and retain data. That trust is less sturdy than it was several years ago because of incidents and successful breaches that have given rise to fears that corporate and personal data are being compromised and misused. Concern is increasing, too, about the ability of information systems to prevent data from being manipulated; the 2016 US election heightened public awareness of that issue. In most cases, data manipulation is a more dangerous threat than data theft.

Right now, this mistrust isn't too great. We're still mostly able to ignore the risks and trust those governments and companies—or, at least, act like we do—because we don't have much choice. We pretend that our Facebook feed is filled with posts from friends, not paid advertisements insinuated into our personal communications. We pretend that our search engines aren't being manipulated by algorithms surreptitiously promoting commercial products. We pretend that the companies entrusted with our data aren't using that data against our interests. We accept all of this because we really have no choice. We ignore all the secrecy because secrecy breeds suspicion.

So far, that's worked. We use our computers and phones. We store our data in the cloud. We have private conversations on Facebook and e-mail. We buy things over the Internet. We buy and use Internet-connected things. And we don't think about it too much.

That could flip at any time. And if it does, it's going to be bad. The ill effects from living in a low-trust society are considerable. Economies suffer. People suffer. Everything suffers.

In 2011, I published *Liars and Outliers*, which looked at security through the lens of trust. Security systems are mechanisms to enforce trust: to ensure that people cooperate with each other and do what's expected. Informally, we enforce that internally with our own moral codes and externally by learning and remembering others' reputations. More formally, we enforce it with rules, laws, and penalties. And we enforce it with security technologies like fences, locks, security cameras, audits, and investigations.

In Chapter 4, I said that everyone wants you to have security, except from them. This is not sustainable. Over the long term, government mass surveillance is not sustainable. We've got to limit it if we want a trustworthy Internet and, by extension, a trustworthy society.

Surveillance capitalism is not sustainable. We've got to limit it, too. As long as surveillance is the business model of the Internet, the companies you entrust with your data and capabilities will never fully support keeping you secure. They will make design decisions that weaken your security against both criminals and governments. We need to change the fabric of the Internet so that it doesn't provide governments with the tools to create a totalitarian state. This isn't going to be easy, and it's not going to happen within the decade. It's not even clear how it could happen in the US; free-speech issues will hamper any legislative efforts to limit commercial surveillance. Even so, I believe it will happen eventually. Perhaps the change will be driven by changing norms. We're starting to chafe under the unremitting extraction of data about both our public and our inner lives—data available to both governments and corporations but not to us. Surveillance capitalism is pervasively damaging to society; sooner or later, society will demand reform.

In order for corporations and governments to be trusted, they need to be trustworthy. This underpins much of what I wrote in Chapter 9. It's not enough for governments to prioritize defense over offense; their priorities must be evident. Government secrecy and duplicity hurt trust.

It's not enough for companies to secure their systems; they need to do it transparently, so that they're seen to be working for the public's benefit and not abusing their positions of power. Every suggestion in this book should be implemented and enforced publicly. Standards should be open. Details of breaches should be disclosed. Enforcement and fines should be public. An insecure Internet+ won't be trusted, but a secure Internet+ must be public to be trusted.

All the suggestions in this book are intended to move us towards an Internet that is fundamentally trustworthy, one where the most powerful actors are prevented from preying on unsuspecting ordinary users. We've got a lot of work to do to get there, and the goal itself may seem a bit utopian; but while we're at it, let's talk about two other key attributes of the ideal Internet we're working towards: resilience and, finally, peace.

A RESILIENT INTERNET

According to sociologist Charles Perrow's theory of complexity, complex systems are less secure than simpler ones and, as a result, attacks and accidents involving complex systems are both more prevalent and more damaging. But Perrow demonstrates that not all complexity is created equal. In particular, complex systems that are both nonlinear and tightly coupled are more fragile.

For example, the air traffic control system is a loosely coupled system. Both individual air traffic control towers and airplanes have failures all the time, but because the different parts of the system only mildly affect the others, the results are rarely catastrophic. Yes, you can read headlines about this or that airport being in chaos as a result of computer problems, but you rarely read about planes crashing into buildings, mountains, or each other.

A row of standing dominos is a linear system. When one topples over, it hits the next domino and causes that one to topple over. Although these chains are large, they topple in an orderly fashion.

The Internet is the opposite: it's both nonlinear in that pieces can have wildly out-of-proportion effects on each other, and tightly coupled in that these effects cascade immediately—characteristics that make catastrophes much more likely. It's so complex that no one understands everything about how it works. It's so complex that it just barely works. It's so complex that we can't predict how it will work in many cases.

We need better security in our large-scale sociotechnical systems, but most of all we need more resilient security.

I have long liked the term "resilience." If you look around, you'll see it used in human psychology, in organizational theory, in disaster recovery, in ecological systems, in materials science, and in systems engineering. Here's a definition from a 1991 book by Aaron Wildavsky called *Searching for Safety*: "Resilience is the capacity to cope with unanticipated dangers after they have become manifest, learning to bounce back."

I have been talking about resilience in IT security for over 15 years. In my 2003 book, *Beyond Fear*, I spent pages on resilience. I wrote:

> Good security systems are resilient. They can withstand failures; a single failure doesn't cause a cascade of other failures. They can withstand attacks, including attackers who cheat. They can withstand new advances in technology. They can fail and recover from failure.

In 2012, the World Economic Forum described cyber resilience as an enabling capability—one that provides physical safety, economic security, and competitive business advantage.

In 2017, the US National Intelligence Council—part of the Office of the Director of National Intelligence—published a comprehensive document looking at long-term security trends. It talked about resilience:

> The most resilient societies will likely be those that unleash and embrace the full potential of all individuals—whether women and minorities or those battered by recent economic and technological trends. They will be moving with, rather than against, historical currents, making use of the ever-expanding scope of human skill to shape the future. In all societies, even in the bleakest circum-

stances, there will be those who choose to improve the welfare, happiness, and security of others—employing transformative technologies to do so at scale. While the opposite will be true as well—destructive forces will be empowered as never before—the central puzzle before governments and societies is how to blend individual, collective, and national endowments in a way that yields sustainable security, prosperity, and hope.

Tactically and technologically, resilience means many different things: multiple layers of defense, isolation, redundancy, and so on. We need to be resilient as a society as well. Much of the damage caused by cyberattacks is psychological. Russia shut off electric power in Ukraine twice, and now Ukrainian citizens have to live with the knowledge that their access to power is fragile. A more resilient power grid would mean a more resilient society.

We can prevent some attacks, but we have to detect and respond to the rest of them after they happen. That process is how we achieve resilience. It was true 15 years ago and, if anything, it is even more true today.

A DEMILITARIZED INTERNET

In Chapter 4, I wrote that we're in the middle of a cyberwar arms race. Arms races are always expensive. They're fueled by ignorance and fear: ignorance of our enemies' capabilities, and fear that theirs are greater than ours. That ignorance and fear is magnified in cyberspace. Remember how hard it was for the US to discern Iraq's nuclear and chemical weapons capabilities? Cyber capabilities are even easier to hide.

This arms race harms our security in two ways. First, it directly reduces security by ensuring that the Internet+ remains insecure. As long as there are countries that need vulnerabilities for cyberweapons, and are willing to discover them themselves or buy them from others, there will be vulnerabilities that don't get patched.

Second, it increases the chances of a cyberwar. Weapons beg to be used, and the more weapons there are in the world, the greater the risk they might be used. The inherent perishability of cyberweapons that I discussed in Chapter 4 makes them attractive to use. The offensive nature of battle-field preparations increases the chance of retaliation, even if that retaliation is based on a misunderstanding. And the attribution gap increases the possibility for misunderstanding—and deliberate deception—especially for countries not privy to the US's intelligence capabilities.

We need to work towards demilitarizing the Internet. It might seem impossible, and in today's geopolitical climate it might very well be, but it's certainly achievable in the long term. It is the only path forward for a sustainable future.

A start would be to move beyond military metaphors for Internet security. For example, conceptualizing it as a public hygiene or pollution problem will lead us towards different sorts of solutions. A 2017 report by the New York Cyber Task Force suggested that governments could tax harmful "emissions" by ISPs—malware, DDoS traffic, and so on—and even implement some sort of cap-and-trade regime. International laws regarding pollution might also provide a useful comparison when wrestling with the international-security issues for the Internet+.

Even more than either of these two things, we need to actively create a peaceful Internet+. The term "cyber peace" has been advanced as an alternative to the increasingly martial rhetoric about cyberspace. Here's Indiana University cybersecurity law professor Scott Shackelford's attempt at defining this nebulous term:

> Cyber peace is not the absence of attacks or exploitations, an idea that could be called negative cyber peace. Rather, it is a network of multilevel regimes working together to promote global, just, and sustainable cybersecurity by clarifying norms for companies and countries alike to help reduce the risk of conflict, crime, and espionage in cyberspace to levels comparable to other business and national security risks. Working together through polycentric partnerships, and with the leadership of engaged individuals and institutions, we can stop cyber war before it starts by laying the groundwork for a positive cyber peace that respects human rights, spreads Internet access, and strengthens governance mechanisms by fostering multi-stakeholder collaboration.

Political scientist Heather Roff agrees, arguing that "cyber peace must be grounded in a conception of positive peace that eliminates structural forms of violence" based on four necessary factors: "a society, trust, governance, and the free flow of information."

In some ways, this sounds like a UN Security Council for the Internet, and we can learn from the successes and failures of that organization. It's a worthy goal, and one we should strive towards.

On a smaller, more immediate scale, there are ways we can work to promote a more just and equitable Internet right now. For all the problems with government and corporate surveillance we have in the US and other Western democracies, and for all the looming dangers to our lives and liberties that I've been describing, it's important to remember that billions of people enjoy considerably less digital freedom and face far more grave risks as a result of their Internet use, in countries like Egypt, Ethiopia, Myanmar, and Turkey.

I am on the board of an organization called Access Now. Our mission is to defend and extend the digital rights of users at risk around the world. One of the services we offer is a Digital Security Helpline, which provides immediate tech support for civil society members who are being spied on and attacked on the Internet. We also provide policy analysis and advocacy on government proposals around the world, advocate for policy changes in different countries, and convene an annual conference on human rights in the digital age.

I've had that organization and its work in the back of my mind as I've been writing this book. Both the problems and solutions I've been talking about focus on the world's liberal democracies. They don't apply as well to countries that use the Internet to find and arrest dissidents, or arrest people who give security training to dissidents. Even so, the recommendations I make would have a positive effect on them as well, even if it's only the democracies that follow through on them. In the meantime, there are groups like Access Now working to improve digital rights around the globe: Paradigm Initiative in Nigeria, SMEX in Lebanon, KICTANet in Kenya, Derechos Digitales in Chile, and so on.

The Internet is often talked about as a societal equalizer, and that's a fair characterization. It circulates and amplifies important ideas and human ideals. It connects people across borders. And it has sparked and enabled a dozen street-level revolutions led by people seeking greater freedoms and a better future. Who knows what the positive potential of the

Internet+ may turn out to be? Of course, the Internet has a dark underbelly as well, and I've spent most of this book talking about problems lurking there. But as with most human endeavors, we need to continue hammering away to shape the emerging Internet+ into a medium that embodies and enables the human ideals of trust, security, resilience, peace, and justice the best it can.

CONCLUSION
Bring Technology and Policy Together

I return to three scenarios repeatedly in this book. The first is a cyber-attack against a power grid. The second is murder by remote hacking of an Internet-connected car. The third is the "click here to kill everybody" scenario, involving replication of a lethal virus by a hacked bio-printer. The first example has already happened. The capability has been demonstrated for the second. The third remains to be seen.

Dan Geer, the security expert, once warned: "A technology that can give you everything you want is a technology that can take away everything that you have." The Internet's benefits to society have been, and will continue to be, enormous. It has already transformed our lives for the better in a multitude of ways, and after only a few decades it's hard to imagine ever going back. Future developments of the Internet+ will be even more transformative: developments in sensors and controllers, algorithms and data, autonomy and cyberphysical systems, AI and robotics. These will make our society as unrecognizable to us today as modern-day society would be to someone from pre-Enlightenment Europe. It's an amazing time to be alive, and I envy the younger generations who have more future ahead of them.

But the risks and dangers are equally transformative. The Internet+

affects the world in a direct physical manner, and that has implications both large and small. The connecting of everything into a single, complex, hyper-connected system quickly makes the risks catastrophic.

Meanwhile, all of our laws, rules, and norms are based on a benign Internet. But the nature of the Internet has changed, and that's the reality we must respond to by pushing governments to act.

Some of my pessimism arises from the extrapolation of technologies. We tend to extrapolate from the world of today, with only a few major changes. My favorite example comes from the 1982 movie *Blade Runner*, which features androids so advanced that they are impossible to identify without specialized equipment. Yet when Deckard—Harrison Ford's character—wants to meet one of them, he uses a coin-operated pay phone because they couldn't imagine cell phones.

We also tend to overestimate the short-term effects of technological change while underestimating the long-term effects. Think of the early years of the Internet. Many people realized it would be used to buy and sell things, but nobody predicted eBay. Many people understood that friends would use it to keep in touch, but nobody predicted Facebook. Again and again, we anticipate the immediate uses of a new technology, but fail to grasp how it will manifest in society. I see the same thing happening with personal digital assistants, robots, blockchain technologies like bitcoin, artificial intelligence, and driverless cars.

What this means is that it's easy to fall into the trap of technical determinism. I can easily map the current trajectories of security. However, I have no idea what new and transformative discoveries and inventions are coming in three, five, or ten years. I can't predict what fundamental advances in computer science will irrevocably change the balance between attack and defense. I can't predict what other technologies might be invented that will profoundly alter the security of the Internet+. I can't predict what sorts of social and political changes might occur that would make the risks in this book less important, or more manageable, or completely irrelevant. Our collective imaginations fail because the future is fundamentally unimaginable.

I do believe, though, that our Internet+ security solutions are ahead of us and not behind us, and that we are much more likely to engineer our way out of the problems we face than we are to restrict our way out of them.

Despite my recommendations in Chapter 6, solutions that require us to significantly constrain the pervasiveness of computers, or the Internet, or any technologies discussed in this book, are unlikely to succeed. The benefits of these technologies are too great, and we are currently too shortsighted to allow anything to get in the way of that.

We have to place our bets on more research, more ideas, more creativity, and more technology. There's no shortage of ideas—both meaningful and incremental, and profound and revolutionary. And while I might not know what the solutions will look like, I have high confidence that they're out there.

For example, I see great promise in the technologies of artificial intelligence and machine learning. Briefly, part of the reason attack is easier than defense is that attackers get to decide the nature of their attacks; they can use the collective strength of people and computers, and target the relative weaknesses of people and computers. Artificial intelligence technologies promise to alter this balance of computers and people, on both the offense and the defense. This will lessen the relative advantages to the attacker afforded by speed, surprise, and complexity.

My pessimism arises more from the US's collective inability to imagine government as a force for good in the world. When I review the current Internet security landscape, I see an environment shaped by corporate decisions to maximize profits and government abdication of its regulatory role to protect all citizens. I see a populace mesmerized by the frankly amazing capabilities of these new networked technologies, and negligent in considering the stupendously profound social repercussions of it all. Our current level of security is determined by the market, and I know—and hopefully have demonstrated—that it will be inadequate for the Internet+.

This is why I spend so much time thinking about public policy. I want to be ready with proposals before a crisis erupts. In a crisis, Congress will require action, and will no doubt employ that false syllogism: "Something must be done. This is something. Therefore, we must do it." It's important to talk now about what good Internet+ security policy will look like, when we have time to do it slowly and carefully, and before a catastrophe occurs.

In this book, I argue for good government doing good. This can be a tough argument to make, and there is a lot of potential for government to be ineffective or even harmful. But I don't see any other option. If government abdicates its responsibility—as it largely has in the US to date—we end up with an insecure Internet+ that only serves short-term commercial and military interests.

Despite the pessimistic tone of much of this book, I am optimistic about cybersecurity in the long term. Eventually, we will solve this.

Otto von Bismarck observed: "Politics is the art of the possible." To that I reply: Technology is the science of the possible. But politics and technology offer different possibilities, and to understand this is to realize that politicians and technologists define "possible" very differently. As a technologist, I want to arrive at the correct answer or the best solution to a problem. A politician, on the other hand, is pragmatic, looking not for what's right or what's best, but for what he or she can actually accomplish.

Today, technology and policy are inextricably intertwined. The scenarios I've outlined—both the technological and economic trends causing them and the political changes needed to fix them—come from my years of involvement in the development of Internet security technology and policy. An understanding of both is critical.

Over the past couple of decades, we've seen many misguided recommendations for Internet security policy. Examples include the FBI's insistence that computer devices be designed to facilitate government access in order to repel the bugbear of "going dark," the vulnerability equities process by which government agencies determine whether to disclose and fix vulnerabilities or use them to attack other systems, the failure of paperless touch-screen voting machines to produce trustworthy elections, and the DMCA. If you followed any of these policy debates as they unfolded, you heard policy makers and technologists talking past each other.

You saw this in Chapters 6, 7, 8, and 9—a bunch of great ideas that won't happen anytime soon. You saw the counterpart to this in Chapter 11—what tech-impaired policy makers might do to make things worse.

The Internet+ will exacerbate most, if not all, of these problems. The growing divide between Washington and Silicon Valley—the mutual mistrust between governments and tech companies—is dangerous. As computer security issues pervade other industries, we'll see similar disconnects between technology and policy—and between technologists and policy makers. British solicitor Nick Bohm eloquently phrased it as "the lawyers and engineers whose arguments pass through one other like angry ghosts."

This division isn't new. Addressing the 2014 Munich Security Conference, Estonian president Toomas Hendrik Ilves observed:

I think much of the problem we face today represents the culmination of a problem diagnosed 55 years ago by C. P. Snow in his essay "The Two Cultures": the absence of dialogue between the scientific-technological and the humanist traditions. When Snow wrote his classic essay, he bemoaned that neither culture understood or impinged on the other. Today, bereft of understanding of fundamental issues and writings in the development of liberal democracy, computer geeks devise ever better ways to track people . . . simply because they can and it's cool. Humanists on the other hand do not understand the underlying technology and are convinced, for example, that tracking meta-data means the government reads their emails.

C. P. Snow's two cultures not only do not talk to each other, they simply act as if the other doesn't exist.

That might have been acceptable in 1959, because technology and policy didn't interact with each other often or as closely as they do now. Today, it's a different story. Technological mishaps can have catastrophic consequences. It's time we crossed the streams. Policy makers and technologists need to work together. They need to learn each other's languages and educate each other.

The solution to this consists of two halves. First, policy makers need to understand technology. In my fantasy world, policy decisions look like they do in *Star Trek: The Next Generation*. There, everyone sits around a conference table, and the technologists explain the meaning of data and scientific realities to Captain Picard. Picard listens, considers the facts and his options, then makes a policy decision informed by science and technology.

That's not the way it works in the real world. Too often, policy makers don't understand science and technology. Too often, they have their agendas and preconceived notions, and they try to force the science to fit. Sometimes they even brag about not understanding technologies. Lobbyists are often happy to provide pseudoscience to match any policies. And their plates are so full with a range of obligations that they don't have the time to fully comprehend the information that's put in front of them.

In Chapter 11, I mentioned Australia's attempts to legislate backdoors in security systems. Answering a press question in 2017, Prime Minister Malcolm Turnbull said: "Well the laws of Australia prevail in Australia, I can assure you of that. The laws of mathematics are very commendable, but the only law that applies in Australia is the law of Australia." This statement, of course, is laughably wrong and attracted widespread, justified mockery. When the laws of Australia and mathematics contradict, the laws of mathematics will prevail every time.

Similarly, I don't think most policy makers fully comprehend the risks posed by large corporate-held databases full of our personal information, or the threats to our nation's critical infrastructure from both hackers and nation-states. I don't think they understand the fundamental concepts of computer security that I enumerated in Chapter 1, or the failures I discussed in Chapters 2 and 3.

Policy must take mathematics, science, and engineering into account. Policy shouldn't pretend that things that are true are not. Policy can't force things to be true that are not. I regard policy as the primary mechanism for addressing our computer security problems. All of our security policy issues will have strong technological components, but we will never get the policy right if policy makers get the technology wrong. This isn't about turning policy makers into technologists, but ensuring that they have a technological intuition that helps them understand technologists and make decisions about technology. Ignorance is no longer an option.

That said, as important as it will be for policy makers to understand technology, that won't be enough. The second half of solving the divide between tech and policy is for technologists to get involved in policy. Not all of them, of course, but we need more public-interest technologists like these people:

Latanya Sweeney directs the Data Privacy Lab at Harvard, where she's a professor of government and technology. She's probably the best analyst of de-anonymization, and regularly demonstrates how different anonymity techniques don't work. She has also exposed bias in Internet algorithms, and has made significant contributions to privacy technologies. In 2014, she spent a year as chief technologist for the Federal Trade Commission.

Susan Landau is currently a professor in cybersecurity at Tufts University. She's a cryptographer and computer security technologist who has worked at both Sun Microsystems and Google. Today, she's easily the best thinker and communicator we have on the value of ubiquitous encryption in the face of the FBI's "going dark" fears, writing books and articles, and testifying before Congress on the topic.

Ed Felten is a Princeton computer science professor who has done considerable security research in a variety of areas. He's probably best known for his analysis of the security of electronic voting machines. In 2010, he was appointed chief technologist for the Federal Trade Commission, and he was deputy US chief technology officer from 2015 to 2017.

I could fill the chapter with names and stories—Ashkan Soltani, Raquel Romano, Chris Soghoian, others—but our needs are much greater than the prominent early adopters who made the leap from technical roles into the development of security policy. Technologists need to permeate policy at all levels, not just in the most visible roles. They need to be on legislative staffs, in regulatory agencies and nongovernment watchdog organizations, members of the press, and think tank policy wonks. We need a lot more of this than we have today.

There are programs to put technologists into policy positions. Tech-Congress is a fellowship program housed at New America, and it places technologists on congressional staffs. The Open Web Fellowship program places technologists within nonprofit organizations. Its focus is currently on organizations that work to protect the open Internet and more broadly to serve the public interest on issues of Internet policy.

Other programs try to harness technology for policy. Code for America is focused on plugging people with engineering and other technology skills into local governments to affect how systems are designed and implemented.

The Electronic Frontier Foundation, where I also serve on the board, has long blended technological and policy expertise. So does the Electronic Privacy Information Center, where I used to serve on the board. Through its Speech, Privacy, and Technology project, the ACLU focuses on the civil liberties impact of new technologies. Other organizations, like Human Rights Watch and Amnesty International, are beginning to tread into this area, albeit more slowly than I would like.

Many universities now offer interdisciplinary degree programs that blend technology and policy. MIT houses the Internet Policy Research Initiative, which offers courses that provide students with an integrated understanding of technology and public policy. Georgetown Law has the Center on Privacy and Technology. Many schools offer joint law and technology degrees. I teach at the Harvard Kennedy School of Government as part of its Digital HKS program.

These are great, but they're still all exceptions. We need to create a viable career path for public-interest technologists. We need courses and degree programs that blend technology and policy. We need internships, fellowships, and full-time jobs in organizations that need these skills. We need technology companies to offer sabbaticals for staff wanting to explore this path, and to value their experience in policy after they return to the business world. We need a career path that ensures that even though newcomers to this field won't earn as much as they would in a high-tech startup, they will have promising professional futures. The security of our computerized and networked society—meaning the security of ourselves, families, homes, businesses, and communities—depends on it.

A good model can be found in public-interest law. In the early 1970s, there was really no such thing. But after the Ford Foundation and other philanthropies decided to support fledgling public-interest law firms, the number of attorneys in the field exploded. In the late 1960s, there were 92 public-interest law centers in the US; by 2000, there were over a thousand. Today, 20% of the graduating class of Harvard Law School go directly into public-interest law, rather than starting at a law firm or a corporation. That experience is valued and serves these lawyers well in their careers, wherever they end up next.

Computer science isn't like that. Practically none of Harvard's graduating class, or that of any other university, go into public-interest technology. It's not a career path that programmers and engineers generally think about. I don't mean to blame the students here. There aren't public-interest jobs waiting for these people, nor does public-interest experience become an important part of their résumés.

This need to combine technology and policy transcends security. Nearly all of the major policy debates of the 21st century will involve technology. Whether the subject is weapons of mass destruction, robots, climate change, food safety, or drones, understanding policy demands understanding the relevant science and technology. If we don't get more technologists working on policy, we'll wind up with bad policy.

More generally, we need to start making moral and ethical and political decisions about how the Internet+ should work. We've built a world where programmers had an inherent right to code the world as they wanted to see it, indemnified against any harm they might have caused along the way. We accepted it because what they decided didn't matter very much. Now it very much matters, and I think this privilege needs to end.

You, the reader, can help bring this all about. We've been mesmerized by the incredible promise of these technologies, while failing to anticipate the problems. My hope is that the news stories of the past couple of years—and this book—have changed that. Now you have to push against the status quo. Encourage your elected officials to take these threats seriously. Make Internet+ security and privacy a campaign issue. It won't matter to our leaders if it doesn't matter to us.

The Internet+ is coming. With little forethought or architecting or planning, it's coming. It's going to change everything in ways we can only imagine and in ways we can't yet imagine. It'll change security, too: more autonomy, more real-world consequences, fewer off switches, and much greater risks.

It's coming faster than most of us think, and certainly too fast for us to prepare for with the tools we have now. We need to do better. We need to get ahead of it. We need to start making better choices. We need to start building security systems as robust as the threats. We need laws and policies that address the threats and the economics and the psychology properly, and won't become obsolete with changing technologies.

Our only hope of getting there is to bring together technologists and policy makers in that mythical *Star Trek* briefing room to work this out. Now.

ACKNOWLEDGMENTS

After a dozen books, you'd think I would have the process down pretty well by now. Even so, every book is different. I started this book too soon after *Data and Goliath* and, as a result, had a few false starts at writing it. I started writing the book you've just read in the summer of 2017, and submitted it for publication at the end of March 2018.

I have an ace team of people who have worked on my recent books, and they all came together for this book as well. Kathleen Seidel is a researcher extraordinaire, who also has a good eye for prose, both macro and micro. Beth Friedman has copyedited everything I've written for 20 years now. She knows me and my writing style, and I don't know how I would manage without her. She not only edited the book before I submitted it to the publisher, but dealt with the in-house copyeditor so I didn't have to. Finally, Rebecca Kessler provided a much-needed developmental edit late in the writing process. She is also invaluable. To those three I added Katherine Mansted, who stepped in late in the process to provide additional research and summarization.

Many people read and commented on all or part of the manuscript in draft. Every mistake they found, or muddied thinking they flagged, made the book better. They are Michael Adame, Ross Anderson, Steve Bass,

Michael Brennan, John Bruce, Cody Charette, John Davis, Judith Donath, Nora Ellingsen, Mieke Eoyang, Greg Falco, Hubert Feyrer, John Fousek, Brett Frischmann, Blair Ganson, Jason Giffey, Jack Goldsmith, Chloe Goodwin, Sarah Grant, Eldar Haber, Bill Herdle, Trey Herr, Christopher Izant, Andrei Jaffe, Danielle Kehl, Eliot Kim, Xia King, Jonathan Korn, Nadiya Kostyuk, Alexander Krey, Lydia Lichlyter, Aleecia McDonald, Daniel Miessler, Adam Montville, Kee Nethery, David O'Brien, Christen Paine, David Perry, Stuart Russell, Martin Schneier, Nick Sinai, Nathaniel Sobel, Hannah Solomon-Strauss, Lance Spitzner, Stephen Taylor, Marc van Zadelhoff, Arun Vishwanath, Sara M. Watson, Jarad Webber, Tom Wheeler, and Ben Wizner. It is no exaggeration to say that this would be a much worse book without them.

W. W. Norton remains a superlative publisher, and I would like to thank my original editor, Jeff Shreve, as well as Brendan Curry, who took over when he left. Jeff signed that too-soon contract and was patient as I flailed about and missed my original deadline. I know it's a cliché to say that my editor never lost faith in me—and honestly, I have no idea what was going on in his head—but he *claimed* to have never lost faith in me. And Norton never took the advance back, even when I offered it. Brendan Curry had an easier time of it; by the time he showed up, I was actually making progress. His work through the publication process was exemplary, especially in the face of my constantly pushing Norton to compress the timeline.

Similarly, Susan Rabiner remains a superlative agent. If it were just negotiating a contract, anyone could do it. But I am continually surprised by how important it is to have someone between myself and the publisher.

I would also like to thank Harvard University—specifically, the Berkman Klein Center for Internet and Society, the Cybersecurity Project at the Belfer Center for Science and International Affairs, and the Harvard Kennedy School of Government in general—for giving me a home to write, speak, and teach. I treasure my colleagues and friends at those institutions, and their ideas and ideals permeate this book. Across Cambridge, I would like to thank my primary employer, Resilient Systems (which became IBM Resilient and which will soon simply be part of IBM Security) for giving me free rein to write and publish this book.

And finally, I would like to thank my wife of 21 years, Karen Cooper, and all my friends and colleagues, for putting up with me while I was writing this book. I tend to have a codependent relationship with my book manuscripts. When they're doing well, I'm okay. When they're experiencing problems, I'm unhappy. Like all books, this one had its moments. I thank you all for your patience and kindness.

NOTES

INTRODUCTION: EVERYTHING IS BECOMING A COMPUTER

1 **A video shows the driver's terrified expression:** Andy Greenberg (21 Jul 2015), "Hackers remotely kill a Jeep on the highway—with me in it," *Wired*, https://www.wired.com/2015/07/hackers-remotely-kill-jeep-highway, https://www.youtube.com/watch?v=MKoSrxBC1xs (video).

1 **They hacked in through the diagnostics port:** Andy Greenberg (1 Aug 2016), "The Jeep hackers are back to prove car hacking can get much worse," *Wired*, https://www.wired.com/2016/08/jeep-hackers-return-high-speed-steering-acceleration-hacks.

1 **They hacked in through the DVD player:** Ishtiaq Rouf et al. (12 Aug 2010), "Security and privacy vulnerabilities of in-car wireless networks: A tire pressure monitoring system case study," *19th USENIX Security Symposium*, http://www.winlab.rutgers.edu/~Gruteser/papers/xu_tpms10.pdf.

1 **through the OnStar navigation system:** Jim Finkle and Bernie Woodall (30 Jul 2015), "Researcher says can hack GM's OnStar app, open vehicle, start engine," *Reuters*, http://www.reuters.com/article/us-gm-hacking-idUSKCN0Q42FI20150730.

1 **and the computers embedded in the tires:** Ishtiaq Rouf et al. (12 Aug 2010), "Security and privacy vulnerabilities of in-car wireless networks: A tire pressure monitoring system case study," *19th USENIX Security Symposium*, http://www.winlab.rutgers.edu/~Gruteser/papers/xu_tpms10.pdf.

1 **via the entertainment system:** Kim Zetter (16 Jun 2016), "Feds say that banned researcher commandeered plane," *Wired*, https://www.wired.com/2015/05/feds-say-banned-researcher-commandeered-plane.

1 **through air-to-ground communications systems:** Sam Grobart (12 Apr 2013), "Hack-

ing an airplane with only an Android phone," *Bloomberg*, http://www.bloomberg.com /news/articles/2013-04-12/hacking-an-airplane-with-only-an-android-phone.

2 **remote hack of a Boeing 757:** Calvin Biesecker (8 Nov 2017), "Boeing 757 testing shows airplanes vulnerable to hacking, DHS says," *Aviation Today*, http://www.aviationtoday .com/2017/11/08/boeing-757-testing-shows-airplanes-vulnerable-hacking-dhs-says.

2 **In 2016, hackers—presumably Russian:** Kim Zetter (12 Jun 2017), "The malware used against the Ukrainian power grid is more dangerous than anyone thought," *Vice Motherboard*, https://motherboard.vice.com/en_us/article/zmeyg8/ukraine -power-grid-malware-crashoverride-industroyer. Kevin Poulsen (12 Jun 2017), "U.S. power companies warned 'nightmare' cyber weapon already causing blackouts," *Daily Beast*, https://www.thedailybeast.com/newly-discovered-nightmare-cyber -weapon-is-already-causing-blackouts.

2 **The CrashOverride attack was different:** Kim Zetter (3 Mar 2016), "Inside the cunning, unprecedented hack of Ukraine's power grid," *Wired*, https://www.wired.com /2016/03/inside-cunning-unprecedented-hack-ukraines-power-grid.

2 **There, the attackers:** Jim Finkle (7 Jan 2016), "U.S. firm blames Russian 'Sandworm' hackers for Ukraine outage," *Reuters*, https://www.reuters.com/article/us-ukraine -cybersecurity-sandworm/u-s-firm-blames-russian-sandworm-hackers-for-ukraine -outage-idUSKBN0UM00N20160108.

2 **One of the station operators recorded:** C&M News (24 Jun 2017), "Watch how hackers took over a Ukrainian power station," *YouTube*, https://www.youtube.com /watch?v=8ThgK1WXUgk.

2 **It had a variety of other "payloads":** Dragos, Inc. (13 Jun 2017), "CRASHOVER-RIDE: Analysis of the threat to electric grid operations," https://dragos.com/blog /crashoverride/CrashOverride-01.pdf.

2 **And while this weapon was fired:** Nicholas Weaver makes this point. Nicholas Weaver (14 Jun 2017), "A cyber-weapon warhead test," *Lawfare*, https://www .lawfareblog.com/cyber-weapon-warhead-test.

2 **In recent years, Russian hackers penetrated:** This operation has been named "Dragonfly." Security Response Attack Investigation Team (20 Oct 2017), "Dragonfly: Western energy sector targeted by sophisticated attack group," *Symantec Corporation*, https://www.symantec.com/connect/blogs/dragonfly-western -energy-sector-targeted-sophisticated-attack-group. Nicole Perlroth and David Sanger (15 Mar 2018), "Cyberattacks put Russian fingers on the switch at power plants, U.S. says," *New York Times*, https://www.nytimes.com/2018/03/15/us/politics /russia-cyberattacks.html.

2 **The hacker wrote a program:** Christopher Meyer (8 Feb 2017), "This teen hacked 150,000 printers to show how the Internet of Things is shit," *Vice Motherboard*, https:// motherboard.vice.com/en_us/article/nzqayz/this-teen-hacked-150000-printers-to -show-how-the-internet-of-things-is-shit.

2 **Earlier in the same year:** Carl Straumsheim (27 Jan 2017), "More anti-Semitic fliers printed at universities," *Inside Higher Ed*, https://www.insidehighered.com/quicktakes /2017/01/27/more-anti-semitic-fliers-printed-universities.

3 **These are still in their infancy:** Jennifer Kite-Powell (29 Oct 2014), "3D printed virus to attack cancer cells," *Forbes*, https://www.forbes.com/sites/jenniferhicks/2014/10 /29/3d-printed-virus-to-attack-cancer-cells/#7a8dbddb104b. Katie Collins (16 Oct

2014), "Meet the biologist hacking 3D printed cancer-fighting viruses," *Wired UK*, https://www.wired.co.uk/article/andrew-hessel-autodesk.

4 **Modern pacemakers:** University of the Basque Country (28 Jan 2015), "Pacemakers with Internet connection, a not-so-distant goal," *Science Daily*, https://www.sciencedaily.com/releases/2015/01/150128113715.htm.

4 **insulin pumps:** Brooke McAdams and Ali Rizvi (4 Jan 2016), "An overview of insulin pumps and glucose sensors for the generalist," *Journal of Clinical Medicine* 5, no. 1, http://www.mdpi.com/2077-0383/5/1/5. Tim Vanderveen (27 May 2014), "From smart pumps to intelligent infusion systems: The promise of interoperability," *Patient Safety and Quality Healthcare*, http://psqh.com/may-june-2014/from-smart-pumps-to-intelligent-infusion-systems-the-promise-of-interoperability.

4 **Pills are becoming smart:** Pam Belluck (13 Nov 2017), "First digital pill approved to worries about biomedical 'Big Brother,'" *New York Times*, https://www.nytimes.com/2017/11/13/health/digital-pill-fda.html.

4 **Smart contact lenses will:** Diego Barretino (25 Jul 2017), "Smart contact lenses and eye implants will give doctors medical insights," *IEEE Spectrum*, https://spectrum.ieee.org/biomedical/devices/smart-contact-lenses-and-eye-implants-will-give-doctors-medical-insights.

4 **Fitness trackers are smart:** Brendan Borrell (29 Jun 2017), "Precise devices: Fitness trackers are more accurate than ever," *Consumer Reports*, https://www.consumerreports.org/fitness-trackers/precise-devices-fitness-trackers-are-more-accurate-than-ever.

4 **a smart collar for your dog:** Anthony Cuthbertson (12 Apr 2016), "This smart collar turns your pet into a living Tamagotchi," *Newsweek*, http://www.newsweek.com/smart-collar-pet-kyon-tamagotchi-gps-dog-446754.

4 **a smart toy for your cat:** Owen Williams (21 Feb 2016), "All I want for Christmas is LG's adorable cat toy," *Next Web*, http://thenextweb.com/gadgets/2016/02/21/all-i-want-for-christmas-is-lgs-adorable-cat-toy.

4 **a smart pen:** Livescribe, Inc. (accessed 24 Apr 2018), "Livescribe Smartpens," http://www.livescribe.com/en-us/smartpen.

4 **a smart toothbrush:** Brandon Griggs (22 Feb 2014), "'Smart' toothbrush grades your brushing habits," *CNN*, http://www.cnn.com/2014/01/09/tech/innovation/smart-toothbrush-kolibree. Sarmistha Acharya (23 Feb 2016), "MWC 2016: Oral-B unveils smart toothbrush that uses mobile camera to help you brush your teeth," *International Business Times*, http://www.ibtimes.co.uk/mwc-2016-oral-b-unveils-smart-toothbrush-that-uses-mobile-camera-help-you-brush-better-1545414.

4 **a smart coffee cup:** Diana Budds (9 Nov 2017), "A smart coffee cup? It's more useful than it sounds," *Fast Company*, https://www.fastcodesign.com/90150019/the-perfect-smart-coffee-cup-is-here.

4 **a smart sex toy:** Phoebe Luckhurst (3 Aug 2017), "These sex toys and smart hook-up apps will make your summer hotter than ever," *Evening Standard*, https://www.standard.co.uk/lifestyle/london-life/these-sex-toys-and-smart-apps-will-make-your-summer-hotter-than-ever-a3603056.html.

4 **a smart Barbie doll:** Samuel Gibbs (13 Mar 2015), "Privacy fears over 'smart' Barbie that can listen to your kids," *Guardian*, https://www.theguardian.com/technology/2015/mar/13/smart-barbie-that-can-listen-to-your-kids-privacy-fears-mattel.

4 **a smart tape measure:** Stanley (accessed 24 Apr 2018), "Smart Measure Pro," http://www.stanleytools.com/explore/stanley-mobile-apps/stanley-smart-measure-pro.

4 **a smart sensor for your plants:** April Glaser (26 Apr 2016), "Dig gardening? Plant some connected tech this spring," *Wired*, https://www.wired.com/2016/04/connected-gardening-tech-iot.

4 **a smart motorcycle helmet:** Samar Warsi (26 Dec 2017), "A motorcycle helmet will call an ambulance and text your family if you have an accident," *Vice Motherboard*, https://motherboard.vice.com/en_us/article/a37bwp/smart-motorcycle-helmet-helli-will-call-ambulance-skully-pakistan.

4 **smart thermostats:** Christopher Snow (14 Mar 2017), "Everyone's buying a smart thermostat—here's how to pick one," *USA Today*, https://www.usatoday.com/story/tech/reviewedcom/2017/03/14/smart-thermostats-are-2017s-hottest-home-gadget-heres-how-to-pick-the-right-one-for-you/99125582.

4 **smart power outlets:** Kashmir Hill and Surya Mattu (7 Feb 2018), "The house that spied on me," *Gizmodo*, https://gizmodo.com/the-house-that-spied-on-me-1822429852.

4 **a smart bathroom scale:** Rose Kennedy (14 Aug 2017), "Want a scale that tells more than your weight? Smart scales are it," *Atlanta Journal-Constitution*, http://www.ajc.com/news/health-med-fit-science/want-scale-that-tells-more-than-your-weight-smart-scales-are/XHpLELYnLgn8cQtBtsay6J.

4 **a smart toilet:** Alina Bradford (1 Feb 2016), "Why smart toilets might actually be worth the upgrade," *CNET*, http://www.cnet.com/how-to/smart-toilets-make-your-bathroom-high-tech.

4 **smart light bulbs:** Alex Colon and Timothy Torres (30 May 2017), "The best smart light bulbs of 2017," *PC Magazine*, https://www.pcmag.com/article2/0,2817,2483488,00.asp.

4 **a smart door lock:** Eugene Kim and Christina Farr (10 Oct 2017), "Amazon is exploring ways to deliver items to your car trunk and the inside of your home," *CNBC*, https://www.cnbc.com/2017/10/10/amazon-is-in-talks-with-phrame-and-is-working-on-a-smart-doorbell.html.

4 **a smart bed:** Adam Gabbatt (5 Jan 2017), "Don't lose your snooze: The technology that's promising a better night's sleep," *Guardian*, https://www.theguardian.com/technology/2017/jan/05/sleep-technology-ces-2017-las-vegas-new-products.

4 **Cities are starting to embed smart sensors:** Matt Hamblen (1 Oct 2015), "Just what IS a smart city?" *Computerworld*, https://www.computerworld.com/article/2986403/internet-of-things/just-what-is-a-smart-city.html.

4 **Smart billboards will recognize you:** Tim Johnson (20 Sep 2017), "Smart billboards are checking you out—and making judgments," *Miami Herald*, http://www.miamiherald.com/news/nation-world/national/article174197441.html.

5 **Those spatial metaphors don't make sense:** This is why I am still using the uppercase "Internet" in this book, even though most style guides now prefer lowercase. One of the premises of this book is that the Internet is a singular connected network—that any part of it can affect any other part of it—and needs to be viewed in this way to properly talk about security.

5 **"the network of physical objects":** Gartner (accessed 24 Apr 2018), "Internet of Things," *Gartner IT Glossary*, https://www.gartner.com/it-glossary/internet-of-things.

5 **In 2017, there were 8.4 billion things:** Gartner (7 Feb 2017), "Gartner says 8.4 bil-

lion connected 'things' will be in use in 2017, up 31 percent from 2016," https://www
.gartner.com/newsroom/id/3598917.

5 **By 2020, there are likely to be:** Tony Danova (2 Oct 2013), "Morgan Stanley: 75 billion
devices will be connected to the Internet of Things by 2020," *Business Insider*, http://
www.businessinsider.com/75-billion-devices-will-be-connected-to-the-internet-by
-2020-2013-10. Peter Brown (25 Jan 2017), "20 billion connected Internet of Things
devices in 2017, IHS Markit says," *Electronics 360*, http://electronics360.globalspec
.com/article/8032/20-billion-connected-internet-of-things-devices-in-2017-ihs
-markit-says. Julia Boorstin (1 Feb 2016), "An Internet of Things that will number
ten billions," *CNBC*, https://www.cnbc.com/2016/02/01/an-internet-of-things-that
-will-number-ten-billions.html. Statista (2018), "Internet of Things (IoT) connected
devices installed base worldwide from 2015 to 2025 (in billions)," https://www
.statista.com/statistics/471264/iot-number-of-connected-devices-worldwide.

6 **your T-shirt someday will:** Michael Sawh (26 Sep 2017), "The best smart clothing:
From biometric shirts to contactless payment jackets," *Wareable*, https://www
.wareable.com/smart-clothing/best-smart-clothing.

6 **"The 'Smart Everything' Trend":** J. R. Raphael (7 Jan 2016), "The 'smart'-everything
trend has officially turned stupid," *Computerworld*, http://www.computerworld.com
/article/3019713/internet-of-things/smart-everything-trend.html.

7 **It's an Internet that senses:** Something that senses, plans, and acts is the classic definition of a robot. Robin R. Murphy (2000), "Robotic paradigms," in *Introduction to AI
Robotics*, MIT Press, https://books.google.com/books/about/?id=RVlnL_X6FrwC.

8 **Or, for short, the Internet+:** In 2016, I tried calling this the "World-Sized Web." "Inter-
net+" is a better term. Bruce Schneier (2 Feb 2016), "The Internet of Things will be the
world's biggest robot," *Forbes*, https://www.forbes.com/sites/bruceschneier/2016/02
/02/the-internet-of-things-will-be-the-worlds-biggest-robot.

10 **It can be a hard argument to make:** Even the conservative *Economist* published an
editorial in 2017 supporting both regulation and liabilities for IoT devices. *Economist*
(8 Apr 2017), "How to manage the computer-security threat," https://www.economist
.com/news/leaders/21720279-incentives-software-firms-take-security-seriously
-are-too-weak-how-manage.

11 **Although this is not a book about:** This is an excellent book on that topic: Alexander
Klimburg (2017), *The Darkening Web: The War for Cyberspace*, Penguin, https://books
.google.com/books/about/?id=kytBvgAACAAJ.

12 **"we're facing 21st-century issues":** Cambridge Cyber Security Summit (4 Oct 2017),
"Transparency, communication and conflict," *CNBC*, https://www.cnbc.com/video
/2017/10/09/cambridge-cyber-security-summit-transparency-communication-and
-conflict.html.

PART I: THE TRENDS

15 **In 2017, a hacker bragged:** Ankit Anubhav (20 Jul 2017), "IoT thermostat bug allows
hackers to turn up the heat," *NewSky Security*, https://blog.newskysecurity.com/iot
-thermostat-bug-allows-hackers-to-turn-up-the-heat-948e554e5e8b.

15 **Separately, a group of researchers:** Lorenzo Franceschi-Bicchierai (7 Aug 2016),
"Hackers make the first-ever ransomware for smart thermostats," *Vice Motherboard*,
https://motherboard.vice.com/en_us/article/aekj9j/internet-of-things-ransomware
-smart-thermostat.

15 **But next time might be my brand:** No, I'm not telling you what brand I have.

16 **crashing airplanes:** Kim Zetter (26 May 2015), "Is it possible for passengers to hack commercial aircraft?" *Wired*, http://www.wired.com/2015/05/possible-passengers -hack-commercial-aircraft. Gerald L. Dillingham, Gregory C. Wilshusen, and Naba-jyoti Barkakati (14 Apr 2015), "Air traffic control: FAA needs a more comprehensive approach to address cybersecurity as agency transitions to NextGen," *GAO-15-370*, US Government Accountability Office, http://www.gao.gov/assets/670/669627.pdf.

16 **disabling cars:** Andy Greenberg (21 Jul 2015), "Hackers remotely kill a Jeep on the highway—with me in it," *Wired*, https://www.wired.com/2015/07/hackers-remotely -kill-jeep-highway, https://www.youtube.com/watch?v=MK0SrxBC1xs (video).

16 **tinkering with medical devices:** Liviu Arsene (20 Nov 2014), "Hacking vulner-able medical equipment puts millions at risk," *Information Week*, http://www .informationweek.com/partner-perspectives/bitdefender/hacking-vulnerable -medical-equipment-puts-millions-at-risk/a/d-id/1319873.

16 **We're worried about being GPS-hacked:** David Hambling (10 Aug 2017), "Ships fooled in GPS spoofing attack suggest Russian cyberweapon," *New Scientist*, https:// www.newscientist.com/article/2143499-ships-fooled-in-gps-spoofing-attack -suggest-russian-cyberweapon.

16 **With smart homes, attacks can mean:** Colin Neagle (2 Apr 2015), "Smart home hacking is easier than you think," *Network World*, http://www.networkworld.com/ article/2905053/security0/smart-home-hacking-is-easier-than-you-think.html.

16 **about 600 million people in the world do:** Ad blockers represent the largest con-sumer boycott in human history. Sean Blanchfield (1 Feb 2017), "The state of the blocked web: 2017 global adblock report," *PageFair*, https://pagefair.com/downloads /2017/01/PageFair-2017-Adblock-Report.pdf.

16 **some sites now employ ad-blocker blockers:** Kate Murphy (20 Feb 2016), "The ad blocking wars," *New York Times*, https://www.nytimes.com/2016/02/21/opinion/ sunday/the-ad-blocking-wars.html.

16 **Spam is an arms race:** Pedro H. Calais Guerra et al. (13–14 Jul 2010), "Exploring the spam arms race to characterize spam evolution," *Electronic Messaging, Anti-Abuse and Spam Conference (CEAS 2010)*, https://honeytarg.cert.br/spampots/papers/ spampots-ceas10.pdf.

17 **"skimmers" to steal card information and PINs:** Alfred Ng (1 Oct 2017), "Credit card thieves are getting smarter. You can, too," *CNET*, https://www.cnet.com/news/credit -card-skimmers-thieves-are-getting-smarter-you-can-too.

17 **remote attacks against ATMs over the Internet:** David Sancho, Numaan Huq, and Massimiliano Michenzi (2017), "Cashing in on ATM malware: A comprehensive look at various attack types," *Trend Micro*, https://documents.trendmicro.com/assets/ white_papers/wp-cashing-in-on-atm-malware.pdf.

1. COMPUTERS ARE STILL HARD TO SECURE

19 **"The only truly secure system":** Quoted in A. K. Dewdney (1 Mar 1989), "Computer recreations: Of worms, viruses and core war," *Scientific American*, http://corewar.co .uk/dewdney/1989-03.htm.

19 **Rod Beckstrom summarized it this way:** Rod Beckstrom (2 Nov 2011), "Statement to the London Conference on Cyberspace, Internet Corporation for Assigned Names

and Numbers (ICANN)," https://www.icann.org/en/system/files/files/beckstrom
-speech-cybersecurity-london-02nov11-en.pdf.

19 **"Security is a process, not a product":** Bruce Schneier (1 Apr 2000), "The process of
security," *Information Security*, https://www.schneier.com/essays/archives/2000/04
/the_process_of_secur.html.

20 **I play Pokémon Go on my phone:** Mystic, level 40. I managed to catch them all for
about a week in August 2017 between when I caught a Farfetch'd in Seoul and when
Mewto was released in Yokohama, and again from November 2017 after I caught my
first Mewto to before Generation 3 was released in December. I travel a lot, and was
able to catch all the regional Pokémon in their original regions. Still, I think it will
be a while before I catch all of the Generation 3 regionals.

20 **We occasionally lose important data:** In late 2017, I had to quickly replace my
iPhone. As part of the process, I enabled iCloud and tried to back up my phone data.
I'm not sure how, but iCloud managed to delete 20 years of calendar history. I don't
know what I would have done if I hadn't had a recent backup.

20 **Some of them are inherent:** Roger A. Grimes (8 Jul 2014), "5 reasons why software
bugs still plague us," *CSO*, https://www.csoonline.com/article/2608330/security/5
-reasons-why-software-bugs-still-plague-us.html. David Heinemeier Hansson (7
Mar 2016), "Software has bugs. This is normal," *Signal v. Noise*, https://m.signalvnoise
.com/software-has-bugs-this-is-normal-f64761a262ca.

20 **Microsoft spent the decade after 2002:** In 2002, Bill Gates sent his landmark "trustworthy computing" memo to all employees. In that same year, Windows development
shut down completely so that every employee could take security training. The company's first Security Development Lifecycle security tools appeared in 2004. Abhishek
Baxi (10 Mar 2014), "From a Bill Gates memo to an industry practice: The story of
Security Development Lifecycle," *Windows Central*, https://www.windowscentral
.com/bill-gates-memo-industry-practice-story-security-development-cycle.

20 **Apple is known for its quality software:** To be fair, the company had some pretty
significant bugs in 2017. Adrian Kingsley-Hughes (19 Dec 2017), "Apple seems to
have forgotten about the whole 'it just works' thing," *ZDNet*, http://www.zdnet.com
/article/apple-seems-to-have-forgotten-about-the-whole-it-just-works-thing.

20 **And NASA had a famous quality control process:** National Research Council (1996),
"Case study: NASA space shuttle flight control software," in *Statistical Software Engineering*, National Academies Press, https://www.nap.edu/read/5018/chapter/4.

21 **NASA still has crazily conservative:** Martha Wetherholt (1 Sep 2015), "NASA's
approach to software assurance," *Crosstalk*, http://static1.1.sqspcdn.com/static/f
/702523/26502332/1441086732177/201509-Wetherholt.pdf.

21 **An example is something called:** Peter Bright (25 Aug 2015), "How security flaws
work: The buffer overflow," *Ars Technica*, https://arstechnica.com/information
-technology/2015/08/how-security-flaws-work-the-buffer-overflow.

21 **We don't know what percentage:** Eric Rescorla (1 Jan 2005), "Is finding security
holes a good idea?" *IEEE Security & Privacy* 3, no. 1, https://dl.acm.org/citation
.cfm?id=1048817. Andy Ozment and Stuart Schechter (1 Jul 2006), "Milk or wine:
Does software security improve with age?" in *Proceedings of the 15th USENIX Security
Symposium*, https://www.microsoft.com/en-us/research/publication/milk-or-wine
-does-software-security-improve-with-age.

21 **It remained undiscovered for two years:** Heather Kelly (9 Apr 2014), "The 'Heart-bleed' security flaw that affects most of the Internet," *CNN*, https://www.cnn.com /2014/04/08/tech/web/heartbleed-openssl/index.html.

21 **The Spectre and Meltdown vulnerabilities:** Andy Greenberg (7 Jan 2018), "Triple Meltdown: How so many researchers found a 20-year-old chip flaw at the same time," *Wired*, https://www.wired.com/story/meltdown-spectre-bug-collision-intel-chip -flaw-discovery.

21 **Keeping IoT devices cheap means:** Sandy Clark et al. (6–10 Dec 2010), "Familiarity breeds contempt: The honeymoon effect and the role of legacy code in zero-day vulnerabilities," in *Proceedings of the 26th Annual Computer Security Applications Conference*, https://dl.acm.org/citation.cfm?id=1920299.

22 **In April 2010, for about 18 minutes:** Nate Anderson (17 Nov 2010), "How China swallowed 15% of 'Net traffic for 18 minutes," *Ars Technica*, https://arstechnica.com/information -technology/2010/11/how-china-swallowed-15-of-net-traffic-for-18-minutes.

22 **Because there's no authentication:** Some meager security features have been added by some large networks, but the document that defines BGP explicitly states: "Secu-rity issues are not discussed in this document." Yakov Rekhter and Tony Li (Mar 1995), "A Border Gateway Protocol 4 (BGP-4)," *Network Working Group, Internet Engi-neering Task Force*, https://tools.ietf.org/html/rfc1771.

22 **We know from documents disclosed:** Axel Arnbak and Sharon Goldberg (30 Jun 2014), "Loopholes for circumventing the Constitution: Unrestrained bulk surveil-lance on Americans by collecting network traffic abroad," *Michigan Telecommuni-cations and Technology Law Review* 21, no. 2, https://repository.law.umich.edu/cgi /viewcontent.cgi?article=1204&context=mttlr. Sharon Goldberg (22 Jun 2017), "Sur-veillance without borders: The 'traffic shaping' loophole and why it matters," *Century Foundation*, https://tcf.org/content/report/surveillance-without-borders-the-traffic -shaping-loophole-and-why-it-matters.

22 **In 2013, one company reported:** Jim Cowie (19 Nov 2013), "The new threat: Targeted Internet traffic misdirection," *Vantage Point*, Oracle + Dyn, https://dyn.com/blog /mitm-internet-hijacking.

22 **In 2014, the Turkish government:** Jim Cowie (19 Nov 2013), "The new threat: Targeted Internet traffic misdirection," *Vantage Point*, Oracle + Dyn, https://dyn.com/blog /mitm-internet-hijacking.

22 **In 2017, traffic to and from:** Dan Goodin (13 Dec 2017), "'Suspicious' event routes traffic for big-name sites through Russia," *Ars Technica*, https://arstechnica.com/information -technology/2017/12/suspicious-event-routes-traffic-for-big-name-sites-through -russia.

22 **a 2008 talk at the DefCon hackers conference:** Dan Goodin (27 Aug 2008), "Hijack-ing huge chunks of the internet: A new How To," *Register*, https://www.theregister.co .uk/2008/08/27/bgp_exploit_revealed.

23 **"It's not that we didn't think about security":** Craig Timberg (30 May 2015), "A flaw in the design," *Washington Post*, http://www.washingtonpost.com/sf/business/2015 /05/30/net-of-insecurity-part-1.

23 **"It is highly desirable that Internet carriers":** Brian E. Carpenter, ed. (Jun 1996), "Architectural principles of the Internet," *Network Working Group, Internet Engineer-ing Task Force*, https://www.ietf.org/rfc/rfc1958.txt.

24 **It makes little sense:** Tyler Moore (2010), "The economics of cybersecurity: Principles

and policy options," *International Journal of Critical Infrastructure Protection*, https://tylermoore.utulsa.edu/ijcip10.pdf.

24 **And as with BGP, it's been 20 years:** In 2017, the switchover was again delayed. Internet Corporation for Assigned Names and Numbers (27 Sep 2017), "KSK rollover postponed," https://www.icann.org/news/announcement-2017-09-27-en.

25 **a Canon Pixma printer:** Michael Jordon (12 Sep 2014), "Hacking Canon Pixma printers: Doomed encryption," *Context Information Security*, https://www.contextis.com/blog/hacking-canon-pixma-printers-doomed-encryption.

25 **a Honeywell Prestige thermostat:** Ralph Kinney (25 May 2017), "Will it run Doom? Smart thermostat running classic FPS game Doom," *Zareview*, https://www.zareview.com/will-run-doom-smart-thermostat-running-classic-fps-game-doom.

25 **a Kodak digital camera:** JJ (1 Mar 2010), "The DoomBox," *Dashfest*, http://www.dashfest.com/?p=113.

25 **Even the best DRM systems:** Kyle Orland (19 Oct 2017), "Denuvo's DRM now being cracked within hours of release," *Ars Technica*, https://arstechnica.com/gaming/2017/10/denuvos-drm-ins-now-being-cracked-within-hours-of-release.

26 **It's an old term from cryptography:** Seth Schoen (17 Mar 2016), "Thinking about the term 'backdoor,'" *Electronic Frontier Foundation*, https://www.eff.org/deeplinks/2016/03/thinking-about-term-backdoor.

26 **When the FBI demands:** Bruce Schneier (18 Feb 2016), "Why you should side with Apple, not the FBI, in the San Bernardino iPhone case," *Washington Post*, https://www.washingtonpost.com/posteverything/wp/2016/02/18/why-you-should-side-with-apple-not-the-fbi-in-the-san-bernardino-iphone-case.

26 **When researchers spot a hard-coded:** Dan Goodin (12 Jan 2016), "Et tu, Fortinet? Hard-coded password raises new backdoor eavesdropping fears," *Ars Technica*, https://arstechnica.com/information-technology/2016/01/et-tu-fortinet-hard-coded-password-raises-new-backdoor-eavesdropping-fears.

26 **All computers can be dragooned:** Maria Korolov (6 Dec 2017), "What is a botnet? And why they aren't going away anytime soon," *CSO*, https://www.csoonline.com/article/3240364/hacking/what-is-a-botnet-and-why-they-arent-going-away-anytime-soon.html.

26 **But today, in computers and on the Internet:** This has been true since the beginning of computer security. Here's a quote from a 1979 journal: "Few if any contemporary computer security controls have prevented a tiger team from easily accessing any information sought." Basically, the attackers always win. Roger R. Schell (Jan–Feb 1979), "Computer security: The Achilles' heel of the electronic Air Force?" *Air University Review* 30, no. 2 (reprinted in *Air & Space Power Journal*, Jan–Feb 2013), http://insct.syr.edu/wp-content/uploads/2015/05/Schell_Achilles_Heel.pdf.

27 **Complexity is the worst enemy of security:** Bruce Schneier (19 Nov 1999), "A plea for simplicity: You can't secure what you don't understand," *Information Security*, https://www.schneier.com/essays/archives/1999/11/a_plea_for_simplicit.html.

27 **And our billions of computers:** David McCandless (24 Sep 2015), "How many lines of code does it take?" *Information Is Beautiful*, http://www.informationisbeautiful.net/visualizations/million-lines-of-code.

27 **Computer security experts like to:** Lily Hay Newman (12 Mar 2017), "Hacker lexicon: What is an attack surface?" *Wired*, https://www.wired.com/2017/03/hacker-lexicon-attack-surface.

27 **Users regularly fail to change:** Robert McMillan (17 Sep 2017), "An unexpected security problem in the cloud," *Wall Street Journal*, https://www.wsj.com/articles /an-unexpected-security-problem-in-the-cloud-1505700061.

27 **In 2017, Stanford University blamed:** Elena Kadavny (1 Dec 2017), "Thousands of records exposed in Stanford data breaches," *Palo Alto Online*, https://www .paloaltoonline.com/news/2017/12/01/thousands-of-records-exposed-in-stanford -data-breaches.

28 **"If we were to score cyber":** Dan Geer (6 Aug 2014), "Cybersecurity as realpolitik," *Black Hat 2014*, http://geer.tinho.net/geer.blackhat.6viii14.txt.

28 **Murder is easy, too:** Aside from those social systems, our internal psychology and moral values mostly keep us from murdering others.

28 **The criminals gained access:** Elizabeth A. Harris et al. (17 Jan 2014), "A sneaky path into Target customers' wallets," *New York Times*, https://www.nytimes.com/2014/01 /18/business/a-sneaky-path-into-target-customers-wallets.html.

29 **So when Dyn went down:** Catalin Cimpanu (30 Mar 2017), "New Mirai botnet slams U.S. college with 54-hour DDoS attack," *Bleeping Computer*, https://www .bleepingcomputer.com/news/security/new-mirai-botnet-slams-us-college-with -54-hour-ddos-attack. Manos Antonakakis et al. (8 Aug 2017), "Understanding the Mirai botnet," in *Proceedings of the 26th USENIX Security Symposium*, https://www .usenix.org/system/files/conference/usenixsecurity17/sec17-antonakakis.pdf.

29 **In 2017, hackers penetrated:** Alex Schiffer (21 Jul 2017), "How a fish tank helped hack a casino," *Washington Post*, https://www.washingtonpost.com/news/innovations /wp/2017/07/21/how-a-fish-tank-helped-hack-a-casino.

29 **And two: it's possible that:** This essay describes an interaction between the way Gmail and Netflix interpret e-mail addresses that results in an insecurity: James Fisher (7 Apr 2018), "The dots do matter: How to scam a Gmail user," *Jameshfisher .com*, https://jameshfisher.com/2018/04/07/the-dots-do-matter-how-to-scam-a -gmail-user.html.

29 **In 2012, someone compromised:** Mat Honan (6 Aug 2012), "How Apple and Amazon security flaws led to my epic hacking," *Wired*, https://www.wired.com/2012/08 /apple-amazon-mat-honan-hacking. Mat Honan (17 Aug 2012), "How I resurrected my digital life after an epic hacking," *Wired*, https://www.wired.com/2012/08/mat -honan-data-recovery.

29 **A vulnerability in Samsung:** Pedro Venda (18 Aug 2015), "Hacking DefCon 23's IoT Village Samsung fridge," *Pen Test Partners*, http://www.pentestpartners.com /blog/hacking-defcon-23s-iot-village-samsung-fridge. John Leyden (25 Aug 2015), "Samsung smart fridge leaves Gmail logins open to attack," *Register*, http://www .theregister.co.uk/2015/08/24/smart_fridge_security_fubar.

29 **The gyroscope on your iPhone:** Yan Michalevsky, Gabi Nakibly, and Dan Boneh (20– 22 Aug 2014), "Gyrophone: Recognizing speech from gyroscope signals," in *Proceedings of the 23rd USENIX Security Symposium*, https://crypto.stanford.edu/gyrophone.

29 **The antivirus software sold by Kaspersky:** Dan Goodin (10 Oct 2017), "How Kaspersky AV reportedly was caught helping Russian hackers steal NSA secrets," *Ars Technica*, https://arstechnica.com/information-technology/2017/10/russian-hackers -reportedly-used-kaspersky-av-to-search-for-nsa-secrets.

30 **The attacker who created the Mirai botnet:** Catalin Cimpanu (30 Mar 2017), "New Mirai botnet slams U.S. college with 54-hour DDoS attack," *Bleeping Computer*,

https://www.bleepingcomputer.com/news/security/new-mirai-botnet-slams-us -college-with-54-hour-ddos-attack.

30 **They can hire ransomware-as-a-service:** Tara Seals (18 May 2016), "Enormous malware as a service infrastructure fuels ransomware epidemic," *Infosecurity Magazine*, https://www.infosecurity-magazine.com/news/enormous-malware-as-a-service.

30 **European companies like HackingTeam:** Aaron Sankin (9 Jul 2015), "Forget Hacking Team—many other companies sell surveillance tech to repressive regimes," *Daily Dot*, https://www.dailydot.com/layer8/hacking-team-competitors.

30 **The malware was created by:** US Department of Justice (28 Nov 2017), "Canadian hacker who conspired with and aided Russian FSB officers pleads guilty," https://www.justice.gov/opa/pr/canadian-hacker-who-conspired-and-aided-russian-fsb -officers-pleads-guilty.

31 **"Class break" is a concept from computer security:** Bruce Schneier (3 Jan 2017), "Class breaks," *Schneier on Security*, https://www.schneier.com/blog/archives/2017 /01/class_breaks.html.

31 **A cryptographic flaw forced the government:** Dan Goodin (6 Nov 2017), "Flaw crippling millions of crypto keys is worse than first disclosed," *Ars Technica*, https:// arstechnica.com/information-technology/2017/11/flaw-crippling-millions-of -crypto-keys-is-worse-than-first-disclosed.

31 **According to a 2011 DHS study:** US Department of Homeland Security (Nov 2012), "National risk estimate: Risks to U.S. critical infrastructure from global positioning system disruptions," https://www.hsdl.org/?abstract&did=739832.

32 **In 2012, this happened to Onity:** Andy Greenberg (26 Nov 2012), "Security flaw in common keycard locks exploited in string of hotel room break-ins," *Forbes*, https:// www.forbes.com/sites/andygreenberg/2012/11/26/security-flaw-in-common -keycard-locks-exploited-in-string-of-hotel-room-break-ins.

32 **It took months for Onity to realize:** Andy Greenberg (6 Dec 2012), "Lock firm Onity starts to shell out for security fixes to hotels' hackable locks," *Forbes*, https://www .forbes.com/sites/andygreenberg/2012/12/06/lock-firm-onity-starts-to-shell-out -for-security-fixes-to-hotels-hackable-locks. Andy Greenberg (15 May 2013), "Hotel lock hack still being used in burglaries months after lock firm's fix," *Forbes*, https:// www.forbes.com/sites/andygreenberg/2013/05/15/hotel-lock-hack-still-being-used -in-burglaries-months-after-lock-firms-fix. Andy Greenberg (1 Aug 2017), "The hotel room hacker," *Wired*, https://www.wired.com/2017/08/the-hotel-hacker.

32 **In 1976, cryptography experts estimated:** Whitfield Diffie and Martin E. Hellman (1 Jun 1977), "Exhaustive cryptanalysis of the NBS Data Encryption Standard," *Computer*, https://www-ee.stanford.edu/~hellman/publications/27.pdf.

32 **In my 1995 book *Applied Cryptography*:** Bruce Schneier (1995), *Applied Cryptography*, 2nd edition, Wiley.

32 **In 1998, the Electronic Frontier Foundation:** Electronic Frontier Foundation (1998), *Cracking DES: Secrets of Encryption Research, Wiretap Politics, and Chip Design*, O'Reilly & Associates.

32 **Fast-forward a half decade:** Stephanie K. Pell and Christopher Soghoian (29 Dec 2014), "Your secret Stingray's no secret anymore: The vanishing government monopoly over cell phone surveillance and its impact on national security and consumer privacy," *Harvard Journal of Law and Technology* 28, no. 1, https://papers.ssrn.com /sol3/papers.cfm?abstract_id=2437678.

33 **Fast-forward another half decade:** Kim Zetter (31 Jul 2010), "Hacker spoofs cell phone tower to intercept calls," *Wired*, https://www.wired.com/2010/07/intercepting-cell-phone-calls.

33 **The result is passwords:** My essay about how to choose a secure password: Bruce Schneier (25 Feb 2014), "Choosing a secure password," *Boing Boing*, https://boingboing.net/2014/02/25/choosing-a-secure-password.html.

33 **In the 1970s, IBM mathematicians:** Don Coppersmith (May 1994), "The Data Encryption Standard (DES) and its strength against attacks," *IBM Journal of Research and Development* 38, no. 3, http://simson.net/ref/1994/coppersmith94.pdf.

33 **The NSA classified IBM's discovery:** Eli Biham and Adi Shamir (1990), "Differential cryptanalysis of DES-like cryptosystems," *Journal of Cryptology* 4, no. 1, https://link.springer.com/article/10.1007/BF00630563.

2. PATCHING IS FAILING AS A SECURITY PARADIGM

34 **"Move fast and break things":** In 2014, Facebook changed its motto. Samantha Murphy (30 Apr 2014), "Facebook changes its 'Move fast and break things' motto," *Mashable*, http://mashable.com/2014/04/30/facebooks-new-mantra-move-fast-with-stability/#ebhnHppqdPq9.

36 **"responsible disclosure":** Stephen A. Shepherd (22 Apr 2003), "How do we define responsible disclosure?" *SANS Institute*, https://www.sans.org/reading-room/white papers/threats/define-responsible-disclosure-932.

36 **Google has an entire team:** Andy Greenberg (16 Jul 2014), "Meet 'Project Zero,' Google's secret team of bug-hunting hackers," *Wired*, https://www.wired.com/2014/07/google-project-zero. Robert Hackett (23 Jun 2017), "Google's elite hacker SWAT team vs. everyone," *Fortune*, http://fortune.com/2017/06/23/google-project-zero-hacker-swat-team.

36 **Despite the seemingly endless stream:** Andy Ozment and Stuart Schechter (1 Jul 2006), "Milk or wine: Does software security improve with age?" in *Proceedings of the 15th USENIX Security Symposium*, https://www.microsoft.com/en-us/research/publication/milk-or-wine-does-software-security-improve-with-age.

37 **Some people don't patch:** Malwarebytes (4 Oct 2017), "PUP reconsideration information: How do we identify potentially unwanted software?" https://www.malwarebytes.com/pup. Chris Hutton (1 Aug 2014), "12 downloads that sneak unwanted software into your PC," *Tom's Guide*, https://www.tomsguide.com/us/top-downloads-unwanted-software,news-19249.html.

37 **Equifax was hacked because:** Cyrus Farivar (15 Sep 2017), "Equifax CIO, CSO 'retire' in wake of huge security breach," *Ars Technica*, https://arstechnica.com/tech-policy/2017/09/equifax-cio-cso-retire-in-wake-of-huge-security-breach.

37 **The Amnesia IoT botnet made use of:** John Leyden (7 Apr 2017), "'Amnesia' IoT botnet feasts on year-old unpatched vulnerability," *Register*, https://www.theregister.co.uk/2017/04/07/amnesia_iot_botnet.

37 **Sometimes, ISPs have the ability:** Fredric Paul (7 Sep 2017), "Fixing, upgrading and patching IoT devices can be a real nightmare," *Network World*, https://www.networkworld.com/article/3222651/internet-of-things/fixing-upgrading-and-patching-iot-devices-can-be-a-real-nightmare.html.

37 **Right now, the only way:** Lucian Constantin (17 Feb 2016), "Hard-coded password exposes up to 46,000 video surveillance DVRs to hacking," *PC World*, https://www

.pcworld.com/article/3034265/hard-coded-password-exposes-up-to-46000-video
-surveillance-dvrs-to-hacking.html.

37 **In 2010, a security researcher analyzed:** Craig Heffner (6 Jul 2010), "How to hack
millions of routers," *DefCon 18*, https://www.defcon.org/images/defcon-18/dc-18
-presentations/Heffner/DEFCON-18-Heffner-Routers.pdf. Craig Heffner (5 Oct 2010),
"DEFCON 18: How to hack millions of routers," *YouTube*, http://www.youtube.com
/watch?v=stnJiPBIM6o.

37 **Things haven't improved since then:** Jennifer Valentino-DeVries (18 Jan 2016),
"Rarely patched software bugs in home routers cripple security," *Wall Street Journal*, https://www.wsj.com/articles/rarely-patched-software-bugs-in-home-routers
-cripple-security-1453136285.

37 **The malware DNSChanger attacks:** Elinor Mills (17 Jun 2008), "New DNSChanger Trojan variant targets routers," *CNET*, http://news.cnet.com/8301-10784_3-9970972-7.html.

37 **In Brazil in 2012, 4.5 million DSL routers:** Graham Cluley (1 Oct 2012), "How millions
of DSL modems were hacked in Brazil, to pay for Rio prostitutes," *Naked Security*,
http://nakedsecurity.sophos.com/2012/10/01/hacked-routers-brazil-vb2012.

37 **In 2013, a Linux worm targeted:** Dan Goodin (27 Nov 2013), "New Linux worm targets routers, cameras, 'Internet of things' devices," *Ars Technica*, http://arstechnica
.com/security/2013/11/new-linux-worm-targets-routers-cameras-Internet-of-things
-devices.

37 **In 2016, the Mirai botnet used:** Robinson Meyer (21 Oct 2016), "How a bunch of hacked
DVR machines took down Twitter and Reddit," *Atlantic*, https://www.theatlantic
.com/technology/archive/2016/10/how-a-bunch-of-hacked-dvr-machines-took
-down-twitter-and-reddit/505073.

37 **it exploited such rookie security mistakes:** Manos Antonakakis et al. (8 Aug 2017),
"Understanding the Mirai botnet," in *Proceedings of the 26th USENIX Security Symposium*, https://www.usenix.org/system/files/conference/usenixsecurity17/sec17
-antonakakis.pdf.

37 **In 2015, Chrysler recalled:** Andy Greenberg (24 Jul 2016), "After Jeep hack, Chrysler
recalls 1.4m vehicles for bug fix," *Wired*, https://www.wired.com/2015/07/jeep-hack
-chrysler-recalls-1-4m-vehicles-bug-fix.

38 **In 2017, Abbott Labs told:** Dan Goodin (30 Aug 2017), "465k patients told to visit
doctor to patch critical pacemaker vulnerability," *Ars Technica*, https://www
.arstechnica.com/information-technology/2017/08/465k-patients-need-a-firmware
-update-to-prevent-serious-pacemaker-hacks.

38 **Kindle does the same thing:** Kyree Leary (27 Apr 2017), "How to update your Kindle
and Kindle Fire devices," *Digital Trends*, https://www.digitaltrends.com/mobile/how
-to-update-your-kindle.

38 **One 2016 survey found:** Flexera Software (13 Mar 2017), *Vulnerability Review 2017*,
https://www.flexera.com/enterprise/resources/research/vulnerability-review.

38 **Android users, for example:** Alex Dobie (16 Sep 2012), "Why you'll never have the
latest version of Android," *Android Central*, http://www.androidcentral.com/why
-you-ll-never-have-latest-version-android.

38 **The result is that about half:** Gregg Keizer (23 Mar 2017), "Google: Half of Android
devices haven't been patched in a year or more," *Computerworld*, https://www
.computerworld.com/article/3184400/android/google-half-of-android-devices
-havent-been-patched-in-a-year-or-more.html.

38 **In 2014, an iOS patch left:** Adrian Kingsley-Hughes (24 Sep 2014), "Apple pulls iOS 8.0.1 update, after killing cell service, Touch ID," *ZDNet*, http://www.zdnet.com/article /apple-pulls-ios-8-0-1-update-after-killing-cell-service-touch-id.

38 **In 2017, a flawed patch:** Dan Goodin (14 Aug 2017), "Update gone wrong leaves 500 smart locks inoperable," *Ars Technica*, https://www.arstechnica.com/information -technology/2017/08/500-smart-locks-arent-so-smart-anymore-thanks-to-botched -update.

38 **In 2018, in response to:** Mathew J. Schwartz (9 Jan 2018), "Microsoft pauses Windows security updates to AMD devices," *Data Breach Today*, https://www.databreachtoday .com/microsoft-pauses-windows-security-updates-to-amd-devices-a-10567.

38 **There are more examples:** Larry Seltzer (15 Dec 2014), "Microsoft update blunders going out of control," *ZDNet*, http://www.zdnet.com/article/has-microsoft-stopped -testing-their-updates.

39 **Maintaining lots of different:** Microsoft currently only supports the four most recent versions of Windows. Microsoft Corporation (accessed 24 Apr 2018), "Windows lifecycle fact sheet," https://support.microsoft.com/en-us/help/13853/windows -lifecycle-fact-sheet.

40 **Some of the organizations affected:** Brian Barrett (14 Jun 2017), "If you still use Windows XP, prepare for the worst," *Wired*, https://www.wired.com/2017/05/still -use-windows-xp-prepare-worst.

40 **About 140 million computers:** Jeff Parsons (15 May 2017), "This is how many computers are still running Windows XP," *Mirror*, https://www.mirror.co.uk/tech/how -many-computers-still-running-10425650.

40 **including most ATMs:** David Sancho, Numaan Huq, and Massimiliano Michenzi (2017), "Cashing in on ATM malware: A comprehensive look at various attack types," *Trend Micro*, https://documents.trendmicro.com/assets/white_papers/wp-cashing -in-on-atm-malware.pdf.

40 **A popular shipboard satellite communications system:** Catalin Cimpanu (26 Oct 2017), "Backdoor account found in popular ship satellite communications system," *Bleeping Computer*, https://www.bleepingcomputer.com/news/security/backdoor -account-found-in-popular-ship-satellite-communications-system.

40 **For an airplane, it can cost:** Lucian Armasu (13 Nov 2017), "Boeing 757 hacked by DHS in cybersecurity test," *Tom's Hardware*, http://www.tomshardware.com/news /boeing-757-remote-hack-test,35911.html.

41 **"false and misleading":** Dan Goodin (30 Aug 2017), "465k patients told to visit doctor to patch critical pacemaker vulnerability," *Ars Technica*, https://arstechnica .com/information-technology/2017/08/465k-patients-need-a-firmware-update-to -prevent-serious-pacemaker-hacks.

41 **The FBI arrested Dmitry Sklyarov:** Electronic Frontier Foundation (1 Jul 2011; last updated 7 Aug 2012), "US v. ElcomSoft Sklyarov," https://www.eff.org/cases/us-v -elcomsoft-sklyarov.

41 **Also in 2001, HP used the law:** John Leyden (31 Jul 2002), "HP invokes DMCA to quash Tru64 bug report," *Register*, https://www.theregister.co.uk/2002/07/31/hp _invokes_dmca_to_quash. Declan McCullagh (2 Aug 2002), "HP backs down on copyright warning," *CNET*, https://www.cnet.com/news/hp-backs-down-on -copyright-warning.

41 **In 2011, Activision used it to shut down:** Electronic Frontier Foundation (1 Mar

2013), "Unintended consequences: Fifteen years under the DMCA," https://www.eff
.org/pages/unintended-consequences-fifteen-years-under-dmca.

42 **In 2016, the Library of Congress:** Charlie Osborne (31 Oct 2016), "US DMCA rules
updated to give security experts legal backing to research," *ZDNet*, http://www
.zdnet.com/article/us-dmca-rules-updated-to-give-security-experts-legal-backing
-to-research.

42 **it's a narrow exemption that's temporary:** Maria A. Pallante (Oct 2015), "Section
1201 rulemaking: Sixth triennial proceeding to determine exemptions to the prohibition on circumvention," *United States Copyright Office*, https://www.copyright.gov
/1201/2015/registers-recommendation.pdf.

42 **In 2008, the Boston MBTA used:** Kim Zetter (9 Sep 2008), "DefCon: Boston subway
officials sue to stop talk on fare card hacks," *Wired*, https://www.wired.com/2008
/08/injunction-requ.

42 **In 2013, Volkswagen sued:** Chris Perkins (14 Aug 2015), "Volkswagen suppressed a
paper about car hacking for 2 years," *Mashable*, http://mashable.com/2015/08/14
/volkswagen-suppress-car-vulnerability.

42 **And in 2016, the Internet security company FireEye:** Kim Zetter (11 Sep 2016),
"A bizarre twist in the debate over vulnerability disclosures," *Wired*, https://www
.wired.com/2015/09/fireeye-enrw-injunction-bizarre-twist-in-the-debate-over
-vulnerability-disclosures.

42 **If you're a young academic:** Electronic Frontier Foundation (21 Jul 2016), "EFF
lawsuit takes on DMCA section 1201: Research and technology restrictions violate
the First Amendment," https://www.eff.org/press/releases/eff-lawsuit-takes-dmca
-section-1201-research-and-technology-restrictions-violate.

42 **"Waterfall" is the term used:** Winston Royce (25–28 Aug 1970), "Managing the development of large software systems," *1970 WESCON Technical Papers* 26, https://books
.google.com/books?id=9U1GAQAAIAAJ.

42 **"Agile" describes the newer model:** Agile Alliance (accessed 24 Apr 2018), "Agile 101,"
https://www.agilealliance.org/agile101.

43 **We need to integrate the two paradigms:** There has been some work integrating
security into agile development practices. Information Security Forum (Oct 2017),
"Embedding Security into Agile Development: Ten Principles for Rapid Development," unpublished draft.

3. KNOWING WHO'S WHO ON THE INTERNET IS GETTING HARDER

44 **"On the Internet, no one knows you're a dog":** Glenn Fleishman (14 Dec 2000),
"Cartoon captures spirit of the Internet," *New York Times*, http://www.nytimes.com
/2000/12/14/technology/cartoon-captures-spirit-of-the-internet.html.

44 **"Remember when, on the Internet":** Kaamran Hafeez (23 Feb 2015), "Cartoon: 'Remember when, on the Internet, nobody knew who you were?'" *New Yorker*, http://www
.kaamranhafeez.com/product/remember-internet-nobody-knew-new-yorker-cartoon.

45 **Tailored Access Operations (TAO) group:** It's now called the Computer Network
Operations group.

45 **In a nutshell, he said:** Rob Joyce (28 Jan 2016), "Disrupting nation state hackers,"
USENIX Enigma 2016, https://www.youtube.com/watch?v=bDJb8WOJYdA (video),
https://www.usenix.org/sites/default/files/conference/protected-files/enigma
_slides_joyce.pdf (slides).

45 **It's how the Chinese hackers breached:** Brendan I. Koerner (23 Oct 2016), "Inside the cyberattack that shocked the U.S. government," *Wired*, https://www.wired.com /2016/10/inside-cyberattack-shocked-us-government.

45 **The 2014 criminal attack against Target Corporation:** Brian Krebs (5 Feb 2014), "Target hackers broke in via HVAC company," *Krebs on Security*, https://krebsonsecurity .com/2014/02/target-hackers-broke-in-via-hvac-company.

45 **From 2011 to 2014, Iranian hackers stole:** Jim Finkle (29 May 2014), "Iranian hackers use fake Facebook accounts to spy on U.S., others," *Reuters*, http://www.reuters .com/article/iran-hackers/iranian-hackers-use-fake-facebook-accounts-to-spy-on -u-s-others-idUSL1N0OE2CU20140529.

45 **The 2015 hacktivist who broke into:** Lorenzo Franceschi-Bicchierai (15 Apr 2016), "The vigilante who hacked Hacking Team explains how he did it," *Vice Motherboard*, https://motherboard.vice.com/en_us/article/3dad3n/the-vigilante-who-hacked -hacking-team-explains-how-he-did-it.

45 **And the 2016 Russian attacks against:** David E. Sanger and Nick Corasanti (14 Jun 2016), "D.N.C. says Russian hackers penetrated its files, including dossier on Donald Trump," *New York Times*, https://www.nytimes.com/2016/06/15/us/politics/russian -hackers-dnc-trump.html.

45 **One survey found that 80% of breaches:** Andras Cser (8 Jul 2016), "The Forrester Wave: Privileged identity management, Q3 2016," *Forrester*, https://www.beyondtrust.com/ wp-content/uploads/forrester-wave-for-privilege-identity-management-2016.pdf.

45 **Google looked at Gmail users:** Kurt Thomas and Angelika Moscicki (9 Nov 2017), "New research: Understanding the root cause of account takeover," *Google Security Blog*, https://security.googleblog.com/2017/11/new-research-understanding-root -cause.html.

46 **They guess the answers to the "secret questions":** Bruce Schneier (9 Feb 2005), "The curse of the secret question," *Schneier on Security*, https://www.schneier.com/essays /archives/2005/02/the_curse_of_the_sec.html.

46 **After receiving bad advice:** Eric Lipton, David E. Sanger, and Scott Shane (13 Dec 2016), "The perfect weapon: How Russian cyberpower invaded the U.S.," *New York Times*, https://www.nytimes.com/2016/12/13/us/politics/russia-hack-election-dnc.html.

46 **Google found and disabled the worm:** Alex Johnson (4 May 2017), "Massive phishing attack targets Gmail users," *NBC News*, https://www.nbcnews.com/tech/security/ massive-phishing-attack-targets-millions-gmail-users-n754501.

46 **An example of something you are is biometrics:** Nary Subramanian (1 Jan 2011), "Biometric authentication," in *Encyclopedia of Cryptography and Security*, Springer, https://link-springer-com/content/pdf/10.1007%2F978-1-4419-5906-5_775.pdf.

46 **These are things you carry with you:** Robert Zuccherato (1 Jan 2011), "Authentication token," in *Encyclopedia of Cryptography and Security*, Springer, https://link-springer -com.ezproxy.cul.columbia.edu/referencework/10.1007%2F978-1-4419-5906-5.

47 **Using two of them together:** J. R. Raphael (30 Nov 2017), "What is two-factor authentication (2FA)? How to enable it and why you should," *CSO*, https://www.csoonline .com/article/3239144/password-security/what-is-two-factor-authentication-2fa -how-to-enable-it-and-why-you-should.html.

47 **This, of course, isn't perfect, either:** Andy Greenberg (26 Jun 2016), "So hey you should stop using texts for two-factor authentication," *Wired*, https://www.wired .com/2016/06/hey-stop-using-texts-two-factor-authentication.

47 **Sprint, T-Mobile, Verizon, and AT&T:** Steve Dent (8 Sep 2017), "U.S. carriers partner on a better mobile authentication system," *Engadget*, https://www.engadget.com/2017/09/08/mobile-authentication-taskforce-att-verizon-tmobile-sprint.

47 **Among other security protections:** Dario Salice (17 Oct 2017), "Google's strongest security, for those who need it most," *Keyword*, https://www.blog.google/topics/safety-security/googles-strongest-security-those-who-need-it-most.

47 **Sticky-note passwords regularly show up:** Here's one example from 2018: Kif Leswing (16 Jan 2018), "A password for the Hawaii emergency agency was hiding in a public photo, written on a Post-it note," *Business Insider*, http://www.businessinsider.com/hawaii-emergency-agency-password-discovered-in-photo-sparks-security-criticism-2018-1.

48 **Your smartphone has evolved into:** Gary Robbins (23 Apr 2017), "The Internet of Things lets you control the world with a smartphone," *San Diego Union Tribune*, http://www.sandiegouniontribune.com/sd-me-connected-home-20170423-story.html.

48 **A hacker can convince a cell provider:** Steven Melendez (18 Jul 2017), "How to steal a phone number and everything linked to it," *Fast Company*, https://www.fastcompany.com/40432975/how-to-steal-a-phone-number-and-everything-linked-to-it.

48 **They'll reset bank accounts:** Alex Perekalin (19 May 2017), "Why two-factor authentication is not enough," *Kaspersky Daily*, https://www.kaspersky.com/blog/ss7-attack-intercepts-sms/16877. Nathaniel Popper (21 Aug 2017), "Identity thieves hijack cellphone accounts to go after virtual currency," *New York Times*, https://www.nytimes.com/2017/08/21/business/dealbook/phone-hack-bitcoin-virtual-currency.html.

49 **This is called a man-in-the-middle attack:** Rapid7 (9 Aug 2017), "Man-in-the-middle (MITM) attacks," *Rapid7 Fundamentals*, https://www.rapid7.com/fundamentals/man-in-the-middle-attacks.

49 **A credit card issuer might flag:** Gartner (accessed 24 Apr 2018), "Reviews for online fraud detection," https://www.gartner.com/reviews/market/OnlineFraudDetectionSystems.

50 **This was one of the techniques:** David Kushner (26 Feb 2013), "The real story of Stuxnet," *IEEE Spectrum*, https://spectrum.ieee.org/telecom/security/the-real-story-of-stuxnet.

50 **For years, though, hackers have been:** Dan Goodin (3 Nov 2017), "Stuxnet-style code signing is more widespread than anyone thought," *Ars Technica*, https://arstechnica.com/information-technology/2017/11/evasive-code-signed-malware-flourished-before-stuxnet-and-still-does. Doowon Kim, Bum Jun Kwon, and Tudor Dumitras (1 Nov 2017), "Certified malware: Measuring breaches of trust in the Windows code-signing PKI," *ACM Conference on Computer and Communications Security (ACM CCS '17)*, http://www.umiacs.umd.edu/~tdumitra/papers/CCS-2017.pdf.

51 **Facebook has a "real name" policy:** Amanda Holpuch (15 Dec 2015), "Facebook adjusts controversial 'real name' policy in wake of criticism," *Guardian*, https://www.theguardian.com/us-news/2015/dec/15/facebook-change-controversial-real-name-policy.

51 **Google requires a phone number:** Eric Griffith (3 Dec 2017), "How to create an anonymous email account," *PC Magazine*, https://www.pcmag.com/article2/0,2817,2476288,00.asp.

52 **He was found by a dogged FBI agent:** Nate Anderson and Cyrus Farivar (3 Oct

2013), "How the feds took down the Dread Pirate Roberts," *Ars Technica*, https://arstechnica.com/tech-policy/2013/10/how-the-feds-took-down-the-dread-pirate-roberts.

52 **Pedophiles have been arrested:** Joseph Cox (15 Jun 2016), "How the feds use Photoshop to track down pedophiles," *Vice Motherboard*, https://motherboard.vice.com/en_us/article/8q8594/enhance-enhance-enhance-how-the-feds-use-photoshop-to-track-down-pedophiles. Tom Kelly (27 Oct 2007), "Ashbourne Interpol officer's role in paedophile suspect hunt," *Heath Chronicle*, http://www.meathchronicle.ie/news/roundup/articles/2007/03/11/1025-ashbourne-interpol-officers-role-in-paedophile-suspect-hunt.

52 **A Belarusian who ran:** Dan Goodin (5 Dec 2017), "Mastermind behind sophisticated, massive botnet outs himself," *Ars Technica*, https://arstechnica.com/tech-policy/2017/12/mastermind-behind-massive-botnet-tracked-down-by-sloppy-opsec.

52 **The Texas hacker Higinio O. Ochoa III:** John Leyden (13 Apr 2012), "FBI track alleged Anon from unsanitised busty babe pic," *Register*, https://www.theregister.co.uk/2012/04/13/fbi_track_anon_from_iphone_photo.

53 **"made significant advances in":** Leon E. Panetta (11 Oct 2012), "Remarks by Secretary Panetta on cybersecurity to the Business Executives for National Security, New York City," *US Department of Defense*, http://archive.defense.gov/transcripts/transcript.aspx?transcriptid=5136.

53 **Other US government officials:** Andy Greenberg (8 Apr 2010), "Security guru Richard Clarke talks cyberwar," *Forbes*, http://www.forbes.com/2010/04/08/cyberwar-obama-korea-technology-security-clarke.html.

53 **"It's amazing the amount of lawyers":** Kim Zetter (29 Jan 2016), "NSA hacker chief explains how to keep him out of your system," *Wired*, https://www.wired.com/2016/01/nsa-hacker-chief-explains-how-to-keep-him-out-of-your-system.

53 **5 Chinese for hacking:** US Department of Justice (19 May 2014), "U.S. charges five Chinese military hackers for cyber espionage against U.S. corporations and a labor organization for commercial advantage," https://www.justice.gov/opa/pr/us-charges-five-chinese-military-hackers-cyber-espionage-against-us-corporations-and-labor.

53 **13 Russians for interfering:** Matt Apuzzo and Sharon LaFraniere (16 Feb 2018), "13 Russians indicted as Mueller reveals effort to aid Trump campaign," *New York Times*, https://www.nytimes.com/2018/02/16/us/politics/russians-indicted-mueller-election-interference.html.

53 **Unless attribution is followed by:** Benjamin Edwards et al. (11 Jan 2017), "Strategic aspects of cyberattack, attribution, and blame," *Proceedings of the National Academy of Sciences of the United States of America* 114, no. 11, http://www.pnas.org/content/pnas/114/11/2825.full.pdf.

54 **The main points are these:** William R. Detlefsen (23 May 2015), "Cyber attacks, attribution, and deterrence: Three case studies," *School of Advanced Military Studies, US Army Command and General Staff College*, http://www.dtic.mil/dtic/tr/fulltext/u2/1001276.pdf. Benjamin Edwards et al. (11 Jan 2017), "Strategic aspects of cyberattack, attribution, and blame," *Proceedings of the National Academy of Sciences of the United States of America* 114, no. 11, http://www.pnas.org/content/114/11/2825.full.pdf. Delbert Tran (16 Aug 2017), "The law of attribution," *Cyber Conflict Project, Yale University*, https://law.yale.edu/system/files/area/center/global/document/2017.05.10_-_law_of_attribution.pdf.

54 **I was on the wrong side of this debate:** Bruce Schneier (11 Dec 2014), "Comments on the Sony hack," *Schneier on Security*, https://www.schneier.com/blog/archives/2014 /12/comments_on_the.html.

54 **It wasn't until the *New York Times* reported:** David E. Sanger and Martin Fackler (18 Jan 2015), "N.S.A. breached North Korean networks before Sony attack, officials say," *New York Times*, https://www.nytimes.com/2015/01/19/world/asia/nsa-tapped -into-north-korean-networks-before-sony-attack-officials-say.html.

55 **Right now, Russia doesn't do much:** When Russia attacked the 2018 Winter Olympics in South Korea, it tried to blame North Korea. Ellen Nakashima (24 Feb 2018), "Russian spies hacked the Olympics and tried to make it look like North Korea did it, U.S. officials say," *Washington Post*, https://www.washingtonpost.com/world/national -security/russian-spies-hacked-the-olympics-and-tried-to-make-it-look-like-north -korea-did-it-us-officials-say/2018/02/24/44b5468e-18f2-11e8-92c9-376b4fe57ff7 _story.html.

4. EVERYONE FAVORS INSECURITY

56 **The FBI wants you to have security:** I'll talk about this in Chapter 11, but here's just one recent example: Cyrus Farivar (7 Mar 2018), "FBI again calls for magical solution to break into encrypted phones," *Ars Technica*, https://arstechnica.com/tech-policy /2018/03/fbi-again-calls-for-magical-solution-to-break-into-encrypted-phones.

57 **"surveillance capitalism":** Shoshana Zuboff (17 Apr 2015), "Big other: Surveillance capitalism and the prospects of an information civilization," *Journal of Information Technology* 30, https://papers.ssrn.com/sol3/papers.cfm?abstract_id=2594754.

57 **Companies are trying to figure out:** Aaron Taube (24 Jan 2014), "Apple wants to use your heart rate and facial expressions to figure out what mood you're in," *Business Insider*, http://www.businessinsider.com/apples-mood-based-ad-targeting-patent -2014-1. Andrew McStay (4 Aug 2015), "Now advertising billboards can read your emotions . . . and that's just the start," *Conversation*, http://theconversation.com/now -advertising-billboards-can-read-your-emotions-and-thats-just-the-start-45519.

57 **They're trying to determine what you're paying attention to:** Andrew McStay (27 Jun 2017), "Tech firms want to detect your emotions and expressions, but people don't like it," *Conversation*, https://theconversation.com/tech-firms-want-to-detect -your-emotions-and-expressions-but-people-dont-like-it-80153. Nick Whigham (13 May 2017), "Glitch in digital pizza advert goes viral, shows disturbing future of facial recognition tech," *News.com.au*, http://www.news.com.au/technology/innovation /design/glitch-in-digital-pizza-advert-goes-viral-shows-disturbing-future-of-facial -recognition-tech/news-story/3b43904b6dd5444a279fd3cd6f8551db.

57 **They're trying to learn what images you respond to:** Pamela Paul (10 Dec 2010), "Flattery will get an ad nowhere," *New York Times*, http://www.nytimes.com/2010 /12/12/fashion/12Studied.html.

58 **No one knows how many online:** Paul Boutin (30 May 2016), "The secretive world of selling data about you," *Newsweek*, http://www.newsweek.com/secretive-world -selling-data-about-you-464789.

58 **That list would include any apps:** Keith Collins (21 Nov 2017), "Google collects Android users' locations even when location services are disabled," *Quartz*, https://qz .com/1131515/google-collects-android-users-locations-even-when-location-services -are-disabled. Arsalan Mosenia et al. (15 Sep 2017), "PinMe: Tracking a smartphone

user around the world," *IEEE Transactions on Multi-Scale Computing Systems* vol. PP, no. 99, http://ieeexplore.ieee.org/document/8038870. Christopher Loran (13 Dec 2017), "How you can be tracked even with your GPS turned off," *Android Authority*, https://www.androidauthority.com/tracked-gps-off-822865.

58 **In 2013, researchers discovered:** Jialiu Lin et al. (5–8 Sep 2012), "Expectation and purpose: Understanding users' mental models of mobile app privacy through crowdsourcing," in *Proceedings of the 2012 International Conference on Ubiquitous Computing*, ACM, https://www.winlab.rutgers.edu/~janne/privacyasexpectations -ubicomp12-final.pdf.

58 **Any Wi-Fi networks your phone connects to:** Retailers are tracking customers using their cell phones' Wi-Fi as they walk around in stores. Stephanie Clifford and Quentin Hardy (14 Jul 2013), "Attention, shoppers: Store is tracking your cell," *New York Times*, http://www.nytimes.com/2013/07/15/business/attention-shopper -stores-are-tracking-your-cell.html.

58 **The company Alphonso provides apps:** Sapna Maheshwari (28 Dec 2017), "That game on your phone may be tracking what you're watching on TV," *New York Times*, https:// www.nytimes.com/2017/12/28/business/media/alphonso-app-tracking.html.

58 **Facebook has a patent on using:** Ben Chen and Facebook Corporation (22 Mar 2016), "Systems and methods for utilizing wireless communications to suggest connections for a user," US Patent 9,294,991, https://patents.justia.comm/patent/9294991.

58 **Did an automatic license plate scanner:** Catherine Crump et al. (17 Jul 2013), "You are being tracked: How license plate readers are being used to record Americans' movements," *American Civil Liberties Union*, https://www.aclu.org/files/assets /071613-aclu-alprreport-opt-v05.pdf.

58 **Surveillance companies know a lot about us:** Dylan Curren (30 Mar 2018), "Are you ready? Here's all the data Facebook and Google have on you," *Guardian*, https:// www.theguardian.com/commentisfree/2018/mar/28/all-the-data-facebook-google -has-on-you-privacy.

58 **We never lie to our search engines:** Settings like Chrome's "incognito mode" or Firefox's "private browsing" keep the browser from saving your browsing history. It does not prevent any websites you visit from tracking you.

59 **Already, all new Toyota cars track speed:** Hans Greimel (6 Oct 2015), "Toyota unveils new self-driving safety tech, targets 2020 autonomous drive," *Automotive News*, http://www.autonews.com/article/20151006/OEM06/151009894/toyota-unveils -new-self-driving-safety-tech-targets-2020-autonomous.

59 **In 2015, John Deere told:** Dana Bartholomew (2015), "Long comment regarding a proposed exemption under 17 U.S.C. 1201," *Deere and Company*, https://copyright.gov /1201/2015/comments-032715/class%2021/John_Deere_Class21_1201_2014.pdf.

60 **Apple censored apps that tracked:** Stuart Dredge (30 Sep 2015), "Apple removed drone-strike apps from App Store due to 'objectionable content,'" *Guardian*, https:// www.theguardian.com/technology/2015/sep/30/apple-removing-drone-strikes-app . Lorenzo Franceschi-Bicchierai (28 Mar 2017), "Apple just banned the app that tracks U.S. drone strikes again," *Vice Motherboard*, https://motherboard.vice.com/en_us /article/538kan/apple-just-banned-the-app-that-tracks-us-drone-strikes-again.

60 **"content that ridicules public figures":** Jason Grigsby (19 Apr 2010), "Apple's policy on satire: 16 apps rejected for 'ridiculing public figures,'" *Cloudfour*, https://cloudfour .com/thinks/apples-policy-on-satire-16-rejected-apps.

60 **in 2017, Apple removed security apps:** Telegraph Reporters (31 Jul 2017), "Apple removes VPN apps used to evade China's internet censorship," *Telegraph*, http://www.telegraph.co.uk/technology/2017/07/31/apple-removes-vpn-apps-used-evade -chinas-internet-censorship.

60 **Google has also banned an app:** AdNauseam (5 Jan 2017), "AdNauseam banned from the Google Web Store," https://adnauseam.io/free-adnauseam.html.

61 **"Some of us have pledged our allegiance":** Bruce Schneier (26 Nov 2012), "When it comes to security, we're back to feudalism," *Wired*, https://www.wired.com/2012/11 /feudal-security.

61 **Companies owning fleets of autonomous cars:** Judith Donath (16 Nov 2017), "Uber-FREE: The ultimate advertising experience," *Medium*, https://medium.com/@ judithd/the-future-of-self-driving-cars-and-of-advertising-will-be-promoted-rides -free-transportation-b5f7acd702d4.

62 **Because the machines use software:** After years of refusing to allow consumers to use refillable pods, Keurig now allows consumers to use any coffee they want, as long as they buy a special add-on. Alex Hern (11 May 2015), "Keurig takes steps towards abandoning coffee-pod DRM," *Guardian*, https://www.theguardian.com/technology /2015/may/11/keurig-takes-steps-towards-abandoning-coffee-pod-drm.

62 **HP printers no longer allow:** Brian Barrett (23 Sep 2016), "HP has added DRM to its ink cartridges. Not even kidding (updated)," *Wired*, https://www.wired.com/2016/09 /hp-printer-drm.

62 **And while some companies have overreached:** Electronic Frontier Foundation (last updated 31 Aug 2004), *Chamberlain Group Inc. v. Skylink Technologies Inc.*, https:// www.eff.org/cases/chamberlain-group-inc-v-skylink-technologies-inc. *Tech Law Journal* (31 Aug 2004), "Federal Circuit rejects anti-circumvention claim in garage door opener case," http://www.techlawjournal.com/topstories/2004/20040831.asp. US Supreme Court (25 Mar 2014), "Opinion," *Lexmark International, Inc. v. Static Control Components, Inc.*, No. 12–873, https://www.supremecourt.gov/opinions/13pdf/12 -873_3dq3.pdf.

63 **The data is owned by the companies:** Hugo Campos (24 Mar 2015), "The heart of the matter," *Slate*, http://www.slate.com/articles/technology/future_tense/2015/03 /patients_should_be_allowed_to_access_data_generated_by_implanted_devices .html.

63 **Similarly, people have been hacking:** Darren Murph (6 Apr 2007), "Mileage maniacs hack Toyota's Prius for 116 mpg," *Engadget*, https://www.engadget.com/2007/04/06 /mileage-maniacs-hack-toyotas-prius-for-116-mpg.

63 **There are hacks and cheat codes:** Jeremy Hoag (13 Mar 2012), "Hack your ride: Cheat codes and workarounds for your car's tech annoyances," *Lifehacker*, http://lifehacker .com/5893227/hack-your-ride-cheat-codes-and-workarounds-for-your-cars-tech -annoyances.

63 **It's no different with automobile:** Michelle V. Rafter (22 Jul 2014), "Decoding what's in your car's black box," *Edmunds*, https://www.edmunds.com/car-technology/car -black-box-recorders-capture-crash-data.html.

63 **Police and insurance companies:** Peter Hall (7 Jun 2014), "Car black box data can be used as evidence," *Morning Call*, http://www.mcall.com/mc-car-black-box-data -can-be-used-as-evidence-story.html.

63 **A California law allowing:** Brian Heaton (27 Mar 2014), "Expert: California car

data privacy bill 'unworkable,'" *Government Technology*, http://www.govtech.com/transportation/Expert-California-Car-Data-Privacy-Bill-Unworkable.html.

63 **And John Deere tractor owners:** Jason Koebler (21 Mar 2017), "Why American farmers are hacking their tractors with Ukrainian firmware," *Vice Motherboard*, https://motherboard.vice.com/en_us/article/xykkkd/why-american-farmers-are-hacking-their-tractors-with-ukrainian-firmware.

63 **For example, some people are hacking:** Jerome Radcliffe (4 Aug 2011), "Hacking medical devices for fun and insulin: Breaking the human SCADA system," *Black Hat 2011*, https://media.blackhat.com/bh-us-11/Radcliffe/BH_US_11_Radcliffe_Hacking_Medical_Devices_WP.pdf. Chuck Seegert (8 Oct 2014), "Hackers develop DIY remote-monitoring for diabetes," *Med Device Online*, http://www.meddeviceonline.com/doc/hackers-develop-diy-remote-monitoring-for-diabetes-0001.

64 **had used it to spy on journalists:** John Scott-Railton et al. (19 Jun 2017), "Reckless exploit: Mexican journalists, lawyers, and a child targeted with NSO spyware," *Citizen Lab*, https://citizenlab.ca/2017/06/reckless-exploit-mexico-nso.

64 **dissidents, political opponents:** John Scott-Railton et al. (29 Jun 2017), "Reckless redux: Senior Mexican legislators and politicians targeted with NSO spyware," *Citizen Lab*, https://citizenlab.ca/2017/06/more-mexican-nso-targets.

64 **international investigators:** John Scott-Railton et al. (10 Jul 2017), "Reckless III: Investigation into Mexican mass disappearance targeted with NSO spyware," *Citizen Lab*, https://citizenlab.ca/2017/07/mexico-disappearances-nso.

64 **lawyers:** John Scott-Railton et al. (2 Aug 2017), "Reckless IV: Lawyers for murdered Mexican women's families targeted with NSO spyware," *Citizen Lab*, https://citizenlab.ca/2017/08/lawyers-murdered-women-nso-group.

64 **anti-corruption groups:** John Scott-Railton et al. (30 Aug 2017), "Reckless V: Director of Mexican anti-corruption group targeted with NSO group's spyware," *Citizen Lab*, https://citizenlab.ca/2017/08/nso-spyware-mexico-corruption.

64 **and people who supported a tax on soft drinks:** John Scott-Railton et al. (11 Feb 2017), "Bitter sweet: Supporters of Mexico's soda tax targeted with NSO exploit links," *Citizen Lab*, https://citizenlab.ca/2017/02/bittersweet-nso-mexico-spyware.

64 **The products of FinFisher:** Bill Marczak et al. (15 Oct 2015), "Pay no attention to the server behind the proxy: Mapping FinFisher's continuing proliferation," *Citizen Lab*, https://citizenlab.ca/2015/10/mapping-finfishers-continuing-proliferation.

65 **And it does—through bribery:** Glenn Greenwald (2014), *No Place to Hide: Edward Snowden, the NSA, and the U.S. Surveillance State*, Metropolitan Books, https://books.google.com/books/?id=AvFzAgAAQBAJ.

65 **collecting cell phone location data:** The cooperation of the telecommunications industry is essential for many of the NSA's collection programs. Mieke Eoyang (6 Apr 2016), "Beyond privacy and security: The role of the telecommunications industry in electronic surveillance," *Aegis Paper Series* No. 1603, Hoover Institution, https://www.hoover.org/research/beyond-privacy-security-role-telecommunications-industry-electronic-surveillance-0.

65 **Similarly, Russia gets bulk access:** Andrei Soldatov and Irina Borogan (8 Sep 2015), "Inside the Red Web: Russia's back door onto the internet—extract," *Guardian*, https://www.theguardian.com/world/2015/sep/08/red-web-book-russia-internet.

65 **Instead, they buy surveillance:** Aaron Sankin (9 Jul 2015), "Forget Hacking Team—

Many other companies sell surveillance tech to repressive regimes," *Daily Dot*, https://www.dailydot.com/layer8/hacking-team-competitors.

65 **They even have a conference, called ISS World:** Patrick Howell O'Neill (20 Jun 2017), "ISS World: The traveling spyware roadshow for dictatorships and democracies," *CyberScoop*, https://www.cyberscoop.com/iss-world-wiretappers-ball-nso-group -ahmed-mansoor.

66 **Moonlight Maze in 1999:** Juan Andres Guerrero-Saade et al. (Apr 2017), "Penquin's moonlit maze: The dawn of nation-state digital espionage," *Kaspersky Lab*, https:// securelist.com/files/2017/04/Penquins_Moonlit_Maze_PDF_eng.pdf.

66 **Titan Rain in the early 2000s:** Richard Norton-Taylor (4 Sep 2007), "Titan Rain: How Chinese hackers targeted Whitehall," *Guardian*, https://www.theguardian.com /technology/2007/sep/04/news.internet.

66 **Buckshot Yankee in 2008:** Ellen Nakashima (8 Dec 2011), "Cyber-intruder sparks response, debate," *Washington Post*, https://www.washingtonpost.com/national /national-security/cyber-intruder-sparks-response-debate/2011/12/06/gIQAxLuFgO _story.html.

66 **Over the years, China has stolen:** Caitlin Dewey (28 May 2013), "The U.S. weapons systems that experts say were hacked by the Chinese," *Washington Post*, https://www .washingtonpost.com/news/worldviews/wp/2013/05/28/the-u-s-weapons-systems -that-experts-say-were-hacked-by-the-chinese.

66 **In 2010, China hacked into Google:** Kim Zetter (12 Jan 2010), "Google to stop censoring search results in China after hack attack," *Wired*, https://www.wired.com/2010 /01/google-censorship-china.

66 **In 2015, we learned that China:** Robert Windrem (10 Aug 2015), "China read emails of top U.S. officials," *NBC News*, https://www.nbcnews.com/news/us-news/china-read -emails-top-us-officials-n406046.

66 **Also in 2015, the Chinese hacked:** Brendan I. Koerner (23 Oct 2016), "Inside the cyberattack that shocked the U.S. government," *Wired*, https://www.wired.com /2016/10/inside-cyberattack-shocked-us-government. Evan Perez (24 Aug 2017), "FBI arrests Chinese national connected to malware used in OPM data breach," *CNN*, http://www.cnn.com/2017/08/24/politics/fbi-arrests-chinese-national-in-opm -data-breach/index.html.

66 **from Russia:** Kaspersky Lab Global Research and Analysis Team (30 Aug 2017), "Introducing White Bear," *SecureList*, https://securelist.com/introducing-whitebear /81638.

66 **China:** British Broadcasting Corporation (29 Mar 2009), "Major cyber spy network uncovered," *BBC News*, http://news.bbc.co.uk/1/hi/world/americas/7970471.stm.

66 **the US:** Boldizsár Bencsáth et al. (14 Oct 2011), "Duqu: A Stuxnet-like malware found in the wild," *Laboratory of Cryptography and System Security, Budapest University of Technology and Economics*, http://www.crysys.hu/publications/files/benc sathPBF11duqu.pdf.

66 **the US and Israel together:** Ellen Nakashima, Greg Miller, and Julie Tate (19 Jun 2012), "U.S., Israel developed Flame computer virus to slow Iranian nuclear efforts, officials say," *Washington Post*, https://www.washingtonpost.com/world/national -security/us-israel-developed-computer-virus-to-slow-iranian-nuclear-efforts -officials-say/2012/06/19/gJQA6xBPoV_story.html.

66 **Spain, and several unidentified countries:** Fahmida Y. Rashid (11 Feb 2014), "The Mask hack 'beyond anything we've seen so far,'" *PC Magazine*, http://securitywatch .pcmag.com/hacking/320622-the-mask-hack-beyond-anything-we-ve-seen-so-far. Brian Donohue (11 Feb 2014), "The Mask: Unveiling the world's most sophisticated APT campaign," *Kaspersky Lab Daily*, https://www.kaspersky.com/blog/the-mask -unveiling-the-worlds-most-sophisticated-apt-campaign/3723. Dan Goodin (8 Aug 2016), "Researchers crack open unusually advanced malware that hid for 5 years," *Ars Technica*, https://arstechnica.com/information-technology/2016/08/researchers -crack-open-unusually-advanced-malware-that-hid-for-5-years.

66 **In 2017, North Korea hacked:** Choe Sang-Hun (10 Oct 2017), "North Korean hackers stole U.S.-South Korean military plans, lawmaker says," *New York Times*, https:// www.nytimes.com/2017/10/10/world/asia/north-korea-hack-war-plans.html.

66 **China, for example, has stolen:** Barack Obama and Xi Jinping (25 Sep 2015), "Remarks by President Obama and President Xi of the People's Republic of China in joint press conference," *White House Office of the Press Secretary*, https://obamawhitehouse .archives.gov/the-press-office/2015/09/25/remarks-president-obama-and-president -xi-peoples-republic-china-joint.

66 **China does seem to have toned down:** Joseph Menn and Jim Finkle (20 Jun 2016), "Chinese economic cyber-espionage plummets in U.S.: Experts," *Reuters*, http://www .reuters.com/article/us-cyber-spying-china/chinese-economic-cyber-espionage -plummets-in-u-s-experts-idUSKCN0Z700D.

66 **Just as the NSA spied on:** Josh Dawsey, Emily Stephenson, and Andrea Peterson (5 Oct 2017), "John Kelly's personal cellphone was compromised, White House believes," *Politico*, https://www.politico.com/story/2017/10/05/john-kelly-cell-phone -compromised-243514.

66 **"You have to kind of salute the Chinese":** Mike Levine (25 Jun 2015), "China is 'leading suspect' in massive hack of US government networks," *ABC News*, http://abcnews .go.com/US/china-leading-suspect-massive-hack-us-government-networks/story ?id=32036222.

67 **One: its budget is significantly larger:** The NSA's budget is classified, but estimated to be around $11 billion. No other country even comes close. Scott Shane (29 Aug 2013), "New leaked document outlines U.S. spending on intelligence agencies," *New York Times*, http://www.nytimes.com/2013/08/30/us/politics/leaked-document -outlines-us-spending-on-intelligence.html. Michael Holt (4 Oct 2015), "Top 15 global intelligence agencies with biggest budgets in the world have tripled since 2009–2016," *LinkedIn*, https://www.linkedin.com/pulse/top-15-global-intelligence -agencies-biggest-budgets-world-holt.

67 **Three: the physical location:** Anne Edmundson et al. (10 Mar 2017), "RAN: Routing around nation-states," *Princeton University*, https://www.cs.princeton.edu/~jrex/papers /ran17.pdf.

67 **China leads the way:** Kiyo Dorrer (31 Mar 2017), "Hello, Big Brother: How China controls its citizens through social media," *Deutsche Welle*, http://www.dw.com/en/hello -big-brother-how-china-controls-its-citizens-through-social-media/a-38243388. Maya Wang (18 Aug 2017), "China's dystopian push to revolutionize surveillance," *Human Rights Watch*, https://www.hrw.org/news/2017/08/18/chinas-dystopian-push -revolutionize-surveillance.

67 **The government's goal is not so much:** Gary King, Jennifer Pan, and Margaret E.

Roberts (May 2013), "How censorship in China allows government criticism but silences collective expression," *American Political Science Review* 107, no. 2, https://gking.harvard.edu/files/censored.pdf.

67 **The Great Firewall of China:** The system can be subverted, but combined with China's surveillance and enforcement regime and the resultant self-censorship, it's very effective. Oliver August (23 Oct 2007), "The Great Firewall: China's misguided—and futile—attempt to control what happens online," *Wired*, https://www.wired.com/2007/10/ff-chinafirewall.

67 **Each citizen will be given a score:** Josh Chin and Gillian Wong (28 Nov 2016), "China's new tool for social control: A credit rating for everything," *Wall Street Journal*, https://www.wsj.com/articles/chinas-new-tool-for-social-control-a-credit-rating-for-everything-1480351590.

68 **France and Germany censor Nazi speech:** Matthew Lasar (22 Jun 2011), "Nazi hunting: How France first 'civilized' the internet," *Ars Technica*, https://arstechnica.com/tech-policy/2011/06/how-france-proved-that-the-internet-is-not-global. Anthony Faiola (6 Jan 2016), "Germany springs to action over hate speech against migrants," *Washington Post*, https://www.washingtonpost.com/world/europe/germany-springs-to-action-over-hate-speech-against-migrants/2016/01/06/6031218e-b315-11e5-8abc-d09392edc612_story.html.

68 **Some say cyberwar is coming:** Richard Clarke and Robert K. Knake (Apr 2010), *Cyber War: The Next Threat to National Security and What to Do about It*, Harper Collins, https://books.google.com/books?id=rNRlR4RGkecC.

68 **Some say cyberwar is here:** David E. Sanger (2018), *The Perfect Weapon: War, Sabotage, and Fear in the Cyber Age*, Crown, https://books.google.com/books?id=htc7DwAAQBAJ.

68 **Some say cyberwar is everywhere:** Fred Kaplan (2016), *Dark Territory: The Secret History of Cyber War*, Simon & Schuster, https://books.google.com/books?id=q1AJCgAAQBAJ.

68 **In truth, "cyberwar" is a term:** Probably the best consensus definition is in the *Tallinn Manual*. NATO Cooperative Cyber Defence Centre of Excellence (Feb 2017), *Tallinn Manual 2.0 on the International Law Applicable to Cyber Operations*, 2nd edition, Cambridge University Press, http://www.cambridge.org/us/academic/subjects/law/humanitarian-law/tallinn-manual-20-international-law-applicable-cyber-operations-2nd-edition.

68 **Stuxnet, discovered in 2010:** David Kushner (26 Feb 2013), "The real story of Stuxnet," *IEEE Spectrum*, https://spectrum.ieee.org/telecom/security/the-real-story-of-stuxnet. Ralph Langner (1 Nov 2013), "To kill a centrifuge," *Langner Group*, https://www.langner.com/wp-content/uploads/2017/03/to-kill-a-centrifuge.pdf. Kim Zetter (2015), *Countdown to Zero Day: Stuxnet and the Launch of the World's First Digital Weapon*, Crown Books, https://books.google.com/books?id=1l2YAwAAQBAJ.

68 **Targets are not limited to:** These are often known as SCADA systems. Alex Hern (17 Oct 2013), "U.S. power plants 'vulnerable to hacking,'" *Guardian*, https://www.theguardian.com/technology/2013/oct/17/us-power-plants-hacking. Jack Wiles et al. (23 Aug 2008), *Techno Security's Guide to Securing SCADA*, Ingress, https://books.google.com/books?id=sHtIdWn1gnAC.

69 **In 2007, Israel attacked:** David A. Fulghum, Robert Wall, and Douglas Barrie (5

Nov 2007), "Details about Israel's high-tech strike on Syria," *Aviation Week Network*, http://aviationweek.com/awin/details-about-israel-s-high-tech-strike-syria.

69 **In 2008, Russia coordinated:** John Markoff (13 Aug 2008), "Before the gunfire, cyberattacks," *New York Times*, http://www.nytimes.com/2008/08/13/technology/13cyber.html.

69 **The US conducted a series:** Alan D. Campen, ed. (1992), *The First Information War: The Story of Communications, Computers, and Intelligence Systems in the Persian Gulf War*, AFCEA International Press, https://archive.org/details/firstinformationoocamp.

69 **In 2016, President Obama acknowledged:** Barack Obama (13 Apr 2016), "Statement by the president on progress in the fight against ISIL," *White House Office of the Press Secretary*, https://obamawhitehouse.archives.gov/the-press-office/2016/04/13/statement-president-progress-fight-against-isil.

69 **In 2017, we learned about a group:** This operation has been named "Dragonfly." Security Response Attack Investigation Team (20 Oct 2017), "Dragonfly: Western energy sector targeted by sophisticated attack group," *Symantec Corporation*, https://www.symantec.com/connect/blogs/dragonfly-western-energy-sector-targeted-sophisticated-attack-group.

69 **In 2016, the Iranians did the same thing:** Joseph Berger (25 Mar 2016), "A dam, small and unsung, is caught up in an Iranian hacking case," *New York Times*, http://www.nytimes.com/2016/03/26/nyregion/rye-brook-dam-caught-in-computer-hacking-case.html.

69 **Experts surmise that these operations:** United States Computer Emergency Readiness Team (20 Oct 2017), "Alert (TA17-293A): Advanced persistent threat activity targeting energy and other critical infrastructure sectors," https://www.us-cert.gov/ncas/alerts/TA17-293A.

69 **"preparing the battlefield":** Seymour M. Hersh (7 Jul 2008), "Preparing the battlefield," *New Yorker*, https://www.newyorker.com/magazine/2008/07/07/preparing-the-battlefield.

69 **It's not just the stronger powers:** Kertu Ruus (2008), "Cyber war I: Estonia attacked from Russia," *European Affairs* 9, no. 1–2, http://www.europeaninstitute.org/index.php/component/content/article?id=67:cyber-war-i-estonia-attacked-from-russia.

69 **Iran attacked Las Vegas's Sands Hotel:** Benjamin Elgin and Michael Riley (12 Dec 2014), "Now at the Sands Casino: An Iranian hacker in every server," *Bloomberg*, http://www.businessweek.com/articles/2014-12-11/iranian-hackers-hit-sheldon-adelsons-sands-casino-in-las-vegas.

69 **These include the US, the UK:** The industry name for these kinds of attackers is APT: advanced persistent threat.

69 **They are the elite few:** Ben Buchanan (Jan 2017), "The legend of sophistication in cyber operations," *Harvard Kennedy School Belfer Center for Science and International Affairs*, https://www.belfercenter.org/publication/legend-sophistication-cyber-operations.

70 **Both of these tiers of countries:** Scott DePasquale and Michael Daly (12 Oct 2016), "The growing threat of cyber mercenaries," *Politico*, https://www.politico.com/agenda/story/2016/10/the-growing-threat-of-cyber-mercenaries-000221.

70 **If an isolated and heavily sanctioned country:** David E. Sanger, David D. Kirkpatrick, and Nicole Perlroth (15 Oct 2017), "The world once laughed at North Korean

cyberpower. No more," *New York Times*, https://www.nytimes.com/2017/10/15/world/asia/north-korea-hacking-cyber-sony.html.

70 **The 2007 document didn't mention:** John D. Negroponte (11 Jan 2007), "Annual threat assessment of the Director of National Intelligence," *Office of the Director of National Intelligence*, http://www.au.af.mil/au/awc/awcgate/dni/threat_assessment_11jan07.pdf.

70 **Even in the 2009 report, "the growing cyber":** Dennis C. Blair (12 Feb 2009), "Annual threat assessment of the intelligence community for the Senate Select Committee on Intelligence," *Office of the Director of National Intelligence*, https://www.dni.gov/files/documents/Newsroom/Testimonies/20090212_testimony.pdf.

70 **By 2010, cyber threats were the first:** Dennis C. Blair (2 Feb 2010), "Annual threat assessment of the U.S. intelligence community for the Senate Select Committee on Intelligence," *Office of the Director of National Intelligence*, https://www.dni.gov/files/documents/Newsroom/Testimonies/20100202_testimony.pdf.

70 **"Our adversaries are becoming more adept":** Daniel R. Coats (11 May 2017), "Statement for the record: Worldwide threat assessment of the US intelligence community: Senate Select Committee on Intelligence," *Office of the Director of National Intelligence*, https://www.dni.gov/files/documents/Newsroom/Testimonies/SSCI%20Unclassified%20SFR%20-%20Final.pdf.

70 **Similarly, the Munich Security Conference:** Toomas Hendrik Ilves (31 Jan 2014), "Rebooting trust? Freedom vs. security in cyberspace," *Office of the President, Republic of Estonia*, https://vp2006-2016.president.ee/en/official-duties/speeches/9796-qrebooting-trust-freedom-vs-security-in-cyberspaceq.

71 **Even a well-targeted cyberweapon like Stuxnet:** Jarrad Shearer (13 Jul 2010; updated 26 Sep 2017), "W32.Stuxnet," *Symantec*, https://www.symantec.com/security_response/writeup.jsp?docid=2010-071400-3123-99.

71 **In 2017, the global shipping giant Maersk:** Iain Thomson (28 Jun 2017), "Everything you need to know about the Petya, er, NotPetya nasty trashing PCs worldwide," *Register*, https://www.theregister.co.uk/2017/06/28/petya_notpetya_ransomware. Josh Fruhlinger (17 Oct 2017), "Petya ransomware and NotPetya: What you need to know now," *CSO*, https://www.csoonline.com/article/3233210/ransomware/petya-ransomware-and-notpetya-malware-what-you-need-to-know-now.html. Nicholas Weaver (28 Jun 2017), "Thoughts on the NotPetya ransomware attack," *Lawfare*, https://lawfareblog.com/thoughts-notpetya-ransomware-attack. Ellen Nakashima (12 Jan 2018), "Russian military was behind 'Notpetya' cyberattack in Ukraine, CIA concludes," *Washington Post*, https://www.washingtonpost.com/world/national-security/russian-military-was-behind-notpetya-cyberattack-in-ukraine-cia-concludes/2018/01/12/048d8506-f7ca-11e7-b34a-b85626af34ef_story.html.

71 **when Iran attacked the Saudi:** Nicole Perlroth (23 Oct 2012), "In cyberattack on Saudi firm, U.S. sees Iran firing back," *New York Times*, http://www.nytimes.com/2012/10/24/business/global/cyberattack-on-saudi-oil-firm-disquiets-us.html.

71 **when North Korea used WannaCry:** David E. Sanger and William J. Broad (4 Mar 2017), "Trump inherits a secret cyberwar against North Korean missiles," *New York Times*, https://www.nytimes.com/2017/03/04/world/asia/north-korea-missile-program-sabotage.html.

71 **In 2012, a senior Russian general:** Mark Galeotti (6 Jul 2014), "The 'Gerasimov Doc-

trine' and Russian non-linear war," *In Moscow's Shadows*, https://inmoscowsshadows
.wordpress.com/2014/07/06/the-gerasimov-doctrine-and-russian-non-linear
-war. Henry Foy (15 Sep 2017), "Valery Gerasimov, the general with a doctrine for
Russia," *Financial Times*, https://www.ft.com/content/7e14a438-989b-11e7-a652
-cde3f882dd7b.

71 **There are cyberattacks that will be:** David E. Sanger and Elisabeth Bumiller (31 May
2011), "Pentagon to consider cyberattacks acts of war," *New York Times*, http://www
.nytimes.com/2011/06/01/us/politics/01cyber.html.

71 **a state that political scientist Lucas Kello calls "unpeace":** Lucas Kello (2017), *The
Virtual Weapon and International Order*, Yale University Press, https://yalebooks.yale
.edu/book/9780300220230/virtual-weapon-and-international-order.

71 **The US responded to the North Korean attack:** Carol Morello and Greg Miller (2
Jan 2015), "U.S. imposes sanctions on N. Korea following attack on Sony," *Washington Post*, https://www.washingtonpost.com/world/national-security/us-imposes
-sanctions-on-n-korea-following-attack-on-sony/2015/01/02/3e5423ae-92af-11e4
-a900-9960214d4cd7_story.html.

71 **The US responded to Russian hacking:** Lauren Gambino and Sabrina Siddiqui (30
Dec 2016), "Obama expels 35 Russian diplomats in retaliation for US election hacking," *Guardian*, https://www.theguardian.com/us-news/2016/dec/29/barack-obama
-sanctions-russia-election-hack.

72 **Cyber policy expert Jason Healey developed:** Jason Healey (2011), "The spectrum
of national responsibility for cyberattacks," *Brown Journal of World Affairs* 18, no.
1, https://www.brown.edu/initiatives/journal-world-affairs/sites/brown.edu
.initiatives.journal-world-affairs/files/private/articles/18.1_Healey.pdf.

72 **Here again, the operations had:** David E. Sanger and William J. Broad (4 Mar 2017),
"Trump inherits a secret cyberwar against North Korean missiles," *New York Times*,
https://www.nytimes.com/2017/03/04/world/asia/north-korea-missile-program
-sabotage.html.

72 **Cyberweapons were used:** Nadiya Kostyuk and Yuri M. Zhukov (10 Nov 2017), "Invisible digital front: Can cyber attacks shape battlefield events?" *Journal of Conflict Resolution*, http://journals.sagepub.com/doi/pdf/10.1177/0022002717737138.

72 **This means that a nation finding itself:** Robert Axelrod and Rum Iliev (28 Jan 2014),
"Timing of cyber conflict," *Proceedings of the National Academy of Sciences of the
United States of America* 111, no. 4, http://www.pnas.org/content/111/4/1298.

72 **While that intellectual-property theft:** Caitlin Dewey (28 May 2013), "The U.S.
weapons systems that experts say were hacked by the Chinese," *Washington Post*,
https://www.washingtonpost.com/news/worldviews/wp/2013/05/28/the-u-s
-weapons-systems-that-experts-say-were-hacked-by-the-chinese. Marcus Weis-
gerber (23 Sep 2015), "China's copycat jet raises questions about F-35," *Defense One*,
http://www.defenseone.com/threats/2015/09/more-questions-f-35-after-new-specs
-chinas-copycat/121859. Justin Ling (24 Mar 2016), "Man who sold F-35 secrets to
China pleads guilty," *Vice News*, https://news.vice.com/article/man-who-sold-f-35
-secrets-to-china-pleads-guilty.

73 **Countries are also getting more brazen:** The Council on Foreign Relations is trying to track all of them. Adam Segal (6 Nov 2017), "Tracking state-sponsored cyber
operations," *Council on Foreign Relations*, https://www.cfr.org/blog/tracking-state
-sponsored-cyber-operations.

73 **Attack is not only easier than defense:** To be fair, just because attack is easier than defense doesn't mean that offensive cyberspace operations are easier than defensive ones. Rebecca Slayton (1 Feb 2017), "What is the cyber offense-defense balance? Conceptions, causes, and assessment," *International Security* 41, no. 3, https://www.mitpressjournals.org/doi/abs/10.1162/ISEC_a_00267?journalCode=isec.

73 **"I think both China and the United States":** Gideon Rachman (5 Jan 2017), "Axis of power," *New World*, BBC Radio 4, http://www.bbc.co.uk/programmes/b086tfbh.

73 **"We have better cyber rocks to throw":** This quote is attributed to several people, but this is the earliest citation I could find: Fred Kaplan (12 Dec 2016), "How the U.S. could respond to Russia's hacking," *Slate*, http://www.slate.com/articles/news_and_politics/war_stories/2016/12/the_u_s_response_to_russia_s_hacking_has_consequences_for_the_future_of.html.

74 **In early 2018, the Indiana hospital Hancock Health:** Charlie Osborne (17 Jan 2018), "US hospital pays $55,000 to hackers after ransomware attack," *ZDNet*, http://www.zdnet.com/article/us-hospital-pays-55000-to-ransomware-operators.

74 **Ransomware is increasingly common:** Brian Krebs (16 Sep 2016), "Ransomware getting more targeted, expensive," *Krebs on Security*, https://krebsonsecurity.com/2016/09/ransomware-getting-more-targeted-expensive.

74 **Kaspersky Lab reported:** Kaspersky Lab (28 Nov 2016), "Story of the year: The ransomware revolution," *Kaspersky Security Bulletin 2016*, https://media.kaspersky.com/en/business-security/kaspersky-story-of-the-year-ransomware-revolution.pdf.

74 **Symantec found that average ransom amounts:** Symantec Corporation (19 Jul 2016), "Ransomware and businesses 2016," https://www.symantec.com/content/en/us/enterprise/media/security_response/whitepapers/ISTR2016_Ransomware_and_Businesses.pdf. Symantec Corporation (26 Apr 2017), "Alarming increase in targeted attacks aimed at politically motivated sabotage and subversion," https://www.symantec.com/about/newsroom/press-releases/2017/symantec_0426_01.

74 **Carbon Black reported that total sales:** Carbon Black (9 Oct 2017), "The ransomware economy," https://cdn.www.carbonblack.com/wp-content/uploads/2017/10/Carbon-Black-Ransomware-Economy-Report-101117.pdf.

75 **All in all, it's a billion-dollar business:** Herb Weisman (9 Jan 2017), "Ransomware: Now a billion dollar a year crime and growing," *NBC News*, https://www.nbcnews.com/tech/security/ransomware-now-billion-dollar-year-crime-growing-n704646. Symantec Corporation (19 Jul 2016), "Ransomware and businesses 2016," http://www.symantec.com/content/en/us/enterprise/media/security_response/whitepapers/ISTR2016_Ransomware_and_Businesses.pdf.

75 **$500 billion:** Luke Graham (7 Feb 2017), "Cybercrime costs the global economy $450 billion: CEO," *CNBC*, https://www.cnbc.com/2017/02/07/cybercrime-costs-the-global-economy-450-billion-ceo.html.

75 **$3 trillion:** Steve Morgan (22 Aug 2016), "Cybercrime damages expected to cost the world $6 trillion by 2021," *CSO*, https://www.csoonline.com/article/3110467/security/cybercrime-damages-expected-to-cost-the-world-6-trillion-by-2021.html.

75 **Additional losses due to intellectual-property theft:** Dennis C. Blair et al. (22 Feb 2017), "Update to the IP Commission Report: The theft of American intellectual property: Reassessments of the challenge and United States Policy," *National Bureau of Asian Research*, http://www.ipcommission.org/report/IP_Commission_Report_Update_2017.pdf.

75 **A thief pretends to be:** Federal Bureau of Investigation (14 Jun 2016), "Business e-mail compromise: The 3.1 billion dollar scam," https://www.ic3.gov/media/2016/160614 .aspx. Brian Krebs (23 Jun 2016), "FBI: Extortion, CEO fraud among top online fraud complaints in 2016," *Krebs on Security*, https://krebsonsecurity.com/2017/06/fbi -extortion-ceo-fraud-among-top-online-fraud-complaints-in-2016.

75 **Or to divert the proceeds:** Kenneth R. Harney (31 Mar 2016), "Scary new scam could swipe all your closing money," *Chicago Tribune*, http://www.chicagotribune.com /classified/realestate/ct-re-0403-kenneth-harney-column-20160331-column.html.

75 **Turns out that the answer is: plenty:** Brian Krebs (12 Oct 2012), "The scrap value of a hacked PC, revisited," *Krebs on Security*, https://krebsonsecurity.com/2012/10/the -scrap-value-of-a-hacked-pc-revisited.

75 **Botnets can be used for all sorts of things:** Dan Goodin (2 Feb 2018), "Crypto-currency botnets are rendering some companies unable to operate," *Ars Technica*, https://arstechnica.com/information-technology/2018/02/cryptocurrency-botnets -generate-millions-but-exact-huge-cost-on-victims.

75 **Hackers use bots to commit click fraud:** White Ops (20 Dec 2016), "The Methbot operation," https://www.whiteops.com/hubfs/Resources/WO_Methbot_Operation _WP.pdf.

76 **"The CaaS model provides easy access":** Rob Wainwright et al. (15 Mar 2017), "Euro-pean Union serious and organized crime threat assessment: Crime in the age of tech-nology," *Europol*, https://www.europol.europa.eu/activities-services/main-reports /european-union-serious-and-organised-crime-threat-assessment-2017.

76 **They sell hacking tools:** Nicolas Rapp and Robert Hackett (25 Oct 2017), "A hacker's tool kit," *Fortune*, http://fortune.com/2017/10/25/cybercrime-spyware-marketplace. Dan Goodin (1 Feb 2018), "New IoT botnet offers DDoSes of once-unimaginable sizes for $20," *Ars Technica*, https://arstechnica.com/information-technology/2018/02/for -sale-ddoses-guaranteed-to-take-down-gaming-servers-just-20.

76 **North Korea is particularly egregious:** Dorothy Denning (20 Feb 2018), "North Korea's growing criminal cyberthreat," *Conversation*, https://theconversation.com /north-koreas-growing-criminal-cyberthreat-89423.

76 **It employs hackers to raise money:** Sam Kim (7 Feb 2018), "Inside North Korea's hacker army," *Bloomberg*, https://www.bloomberg.com/news/features/2018-02-07 /inside-kim-jong-un-s-hacker-army.

76 **it stole $81 million from Bangladesh Bank:** Kim Zetter (17 Jun 2016), "That insane, $81M Bangladesh bank heist? Here's what we know," *Wired*, https://www.wired.com /2016/05/insane-81m-bangladesh-bank-heist-heres-know.

76 **We've seen webcams, DVRs:** Brian Krebs (16 Oct 2016), "Hacked cameras, DVRs powered today's massive internet outage," *Krebs on Security*, https://krebsonsecurity .com/2016/10/hacked-cameras-dvrs-powered-todays-massive-internet-outage.

76 **We've seen home appliances:** Proofpoint (16 Jan 2014), "Your fridge is full of spam: Proof of an IoT-driven attack," https://www.proofpoint.com/us/threat-insight/post /Your-Fridge-is-Full-of-SPAM. Dan Goodin (17 Jan 2014), "Is your refrigerator really part of a massive spam-sending botnet?" *Ars Technica*, https://arstechnica.com /information-technology/2014/01/is-your-refrigerator-really-part-of-a-massive-spam -sending-botnet.

76 **Attackers have bricked IoT devices:** Pierluigi Paganini (12 Apr 2017), "The rise of the

IoT botnet: Beyond the Mirai bot," *InfoSec Institute*, http://resources.infosecinstitute
.com/rise-iot-botnet-beyond-mirai-bot.

76 **Dick Cheney's heart defibrillator:** Dana Ford (24 Aug 2013), "Cheney's defibrillator
was modified to prevent hacking," *CNN*, http://www.cnn.com/2013/10/20/us/dick
-cheney-gupta-interview/index.html.

76 **In 2017, a man sent a tweet:** David Kravets (17 Mar 2017), "Man accused of sending a seizure-inducing tweet charged with cyberstalking," *Ars Technica*, https://
arstechnica.com/tech-policy/2017/03/man-arrested-for-allegedly-sending
-newsweek-writer-a-seizure-inducing-tweet.

77 **Also in 2017, WikiLeaks published information:** Steve Overly (8 Mar 2017), "What
we know about car hacking, the CIA and those WikiLeaks claims," *Washington
Post*, https://www.washingtonpost.com/news/innovations/wp/2017/03/08/what
-we-know-about-car-hacking-the-cia-and-those-wikileaks-claims.

77 **Hackers have demonstrated ransomware:** Lorenzo Franceschi-Bicchierai (7 Aug
2016), "Hackers make the first-ever ransomware for smart thermostats," *Vice Motherboard*, https://motherboard.vice.com/en_us/article/aekj9j/Internet-of-things
-ransomware-smart-thermostat.

77 **In 2017, an Austrian hotel:** David Z. Morris (29 Jan 2017), "Hackers hijack hotel's
smart locks, demand ransom," *Fortune*, http://fortune.com/2017/01/29/hackers
-hijack-hotels-smart-locks.

77 **In 2017, the NotPetya ransomware:** Russell Brandom (12 May 2017), "UK hospitals
hit with massive ransomware attack," *Verge*, https://www.theverge.com/2017/5/12
/15630354/nhs-hospitals-ransomware-hack-wannacry-bitcoin. April Glaser (27
Jun 2017), "U.S. hospitals have been hit by the global ransomware attack," *Recode*,
https://www.recode.net/2017/6/27/15881666/global-eu-cyber-attack-us-hackers-nsa
-hospitals.

77 **delay surgeries:** Denis Campbell and Haroon Siddique (15 May 2017), "Operations
cancelled as Hunt accused of ignoring cyber-attack warnings," *Guardian*, https://
www.theguardian.com/technology/2017/may/15/warning-of-nhs-cyber-attack-was
-not-acted-on-cybersecurity.

77 **route incoming emergency patients elsewhere:** ITV (16 May 2017), "NHS cyber
attack: Hospitals no longer diverting patients," http://www.itv.com/news/2017-05
-16/nhs-cyber-attack-hospitals-no-longer-diverting-patients.

77 **We saw the harbinger of this trend:** Sean Gallagher (25 Oct 2016), "How one rent
-a-botnet army of cameras, DVRs caused Internet chaos," *Ars Technica*, https://
arstechnica.com/information-technology/2016/10/inside-the-machine-uprising
-how-cameras-dvrs-took-down-parts-of-the-internet.

5. RISKS ARE BECOMING CATASTROPHIC

78 **You'll see it called the "CIA triad":** Mike Gault (20 Dec 2016), "The CIA secret to
cybersecurity that no one seems to get," *Wired*, https://www.wired.com/2015/12/the
-cia-secret-to-cybersecurity-that-no-one-seems-to-get.

78 **theft of celebrity photos from Apple's iCloud:** Jon Blistein (15 Mar 2016), "Hacker
pleads guilty to stealing celebrity nude photos," *Rolling Stone*, https://www
.rollingstone.com/movies/news/hacker-pleads-guilty-to-stealing-celebrity-nude
-photos-20160315.

78 **breach of the Ashley Madison adultery site:** Nate Lord (27 Jul 2017), "A timeline of the Ashley Madison hack," *Digital Guardian*, https://digitalguardian.com/blog/timeline -ashley-madison-hack.

78 **Russians hacked the Democratic National Committee:** Eric Lipton, David E. Sanger, and Scott Shane (13 Dec 2016), "The perfect weapon: How Russian cyber-power invaded the U.S.," *New York Times*, https://www.nytimes.com/2016/12/13/us/ politics/russia-hack-election-dnc.html.

78 **stole 150 million personal records from Equifax:** Stacy Cowley (2 Oct 2017), "2.5 million more people potentially exposed in Equifax breach," *New York Times*, https:// www.nytimes.com/2017/10/02/business/equifax-breach.html.

79 **Office of Personnel Management data breach:** Brendan I. Koerner (23 Oct 2016), "Inside the cyberattack that shocked the U.S. government," *Wired*, https://www .wired.com/2016/10/inside-cyberattack-shocked-us-government. Evan Perez (24 Aug 2017), "FBI arrests Chinese national connected to malware used in OPM data breach," *CNN*, http://www.cnn.com/2017/08/24/politics/fbi-arrests-chinese -national-in-opm-data-breach/index.html.

79 **One way of thinking about this:** Ross Anderson uses this language in his writ-ings. Eireann Leverett, Richard Clayton, and Ross Anderson (6 Jun 2017), "Standard-ization and certification of the 'Internet of Things,'" *Institute for Consumer Policy*, https://www.conpolicy.de/en/news-detail/standardization-and-certification-of-the -internet-of-things.

79 **In 2007, the Idaho National Laboratory:** Kim Zetter (26 Sep 2007), "Simulated cyberattack shows hackers blasting away at the power grid," *Wired*, https://www .wired.com/2007/09/simulated-cyber.

79 **In 2015, someone hacked into an unnamed steel mill:** Kim Zetter (1 Jan 2015), "A cyberattack has caused confirmed physical damage for the second time ever," *Wired*, https://www.wired.com/2015/01/german-steel-mill-hack-destruction.

79 **in 2016, the Department of Justice indicted an Iranian hacker:** Joseph Berger (25 Mar 2016), "A dam, small and unsung, is caught up in an Iranian hacking case," *New York Times*, http://www.nytimes.com/2016/03/26/nyregion/rye-brook-dam-caught -in-computer-hacking-case.html.

80 **"Accidents and, thus, potential catastrophes":** Charles Perrow (1999), *Normal Acci-dents: Living with High-Risk Technologies*, Princeton University Press, https://www .amazon.com/Normal-Accidents-Living-High-Risk-Technologies/dp/0691004129.

80 **In 2015, an 18-year-old outfitted a drone:** Michael Martinez, John Newsome, and Rene Marsh (21 Jul 2015), "Handgun-firing drone appears legal in video, but FAA, police probe further," *CNN*, http://www.cnn.com/2015/07/21/us/gun-drone -connecticut/index.html.

80 **Someone could also take control:** Jordan Golson (2 Aug 2016), "Jeep hackers at it again, this time taking control of steering and braking systems," *Verge*, https:// www.theverge.com/2016/8/2/12353186/car-hack-jeep-cherokee-vulnerability-miller -valasek.

80 **hack a hospital drug pump:** Kim Zetter (8 Jun 2015), "Hacker can send fatal dose to hospital drug pumps," *Wired*, https://www.wired.com/2015/06/hackers-can-send -fatal-doses-hospital-drug-pumps.

80 **So are airplanes:** Kim Zetter (26 May 2015), "Is it possible for passengers to hack commercial aircraft?" *Wired*, https://www.wired.com/2015/05/possible-passengers

-hack-commercial-aircraft. Anthony Cuthbertson (20 Dec 2016), "Hackers expose security flaws with major airlines," *Newsweek*, http://www.newsweek.com/hackers -hijack-planes-flight-system-flaw-534071.

80 **commercial ships:** Jack Morse (18 Jul 2017), "Remotely hacking ships shouldn't be this easy, and yet . . ." *Mashable*, http://mashable.com/2017/07/18/hacking-boats-is -fun-and-easy.

80 **electronic road signs:** Jill Scharr (6 Jun 2014), "Hacking an electronic highway sign is way too easy," *Tom's Guide*, https://www.tomsguide.com/us/highway-signs-easily -hacked,news-18915.html.

80 **tornado sirens:** Robert McMillan (12 Apr 2017), "Tornado-siren false alarm shows radio-hacking risk," *Wall Street Journal*, https://www.wsj.com/articles/tornado-siren -false-alarm-shows-radio-hacking-risk-1492042082.

80 **Nuclear weapons systems are almost:** John Denley (28 Sep 2017), "No nuclear weapon is safe from cyberattacks," *Wired*, https://www.wired.co.uk/article/no -nuclear-weapon-is-safe-from-cyberattacks.

80 **Satellites, too:** Gregory Falco (Mar 2018), "The Vacuum of Space Cyber Security," *Cyber Security Project, Harvard Kennedy School Belfer Center for Science and International Affairs*, unpublished draft.

80 **Attacks against the integrity of data:** Neal A. Pollar, Adam Segal, and Matthew G. DeVost (16 Jan 2018), "Trust war: Dangerous trends in cyber conflict," *War on the Rocks*, https://warontherocks.com/2018/01/trust-war-dangerous-trends-cyber -conflict.

80 **In 2016, Russian government hackers:** Rick Maese and Matt Bonesteel (9 Dec 2016), "World Anti-Doping Agency report details scope of massive Russian scheme," *Washington Post*, https://www.washingtonpost.com/news/early-lead/wp/2016/12/09 /wada-report-details-scope-of-massive-russian-doping-scheme.

80 **In 2017, hackers—possibly hired:** Karen DeYoung and Ellen Nakashima (16 Jul 2016), "UAE orchestrated hacking of Qatari government sites, sparking regional upheaval, according to U.S. intelligence officials," *Washington Post*, https://www .washingtonpost.com/world/national-security/uae-hacked-qatari-government -sites-sparking-regional-upheaval-according-to-us-intelligence-officials/2017/07 /16/00c46e54-698f-11e7-8eb5-cbccc2e7bfbf_story.html.

80 **There is evidence that the Russians:** Nicole Perlroth, Michael Wines, and Matthew Rosenberg (1 Sep 2017), "Russian election hacking efforts, wider than previously known, draw little scrutiny," *New York Times*, https://www.nytimes.com/2017/09/01 /us/politics/russia-election-hacking.html.

81 **"Most of the public discussion":** James R. Clapper (26 Feb 2015), "Statement for the record: Worldwide threat assessment of the US intelligence community: Senate Armed Services Committee," *Office of the Director of National Intelligence*, http:// www.dni.gov/files/documents/Unclassified_2015_ATA_SFR_-_SASC_FINAL.pdf.

81 **then–director of national intelligence James Clapper:** Ashley Carman (11 Sep 2015), "'Information integrity' among top cyber priorities for U.S. gov't, Clapper says," *SC Magazine*, http://www.scmagazine.com/intelligence-committee-hosts -cybersecurity-hearing/article/438202.

81 **then–NSA director Mike Rogers:** Katie Bo Williams (27 Sep 2015), "Officials worried hackers will change your data, not steal it," *Hill*, http://thehill.com/policy/cyber security/254977-officials-worried-hackers-will-change-your-data-not-steal-it.

81 **"Future cyber operations will almost certainly":** James R. Clapper (9 Feb 2016), "Statement for the record: Worldwide threat assessment of the US intelligence community: Senate Armed Services Committee," *Office of the Director of National Intelligence*, https://www.dni.gov/files/documents/SASC_Unclassified_2016_ATA_SFR _FINAL.pdf.

81 **Between 2014 and 2016:** Shaun Waterman (20 Jul 2016), "Bank regulators briefed on Treasury-led cyber drill," *Fed Scoop*, https://www.fedscoop.com/us-treasury -cybersecurity-drill-july-2016.

81 **and then established a program:** Telis Demos (3 Dec 2017), "Banks build line of defense for doomsday cyberattack," *Wall Street Journal*, https://www.wsj.com/articles /banks-build-line-of-defense-for-doomsday-cyberattack-1512302401.

82 **The machine-learning algorithm modifies:** Ben Buchanan and Taylor Miller (Jun 2017), "Machine Learning for Policymakers: What It Is and Why It Matters," *Cyber Security Project, Harvard Kennedy School Belfer Center for Science and International Affairs*, https://www.belfercenter.org/sites/default/files/files/publication/Machine LearningforPolicymakers.pdf.

82 **They categorize photographs and translate text:** Sam Wong (30 Nov 2016), "Google Translate AI invents its own language to translate with," *New Scientist*, https://www .newscientist.com/article/2114748-google-translate-ai-invents-its-own-language-to -translate-with. Cade Metz (9 May 2017), "Facebook's new AI could lead to translations that actually make sense," *Wired*, https://www.wired.com/2017/05/facebook -open-sources-neural-networks-speed-translations.

82 **They play Go as well as a master:** Elizabeth Gibney (17 Jan 2016), "Google AI algorithm masters ancient game of Go," *Nature* 529, http://www.nature.com/news/google -ai-algorithm-masters-ancient-game-of-go-1.19234.

82 **read X-rays and diagnose cancers:** Andre Esteva et al. (25 Jan 2017), "Dermatologist -level classification of skin cancer with deep neural networks," *Nature* 542, https:// www.nature.com/nature/journal/v542/n7639/full/nature21056.html.

82 **inform bail, sentencing, and parole decisions:** Julia Angwin et al. (23 May 2016), "Machine bias," *ProPublica*, https://www.propublica.org/article/machine-bias-risk -assessments-in-criminal-sentencing.

82 **They analyze speech to assess suicide risk:** Peter Holley (26 Sep 2017), "Teenage suicide is extremely difficult to predict. That's why some experts are turning to machines for help," *Washington Post*, https://www.washingtonpost.com/amphtml /news/innovations/wp/2017/09/25/teenage-suicide-is-extremely-difficult-to -predict-thats-why-some-experts-are-turning-to-machines-for-help.

82 **analyze faces to predict homosexuality:** To be fair, there are a lot of questions about this research. Yilun Wang and Michal Kosinski (15 Feb 2017; last updated 16 Oct 2017), "Deep neural networks are more accurate than humans at detecting sexual orientation from facial images," *Open Science Framework*, https://osf.io/zn79k.

82 **predicting the quality of fine Bordeaux wine:** Orley Ashenfelter (29 May 2008), "Predicting the quality and prices of Bordeaux wine," *Economic Journal*, http:// onlinelibrary.wiley.com/doi/10.1111/j.1468-0297.2008.02148.x/abstract.

82 **hiring blue-collar employees:** Mitchell Hoffman, Lisa Kahn, and Danielle Li (Nov 2015), "Discretion in hiring," *National Bureau of Economic Research*, https://www .nber.org/papers/w21709.pdf.

82 **deciding whether to punt in football:** Adam Himmelsbach (18 Aug 2012), "Punting

less can be rewarding, but coaches aren't risking jobs on it," *New York Times*, http://www.nytimes.com/2012/08/19/sports/football/calculating-footballs-risk-of-not-punting-on-fourth-down.html.

82 **Machine learning is used to detect:** Sally Adee (17 Aug 2016), "Scammer AI can tailor clickbait to you for phishing attacks," *New Scientist*, https://www.newscientist.com/article/2101483-scammer-ai-can-tailor-clickbait-to-you-for-phishing-attacks.

82 **For example, Deep Patient:** Riccardo Miotto, Brian A. Kidd, and Joel T. Dudley (17 May 2016), "Deep Patient: An unsupervised representation to predict the future of patients from the electronic health records," *Scientific Reports* 6, no. 26094, https://www.nature.com/articles/srep26094.

83 **But although the system works:** Will Knight (11 Apr 2017), "The dark secret at the heart of AI," *MIT Technology Review*, https://www.technologyreview.com/s/604087/the-dark-secret-at-the-heart-of-ai.

83 **A 2014 book, *Autonomous Technologies*:** William Messner, ed. (2014), *Autonomous Technologies: Applications That Matter*, SAE International, http://books.sae.org/jpf-auv-004.

84 **One research project focused on:** Anh Nguyen, Jason Yosinski, and Jeff Clune (2 Apr 2015), "Deep neural networks are easily fooled: High confidence predictions for unrecognizable images," in *Proceedings of the 2015 IEEE Conference on Computer Vision and Pattern Recognition (CVPR '15)*, https://arxiv.org/abs/1412.1897.

84 **A related research project was able:** Christian Szegedy et al. (19 Feb 2014), "Intriguing properties of neural networks," in *Conference Proceedings: International Conference on Learning Representations (ICLR) 2014*, https://arxiv.org/abs/1312.6199.

84 **Yet another project tricked an algorithm:** Andrew Ilyas et al. (20 Dec 2017), "Partial information attacks on real-world AI," *LabSix*, http://www.labsix.org/partial-information-adversarial-examples.

85 **Like the Microsoft chatbot Tay:** James Vincent (24 Mar 2016), "Twitter taught Microsoft's AI chatbot to be a racist asshole in less than a day," *Verge*, https://www.theverge.com/2016/3/24/11297050/tay-microsoft-chatbot-racist.

85 **In 2017, Dow Jones accidentally:** Timothy B. Lee (10 Oct 2017), "Dow Jones posts fake story claiming Google was buying Apple," *Ars Technica*, https://arstechnica.com/tech-policy/2017/10/dow-jones-posts-fake-story-claiming-google-was-buying-apple.

85 **Within minutes, a trillion dollars:** Bob Pisani (21 Apr 2015), "What caused the flash crash? DFTC, DOJ weigh in," *CNBC*, https://www.cnbc.com/2015/04/21/what-caused-the-flash-crash-cftc-doj-weigh-in.html.

85 **in 2013, hackers broke into the Associated Press's:** Edmund Lee (24 Apr 2013), "AP Twitter account hacked in market-moving attack," *Bloomberg*, https://www.bloomberg.com/news/articles/2013-04-23/dow-jones-drops-recovers-after-false-report-on-ap-twitter-page.

85 **We should also expect autonomous:** George Dvorsky (11 Sep 2017), "Hackers have already started to weaponize artificial intelligence," *Gizmodo*, https://gizmodo.com/hackers-have-already-started-to-weaponize-artificial-in-1797688425.

85 **The Cyber Grand Challenge was similar:** Cade Metz (6 Jul 2016), "DARPA goes full *Tron* with its grand battle of the hack bots," *Wired*, https://www.wired.com/2016/07/__trashed-19.

85 **One program found:** Matthew Braga (16 Jun 2016), "In the future, we'll leave software bug hunting to the machines," *Vice Motherboard*, https://motherboard.vice.com/en

_us/article/mg73a8/cyber-grand-challenge. Cade Metz (5 Aug 2016), "Hackers don't have to be human anymore. This bot battle proves it," *Wired*, https://www.wired.com /2016/08/security-bots-show-hacking-isnt-just-humans.

85 **In a later contest that had both:** Sharon Gaudin (5 Aug 2016), "'Mayhem' takes first in DARPA hacking challenge," *Computerworld*, https://www.computerworld.com /article/3104891/security/mayhem-takes-first-in-darpas-all-computer-hacking -challenge.html.

85 **Attackers will use software to:** Kevin Townsend (29 Nov 2016), "How machine learning will help attackers," *Security Week*, http://www.securityweek.com/how-machine -learning-will-help-attackers.

85 **Most security experts expect:** Cylance (1 Aug 2017), "Black Hat attendees see AI as double-edged sword," https://www.cylance.com/en_us/blog/black-hat-attendees -see-ai-as-double-edged-sword.html.

86 **"Artificial intelligence and machine learning":** Greg Allen and Taniel Chan (13 Jul 2017), "Artificial intelligence and national security," *Harvard Kennedy School Belfer Center for Science and International Affairs*, https://www.belfercenter.org/sites/default /files/files/publication/AI%20NatSec%20-%20final.pdf.

86 **in robots to remotely take control of them:** Matt Burgess (22 Aug 2017), "Ethical hackers have turned this robot into a stabbing machine," *Wired*, https://www.wired .co.uk/article/hacked-robots-pepper-nao-alpha-2-stab-screwdriver.

86 **in teleoperated surgical robots:** Tamara Bonaci et al. (17 Apr 2015), "To make a robot secure: An experimental analysis of cyber security threats against teleoperated surgical robotics," *ArXiv* 1504.04339v1, https://arxiv.org/pdf/1504.04339v1.pdf. Darlene Storm (27 Apr 2015), "Researchers hijack teleoperated surgical robot: Remote surgery hacking threats," *Computerworld*, https://www.computerworld.com/article/2914741 /cybercrime-hacking/researchers-hijack-teleoperated-surgical-robot-remote -surgery-hacking-threats.html.

86 **and industrial robots:** Thomas Fox-Brewster (3 May 2017), "Catastrophe warning: Watch an industrial robot get hacked," *Forbes*, https://www.forbes.com/sites/ thomasbrewster/2017/05/03/researchers-hack-industrial-robot-making-a-drone-rotor.

86 **Autonomous military systems deserve:** Paul Scharre (24 Apr 2017), *Army of None: Autonomous Weapons and the Future of War*, W. W. Norton, https://books.google.com /books?id=sjMsDwAAQBAJ.

86 **The US Department of Defense defines:** Heather Roff (9 Feb 2016), "Distinguishing autonomous from automatic weapons," *Bulletin of the Atomic Scientists*, http:// thebulletin.org/autonomous-weapons-civilian-safety-and-regulation-versus -prohibition/distinguishing-autonomous-automatic-weapons.

86 **If they are autonomous:** Paul Scharre (29 Feb 2016), "Autonomous weapons and operational risk," *Center for a New American Security*, https://www.cnas.org/publications /reports/autonomous-weapons-and-operational-risk.

86 **Technologists Bill Gates, Elon Musk, and Stephen Hawking:** Michael Sainato (19 Aug 2015), "Stephen Hawking, Elon Musk, and Bill Gates warn about artificial intelligence," *Observer*, http://observer.com/2015/08/stephen-hawking-elon-musk-and-bill -gates-warn-about-artificial-intelligence.

86 **The risks might be remote:** Stuart Russell et al. (11 Jan 2015), "An open letter: Research priorities for robust and beneficial artificial intelligence," *Future of Life Institute*, https://futureoflife.org/ai-open-letter.

86 **I am less worried about AI:** These two essays talk about that: Ted Chiang (18 Dec 2017), "Silicon Valley is turning into its own worst fear," *BuzzFeed*, https://www .buzzfeed.com/tedchiang/the-real-danger-to-civilization-isnt-ai-its-runaway. Charlie Stross (Jan 2018), "Dude, you broke the future!" *Charlie's Diary*, http://www .antipope.org/charlie/blog-static/2018/01/dude-you-broke-the-future.html.

87 **"Long before we see such machines arising":** Rodney Brooks (7 Sep 2017), "The seven deadly sins of predicting the future of AI," http://rodneybrooks.com/the-seven -deadly-sins-of-predicting-the-future-of-ai.

87 **For example, there is widespread suspicion:** Sean Gallagher (15 Nov 2016), "Chinese company installed secret backdoor on hundreds of thousands of phones," *Ars Technica*, https://arstechnica.com/information-technology/2016/11/chinese-company -installed-secret-backdoor-on-hundreds-of-thousands-of-phones.

87 **computer security products from Kaspersky Lab:** Cyrus Farivar (11 Jul 2017), "Kaspersky under scrutiny after Bloomberg story claims close links to FSB," *Ars Technica*, https://arstechnica.com/information-technology/2017/07/kaspersky -denies-inappropriate-ties-with-russian-govt-after-bloomberg-story.

87 **In 2018, US intelligence officials:** Selena Larson (14 Feb 2018), "The FBI, CIA and NSA say Americans shouldn't use Huawei phones," *CNN*, http://money.cnn.com/2018/02 /14/technology/huawei-intelligence-chiefs/index.html.

87 **Back in 1997, the Israeli company Check Point:** Emily G. Cohen (7 Jul 1997), "Check Point response to Mossad rumor," *Firewalls Mailing List*, Great Circle Associates, http://old.greatcircle.com/firewalls/mhonarc/firewalls.199707/msg00223.html.

87 **In the US, the NSA secretly installed:** Julia Angwin et al. (15 Aug 2015), "AT&T helped U.S. spy on Internet on a vast scale, *New York Times*, https://www.nytimes.com/2015 /08/16/us/politics/att-helped-nsa-spy-on-an-array-of-internet-traffic.html.

87 **They demonstrate the vulnerability:** Arnd Weber et al. (22 Mar 2018), "Sovereignty in information technology: Security, safety and fair market access by openness and control of the supply chain," *Karlsruher Institut für Technologie*, http://www.itas.kit .edu/pub/v/2018/weua18a.pdf.

88 **Adding a backdoor onto a computer chip:** Georg T. Becker et al. (Jan 2014), "Stealthy dopant-level hardware Trojans: Extended version," *Journal of Cryptographic Engineering* 4, https://link.springer.com/article/10.1007/s13389-013-0068-0.

88 **China demands to see source code:** Paul Mozur (28 Jan 2015), "New rules in China upset Western tech companies," *New York Times*, https://www.nytimes.com /2015/01/29/technology/in-china-new-cybersecurity-rules-perturb-western-tech -companies.html.

88 **So does the US:** Zack Whittaker (17 Mar 2016), "U.S. government pushed tech firms to hand over source code," *ZDNet*, http://www.zdnet.com/article/us-government -pushed-tech-firms-to-hand-over-source-code.

88 **Kaspersky offered to let any government:** John Leyden (23 Oct 2017), "'We've nothing to hide': Kaspersky Lab offers to open up source code," *Register*, https://www .theregister.co.uk/2017/10/23/kaspersky_source_code_review.

88 **In 2017, HP Enterprise faced criticism:** Joel Schectman, Dustin Volz, and Jack Stubbs (2 Oct 2017), "HP Enterprise let Russia scrutinize cyberdefense system used by Pentagon," *Reuters*, https://www.reuters.com/article/us-usa-cyber-russia-hpe -specialreport/special-report-hp-enterprise-let-russia-scrutinize-cyberdefense -system-used-by-pentagon-idUSKCN1C716M.

88 **According to NSA documents:** Whether they were successful or not was deliberately withheld by the *New York Times*, citing national security concerns. My guess is that they were successful. David E. Sanger and Nicole Perlroth (23 Mar 2014), "N.S.A. breached Chinese servers seen as security threat," *New York Times*, https://www.nytimes.com/2014/03/23/world/asia/nsa-breached-chinese-servers-seen-as-spy-peril.html.

88 **We know from the Snowden documents:** The one document we have shows the NSA intercepting devices "bound for the Syrian Telecommunications Establishment (STE) to be used as part of their internet backbone." Chief (name redacted), Access and Target Development (S3261) (Jun 2010), "Stealthy techniques can crack some of SIGINT's hardest targets," *SID Today*, http://www.spiegel.de/media/media-35669.pdf. Sean Gallagher (14 May 2014), "Photos of an NSA 'upgrade' factory show Cisco router getting implant," *Ars Technica*, https://arstechnica.com/tech-policy/2014/05/photos-of-an-nsa-upgrade-factory-show-cisco-router-getting-implant.

88 **That was done without Cisco's knowledge:** Darren Pauli (18 Mar 2015), "Cisco posts kit to empty houses to dodge NSA chop shops," *Register*, https://www.theregister.co.uk/2015/03/18/want_to_dodge_nsa_supply_chain_taps_ask_cisco_for_a_dead_drop.

88 **in Juniper firewalls:** Kim Zetter (19 Dec 2015), "Secret code found in Juniper's firewalls shows risk of government backdoors," *Wired*, https://www.wired.com/2015/12/juniper-networks-hidden-backdoors-show-the-risk-of-government-backdoors.

88 **and D-Link routers:** Jeremy Kirk (14 Oct 2013), "Backdoor found in D-Link router firmware code," *InfoWorld*, http://www.infoworld.com/article/2612384/network-router/backdoor-found-in-d-link-router-firmware-code.html.

88 **One report said that 4.2 million fake apps:** Gio Benitez (7 Nov 2017), "How to protect yourself from downloading fake apps and getting hacked," *ABC News*, http://abcnews.go.com/US/protect-downloading-fake-apps-hacked/story?id=50972286.

88 **This included a fake WhatsApp app:** Lorenzo Franceschi-Bicchierai (3 Nov 2017), "More than 1 million people downloaded a fake WhatsApp Android app," *Vice Motherboard*, https://motherboard.vice.com/en_us/article/evbakk/fake-whatsapp-android-app-1-million-downloads.

88 **Hackers linked to China compromised:** Lucian Constantin (18 Sep 2017), "Malware-infected CCleaner installer distributed to users via official servers for a month," *Vice Motherboard*, https://motherboard.vice.com/en_us/article/a3kgpa/ccleaner-backdoor-malware-hack. Thomas Fox-Brewster (21 Sep 2017), "Avast: The 2.3M CCleaner hack was a sophisticated assault on the tech industry," *Forbes*, https://www.forbes.com/sites/thomasbrewster/2017/09/21/avast-ccleaner-attacks-target-tech-industry.

89 **Unknown hackers corrupted:** Andy Greenberg (7 Jul 2017), "The Petya plague exposes the threat of evil software updates," *Wired*, https://www.wired.com/story/petya-plague-automatic-software-updates.

89 **Another group used fake antivirus updates:** Joseph Graziano (21 Nov 2013), "Fake AV software updates are distributing malware," *Symantec Corporation*, https://www.symantec.com/connect/blogs/fake-av-software-updates-are-distributing-malware.

89 **Researchers demonstrated how to hack:** Omer Shwartz et al. (14 Aug 2017), "Shattered trust: When replacement smartphone components attack," in *Proceedings of*

the 11th USENIX Workshop on Offensive Technologies (WOOT 17), https://www.usenix
.org/conference/woot17/workshop-program/presentation/shwartz.

89 **And there are enough similar attacks:** Mike Murphy (18 Dec 2017), "Think twice
about buying internet-connected devices off eBay," *Quartz*, https://qz.com/1156059
/dont-buy-second-hand-internet-connected-iot-devices-from-sites-like-ebay-ebay.

89 **In 2018, the African Union discovered:** Aaron Maasho (29 Jan 2018), "China denies
report it hacked African Union headquarters," *Reuters*, https://www.reuters.com
/article/us-africanunion-summit-china/china-denies-report-it-hacked-african
-union-headquarters-idUSKBN1FI2I5.

89 **I am reminded of the US embassy:** Elaine Sciolino (15 Nov 1988), "The bugged
embassy case: What went wrong," *New York Times*, http://www.nytimes.com/1988
/11/15/world/the-bugged-embassy-case-what-went-wrong.html.

89 **"An aggressor nation or extremist group":** Elisabeth Bumiller and Thom Shanker
(11 Oct 2012), "Panetta warns of dire threat of cyberattack," *New York Times*, http://www
.nytimes.com/2012/10/12/world/panetta-warns-of-dire-threat-of-cyberattack.html.

90 **"Cyber threats also pose an increasing risk":** Daniel R. Coats (11 May 2017), "Statement for the record: Worldwide threat assessment of the US intelligence community:
Senate Select Committee on Intelligence," *Office of the Director of National Intelligence*, https://www.dni.gov/files/documents/Newsroom/Testimonies/SSCI%20
Unclassified%20SFR%20-%20Final.pdf.

90 **"The potential for surprise in the cyber realm":** Daniel R. Coats (13 Feb 2018), "State-
ment for the record: Worldwide threat assessment of the US intelligence community,"
Office of the Director of National Intelligence, https://www.dni.gov/files/documents
/Newsroom/Testimonies/2018-ATA---Unclassified-SSCI.pdf.

90 **In 2015, Lloyd's of London developed:** Simon Ruffle et al. (6 Jul 2015), "Business
blackout: The insurance implications of a cyber attack on the U.S. power grid,"
Lloyd's Cambridge Centre for Risk Studies, https://www.lloyds.com/news-and-insight
/risk-insight/library/society-and-security/business-blackout.

90 **Someone with a gun can do more damage:** Stephen Paddock is an example of this.
Alex Horton (3 Oct 2017), "The Las Vegas shooter modified a dozen rifles to shoot
like automatic weapons," *Washington Post*, https://www.washingtonpost.com/news
/checkpoint/wp/2017/10/02/video-from-las-vegas-suggests-automatic-gunfire-heres
-what-makes-machine-guns-different.

91 **That gun-carrying drone will become:** ReprapAlgarve (23 Sep 2016), "DIY 3D printed
assassination drone," *YouTube*, https://www.youtube.com/watch?v=N3mdUjT6C5w.

91 **Liberal democracies are more vulnerable:** Jack Goldsmith and Stuart Russell (5 Jun
2018), "Strengths Become Vulnerabilities: How a Digital World Disadvantages the
United States in Its International Relations," *Aegis Series Paper*, Hoover Working
Group on National Security, Technology, and Law, https://www.hoover.org/sites/
default/files/research/docs/381100534-strengths-become-vulnerabilities.pdf

92 **"Our economy is more digitalized":** Barack Obama (16 Dec 2016), "Press conference
by the president," *White House Office of the Press Secretary*, https://obamawhitehouse
.archives.gov/the-press-office/2016/12/16/press-conference-president.

92 **This asymmetry makes deterrence more difficult:** Joseph Nye has written
extensively about deterrence in cyberspace. Joseph S. Nye Jr. (1 Feb 2017), "Deterrence and dissuasion in cyberspace," *International Security* 41, no. 3, https://www
.mitpressjournals.org/doi/pdf/10.1162/ISEC_a_00266.

92 **The technologies that we most feared:** Rochelle F. H. Bohaty (12 Jan 2008), "Danger-ously vulnerable," *Chemical & Engineering News*, http://pubs.acs.org/cen/email/html/cen_87_i02_8702gov2.html.

92 **Cyberweapons have been invoked:** Also, biological attacks and cyberattacks are both much harder to attribute than the others, making them even scarier.

93 **Electromagnetic pulse weapons are:** Peter Vincent Pry (8 May 2014), "Electromag-netic pulse: Threat to critical infrastructure," *Testimony before the Subcommittee on Cybersecurity, Infrastructure Protection and Security Technologies, House Commit-tee on Homeland Security*, http://docs.house.gov/meetings/HM/HM08/20140508/102200/HHRG-113-HM08-Wstate-PryP-20140508.pdf. William R. Graham and Peter Vincent Pry (12 Oct 2017), "North Korea nuclear EMP attack: An existential threat," *US House of Representatives Committee on Homeland Security, Subcommittee on Over-sight and Management Efficiency Hearing*, http://docs.house.gov/meetings/HM/HM09/20171012/106467/HHRG-115-HM09-Wstate-PryP-20171012.pdf.

93 **I'm sure that future technological developments:** The term "weapon of mass destruction" is now being used for pretty much everything. The FBI referred to the Boston Marathon bombers' pressure-cooker bombs as weapons of mass destruc-tion. Federal Bureau of Investigation (accessed 24 Apr 2018), "Weapons of mass destruction," http://www.fbi.gov/about-us/investigate/terrorism/wmd/wmd_faqs. Brian Palmer (31 Mar 2010), "When did IEDs become WMD?" *Slate*, http://www.slate.com/articles/news_and_politics/explainer/2010/03/when_did_ieds_become_wmd.html.

93 **"Terrorists—to include the Islamic State":** Daniel R. Coats (11 May 2017), "State-ment for the record: Worldwide threat assessment of the US intelligence community: Senate Select Committee on Intelligence," *Office of the Director of National Intelli-gence*, https://www.dni.gov/files/documents/Newsroom/Testimonies/SSCI%20Unclassified%20SFR%20-%20Final.pdf.

93 **"If there was even a 1 percent chance":** Ron Suskind (2006), *The One Percent Doctrine: Deep inside America's Pursuit of Its Enemies since 9/11*, Simon & Schuster, https://www.amazon.com/dp/B000NY12N2/ref=dp-kindle-redirect?_encoding=UTF8&btkr=1.

94 **I have long thought:** James Barron (15 Aug 2003), "The blackout of 2003," *New York Times*, http://www.nytimes.com/2003/08/15/nyregion/blackout-2003-overview-power-surge-blacks-northeast-hitting-cities-8-states.html.

94 **It wasn't deliberate by any stretch:** US-CERT National Cyber Awareness System (Dec 2003), "2003 CERT Advisories," *Carnegie Mellon Software Engineering Institute*, https://www.cert.org/historical/advisories/CA-2003-20.cfm.

94 **The official report on the blackout:** Paul F. Barber et al. (13 Jul 2004), "Technical analysis of the August 13, 2003 blackout," *North American Electric Reliability Council*, http://www.nerc.com/docs/docs/blackout/NERC_Final_Blackout_Report_07_13_04.pdf. U.S.-Canada Power System Outage Task Force (1 Apr 2004), "Final report on the August 14, 2003 blackout in the United States and Canada: Causes and recommen-dations," https://energy.gov/sites/prod/files/oeprod/DocumentsandMedia/Blackout Final-Web.pdf.

94 **Similarly, the authors of the Mirai botnet:** Brian Krebs (18 Jan 2017), "Who is Anna-Senpai, the Mirai worm author?" *Krebs on Security*, https://krebsonsecurity.com/2017/01/who-is-anna-senpai-the-mirai-worm-author.

94 **In fact, three college students wrote:** Garrett M. Graff (13 Dec 2017), "How a dorm

room Minecraft scam brought down the Internet," *Wired*, https://www.wired.com /story/mirai-botnet-minecraft-scam-brought-down-the-internet.

94 **But it erased all data on over 30,000 hard drives:** Parmy Olson (9 Nov 2012), "The day a computer virus came close to plugging Gulf Oil," *Forbes*, https://www.forbes.com /sites/parmyolson/2012/11/09/the-day-a-computer-virus-came-close-to-plugging -gulf-oil.

94 **The shipping giant Maersk was hit:** Iain Thomson (16 Aug 2017), "NotPetya ransomware attack cost us $300m—shipping giant Maersk," *Register*, https://www .theregister.co.uk/2017/08/16/notpetya_ransomware_attack_cost_us_300m_says _shipping_giant_maersk.

95 **To this we can add mass murder:** Elton Hobson (24 Nov 2017), "Powerful video warns of the danger of autonomous 'slaughterbot' drone swarms," *Global News*, https:// globalnews.ca/news/3880186/powerful-video-warns-of-the-danger-of-autonomous -slaughterbot-drone-swarms.

95 **malicious code received from space aliens:** Michael Hippke and John G. Learned (6 Feb 2018), "Interstellar communication. IX. Message decontamination is possible," *ArXiv* 1802.02180v1, https://arxiv.org/pdf/1802.02180.pdf.

95 **all the things we haven't thought of yet:** I've heard the term "BRINE" used as an acronym to refer to "biology, robotics, information, nanotechnology, and energy." James Kadtke and Linton Wells II (4 Sep 2014), "Policy challenges of accelerating technological change: Security policy and strategy implications of parallel scientific revolutions," *Center for Technology and National Security Policy, National Defense University*, http://ctnsp.dodlive.mil/files/2014/09/DTP106.pdf.

95 **They put less money into:** Bruce Russett et al. (Dec 1994), "Did Americans' expectations of nuclear war reduce their savings?" *International Studies Quarterly* 38, http://www.jstor.org/discover/10.2307/2600866?uid=3739256&uid=2&uid=4&sid =21103807505461.

95 **Some people decided not to have children:** William R. Beardslee (Mar–Apr 1983), "Adolescents and the threat of nuclear war: The evolution of a perspective," *Yale Journal of Biology and Medicine* 56, http://www.ncbi.nlm.nih.gov/pmc/articles/PMC 2589708/pdf/yjbm00104-0020.pdf.

95 **Over the years, there were plenty:** Union of Concerned Scientists (20 Apr 2015), "Close calls with nuclear weapons," http://www.ucsusa.org/sites/default/files/attach/2015 /04/Close%20Calls%20with%20Nuclear%20Weapons.pdf. Future of Life Institute (1 Feb 2016), "Accidental nuclear war: A timeline," https://futureoflife.org/background /nuclear-close-calls-a-timeline.

95 **The Cuban Missile Crisis is probably:** Benjamin Schwarz (1 Jan 2013), "The real Cuban missile crisis," *Atlantic*, https://www.theatlantic.com/magazine/archive/2013 /01/the-real-cuban-missile-crisis/309190.

95 **although the 1983 false alarm is a close second:** Sewell Chan (18 Sep 2017), "Stanislav Petrov, Soviet officer who helped avert nuclear war," *New York Times*, https://www .nytimes.com/2017/09/18/world/europe/stanislav-petrov-nuclear-war-dead.html.

95 **although much less damaging than:** Laura Geggel (9 Feb 2016), "The odds of dying," *Live Science*, https://www.livescience.com/3780-odds-dying.html.

95 **But instead of regarding it as:** As amazing as it seems today, immediately after 9/11, people actually believed that terrorist attacks of that magnitude would happen every few months. Pew Research Center (Apr 2013), "Apr 18–21 2013, omnibus, final

topline, N=1,002," *Pew Research Center*, http://www.people-press.org/files/legacy -questionnaires/4-23-13%20topline%20for%20release.pdf.

95 **the Boston Marathon bombings:** Adam Gabbatt (23 Apr 2013), "Boston Marathon bombing injury toll rises to 264," *Guardian*, http://www.theguardian.com/world /2013/apr/23/boston-marathon-injured-toll-rise.

95 **Bathtubs, home appliances, and deer:** National Safety Council (accessed 24 Apr 2018), "What are the odds of dying from . . . ," http://www.nsc.org/learn/safety -knowledge/Pages/injury-facts-chart.aspx (text, chart), http://injuryfacts.nsc.org /all-injuries/preventable-death-overview/odds-of-dying (graphic). Kevin Gipson and Adam Suchy (Sep 2011), "Instability of televisions, furniture, and appliances: Estimated and reported fatalities, 2011 report," *Consumer Product Safety Commission*, https://web.archive.org/web/20111007090947/http://www.cpsc.gov/library/foia /foia11/os/tipover2011.pdf.

95 **But while we seem to be coming out of:** John Mueller and Mark G. Stewart (1 Jul 2012), "The terrorism delusion: America's overwrought response to September 11," *International Security* 37, no. 1, https://politicalscience.osu.edu/faculty/jmueller/absisfin.pdf.

95 **In general, people are very bad at:** Daniel Gilbert (2 Jul 2006), "If only gay sex caused global warming," *Los Angeles Times*, http://articles.latimes.com/2006/jul/02/opinion /op-gilbert2. Bruce Schneier (13 Jun 2008), "The psychology of security," *AfricaCrypt 2008*, https://www.schneier.com/academic/archives/2008/01/the_psychology_of _se.html.

96 **I coined the term in 2005:** Bruce Schneier (8 Sep 2005), "Terrorists don't do movie plots," *Wired*, http://www.wired.com/2005/09/terrorists-dont-do-movie-plots.

96 **One: we are a species of storytellers:** Bruce Schneier (31 Jul 2012), "Drawing the wrong lessons from horrific events," *CNN*, http://www.cnn.com/2012/07/31/opinion /schneier-aurora-aftermath/index.html.

96 **And two: it makes no sense:** Bruce Schneier (Nov 2009), "Beyond security theater," *New Internationalist*, https://www.schneier.com/essays/archives/2009/11/beyond _security_thea.html.

PART II: THE SOLUTIONS

100 **Today, spam still constitutes:** Statista (Oct 2017), "Global spam volume as percentage of total e-mail traffic from January 2014 to September 2017, by month," https:// www.statista.com/statistics/420391/spam-email-traffic-share.

100 **but 99.99% of it is blocked:** Jordan Robertson (19 Jan 2016), "E-mail spam goes artisanal," *Bloomberg*, https://www.bloomberg.com/news/articles/2016-01-19/e-mail -spam-goes-artisanal.

100 **The EU's Payment Services Directives:** Steven J. Murdoch (3 Oct 2017), "Liability for push payment fraud pushed onto the victims," *Bentham's Gaze*, https://www .benthamsgaze.org/2017/10/03/liability-for-push-payment-fraud-pushed-onto-the -victims. Steven J. Murdoch and Ross Anderson (9 Nov 2014), "Security protocols and evidence: Where many payment systems fail," *FC 2014: International Conference on Financial Cryptography and Data Security*, https://link.springer.com/chapter/10 .1007/978-3-662-45472-5_2.

100 **Amazingly, the UK may make this:** Patrick Jenkins and Sam Jones (25 May 2016), "Bank customers may cover cost of fraud under new UK proposals," *Financial Times*, https://www.ft.com/content/e335211c-2105-11e6-aa98-db1e01fabc0c.

100 **And similarly, in the US:** Federal Trade Commission (Aug 2012), "Lost or stolen credit, ATM, and debit cards," https://www.consumer.ftc.gov/articles/0213-lost-or -stolen-credit-atm-and-debit-cards.

101 **"security is a tax on the honest":** Bruce Schneier (2012), *Liars and Outliers: Enabling the Trust That Society Needs to Thrive*, Wiley, http://www.wiley.com/WileyCDA/Wiley Title/productCd-1118143302.html.

101 **"guard labor":** Arjun Jayadev and Samuel Bowles (Apr 2006), "Guard labor," *Journal of Development Economics* 79, no. 2, http://www.sciencedirect.com/science/article/pii /S0304387806000125.

101 **The tech analyst firm Gartner estimates:** Gartner (16 Aug 2017), "Gartner says worldwide information security spending will grow 7 percent to reach $86.4 billion in 2017," https://www.gartner.com/newsroom/id/3784965.

101 **If we want more security:** Allison Gatlin (8 Feb 2016), "Cisco, IBM, Dell M&A brawl may whack Symantec, Palo Alto, Fortinet," *Investor's Business Daily*, https://www .investors.com/news/technology/cisco-ibm-dell-ma-brawl-whacks-symantec-palo -alto-fortinet.

102 **A 2017 Ponemon Institute report concluded:** Ponemon Institute (20 Jun 2017) "2017 cost of data breach study," http://info.resilientsystems.com/hubfs/IBM_Resilient _Branded_Content/White_Papers/2017_Global_CODB_Report_Final.pdf.

102 **A Symantec report estimated:** Symantec Corporation (23 Jan 2018), "2017 Norton cyber security insights report: Global results," https://www.symantec.com/content /dam/symantec/docs/about/2017-ncsir-global-results-en.pdf.

103 **"We found that resulting values are":** I was a member of the steering committee for this research project. Paul Dreyer et al. (14 Jan 2018), "Estimating the global cost of cyber risk," RAND Corporation, https://www.rand.org/pubs/research _reports/RR2299.html.

6. WHAT A SECURE INTERNET+ LOOKS LIKE

105 **"disconcerting lack of regard":** Finn Lützow-Holm Myrstad (1 Dec 2016), "#Toyfail: An analysis of consumer and privacy issues in three internet-connected toys," *Forbrukerrådet*, https://consumermediallc.files.wordpress.com/2016/12/toyfail_report _desember2016.pdf.

106 **Germany banned My Friend Cayla:** Philip Oltermann (17 Feb 2017), "German parents told to destroy doll that can spy on children," *Guardian*, https://www.theguardian .com/world/2017/feb/17/german-parents-told-to-destroy-my-friend-cayla-doll-spy -on-children.

106 **Mattel's Hello Barbie had:** Samuel Gibbs (26 Nov 2015), "Hackers can hijack Wi-Fi Hello Barbie to spy on your children," *Guardian*, https://www.theguardian.com /technology/2015/nov/26/hackers-can-hijack-wi-fi-hello-barbie-to-spy-on-your -children.

106 **In 2017, the consumer credit-reporting agency Equifax:** Tara Siegel Bernard et al. (7 Sep 2017), "Equifax says cyberattack may have affected 143 million in the U.S.," *New York Times*, https://www.nytimes.com/2017/09/07/business/equifax-cyberattack .html. Stacy Cowley (2 Oct 2017), "2.5 million more people potentially exposed in Equifax breach," *New York Times*, https://www.nytimes.com/2017/10/02/business /equifax-breach.html.

106 **The attackers used a critical vulnerability:** Lukasz Lenart (9 Mar 2017), "S2-045:

Possible remote code execution when performing file upload based on Jakarta Multipart parser," *Apache Struts 2 Documentation*, https://cwiki.apache.org/confluence /display/WW/S2-045. Dan Goodin (9 Mar 2017), "Critical vulnerability under 'massive' attack imperils high-impact sites," *Ars Technica*, https://arstechnica.com /information-technology/2017/03/critical-vulnerability-under-massive-attack -imperils-high-impact-sites.

106 **Equifax had been notified by Apache:** Dan Goodin (2 Oct 2017), "A series of delays and major errors led to massive Equifax breach," *Ars Technica*, https://arstechnica .com/information-technology/2017/10/a-series-of-delays-and-major-errors-led-to -massive-equifax-breach.

106 **but didn't get around to installing:** Cyrus Farivar (15 Sep 2017), "Equifax CIO, CSO 'retire' in wake of huge security breach," *Ars Technica*, https://arstechnica.com/tech -policy/2017/09/equifax-cio-cso-retire-in-wake-of-huge-security-breach.

106 **The company's insecurity was incredible:** James Scott (20 Sep 2017), "Equifax: America's in-credible insecurity," *Institute for Critical Infrastructure Technology*, http://icitech.org/wp-content/uploads/2017/09/ICIT-Analysis-Equifax-Americas -In-Credible-Insecurity-Part-One.pdf.

106 **"laughably bad":** Bruce Schneier (1 Nov 2017), "Testimony and statement for the record: Hearing on 'securing consumers' credit data in the age of digital commerce' before the Subcommittee on Digital Commerce and Consumer Protection Committee on Energy and Commerce, United States House of Representatives," http://docs .house.gov/meetings/IF/IF17/20171101/106567/HHRG-115-IF17-Wstate-SchneierB -20171101.pdf.

106 **Equifax had a history of security failures:** Thomas Fox-Brewster (8 Sep 2017), "A brief history of Equifax security fails," *Forbes*, https://www.forbes.com/sites/ thomasbrewster/2017/09/08/equifax-data-breach-history.

106 **"security by design":** Here's one example of what that means: Open Web Application Security Project (last modified 3 Aug 2016), "Security by design principles," https:// www.owasp.org/index.php/Security_by_Design_Principles.

109 **Those principles, and some of the items:** Jonathan Zittrain et al. (Feb 2018), "'Don't Panic' Meets the Internet of Things: Recommendations for a Responsible Future," *Berklett Cybersecurity Project, Berkman Center for Internet and Society at Harvard University*, unpublished draft.

109 **While researching for this book:** Bruce Schneier (9 Feb 2017), "Security and privacy guidelines for the Internet of Things," *Schneier on Security*, https://www.schneier .com/blog/archives/2017/02/security_and_pr.html.

110 **anonymizing data is much harder:** Latanya Sweeney has done some amazing work reidentifying anonymized data. Here are some examples: Latanya Sweeney (accessed 24 Apr 2018), "Research accomplishments of Latanya Sweeney, Ph.D.: Policy and law: Identifiability of de-identified data," http://latanyasweeney.org/work /identifiability.html.

110 **Much of this data will be in the cloud:** This is not uniformly believed. For example: Debra Littlejohn Shinder (27 Jul 2016), "From mainframe to cloud: It's technology déjà vu all over again," *TechTalk*, https://techtalk.gfi.com/from-mainframe-to-cloud-its -technology-deja-vu-all-over-again.

111 **At a high level, we expect accuracy:** Software and Information Industry Association (15 Sep 2017), "Principles for ethical data use," *SIAA Issue Brief*, http://www.siia.net

/Portals/0/pdf/Policy/Principles%20for%20Ethical%20Data%20Use%20SIIA%20 Issue%20Brief.pdf?ver=2017-09-15-130746-523. Erica Kochi et al. (12 Mar 2018), "How to prevent discriminatory outcomes in machine learning," Global Future Council on Human Rights 2016–2018, World Economic Forum, http://www3.weforum.org /docs/WEF_40065_White_Paper_How_to_Prevent_Discriminatory_Outcomes _in_Machine_Learning.pdf.

111 **Some machine-learning algorithms have:** Will Knight (11 Apr 2017), "The dark secret at the heart of AI," *MIT Technology Review*, https://www.technologyreview .com/s/604087/the-dark-secret-at-the-heart-of-ai.

112 **Think of them as black boxes:** For more on secret algorithms, I recommend this book: Frank Pasquale (2015), *The Black Box Society: The Secret Algorithms That Control Money and Information*, Harvard University Press, http://www.hup.harvard.edu /catalog.php?isbn=9780674368279.

112 **Even if an algorithm can't be made public:** Larry Hardesty (27 Oct 2016), "Making computers explain themselves," *MIT News*, http://news.mit.edu/2016/making -computers-explain-themselves-machine-learning-1028. Sara Castellanos and Steven Norton (10 Aug 2017), "Inside DARPA's push to make artificial intelligence explain itself," *Wall Street Journal*, https://blogs.wsj.com/cio/2017/08/10/inside-darpas-push -to-make-artificial-intelligence-explain-itself. Matthew Hutson (31 May 2017), "Q&A: Should artificial intelligence be legally required to explain itself?" *Science*, http:// www.sciencemag.org/news/2017/05/qa-should-artificial-intelligence-be-legally -required-explain-itself.

112 **That is, we can demand:** The EU's General Data Protection Regulation includes some form of a "right to an explanation." Experts are still arguing about how extensive that right is. Bryce Goodman and Seth Flaxman (28 Jun 2016), "European Union regulations on algorithmic decision-making and a 'right to explanation,'" *2016 ICML Workshop on Human Interpretability in Machine Learning*, https://arxiv.org/abs/1606 .08813. Sandra Wachter, Brent Mittelstadt, and Luciano Floridi (24 Jan 2017), "Why a right to explanation of automated decision-making does not exist in the General Data Protection Regulation," *International Data Privacy Law 2017*, https://papers.ssrn .com/sol3/papers.cfm?abstract_id=2903469.

112 **Because of the way machine learning works:** Will Knight (11 Apr 2017), "The dark secret at the heart of AI," *MIT Technology Review*, https://www.technologyreview .com/s/604087/the-dark-secret-at-the-heart-of-ai.

112 **and requiring them often reduces the accuracy:** Cliff Kuang (21 Nov 2017), "Can A.I. be taught to explain itself?" *New York Times Magazine*, https://www.nytimes.com /2017/11/21/magazine/can-ai-be-taught-to-explain-itself.html.

112 **So maybe what we really want:** Nicholas Diakopoulos et al. (17 Nov 2016), "Principles for accountable algorithms and a social impact statement for algorithms," *Fairness, Accountability, and Transparency in Machine Learning*, https://www.fatml .org/resources/principles-for-accountable-algorithms.

112 **Or contestability:** Tad Hirsch (9 Sep 2017), "Designing contestability: Interaction design, machine learning, and mental health," *2017 Conference on Designing Interactive Systems*, https://dl.acm.org/citation.cfm?doid=3064663.3064703.

112 **Maybe all we need is auditability:** Christian Sandvig et al. (22 May 2014), "Auditing algorithms: Research methods for detecting discrimination on Internet platforms," *64th Annual Meeting of the International Communication Association*, http://

www-personal.umich.edu/~csandvig/research/Auditing%20Algorithms%20
--%20Sandvig%20--%20ICA%202014%20Data%20and%20Discrimination%20
Preconference.pdf. Philip Adler et al. (23 Feb 2016), "Auditing black-box models for
indirect influence," *2016 IEEE 16th International Conference on Data Mining (ICDM)*,
http://ieeexplore.ieee.org/document/7837824.

112 **After all, what we want to know:** Julia Angwin et al. (23 May 2016), "Machine bias,"
ProPublica, https://www.propublica.org/article/machine-bias-risk-assessments-in
-criminal-sentencing.

113 **A 2011 report calculated that:** Melissa E. Hathaway and John E. Savage (9 Mar 2012),
"Stewardship of cyberspace: Duties for internet service providers," *CyberDialogue
2012, University of Toronto*, https://www.belfercenter.org/sites/default/files/legacy
/files/cyberdialogue2012_hathaway-savage.pdf.

113 **This centralization might be bad:** Many of the suggestions in this chapter are
taken from this report: Melissa E. Hathaway and John E. Savage (9 Mar 2012), "Stewardship of cyberspace: Duties for internet service providers," *CyberDialogue 2012,
University of Toronto*, https://www.belfercenter.org/sites/default/files/legacy/files
/cyberdialogue2012_hathaway-savage.pdf.

113 **Some ISPs are already blocking:** Linda Rosencrance (10 Jun 2008), "3 top ISPs to
block access to sources of child porn," *Computerworld*, https://www.computerworld
.com/article/2535175/networking/3-top-isps-to-block-access-to-sources-of-child
-porn.html.

113 **Certainly, ISPs are in the best position:** Engineers are working on a security system where routers can query a centralized database and learn where an IoT device
needs to connect and what information it's allowed to send and receive. It's called
Manufacturer Usage Descriptions. The router can restrict the device's connectivity
to just that, greatly improving security. I'm not claiming that this is the correct way
to implement security, but it's an idea that needs further examination. Eliot Lear,
Ralph Droms, and Dan Romascanu (24 Oct 2017), "Manufacturer Usage Description
specification," *Internet Engineering Task Force*, https://datatracker.ietf.org/doc/draft
-ietf-opsawg-mud. Max Pritikin et al. (30 Oct 2017), "Bootstrapping remote secure
key infrastructures (BRSKI)," *Internet Engineering Task Force*, https://datatracker.ietf
.org/doc/draft-ietf-anima-bootstrapping-keyinfra.

114 **This list draws from a paper:** Many of the suggestions in this chapter are taken
from this report. Melissa E. Hathaway and John E. Savage (9 Mar 2012), "Stewardship of cyberspace: Duties for internet service providers," *CyberDialogue 2012, University of Toronto*, https://www.belfercenter.org/sites/default/files/legacy/files/cyber
dialogue2012_hathaway-savage.pdf.

114 **at the time I called it "catastrophic":** Bruce Schneier (9 Apr 2014), "Heartbleed,"
Schneier on Security, https://www.schneier.com/blog/archives/2014/04/heartbleed
.html.

114 **17% of the Internet's web servers:** Paul Mutton (8 Apr 2014), "Half a million widely
trusted websites vulnerable to Heartbleed bug," *Netcraft*, https://news.netcraft
.com/archives/2014/04/08/half-a-million-widely-trusted-websites-vulnerable-to
-heartbleed-bug.html.

115 **The result was that the vulnerability:** Ben Grubb (11 Apr 2014), "Man who introduced serious 'Heartbleed' security flaw denies he inserted it deliberately," *Sydney
Morning Herald*, http://www.smh.com.au/it-pro/security-it/man-who-introduced

-serious-heartbleed-security-flaw-denies-he-inserted-it-deliberately-20140410
-zqta1.html. Alex Hern (11 Apr 2014), "Heartbleed: Developer who introduced the
error regrets 'oversight,'" *Guardian*, https://www.theguardian.com/technology/2014
/apr/11/heartbleed-developer-error-regrets-oversight.

115 **In response to Heartbleed:** Steven J. Vaughan-Nichols (28 Apr 2014), "Cash, the Core
Infrastructure Initiative, and open source projects," *ZDNet*, http://www.zdnet.com
/article/cash-the-core-infrastructure-initiative-and-open-source-projects.

115 **That was okay when the Internet was:** Alex McKenzie (5 Dec 2009), "Early sketch
of ARPANET's first four nodes," *Scientific American*, https://www.scientificamerican
.com/gallery/early-sketch-of-arpanets-first-four-nodes.

115 **These are companies you have likely never heard of:** Yudhanjaya Wijeratne (28
Jun 2016), "The seven companies that really own the Internet," *Icarus Wept*, http://
icaruswept.com/2016/06/28/who-owns-the-internet.

116 **They gained access to the pipeline's control system:** Dan Goodin (10 Dec 2014),
"Hack said to cause fiery pipeline blast could rewrite history of cyberwar," *Ars Technica*, https://arstechnica.com/information-technology/2014/12/hack-said-to-cause
-fiery-pipeline-blast-could-rewrite-history-of-cyberwar.

116 **In 2013, we learned that the NSA had hacked:** Simon Romero (9 Sep 2013), "N.S.A.
spied on Brazilian oil company, report says," *New York Times*, http://www.nytimes.com
/2013/09/09/world/americas/nsa-spied-on-brazilian-oil-company-report-says.html.

116 **In 2017, someone was able to spoof:** David Hambling (10 Aug 2017), "Ships fooled
in GPS spoofing attack suggest Russian cyberweapon," *New Scientist*, https://www
.newscientist.com/article/2143499-ships-fooled-in-gps-spoofing-attack-suggest
-russian-cyberweapon.

116 **In the US, a series of documents:** Office of Homeland Security (15 Jul 2002), "National
strategy for homeland security," https://www.hsdl.org/?view&did=856. George W.
Bush (5 Feb 2003), "The national strategy for the physical protection of critical infrastructures and key assets," *Office of the President of the United States*, https://www
.hsdl.org/?abstract&did=1041. Homeland Security Council (5 Oct 2007), "National
strategy for homeland security," https://www.dhs.gov/xlibrary/assets/nat_strat
_homelandsecurity_2007.pdf. George W. Bush (28 Feb 2003), "Directive on management of domestic incidents," *Office of the Federal Register*, https://www.hsdl.org
/?view&did=439105. George W. Bush (17 Dec 2003), "Directive on national prepared-
ness," *Office of the Federal Register*, https://www.hsdl.org/?view&did=441951.

116 **16 "critical infrastructure sectors":** Barack Obama (12 Feb 2013), "Directive on critical infrastructure security and resilience," *White House Office*, https://www.hsdl.org
/?view&did=731087.

117 **"national security, energy and power":** Donald J. Trump (Dec 2017), "National
security strategy of the United States of America," https://www.whitehouse.gov/wp
-content/uploads/2017/12/NSS-Final-12-18-2017-0905.pdf.

117 **Some people add election systems:** Lawrence Norden and Christopher Famighetti
(15 Sep 2015), "America's voting machines at risk," *Brennan Center for Justice, New
York University School of Law*, https://www.brennancenter.org/publication/americas
-voting-machines-risk.

117 **That statistic comes from a 2002 document:** Office of Homeland Security (15
Jul 2002), "National strategy for homeland security," https://www.hsdl.org/?view
&did=856.

117 **and seems to be a rough guess:** One document I found said that only 8% of all utilities are privately owned, but that they generate 75% of the nation's power. Christopher Bellavita (16 Mar 2009), "85% of what you know about homeland security is probably wrong," *Homeland Security Watch*, http://www.hlswatch.com/2009/03/16 /85-percent-is-wrong.

117 **Certainly, it depends on which industry:** Midwest Publishing Company (accessed 24 Apr 2018), "Electric utility industry overview," http://www.midwestpub.com /electricutility_overview.php.

118 **That we need to secure:** Here's one report: President's National Infrastructure Advisory Council (14 Aug 2017), "Securing cyber assets: Addressing urgent cyber threats to critical infrastructure," https://www.dhs.gov/sites/default/files/publications/ niac-cyber-study-draft-report-08-15-17-508.pdf.

118 **"Collect it all":** Glenn Greenwald (15 Jul 2013), "The crux of the NSA story in one phrase: 'Collect it all,'" *Guardian*, https://www.theguardian.com/commentisfree /2013/jul/15/crux-nsa-collect-it-all.

119 **"end-to-end principle":** Jerome H. Saltzer, David P. Reed, and David D. Clark (1 Nov 1984), "End-to-end arguments in system design," *ACM Transactions on Computer Systems* 2, no. 4, http://web.mit.edu/Saltzer/www/publications/endtoend/endtoend.pdf.

119 **And by the way:** Tim Wu (6 Dec 2017), "How the FCC's net neutrality plan breaks with 50 years of history," *Wired*, https://www.wired.com/story/how-the-fccs-net -neutrality-plan-breaks-with-50-years-of-history.

7. HOW WE CAN SECURE THE INTERNET+

121 **There are four basic ways:** ISO 27001 is a good example. International Organization for Standardization (accessed 24 Apr 2018), "ISO/IEC 27000 family: Information security management systems," http://www.iso.org/iso/home/standards/ management-standards/iso27001.htm.

122 **There's a distinction in law:** Pierre J. Schlag (Dec 1985), "Rules and standards," *UCLA Law Review* 33, https://lawweb.colorado.edu/profiles/pubpdfs/schlag/schlag UCLALR.pdf. Julia Black (28 Mar 2007), "Principles based regulation: Risks, challenges and opportunities," *University of Sydney*, http://eprints.lse.ac.uk/62814/1 /__lse.ac.uk_storage_LIBRARY_Secondary_libfile_shared_repository_Content _Black,%20J_Principles%20based%20regulation_Black_Principles%20based%20 regulation_2015.pdf.

122 **It's called "outcomes-based regulation":** Cary Coglianese (2016), "Performance-based regulation: Concepts and challenges," in Francesca Bignami and David Zaring, eds., *Comparative Law and Regulation: Understanding the Global Regulatory Process*, Edward Elgar Publishing, http://onlinepubs.trb.org/onlinepubs/PBRLit /Coglianese3.pdf.

123 **Think of the difference between:** The 1999 Gramm-Leach-Bliley regulations on financial institutions are a good example. The rules don't specify what to do. Instead, they specify how to approach the problem and insist that affected institutions establish reasonable safeguards. The result is that those institutions have flexibility in complying, and the regulatory agencies have flexibility in enforcement. The downside is that "reasonable" is often interpreted as "everyone else is doing it," which results in a herd mentality that can be hard to change. Lorrie Faith Cranor et al. (11 Jun 2013), "Are they actually any different? Comparing thousands of financial

institutions' privacy practices," *Twelfth Workshop on the Economics of Information Security (WEIS 2013)*, https://www.blaseur.com/papers/financial-final.pdf.

123 **"Framework for Improving Critical Infrastructure Cybersecurity":** National Institute of Standards and Technology (revised 5 Dec 2017), "Framework for improving critical infrastructure cybersecurity, version 1.1 draft 2," https://www.nist.gov/sites/default/files/documents/2017/12/05/draft-2_framework-v1-1_without-markup.pdf.

123 **Unfortunately, the NIST Cybersecurity Framework:** Donald J. Trump (11 May 2017), "Presidential executive order on strengthening the cybersecurity of federal networks and critical infrastructure," *Office of the President of the United States*, https://www.whitehouse.gov/presidential-actions/presidential-executive-order-strengthening-cybersecurity-federal-networks-critical-infrastructure.

123 **It also uses a NIST standard:** Christina McGhee (21 May 2014), "DoD turns to FedRAMP and cloud brokering," *FCW*, https://fcw.com/articles/2014/05/21/drill-down-dod-fedramp-and-cloud-brokering.aspx.

124 **Equifax's CEO didn't get his $5.2 million:** Michael Rapaport and Theo Francis (26 Sep 2017), "Equifax says departing CEO won't get $5.2 million in severance pay," *Wall Street Journal*, https://www.wsj.com/articles/equifax-says-departing-ceo-wont-get-5-2-million-in-severance-pay-1506449778. Maria Lamagna (26 Sep 2017), "After breach, Equifax CEO leaves with $18 million pension, and possibly more," *MarketWatch*, https://www.marketwatch.com/story/equifax-ceo-leaves-with-18-million-pension-and-maybe-more-2017-09-26.

124 **His failed bet cost the company:** Catalin Cimpanu (11 Nov 2017), "Hack cost Equifax only $87.5 million—for now," *Bleeping Computer*, https://www.bleepingcomputer.com/news/business/hack-cost-equifax-only-87-5-million-for-now.

124 **The *Deepwater Horizon* disaster cost BP:** Nathan Bomey (14 Jul 2016), "BP's Deepwater Horizon costs total $62B," *USA Today*, https://www.usatoday.com/story/money/2016/07/14/bp-deepwater-horizon-costs/87087056.

124 **We are biased towards preferring:** Daniel Kahneman and Amos Tversky (Mar 1979), "Prospect theory: An analysis of decision under risk," *Econometrica* 47, no. 2, https://www.princeton.edu/~kahneman/docs/Publications/prospect_theory.pdf.

125 **This doesn't mean that no one ever:** Bruce Schneier (Jul/Aug 2008), "How the human brain buys security," *IEEE Security & Privacy*, https://www.schneier.com/essays/archives/2008/07/how_the_human_brain.html.

125 **Equifax learned about its 2017 hack in July:** Dan Goodin (2 Oct 2017), "A series of delays and major errors led to massive Equifax breach," *Ars Technica*, https://arstechnica.com/information-technology/2017/10/a-series-of-delays-and-major-errors-led-to-massive-equifax-breach.

125 **When Yahoo was hacked in 2014:** Jamie Condliffe (15 Dec 2016), "A history of Yahoo hacks," *MIT Technology Review*, https://www.technologyreview.com/s/603157/a-history-of-yahoo-hacks.

125 **Uber, for a year:** Andy Greenberg (21 Nov 2017), "Hack brief: Uber paid off hackers to hide a 57-million user data breach," *Wired*, https://www.wired.com/story/uber-paid-off-hackers-to-hide-a-57-million-user-data-breach.

125 **One study found that stock prices:** Russell Lange and Eric W. Burger (27 Dec 2017), "Long-term market implications of data breaches, not," *Journal of Information Privacy and Security*, http://www.tandfonline.com/doi/full/10.1080/15536548.2017.1394070.

126 **Something like 90% of the Internet's infrastructure:** Ash Carter (17 Apr 2015),

"The Department of Defense cyber strategy," *US Department of Defense*, https://www.defense.gov/Portals/1/features/2015/0415_cyber-strategy/Final_2015_DoD_CYBER_STRATEGY_for_web.pdf.

126 **Author John Greer proposes sending:** John Michael Greer (2011), *The Wealth of Nature: Economics as if Survival Mattered*, New Society Publishers, https://books.google.com/books?id=h3-eVcJImqMC.

127 **Arthur Andersen was a "Big Five":** Flynn McRoberts et al. (1 Sep 2002), "The fall of Andersen," *Chicago Tribune*, http://www.chicagotribune.com/news/chi-0209010315sep01-story.html.

127 **In 2015, Volkswagen was caught cheating:** Megan Gross (3 Mar 2016), "Volkswagen details what top management knew leading up to emissions revelations," *Ars Technica*, http://arstechnica.com/cars/2016/03/volkswagen-says-ceo-was-in-fact-briefed-about-emissions-issues-in-2014. Danielle Ivory and Keith Bradsher (8 Oct 2015), "Regulators investigating 2nd VW computer program on emissions," *New York Times*, http://www.nytimes.com/2015/10/09/business/international/vw-diesel-emissions-scandal-congressional-hearing.html. Guilbert Gates et al. (8 Oct 2015; revised 28 Apr 2016), "Explaining Volkswagen's emissions scandal," *New York Times*, http://www.nytimes.com/interactive/2015/business/international/vw-diesel-emissions-scandal-explained.html.

127 **The company was hit with fines and penalties:** Jan Schwartz and Victoria Bryan (29 Sep 2017), "VW's Dieselgate bill hits $30 bln after another charge," *Reuters*, https://www.reuters.com/article/legal-uk-volkswagen-emissions/vws-dieselgate-bill-hits-30-bln-after-another-charge-idUSKCN1C4271.

127 **Note: one VW manager and one engineer:** Bill Vlasic (6 Dec 2017), "Volkswagen official gets 7-year term in diesel-emissions cheating," *New York Times*, https://www.nytimes.com/2017/12/06/business/oliver-schmidt-volkswagen.html.

128 **Under current law in the US:** Albert Bianchi Jr., Michelle L. Dama, and Adrienne S. Ehrhardt (3 Mar 2017), "Executives and board members could face liability for data breaches," *National Law Review*, https://www.natlawreview.com/article/executives-and-board-members-could-face-liability-data-breaches. Joseph B. Crace Jr. (3 Apr 2017), "When does data breach liability extend to the boardroom?" *Law 360*, https://www.law360.com/articles/907786.

128 **In the UK, the CEO of TalkTalk:** Matt Burgess (1 Feb 2017), "TalkTalk's chief executive Dido Harding has resigned," *Wired*, https://www.wired.co.uk/article/talktalk-dido-harding-resign-quit.

128 **According to Sarbanes-Oxley:** Darren C. Skinner (1 Jun 2006), "Director responsibilities and liability exposure in the era of Sarbanes-Oxley," *Practical Lawyer*, https://www.apks.com/en/perspectives/publications/2006/06/director-responsibilities-and-liability-exposure.

128 **The law's reality might be much less:** Mary Jo White and Andrew J. Ceresney (19 May 2017), "Individual accountability: Not always accomplished through enforcement," *New York Law Journal*, http://www.law.com/newyorklawjournal/almID/1202786743746.

128 **We need to think about doing:** Charles Cresson Wood (4 Dec 2016), "Solving the information security & privacy crisis by expanding the scope of top management personal liability," *Journal of Legislation* 43, no. 1, http://scholarship.law.nd.edu/jleg/vol43/iss1/5.

129 **They were able to steal the codes:** Earlence Fernandes, Jaeyeon Jung, and Atul Prakash (18 Aug 2016), "Security analysis of emerging smart home applications," *2016 IEEE Symposium on Security and Privacy*, http://ieeexplore.ieee.org/document /7546527.

129 **If you read SmartThings Inc.'s terms of service:** SmartThings Inc. (accessed 24 Apr 2018), "Welcome to SmartThings!" https://www.smartthings.com/terms.

129 **These are the "terms of service":** This has been called "the biggest lie on the Internet." Jonathan A. Obar and Anne Oeldorf-Hirsch (24 Aug 2016), "The biggest lie on the Internet: Ignoring the privacy policies and terms of service policies of social networking services," *44th Research Conference on Communication, Information and Internet Policy 2016 (TPRC 44)*, https://papers.ssrn.com/sol3/papers.cfm?abstract _id=2757465.

129 **Not that it would matter if you did:** This right has been challenged in court, and today there are some limits to what companies can do in their terms of service. Juliet Moringiello and John Ottaviani (7 May 2016), "Online contracts: We may modify these at any time, right?" *Business Law Today*, https://www.americanbar.org /publications/blt/2016/05/07_moringiello.html.

129 **Such agreements force unhappy users:** Jessica Silver-Greenberg and Robert Gebeloff (31 Oct 2015), "Arbitration everywhere, stacking the deck of justice," *New York Times*, https://www.nytimes.com/2015/11/01/business/dealbook/arbitration -everywhere-stacking-the-deck-of-justice.html.

130 **Judges have tended to blame hackers:** Jane Chong (30 Oct 2013), "We need strict laws if we want more secure software," *New Republic*, https://newrepublic.com/article /115402/sad-state-software-liability-law-bad-code-part-4.

130 **This is why it is so hard to sue:** Brenda R. Sharton and David S. Kantrowitz (22 Sep 2017), "Equifax and why it's so hard to sue a company for losing your personal information," *Harvard Business Review*, https://hbr.org/2017/09/equifax-and-why-its -so-hard-to-sue-a-company-for-losing-your-personal-information.

130 **But it could not prove:** Janis Kestenbaum, Rebecca Engrav, and Erin Earl (6 Oct 2017), "4 takeaways from *FTC v. D-Link Systems*," *Law 360*, https://www.law360.com /cybersecurity-privacy/articles/971473.

130 **The FTC found that LabMD had not:** Federal Trade Commission (29 Jul 2016), "In the matter of LabMD, Inc., a corporation: Opinion of the commission," Docket No. 9357, https://www.ftc.gov/system/files/documents/cases/160729labmd-opinion.pdf.

131 **The signs are that the court:** Craig A. Newman (18 Dec 2017), "LabMD appeal has privacy world waiting," *Lexology*, https://www.lexology.com/library/detail .aspx?g=129a4ea7-cc38-4976-94af-3f09e8e280d0.

131 **The hotel chains' 2014 class-action lawsuit:** Andy Greenberg (15 May 2013), "Hotel lock hack still being used in burglaries months after lock firm's fix," *Forbes*, https:// www.forbes.com/sites/andygreenberg/2013/05/15/hotel-lock-hack-still-being-used -in-burglaries-months-after-lock-firms-fix.

131 **"Public policy demands that responsibility":** Roger J. Traynor (5 Jul 1944), *Escola v. Coca Cola Bottling Co. of Fresno*, S.F. 16951, Supreme Court of California, https:// repository.uchastings.edu/cgi/viewcontent.cgi?article=1150&context=traynor _opinions.

131 **This is the way wiretap law works:** United States Code (2011), "18 U.S. Code §2520— Recovery of civil damages authorized," in *United States Code*, 2006 edition, Supp.

5, Title 18—Crimes and Criminal Procedure, https://www.gpo.gov/fdsys/search
/pagedetails.action?packageId=USCODE-2011-title18&granuleId=USCODE-2011
-title18-partI-chap119-sec2520.

131 **This is also the way copyright law works:** US Copyright Office (Oct 2009; accessed
24 Apr 2018), "504. Remedies for infringement: Damages and profits," in *Copyright
Law of the United States* (Title 17), Chapter 5: "Copyright Notice, Deposit, and Regis-
tration," https://www.copyright.gov/title17/92chap5.html.

132 **When connected versions of these things:** This article nicely lays out the liability
arguments: Donna L. Burden and Hilarie L. Henry (1 Aug 2015), "Security software
vendors battle against impending strict products liability," *Product Liability Committee Newsletter*, International Association of Defense Counsel, http://www.iadclaw
.org/securedocument.aspx?file=1/19/Product_Liability_August_2015.pdf.

132 **This happened in the 1980s:** Greg Reigel et al. (13 Oct 2015), "GARA: The General
Aviation Revitalization Act of 1994," *GlobalAir.com*, https://blog.globalair.com/post
/GARA-the-General-Aviation-Revitalization-Act-of-1994.aspx.

132 **Where there is risk of liability:** Adam Janofsky (17 Sep 2017), "Insurance grows for
cyberattacks," *Wall Street Journal*, https://www.wsj.com/articles/insurance-grows
-for-cyberattacks-1505700360.

132 **If we require people who purchase:** Paul Christiano (17 Feb 2018), "Liability insurance," *Sideways View*, https://sideways-view.com/2018/02/17/liability-insurance.

133 **Perhaps it would be more accurate:** Paul Merrey et al. (12 Jul 2017), "Seizing the
cyber insurance opportunity," *KPMG International*, https://home.kpmg.com/xx/en
/home/insights/2017/06/seizing-the-cyber-insurance-opportunity.html. US House
of Representatives (22 Mar 2016), "The role of cyber insurance in risk management,"
Hearing before the Subcommittee on Cybersecurity, Infrastructure Protection, and
Security Technologies of the Committee on Homeland Security, https://www.gpo
.gov/fdsys/pkg/CHRG-114hhrg22625/html/CHRG-114hhrg22625.htm.

133 **Insurance companies are starting to figure out:** Adam Janofsky (17 Sep 2017),
"Cyberinsurers look to measure risk," *Wall Street Journal*, https://www.wsj.com/articles
/cyberinsurers-look-to-measure-risk-1505700301.

133 **They're surveillance devices by design:** There are some pretty horrendous baby
monitor security stories. Craig Silverman (24 Jul 2015), "7 creepy baby monitor stories
that will terrify all parents," *BuzzFeed*, https://www.buzzfeed.com/craigsilverman
/creeps-hack-baby-monitors-and-say-terrifying-thing.

133 **Many brands are hackable:** Carl Franzen (4 Aug 2017), "How to find a hack-proof
baby monitor," *Lifehacker*, https://offspring.lifehacker.com/how-to-find-a-hack
-proof-baby-monitor-1797534985.

133 **"[Our] technology transmits a secure":** Amazon.com (accessed 24 Apr 2018), "VTech
DM111 audio baby monitor with up to 1,000 ft of range, 5-level sound indicator, digi-
tized transmission & belt clip," https://www.amazon.com/VTech-DM111-Indicator
-Digitized-Transmission/dp/B00JEV5UI8/ref=pd_lpo_vtph_75_bs_lp_t_1.

134 **I couldn't tell the good from the bad:** I found one security assessment of a few
brands. Mark Stanislav and Tod Beardsley (29 Sep 2015), "Hacking IoT: A case study
on baby monitor exposure and vulnerabilities," *Rapid7*, https://www.rapid7.com/docs
/Hacking-IoT-A-Case-Study-on-Baby-Monitor-Exposures-and-Vulnerabilities.pdf.

134 **"lemons market":** George A. Akerlof (1 Aug 1970), "The market for 'lemons': Quality

uncertainty and the market mechanism," *Quarterly Journal of Economics* 84, no. 3, https://academic.oup.com/qje/article-abstract/84/3/488/1896241.

134 **The result is that insecure products:** Bruce Schneier (19 Apr 2007), "How security companies sucker us with lemons," *Wired*, https://www.wired.com/2007/04/security matters-0419.

134 **There is nothing like this today:** One study estimated it would take average consumers 244 hours/year to read all of the privacy policies they agree to. Aleecia M. McDonald and Lorrie Faith Cranor (1 Oct 2008), "The cost of reading privacy policies," *I/S: A Journal of Law and Policy for the Information Society*, 2008 Privacy Year in Review issue, http://lorrie.cranor.org/pubs/readingPolicyCost-authorDraft.pdf.

135 **"Please be aware that if":** Samsung (accessed 24 Apr 2018), "Samsung local privacy policy—SmartTV supplement," http://www.samsung.com/hk_en/info/privacy /smarttv.

135 **in the UK:** Samuel Gibbs (24 Jul 2017), "Smart fridges and TVs should carry security rating, police chief says," *Guardian*, https://www.theguardian.com/technology/2017 /jul/24/smart-tvs-fridges-should-carry-security-rating-police-chief-says.

135 **the EU:** Catherine Stupp (5 Oct 2016), "Commission plans cybersecurity rules for internet-connected machines," *Euractiv*, http://www.euractiv.com/section/innovation -industry/news/commission-plans-cybersecurity-rules-for-internet-connected -machines. John E. Dunn (11 Oct 2016), "The EU's latest idea to secure the Internet of Things? Sticky labels," *Naked Security*, https://nakedsecurity.sophos.com/2016/10/11 /the-eus-latest-idea-to-secure-the-internet-of-things-sticky-labels.

135 **Australia:** Denham Sadler (23 Oct 2017), "Security ratings for IoT devices?" *InnovationAus.com*, http://www.innovationaus.com/2017/10/Security-ratings-for-IoT -devices.

136 **Companies could display a label:** US Congress (1 Aug 2017), "S.1691—Internet of Things (IoT) Cybersecurity Improvement Act of 2017," https://www.congress.gov/bill /115th-congress/senate-bill/1691/actions. Morgan Chalfant (27 Oct 2017), "Dems push for program to secure internet-connected devices," *Hill*, http://thehill.com/policy /cybersecurity/357509-dems-push-for-program-to-secure-internet-connected -devices.

136 **Consumers Union—the organization behind:** *Consumer Reports* (6 Mar 2017), "Consumer Reports launches digital standard to safeguard consumers' security and privacy in complex marketplace," https://www.consumerreports.org/media -room/press-releases/2017/03/consumer_reports_launches_digital_standard_to _safeguard_consumers_security_and_privacy_in_complex_marketplace.

136 **Who Has Your Back? project:** Nate Cardozo et al. (Jul 2017), "Who Has Your Back? 2017," *Electronic Frontier Foundation*, https://www.eff.org/files/2017/07/08 /whohasyourback_2017.pdf.

136 **Ranking Digital Rights initiative:** Rebecca MacKinnon et al. (March 2017), "2017 corporate accountability index," *Ranking Digital Rights*, https://rankingdigitalrights .org/index2017/assets/static/download/RDRindex2017report.pdf.

137 **And we can do much of this:** Peter "Mudge" Zatko has some interesting ideas in this area and has set up a cyber underwriters lab to test software security. Kim Zetter (29 Jul 2016), "A famed hacker is grading thousands of programs—and may revolutionize software in the process," *Intercept*, https://theintercept.com/2016/07/29/a-famed

-hacker-is-grading-thousands-of-programs-and-may-revolutionize-software-in-the
-process.

137 **In the US, 48 states have:** Foley & Lardner LLP (17 Jan 2018), "State data breach
notification laws," https://www.foley.com/state-data-breach-notification-laws.

137 **There have been several failed attempts:** Selena Larson (1 Dec 2017), "Senators introduce data breach disclosure bill," *CNN*, http://money.cnn.com/2017/12/01/technology
/bill-data-breach-laws/index.html.

138 **Not only will improved vulnerability disclosure:** The results of this have been a
mixed bag. For example, we know that while a data breach has short-term effects
on the company, it has minimal effect on stock price after two weeks. Russell Lange
and Eric W. Burger (27 Dec 2017), "Long-term market implications of data breaches,
not," *Journal of Information Privacy and Security*, http://www.tandfonline.com/doi
/full/10.1080/15536548.2017.1394070.

138 **"Stop.Think.Connect." campaign:** US Department of Homeland Security (accessed
24 Apr 2018), "Stop.Think.Connect.," https://www.dhs.gov/stopthinkconnect.

139 **Today, a lot of security advice:** Bruce Schneier (Sep/Oct 2013), "Security design:
Stop trying to fix the user," *IEEE Security & Privacy*, https://www.schneier.com/blog
/archives/2016/10/security_design.html.

140 **Existing organizations for software professionals:** Here are some examples: IEEE
(accessed 24 Apr 2018), "IEEE Computer Society Certification and Credential Program," https://www.computer.org/web/education/certifications. Association for
Computing Machinery (accessed 24 Apr 2018), "Skillsoft Learning Collections,"
https://learning.acm.org/e-learning/skillsoft. (ISC)² (accessed 24 Apr 2018), "(ISC)²
information security certifications," https://www.isc2.org/Certifications.

140 **The International Organization for Standardization (ISO):** International Organization for Standardization (accessed 24 Apr 2018), "ISO/IEC 27000 family: Information security management systems," http://www.iso.org/iso/home/standards
/management-standards/iso27001.htm.

141 **Various reports forecast 1.5 million:** Julie Peeler and Angela Messer (17 Apr 2015),
"(ISC)² study: Workforce shortfall due to hiring difficulties despite rising salaries,
increased budgets and high job satisfaction rate," *(ISC)² Blog*, http://blog.isc2.org/
isc2_blog/2015/04/isc-study-workforce-shortfall-due-to-hiring-difficulties-despite
-rising-salaries-increased-budgets-a.html. Jeff Kauflin (16 Mar 2017), "The fast
-growing job with a huge skills gap: Cyber security," *Forbes*, https://www.forbes.com
/sites/jeffkauflin/2017/03/16/the-fast-growing-job-with-a-huge-skills-gap-cyber
-security. ISACA (Jan 2016), "2016 cybersecurity skills gap," https://image-store
.slidesharecdn.com/be4eaf1a-eea6-4b97-b36e-b62dfc8dcbae-original.jpeg. Steve
Morgan (2017), "Cybersecurity jobs report: 2017 edition," *Herjavec Group*, https://www
.herjavecgroup.com/wp-content/uploads/2017/06/HG-and-CV-The-Cybersecurity
-Jobs-Report-2017.pdf.

141 **"The cybersecurity skills shortage represents":** John Oltsik (14 Nov 2017), "Research
confirms the cybersecurity skills shortage is an existential threat," *CSO*, https://www
.csoonline.com/article/3237049/security/research-confirms-the-cybersecurity
-skills-shortage-is-an-existential-threat.html.

142 **a cyber Manhattan Project:** Mark Goodman (21 Jan 2015), "We need a Manhattan project for cyber security," *Wired*, https://www.wired.com/2015/01/we-need-a
-manhattan-project-for-cyber-security.

142 **a cyber moonshot:** Accenture (2 Oct 2017), "Defining a cyber moon shot," https://www.accenture.com/t20171004T064630Z__w__/us-en/_acnmedia/PDF-62/Accenture-Defining-Cyber-Moonshot-POV.pdf.

8. GOVERNMENT IS WHO ENABLES SECURITY

144 **A modern airplane has upwards of:** Faye Bowers (29 Oct 1997), "Building a 747: 43 days and 3 million fasteners," *Christian Science Monitor,* https://www.csmonitor.com/1997/1029/102997.us.us.2.html.

144 **182 times in 2017:** My average speed was 27 miles per hour. That's a calm year for me; in 2015, my average speed was 33 miles per hour.

144 **It wasn't always like this:** This is a good summary: Mark Hansen, Carolyn McAndrews, and Emily Berkeley (Jul 2008), "History of aviation safety oversight in the United States," DOT/FAA/AR-08-39, *National Technical Information Service,* http://www.tc.faa.gov/its/worldpac/techrpt/ar0839.pdf.

144 **The result is that today:** The taxi ride to the airport is the most dangerous part of the trip.

145 **Whenever industry groups write about this:** Here's one example: Coalition for Cybersecurity and Policy and Law (26 Oct 2017), "New whitepaper: Building a national cybersecurity strategy: Voluntary, flexible frameworks," *Center for Responsible Enterprise and Trade,* https://create.org/news/new-whitepaper-building-national-cybersecurity-strategy.

145 **The Federal Aviation Administration has:** April Glaser (15 Mar 2017), "Federal privacy laws won't necessarily protect you from spying drones," *Recode,* https://www.recode.net/2017/3/15/14934050/federal-privacy-laws-spying-drones-senate-hearing.

148 **in 2006, Netflix published 100 million:** Katie Hafner (2 Oct 2006), "And if you liked the movie, a Netflix contest may reward you handsomely," *New York Times,* http://www.nytimes.com/2006/10/02/technology/02netflix.html.

148 **Researchers were able to de-anonymize:** Arvind Narayanan and Vitaly Shmatikov (18 May 2008), "Robust de-anonymization of large sparse datasets," *2008 IEEE Symposium on Security and Privacy (SP '08),* https://dl.acm.org/citation.cfm?id=1398064.

148 **which surprised pretty much everyone:** Paul Ohm (13 Aug 2009), "Broken promises of privacy: Responding to the surprising failure of anonymization," *UCLA Law Review* 57, https://papers.ssrn.com/sol3/papers.cfm?abstract_id=1450006.

148 **The FTC took action against Netflix:** Ryan Singel (12 Mar 2010), "Netflix cancels recommendation contest after privacy lawsuit," *Wired,* https://www.wired.com/2010/03/netflix-cancels-contest.

149 **Today, both the FCC and the SEC:** This idea is fleshed out here: Melissa E. Hathaway and John N. Stewart (25 Jul 2014), "Taking control of our cyber future," *Georgetown Journal of International Affairs,* https://www.georgetownjournalofinternationalaffairs.org/online-edition/cyber-iv-feature-taking-control-of-our-cyber-future.

149 **A research group advising the European Commission:** Eireann Leverett, Richard Clayton, and Ross Anderson (6 Jun 2017), "Standardization and certification of the 'Internet of Things,'" *Institute for Consumer Policy,* https://www.conpolicy.de/en/news-detail/standardization-and-certification-of-the-internet-of-things.

149 **Ashkan Soltani, former chief technologist:** Jedidiah Bracy (7 Apr 2016), "McSweeny, Soltani, and regulating the IoT," *International Association of Privacy Professionals,* https://iapp.org/news/a/mcsweeney-soltani-and-regulating-the-iot.

149 **University of Washington law professor Ryan Calo:** Ryan Calo (15 Sep 2014), "The case for a federal robotics commission," *Brookings Institution*, https://www.brookings .edu/research/the-case-for-a-federal-robotics-commission.

149 **And Matthew Scherer of George Mason University:** Matthew U. Scherer (Spring 2016), "Regulating artificial intelligence systems: Risks, challenges, competencies, and strategies," *Harvard Journal of Law & Technology* 29, no. 2, http://jolt.law.harvard .edu/articles/pdf/v29/29HarvJLTech353.pdf.

149 **Israel created its National Cyber Bureau:** National Cyber Bureau (2 Jun 2013), "Mission of the bureau," *Prime Minister's Office*, http://www.pmo.gov.il/English /PrimeMinistersOffice/DivisionsAndAuthorities/cyber/Pages/default.aspx.

149 **The UK created the National Cyber Security Centre:** National Cyber Security Centre (9 Jun 2017; accessed 24 Apr 2018), "About the NCSC," https://www.ncsc.gov.uk /information/about-ncsc.

150 **One: governments tend to regulate industries:** Andrew Odlyzko (1 Mar 2009), "Network neutrality, search neutrality, and the never-ending conflict between efficiency and fairness in markets," *Review of Network Economics* 8, no. 1, https://www .degruyter.com/view/j/rne.2009.8.issue-1/rne.2009.8.1.1169/rne.2009.8.1.1169.xml.

151 **The agency doesn't conduct the testing itself:** Food and Drug Administration (accessed 24 Apr 2018), "The FDA's role in medical device cybersecurity," https:// www.fda.gov/downloads/MedicalDevices/DigitalHealth/UCM544684.pdf.

151 **Rules for privacy of patients' medical data:** Charles Ornstein (17 Nov 2015), "Federal privacy law lags far behind personal-health technologies," *Washington Post*, https:// www.washingtonpost.com/news/to-your-health/wp/2015/11/17/federal-privacy-law -lags-far-behind-personal-health-technologies.

151 **And sometimes the FDA fights back:** Russell Brandom (25 Nov 2013), "Body blow: How 23andMe brought down the FDA's wrath," *Verge*, https://www.theverge.com /2013/11/25/5144928/how-23andme-brought-down-fda-wrath-personal-genetics -wojcicki. Gina Kolata (6 Apr 2017), "F.D.A. will allow 23andMe to sell genetic tests for disease risk to consumers," *New York Times*, https://www.nytimes.com/2017/04 /06/health/fda-genetic-tests-23andme.html.

151 **In 2015, the FTC sued Wyndham Hotels:** Electronic Privacy Information Center (24 Aug 2015), "FTC v. Wyndham," https://epic.org/amicus/ftc/wyndham.

152 **The Federal Court of Appeals sided with:** Federal Trade Commission (9 Dec 2015), "Wyndham settles FTC charges it unfairly placed consumers' payment card information at risk," https://www.ftc.gov/news-events/press-releases/2015/12/wyndham -settles-ftc-charges-it-unfairly-placed-consumers-payment.

152 **It took 13 years for Facebook:** Josh Constine (27 Jun 2017), "Facebook now has 2 billion monthly users . . . and responsibility," *TechCrunch*, https://techcrunch.com /2017/06/27/facebook-2-billion-users.

153 **The law makes an important distinction:** Eric R. Hinz (1 Nov 2012), "A distinctionless distinction: Why the RCS/ECS distinction in the Stored Communications Act does not work," *Notre Dame Law Review* 88, no. 1, https://scholarship.law.nd.edu/cgi /viewcontent.cgi?referer=&httpsredir=1&article=1115&context=ndlr.

153 **The logic behind that old law:** David Kravets (21 Oct 2011), "Aging 'privacy' law leaves cloud email open to cops," *Wired*, https://www.wired.com/2011/10/ecpa-turns -twenty-five.

154 **The big tech companies are spending:** Olivia Solon and Sabrina Siddiqui (3 Sep

2017), "Forget Wall Street: Silicon Valley is the new political power in Washington," *Guardian*, https://www.theguardian.com/technology/2017/sep/03/silicon-valley -politics-lobbying-washington.

154 **Google alone spent $6 million:** Jonathan Taplin (30 Jul 2017), "Why is Google spending record sums on lobbying Washington?" *Guardian*, https://www.theguardian .com/technology/2017/jul/30/google-silicon-valley-corporate-lobbying-washington -dc-politics.

154 **One is the way developers of fitness devices:** Alex Ruoff (29 Jul 2016), "Fitness trackers, wellness apps won't be regulated by FDA," *Bureau of National Affairs*, https:// www.bna.com/fitness-trackers-wellness-n73014445597. Food and Drug Administration, Center for Devices and Radiological Health (29 Jul 2016), "General wellness: Policy for low risk devices, guidance for industry and Food and Drug Administration staff," *Federal Register*, https://www.federalregister.gov/documents/2016/07/29 /2016-17902/general-wellness-policy-for-low-risk-devices-guidance-for-industry -and-food-and-drug-administration.

154 **Data brokers have performed similar:** Brian Fung (29 Mar 2017), "What to expect now that Internet providers can collect and sell your Web browser history," *Washington Post*, https://www.washingtonpost.com/news/the-switch/wp/2017/03/29/what-to-expect -now-that-internet-providers-can-collect-and-sell-your-web-browser-history.

154 **"Power interprets regulation as damage":** Yochai Benkler and Julie Cohen (17 Nov 2017), "Networks 2" (conference session), *After the Digital Tornado Conference, Wharton School, University of Pennsylvania*, http://digitaltornado.net. Supernova Group (19 Nov 2017), "After the Tornado 05: Networks 2," *YouTube*, https://www.youtube.com /watch?v=pCGZ8tIrrIU.

154 **the CAN-SPAM Act that didn't stop spam:** It made things worse, since it superseded stronger state laws and took away individuals' ability to bring lawsuits. Brian Krebs (2 Jul 2017), "Is it time to can the CAN-SPAM Act?" *Krebs on Security*, https:// krebsonsecurity.com/2017/07/is-it-time-to-can-the-can-spam-act.

154 **legal action against robocallers:** Mitchell J. Katz (13 Jan 2017), "FTC announces crackdown on two massive illegal robocall operations," *Federal Trade Commission*, https:// www.ftc.gov/news-events/press-releases/2017/01/ftc-announces-crackdown-two -massive-illegal-robocall-operations. Mike Snider (22 Jun 2017), "FCC hits robocaller with agency's largest-ever fine of $120 million," *USA Today*, https://www.usatoday .com/story/tech/news/2017/06/22/fcc-hits-robocaller-agencys-largest-ever-fine-120 -million/103102546.

154 **"do not call" list violators:** Mitchell J. Katz (6 Jun 2017), "FTC and DOJ case results in historic decision awarding $280 million in civil penalties against Dish Network and strong injunctive relief for Do Not Call violations," *Federal Trade Commission*, https:// www.ftc.gov/news-events/press-releases/2017/06/ftc-doj-case-results-historic -decision-awarding-280-million-civil.

154 **deceptive telco advertisers:** Mitchell J. Katz (11 Mar 2015), "FTC charges DIRECTV with deceptively advertising the cost of its satellite television service," *Federal Trade Commission*, https://www.ftc.gov/news-events/press-releases/2015/03/ftc-charges -directv-deceptively-advertising-cost-its-satellite.

154 **excessive data collection by toys:** Cecilia Kang (8 Jan 2018), "Toymaker VTech settles charges of violating child privacy law," *New York Times*, https://www.nytimes .com/2018/01/08/business/vtech-child-privacy.html.

154 **and televisions:** Juliana Gruenwald Henderson (6 Feb 2017), "VIZIO to pay $2.2 million to FTC, state of New Jersey to settle charges it collected viewing histories on 11 million smart televisions without users' consent," *Federal Trade Commission*, https://www.ftc.gov/news-events/press-releases/2017/02/vizio-pay-22-million-ftc -state-new-jersey-settle-charges-it.

155 **This way of thinking will become:** There are conflicting takes on this in the computer security field. Adam Thierer (11 Mar 2012), "Avoiding a precautionary principle for the Internet," *Forbes*, https://www.forbes.com/sites/adamthierer/2012/03 /11/avoiding-a-precautionary-principle-for-the-internet. Andy Stirling (8 Jul 2013), "Why the precautionary principle matters," *Guardian*, https://www.theguardian .com/science/political-science/2013/jul/08/precautionary-principle-science-policy.

155 **We don't want to—and can't:** Kevin Kelly has written about how to be deliberate in deciding which technologies society should use, and how to roll them out. Kevin Kelly (2010), *What Technology Wants*, Viking, https://books.google.com/books?id =_ToftPd4R8UC.

156 **International cooperation is coming:** It's starting. This arrest was made by Spanish police, with support from the FBI; Romanian, Belarusian, and Taiwanese authorities; and several cybersecurity companies. Micah Singleton (26 Mar 2018), "Europol arrests suspects in bank heists that stole $1.2 billion using malware," *Verge*, https:// www.theverge.com/2018/3/26/17165300/europol-arrest-suspect-bank-heists-1-2 -billion-cryptocurrency-malware.

156 **There are hacker havens:** Noah Rayman (7 Aug 2014), "The world's top 5 cybercrime hotspots," *Time*, http://time.com/3087768/the-worlds-5-cybercrime-hotspots.

157 **Some states, like North Korea:** Christine Kim (27 Jul 2017), "North Korea hacking increasingly focused on making money more than espionage: South Korea study," *Reuters*, https://www.reuters.com/article/us-northkorea-cybercrime/north-korea -hacking-increasingly-focused-on-making-money-more-than-espionage-south -korea-study-idUSKBN1AD0BO.

157 **The treaty provides a framework:** Council of Europe (accessed 24 Apr 2018), "Details of Treaty No. 185: Convention on Cybercrime," https://www.coe.int/en/web /conventions/full-list/-/conventions/treaty/185.

157 **At the extreme, large and powerful countries:** Bruce Sterling (22 Dec 2015), "Respecting Chinese and Russian cyber-sovereignty in the formerly global internet," *Wired*, https://www.wired.com/beyond-the-beyond/2015/12/respecting -chinese-and-russian-cyber-sovereignty-in-the-formerly-global-internet. Andrea Limbago (13 Dec 2016), "The global push for cyber sovereignty is the beginning of cyber fascism," *Hill*, http://thehill.com/blogs/congress-blog/technology/310382-the -global-push-for-cyber-sovereignty-is-the-beginning-of. Vladimir Mikheev (22 Mar 2017), "Why do Beijing and Moscow embrace cyber sovereignty?" *Russia beyond the Headlines*, https://www.rbth.com/opinion/2017/03/22/why-do-beijing-and-moscow -embrace-cyber-sovereignty_725018.

157 **Political scientist Joseph Nye believes:** Joseph S. Nye (forthcoming), "Normative restraints on cyber conflict," *Cyber Security*.

158 **The UN had its GGE:** United Nations General Assembly (24 Jun 2013), "Report of the Group of Governmental Experts on Developments in the Field of Information and Telecommunications in the Context of International Security," *Resolution A/68/98*, http://www.un.org/ga/search/view_doc.asp?symbol=A/68/98.

158 **These were immediately blocked:** Stefan Soesanto and Fosca D'Incau (15 Aug 2017), "The UN GGE is dead: Time to fall forward," *European Council on Foreign Relations*, http://www.ecfr.eu/article/commentary_time_to_fall_forward_on_cyber_governance.

158 **Cyberweapons are easy to hide:** Ariel Rabkin (3 Mar 2015), "Cyber-arms cannot be controlled by treaties," *American Enterprise Institute*, https://www.aei.org/publication/cyber-arms-cannot-be-controlled-by-treaties.

158 **In a 2014 report, cyber policy expert:** Jason Healey (Apr 2014), "Risk nexus: Beyond data breaches: Global interconnections of cyber risk," *Atlantic Council*, http://publications.atlanticcouncil.org/cyberrisks//risk-nexus-september-2015-overcome-by-cyber-risks.pdf.

158 **In the same year, Matt Thomlinson:** Matt Thomlinson (31 Jan 2014), "Microsoft announces Brussels Transparency Center at Munich Security Conference," *Microsoft on the Issues*, https://blogs.microsoft.com/on-the-issues/2014/01/31/microsoft-announces-brussels-transparency-center-at-munich-security-conference.

158 **Microsoft's president and chief legal officer:** Brad Smith (14 Feb 2017), "The need for a Digital Geneva Convention," *Microsoft on the Issues*, https://blogs.microsoft.com/on-the-issues/2017/02/14/need-digital-geneva-convention.

158 **Google has its own proposal:** Kent Walker (31 Oct 2017), "Digital security and due process: Modernizing cross-border government access standards for the cloud era," *Google*, https://blog.google/documents/2/CrossBorderLawEnforcementRequestsWhitePaper_2.pdf.

9. HOW GOVERNMENTS CAN PRIORITIZE DEFENSE OVER OFFENSE

160 **"defense dominant" strategy:** Jason Healey (Jan 2017), "A nonstate strategy for saving cyberspace," *Atlantic Council Strategy Paper* No. 8, Atlantic Council, http://www.atlanticcouncil.org/images/publications/AC_StrategyPapers_No8_Saving_Cyberspace_WEB.pdf.

160 **The NSA has two missions:** John Ferris (1 Mar 2010), "Signals intelligence in war and power politics, 1914–2010," in *The Oxford Handbook of National Security Intelligence*, Oxford, http://www.oxfordhandbooks.com/view/10.1093/oxfordhb/9780195375886.001.0001/oxfordhb-9780195375886-e-0010.

162 **to criminals on the black market:** Dancho Danchev (2 Nov 2008), "Black market for zero day vulnerabilities still thriving," *ZDNet*, http://www.zdnet.com/blog/security/black-market-for-zero-day-vulnerabilities-still-thriving/2108. Dan Patterson (9 Jan 2017), "Gallery: The top zero day Dark Web markets," *TechRepublic*, https://www.techrepublic.com/pictures/gallery-the-top-zero-day-dark-web-markets.

162 **and to governments:** Andy Greenberg (21 Mar 2012), "Meet the hackers who sell spies the tools to crack your PC (and get paid six-figure fees)," *Forbes*, http://www.forbes.com/sites/andygreenberg/2012/03/21/meet-the-hackers-who-sell-spies-the-tools-to-crack-your-pc-and-get-paid-six-figure-fees.

162 **Companies like Azimuth sell:** Joseph Cox and Lorenzo Franceschi-Bicchierai (7 Feb 2018), "How a tiny startup became the most important hacking shop you've never heard of," *Vice Motherboard*, https://motherboard.vice.com/en_us/article/8xdayg/iphone-zero-days-inside-azimuth-security.

162 **And while vendors offer bounties:** Adam Segal (19 Sep 2016), "Using incentives to shape the zero-day market," *Council on Foreign Relations*, https://www.cfr.org/report/using-incentives-shape-zero-day-market.

162 **the not-for-profit Tor Project:** Tor Project (last updated 20 Sep 2017), "Policy [re Tor bug bounties]," *Hacker One, Inc.*, https://hackerone.com/torproject.

162 **the cyberweapons manufacturer Zerodium:** Zerodium (13 Sep 2017; expired 1 Dec 2017), "Tor browser zero-day exploits bounty (expired)," https://zerodium.com/tor.html.

163 **"Every offensive weapon is":** Jack Goldsmith (12 Apr 2014), "Cyber paradox: Every offensive weapon is a (potential) chink in our defense—and vice versa," *Lawfare*, http://www.lawfareblog.com/2014/04/cyber-paradox-every-offensive-weapon-is-a-potential-chink-in-our-defense-and-vice-versa.

163 **Many people have weighed in:** Joel Brenner (14 Apr 2014), "The policy tension on zero-days will not go away," *Lawfare*, http://www.lawfareblog.com/2014/04/the-policy-tension-on-zero-days-will-not-go-away.

163 **Activist and author Cory Doctorow:** Cory Doctorow (11 Mar 2014), "If GCHQ wants to improve national security it must fix our technology," *Guardian*, http://www.theguardian.com/technology/2014/mar/11/gchq-national-security-technology.

163 **I have said similar things:** Bruce Schneier (20 Feb 2014), "It's time to break up the NSA," *CNN*, http://edition.cnn.com/2014/02/20/opinion/schneier-nsa-too-big/index.html.

163 **Computer security expert Dan Geer:** Dan Geer (3 Apr 2013), "Three policies," http://geer.tinho.net/three.policies.2013Apr03Wed.PDF.

163 **Both Microsoft's Brad Smith:** Brad Smith (14 May 2017), "The need for urgent collective action to keep people safe online: Lessons from last week's cyberattack," *Microsoft on the Issues*, https://blogs.microsoft.com/on-the-issues/2017/05/14/need-urgent-collective-action-keep-people-safe-online-lessons-last-weeks-cyberattack.

163 **and Mozilla:** Heather West (7 Mar 2017), "Mozilla statement on CIA/WikiLeaks," *Open Policy & Advocacy*, https://blog.mozilla.org/netpolicy/2017/03/07/mozilla-statement-on-cia-wikileaks. Jochai Ben-Avie (3 Oct 2017), "Vulnerability disclosure should be part of new EU cybersecurity strategy," *Open Policy & Advocacy*, https://blog.mozilla.org/netpolicy/2017/10/03/vulnerability-disclosure-should-be-in-new-eu-cybersecurity-strategy.

163 **"We recommend that the National Security Council":** Richard A. Clarke et al. (12 Dec 2013), "Liberty and security in a changing world," *President's Review Group on Intelligence and Communications Technologies*, https://obamawhitehouse.archives.gov/sites/default/files/docs/2013-12-12_rg_final_report.pdf.

163 **If we give up our own offensive:** Both the NSA and the FBI have made that argument. David E. Sanger (28 Apr 2014), "White House details thinking on cybersecurity flaws," *New York Times*, http://www.nytimes.com/2014/04/29/us/white-house-details-thinking-on-cybersecurity-gaps.html.

163 **"The idea that these problems":** Rick Ledgett (7 Aug 2017), "No, the U.S. government should not disclose all vulnerabilities in its possession," *Lawfare*, https://www.lawfareblog.com/no-us-government-should-not-disclose-all-vulnerabilities-its-possession.

164 **Some are what the NSA calls "NOBUS":** Andrea Peterson (4 Oct 2013), "Why everyone is left less secure when the NSA doesn't help fix security flaws," *Washington Post*, https://www.washingtonpost.com/news/the-switch/wp/2013/10/04/why-everyone-is-left-less-secure-when-the-nsa-doesnt-help-fix-security-flaws.

164 **If a vulnerability is NOBUS:** Lily Hay Newman (16 Jun 2017), "Why governments won't

let go of secret software bugs," *Wired*, https://www.wired.com/2017/05/governments-wont-let-go-secret-software-bugs.

164 **In 2014, then–White House cybersecurity coordinator:** Michael Daniel (28 Apr 2014), "Heartbleed: Understanding when we disclose cyber vulnerabilities," *Office of the President of the United States*, http://www.whitehouse.gov/blog/2014/04/28/heart bleed-understanding-when-we-disclose-cyber-vulnerabilities.

164 **In 2016, the official, heavily redacted:** Andrew Crocker (19 Jan 2016), "EFF pries more information on zero days from the government's grasp," *Electronic Frontier Foundation*, https://www.eff.org/deeplinks/2016/01/eff-pries-more-transparency-zero-days-governments-grasp.

164 **In 2017, new cybersecurity coordinator:** [Office of the President of the United States] (15 Nov 2017), "Vulnerabilities equities policy and process for the United States government," https://www.whitehouse.gov/sites/whitehouse.gov/files/images/External%20-%20Unclassified%20VEP%20Charter%20FINAL.PDF. Rob Joyce (15 Nov 2017), "Improving and making the vulnerability equities process transparent is the right thing to do," *Wayback Machine*, https://web.archive.org/web/20171115151504/https://www.whitehouse.gov/blog/2017/11/15/improving-and-making-vulnerability-equities-process-transparent-right-thing-do.

164 **For example, ETERNALBLUE:** Ellen Nakashima and Craig Timberg (16 May 2017), "NSA officials worried about the day its potent hacking tool would get loose. Then it did," *Washington Post*, https://www.washingtonpost.com/business/technology/nsa-officials-worried-about-the-day-its-potent-hacking-tool-would-get-loose-then-it-did/2017/05/16/50670b16-3978-11e7-a058-ddbb23c75d82_story.html.

165 **Any process that allows such a serious:** The NSA eventually disclosed the vulnerability, but that was after the Russians stole it. Dan Goodin (17 May 2017), "Fearing Shadow Brokers leak, NSA reported critical flaw to Microsoft," *Ars Technica*, https://arstechnica.com/information-technology/2017/05/fearing-shadow-brokers-leak-nsa-reported-critical-flaw-to-microsoft.

165 **Vulnerabilities are independently discovered:** Andy Greenberg (7 Jan 2018), "Triple Meltdown: How so many researchers found a 20-year-old chip flaw at the same time," *Wired*, https://www.wired.com/story/meltdown-spectre-bug-collision-intel-chip-flaw-discovery.

165 **This implies that if the US government:** In 2017, I tried to estimate the annual rate of rediscovery, using available data sets, and found it to be between 11% and 22%. Independently, a group of researchers from the RAND Corporation tried to estimate it as well, using different assumptions and a different data set; they found the rate to be less than 6%. We're all blind folks touching different parts of the elephant. We each extrapolate from our own tiny pieces of data. Clearly we're not going to learn much about the NSA's capabilities this way. Trey Herr, Bruce Schneier, and Christopher Morris (7 Mar 2017), "Taking stock: Estimating vulnerability recovery," *Belfer Cyber Security Project White Paper Series, Harvard Kennedy School Belfer Center for Science and International Affairs*, https://papers.ssrn.com/sol3/papers.cfm?abstract_id=2928758. Lillian Ablon and Timothy Bogart (9 Mar 2017), "Zero days, thousands of nights: The life and times of zero-day vulnerabilities and their exploits," *RAND Corporation*, https://www.rand.org/pubs/research_reports/RR1751.html.

165 **Plus, NOBUS doesn't take into account:** Scott Shane, Matthew Rosenberg, and Andrew W. Lehren (7 Mar 2017), "WikiLeaks releases trove of alleged C.I.A. hacking

documents," *New York Times*, https://www.nytimes.com/2017/03/07/world/europe /wikileaks-cia-hacking.html.https://www.nytimes.com/2017/11/12/us/nsa-shadow -brokers.html. Scott Shane, Nicole Perlroth, and David E. Sanger (12 Nov 2017), "Security breach and spilled secrets have shaken the N.S.A. to its core," *New York Times*, https://www.nytimes.com/2017/11/12/us/nsa-shadow-brokers.html.

165 **These included some pretty nasty:** Bruce Schneier (28 Jul 2017), "Zero-day vulnerabilities against Windows in the NSA tools released by the Shadow Brokers," *Schneier on Security*, https://www.schneier.com/blog/archives/2017/07/zero-day_vulner .html.

165 **Maybe nobody else could have:** Dan Goodin (16 Apr 2017), "Mysterious Microsoft patch killed 0-days released by NSA-leaking Shadow Brokers," *Ars Technica*, https:// arstechnica.co.uk/information-technology/2017/04/purported-shadow-brokers -0days-were-in-fact-killed-by-mysterious-patch.

165 **In 2015, we learned that:** National Security Agency/Central Security Service (30 Oct 2015), "Discovering IT problems, developing solutions, sharing expertise," https:// www.nsa.gov/news-features/news-stories/2015/discovering-solving-sharing-it -solutions.shtml.

165 **"Every year the government only keeps":** Jason Healey (1 Nov 2016), "The U.S. government and zero-day vulnerabilities: From pre-Heartbleed to the Shadow Brokers," *Columbia Journal of International Affairs*, https://jia.sipa.columbia.edu/online -articles/healey_vulnerability_equities_process.

166 **It's clear to many observers:** Bruce Schneier (19 May 2014), "Should U.S. hackers fix cybersecurity holes or exploit them?" *Atlantic*, https://www.schneier.com/essays /archives/2014/05/should_us_hackers_fi.html. Ari Schwartz and Rob Knake (1 Jun 2016), "Government's role in vulnerability disclosure: Creating a permanent and accountable vulnerability equities process," *Harvard Kennedy School Belfer Center for Science and International Affairs*, https://www.belfercenter.org/publication /governments-role-vulnerability-disclosure-creating-permanent-and-accountable. Jason Healey (1 Nov 2016), "The U.S. government and zero-day vulnerabilities: From pre -Heartbleed to the Shadow Brokers," *Columbia Journal of International Affairs*, https:// jia.sipa.columbia.edu/online-articles/healey_vulnerability_equities_process.

166 **Instead, it's making us much less secure:** Oren J. Falkowitz (10 Jan 2017), "U.S. cyber policy makes Americans vulnerable to our own government," *Time*, http://time.com /4625798/donald-trump-cyber-policy.

167 **The NSA participated in the process:** John Gilmore (6 Sep 2013), "Re: [Cryptography] opening discussion: Speculation on 'BULLRUN,' " *Mail Archive*, https://www.mail -archive.com/cryptography@metzdowd.com/msg12325.html.

167 **"devastating effect" on security:** Niels Ferguson and Bruce Schneier (Dec 2003), "A cryptographic evaluation of IPsec," *Counterpane Internet Security*, https://www .schneier.com/academic/paperfiles/paper-ipsec.pdf.

167 **A second example: in the secret:** Elad Barkan, Eli Biham, and Nathan Keller (17 Sep 2003), "Instant ciphertext-only cryptanalysis of GSM encrypted communication," http://cryptome.org/gsm-crack-bbk.pdf.

167 **Both of these were probably part:** Nicole Perlroth, Jeff Larson, and Scott Shane (5 Sep 2013), "Secret documents reveal N.S.A. campaign against encryption," *New York Times*, http://www.nytimes.com/interactive/2013/09/05/us/documents-reveal-nsa -campaign-against-encryption.html. Nicole Perlroth, Jeff Larson, and Scott Shane

(5 Sep 2013), "N.S.A. able to foil basic safeguards of privacy on web," *New York Times*, http://www.nytimes.com/2013/09/06/us/nsa-foils-much-internet-encryption.html. Julian Ball, Julian Borger, and Glenn Greenwald (6 Sep 2013), "Revealed: How US and UK spy agencies defeat internet privacy and security," *Guardian*, https://www .theguardian.com/world/2013/sep/05/nsa-gchq-encryption-codes-security.

168 **CALEA, the Communications Assistance for Law Enforcement Act:** Albert Gidari (22 Feb 2016), "More CALEA and why it trumps the FBI's All Writs Act order," *Center for Internet and Society, Stanford Law School*, http://cyberlaw.stanford.edu/blog/2016 /02/more-calea-and-why-it-trumps-fbis-all-writs-act-order.

168 **AmberJack is another:** InfoSec Institute (8 Jan 2016), "Cellphone surveillance: The secret arsenal," http://resources.infosecinstitute.com/cellphone-surveillance-the -secret-arsenal.

168 **This enables collection of identification:** Joel Hruska (17 Jun 2014), "Stingray, the fake cell phone tower cops and carriers use to track your every move," *Extreme Tech*, http://www.extremetech.com/mobile/184597-stingray-the-fake-cell-phone-tower -cops-and-providers-use-to-track-your-every-move.

168 **Only a few years ago, the FBI:** Kim Zetter (19 Jun 2014), "Emails show feds asking Florida cops to deceive judges," *Wired*, http://www.wired.com/2014/06/feds-told -cops-to-deceive-courts-about-stingray.

168 **When it seemed possible that local police:** Nathan Freed Wessler (3 Jun 2014), "U.S. marshals seize local cops' cell phone tracking files in extraordinary attempt to keep information from public," *American Civil Liberties Union*, https://www.aclu .org/blog/national-security-technology-and-liberty/us-marshals-seize-local-cops -cell-phone-tracking-files.

169 **As recently as 2015, St. Louis police:** Robert Patrick (19 Apr 2015), "Controversial secret phone tracker figured in dropped St. Louis case," *St. Louis Post-Dispatch*, http://www.stltoday.com/news/local/crime-and-courts/controversial-secret -phone-tracker-figured-in-dropped-st-louis-case/article_fbb82630-aa7f-5200-b221 -a7f90252b2d0.html. Cyrus Farivar (29 Apr 2015), "Robbery suspect pulls guilty plea after stingray disclosure, case dropped," *Ars Technica*, http://arstechnica.com/tech -policy/2015/04/29/alleged-getaway-driver-challenges-stingray-use-robbery-case -dropped.

169 **What was once a secret NSA:** Stephanie K. Pell and Christopher Soghoian (29 Dec 2014), "Your secret Stingray's no secret anymore: The vanishing government monop- oly over cell phone surveillance and its impact on national security and consumer privacy," *Harvard Journal of Law and Technology* 28, no. 1, https://papers.ssrn.com /sol3/papers.cfm?abstract_id=2437678.

169 **In 2010, hackers were demonstrating:** Kim Zetter (21 Jul 2010), "Hacker spoofs cell phone tower to intercept calls," *Wired*, http://www.wired.com/2010/07/intercepting -cell-phone-calls.

169 **By 2014, dozens of IMSI-catchers:** Ashkan Soltani and Craig Timberg (17 Sep 2014), "Tech firm tries to pull back curtain on surveillance efforts in Washington," *Washing- ton Post*, http://www.washingtonpost.com/world/national-security/researchers-try -to-pull-back-curtain-on-surveillance-efforts-in-washington/2014/09/17/f8c1f590 -3e81-11e4-b03f-de718edeb92f_story.html.

169 **Now, you can browse the Chinese:** A Mr. Mark Lazarte sells a PKI 1640 IMSI-catcher for $1,800. It seems to be made in Guangdong, China. Mark Lazarte (accessed 24

Apr 2018), "IMSI catcher," *Alibaba*, https://www.alibaba.com/product-detail/IMSI
-catcher_135958750.html.

169 **We know from the Snowden documents:** Charlie Savage et al. (4 Jun 2015), "Hunting for hackers, NSA secretly expands Internet spying at U.S. border," *New York
Times*, https://www.nytimes.com/2015/06/05/us/hunting-for-hackers-nsa-secretly
-expands-internet-spying-at-us-border.html.

170 **That same phone-switch wiretapping capability:** Vassilis Prevelakis and Diomidis
Spinellis (29 Jun 2007), "The Athens affair," *IEEE Spectrum*, https://spectrum.ieee.org
/telecom/security/the-athens-affair.

170 **CALEA inadvertently caused vulnerabilities:** Tom Cross (3 Feb 2010), "Exploiting
lawful intercept to wiretap the Internet," *Black Hat DC 2010*, http://www.blackhat
.com/presentations/bh-dc-10/Cross_Tom/BlackHat-DC-2010-Cross-Attacking
-LawfulI-Intercept-wp.pdf.

170 **"when the NSA tested CALEA-compliant switches":** Quoted in Susan Landau (1
Mar 2016), "Testimony for House Judiciary Committee hearing on 'The encryption
tightrope: Rebalancing Americans' security and privacy,'" https://judiciary.house
.gov/wp-content/uploads/2016/02/Landau-Written-Testimony.pdf.

170 **Even former NSA and CIA director Michael Hayden:** Andrea Peterson (4 Oct 2013),
"Why everyone is left less secure when the NSA doesn't help fix security flaws," *Washington Post*, https://www.washingtonpost.com/news/the-switch/wp/2013/10/04
/why-everyone-is-left-less-secure-when-the-nsa-doesnt-help-fix-security-flaws.

170 **"the NOBUS comfort zone is":** Michael V. Hayden (17 May 2017), "The equities decision: Deciding when to exploit or defend," *Chertoff Group*, http://www.chertoffgroup
.com/point-of-view/109-the-chertoff-group-point-of-view/665-the-equities-decision
-deciding-when-to-exploit-or-defend.

172 **I, and many security technologists:** Harold Abelson et al. (7 Jul 2015), "Keys under
doormats: Mandating insecurity by requiring government access to all data and
communications," *MIT CSAIL Technical Report 2015-026, MIT Computer Science and
Artificial Intelligence Laboratory*, https://dspace.mit.edu/handle/1721.1/97690.

173 **the UK's National Cyber Security Centre:** I have heard it referred to as GCHQ's
London branch.

173 **Unfortunately, in 2016, the NSA underwent:** Ellen Nakashima (2 Feb 2016),
"National Security Agency plans major reorganization," *Washington Post*, https://
www.washingtonpost.com/world/national-security/national-security-agency
-plans-major-reorganization/2016/02/02/2a66555e-c960-11e5-a7b2-5a2f824b02c9
_story.html.

173 **If the NSA is ever to be trusted:** Nicholas Weaver makes this point well. Nicholas
Weaver (10 Feb 2016), "Trust and the NSA reorganization," *Lawfare*, https://www
.lawfareblog.com/trust-and-nsa-reorganization.

174 **Because it was an iPhone 5C:** Samantha Masunaga (2 Oct 2017), "FBI doesn't have to
say who unlocked San Bernardino shooter's iPhone, judge rules," *Los Angeles Times*,
http://beta.latimes.com/business/la-fi-tn-fbi-iphone-20171002-story.html.

174 **Apple resisted the FBI's demand:** Arash Khamooshi (3 Mar 2016), "Breaking down
Apple's iPhone fight with the U.S. government," *New York Times*, https://www.nytimes
.com/interactive/2016/03/03/technology/apple-iphone-fbi-fight-explained.html.

174 **Eventually, the FBI got some unidentified:** Thomas Fox-Brewster (26 Feb 2018), "The
feds can now (probably) unlock every iPhone model in existence," *Forbes*, https://

www.forbes.com/sites/thomasbrewster/2018/02/26/government-can-access-any
-apple-iphone-cellebrite. Sean Gallagher (28 Feb 2018), "Cellebrite can unlock any
iPhone (for some values of 'any')," *Ars Technica*, https://arstechnica.com/information
-technology/2018/02/cellebrite-can-unlock-any-iphone-for-some-values-of-any.

174 **to break into the phone without Apple's help:** Matt Zapotosky (28 Mar 2016), "FBI
has accessed San Bernardino shooter's phone without Apple help," *Washington Post*,
https://www.washingtonpost.com/world/national-security/fbi-has-accessed-san
-bernardino-shooters-phone-without-apples-help/2016/03/28/e593a0e2-f52b-11e5
-9804-537defcc3cf6_story.html. David Kravets (1 Oct 2017), "FBI may keep secret the
name of vendor that cracked terrorist's iPhone," *Ars Technica*, https://arstechnica
.com/tech-policy/2017/10/fbi-does-not-have-to-disclose-payments-to-vendor-for
-iphone-cracking-tool.

174 **"Don't Panic":** Jonathan Zittrain et al. (Feb 2016), "Don't panic: Making progress on
the 'going dark' debate," *Berkman Center for Internet and Society, Harvard University*,
https://cyber.harvard.edu/pubrelease/dont-panic/Dont_Panic_Making_Progress
_on_Going_Dark_Debate.pdf.

175 **All the agency's current employees:** Susan Landau (2017), *Listening In: Cybersecurity in an Insecure Age*, Yale University Press, https://books.google.com/books
?id=QZ47DwAAQBAJ.

175 **"The FBI will need an investigative center":** Susan Landau (1 Mar 2016), "Testimony
for House Judiciary Committee hearing on 'The encryption tightrope: Rebalancing
Americans' security and privacy,'" https://judiciary.house.gov/wp-content/uploads
/2016/02/Landau-Written-Testimony.pdf.

175 **In addition to better computer forensics:** Steven M. Bellovin et al. (19 Aug 2014),
"Lawful hacking: Using existing vulnerabilities for wiretapping on the Internet,"
Northwestern Journal of Technology and Intellectual Property 12, no. 1, https://www
.ssrn.com/abstract=2312107.

176 **If the FBI is going to attract:** They're trying. Federal Bureau of Investigation (29 Dec
2014), "Most wanted talent: Seeking tech experts to become cyber special agents,"
https://www.fbi.gov/news/stories/fbi-seeking-tech-experts-to-become-cyber
-special-agents.

176 **The reality always falls short:** Neil Robinson and Emma Disley (10 Sep 2010), "Incentives and challenges for information sharing in the context of network and information security," *European Network and Information Security Agency*, https://www
.enisa.europa.eu/publications/incentives-and-barriers-to-information-sharing/at
_download/fullReport.

176 **This is rational:** Lawrence A. Gordon, Martin P. Loeb, and William Lucyshyn (Feb
2003), "Sharing information on computer systems security: An economic analysis,"
Journal of Accounting and Public Policy 22, no. 6, http://citeseerx.ist.psu.edu/viewdoc
/download?doi=10.1.1.598.6498&rep=rep1&type=pdf.

177 **The FAA maintains an anonymous database:** US Department of Homeland Security
(10 Sep 2015), "Enhancing resilience through cyber incident data sharing and analysis," https://www.dhs.gov/sites/default/files/publications/Data%20Categories%20
White%20Paper%20-%20508%20compliant.pdf.

177 **Another idea is to create:** Jonathan Bair et al. (forthcoming), "That was close!
Reward reporting of cybersecurity 'near misses,'" *Colorado Technology Law Journal*
16, no. 2, https://papers.ssrn.com/sol3/papers.cfm?abstract_id=3081216.

177 **This NCSB would investigate:** Neil Robinson (19 Jun 2012), "The case for a cyber-security safety board: A global view on risk," *RAND Blog*, https://www.rand .org/blog/2012/06/the-case-for-a-cyber-security-safety-board-a-global.html.

177 **the NTSB's annual "Most Wanted List":** National Transportation Safety Board (accessed 24 Apr 2018), "2017–2018 most wanted list," https://www.ntsb.gov/safety /mwl/Pages/default.aspx.

177 **the most critical changes needed:** Ben Rothke (19 Feb 2015), "It's time for a National Cybersecurity Safety Board (NCSB)," *CSO*, https://www.csoonline.com/article /2886326/security-awareness/it-s-time-for-a-national-cybersecurity-safety-board -ncsb.html.

177 **Nongovernmental networks like:** Sean Michael Kerner (27 Oct 2017), "Cyber Threat Alliance adds new members to security sharing group," *eWeek*, http://www.eweek.com /security/cyber-threat-alliance-adds-new-members-to-security-sharing-group.

178 **We also can't expect corporations:** The US indicted five members of the Chinese People's Liberation Army for these hacks in 2014. Michael S. Schmidt and David E. Sanger (19 May 2014), "5 in China army face U.S. charges of cyberattacks," *New York Times*, https://www.nytimes.com/2014/05/20/us/us-to-charge-chinese-workers -with-cyberspying.html.

178 **We shouldn't expect the Democratic and Republican:** Nicole Gaouette (10 Jan 2017), "FBI's Comey: Republicans also hacked by Russia," *CNN*, http://www.cnn.com /2017/01/10/politics/comey-republicans-hacked-russia/index.html.

178 **Is it a Cyber National Guard?:** In 2017, Representative Will Hurd proposed this. Frank Konkel (21 Jun 2017), "Lawmaker: Cyber National Guard could fill federal work-force gaps," *Nextgov*, http://www.nextgov.com/cybersecurity/2017/06/lawmaker -cyber-national-guard-could-fill-federal-workforce-gaps/138851.

179 **Estonia has a volunteer Cyber Defence Unit:** Monica M. Ruiz (9 Jan 2018), "Is Esto-nia's approach to cyber defense feasible in the United States?" *War on the Rocks*, https://warontherocks.com/2018/01/estonias-approach-cyber-defense-feasible -united-states.

10. PLAN B: WHAT'S LIKELY TO HAPPEN

180 **Despite some very strong words:** Martin Matishak (1 Jan 2018), "After Equifax breach, anger but no action in Congress," *Politico*, https://www.politico.com/story /2018/01/01/equifax-data-breach-congress-action-319631.

180 **Even a bill imposing the tiniest:** Robert McLean (15 Sep 2017), "Elizabeth Warren's Equifax bill would make credit freezes free," *CNN*, http://money.cnn.com/2017/09/15 /pf/warren-schatz-equifax/index.html.

180 **The only thing Congress did:** Devin Coldewey (24 Oct 2017), "Congress votes to disallow consumers from suing Equifax and other companies with arbitration agreements," *TechCrunch*, https://techcrunch.com/2017/10/24/congress-votes-to -disallow-consumers-from-suing-equifax-and-other-companies-with-arbitration -agreements/amp.

180 *Story two:* **The 2017 Internet of Things:** Mark R. Warner (1 Aug 2017), "Senators introduce bipartisan legislation to improve cybersecurity of 'Internet of things' (IoT) devices," https://www.warner.senate.gov/public/index.cfm/2017/8/enators-introduce -bipartisan-legislation-to-improve-cybersecurity-of-internet-of-things-iot-devices.

180 *Story three:* **In 2016, President Obama:** Barack Obama (9 Feb 2016), "Presidential

executive order: Commission on Enhancing National Cybersecurity," *Office of the President of the United States*, https://www.whitehouse.gov/the-press-office/2016/02 /09/executive-order-commission-enhancing-national-cybersecurity.

181 **At the end of that year:** Thomas E. Donilon et al. (1 Dec 2016), "Report on securing and growing the digital economy," *Commission on Enhancing National Cybersecurity*, https://www.nist.gov/sites/default/files/documents/2016/12/02/cybersecurity -commission-report-final-post.pdf.

181 **It's almost two years later:** Donald J. Trump (11 May 2017), "Presidential executive order on strengthening the cybersecurity of federal networks and critical infrastructure," *Office of the President of the United States*, https://www.whitehouse.gov /presidential-actions/presidential-executive-order-strengthening-cybersecurity -federal-networks-critical-infrastructure.

181 **No agency has yet followed that policy:** Nick Marinos (13 Feb 2018), "Critical infrastructure protection: Additional actions are essential for assessing cybersecurity framework adoption," *GAO-18-211, US Government Accountability Office*, https://www .gao.gov/assets/700/690112.pdf.

181 **The rest of the report has been ignored:** You could blame it on the dysfunctional administration, but I don't believe it would have fared much better in a different administration.

182 **Some observers have noted parallels:** *Economist* (8 Apr 2017), "How to manage the computer-security threat," https://www.economist.com/news/leaders/21720279 -incentives-software-firms-take-security-seriously-are-too-weak-how-manage.

182 **It was the 1965 publication of:** Christopher Jensen (26 Nov 2015), "50 years ago, *Unsafe at Any Speed* shook the auto world," *New York Times*, https://www.nytimes .com/2015/11/27/automobiles/50-years-ago-unsafe-at-any-speed-shook-the-auto -world.html.

184 **The GDPR—General Data Protection Regulation:** European Union (27 Apr 2016), "Regulation (EU) 2016/679 of the European Parliament and of the Council of 27 April 2016 on the protection of natural persons with regard to the processing of personal data and on the free movement of such data, and repealing Directive 95/46/EC (General Data Protection Regulation)," *Official Journal of the European Union*, http://eur -lex.europa.eu/eli/reg/2016/679/oj.

184 **For example, the GDPR mandates that:** This is a good short summary: Cennydd Bowles (12 Jan 2018), "A techie's rough guide to GDPR," https://www.cennydd.com /writing/a-techies-rough-guide-to-gdpr.

184 **The GDPR's regulations only affect:** Mark Scott and Laurens Cerulus (31 Jan 2018), "Europe's new data protection rules export privacy standards worldwide," *Politico*, https://www.politico.eu/article/europe-data-protection-privacy-standards-gdpr -general-protection-data-regulation.

185 **If companies have to explain:** This is already happening. In response to the GDPR, PayPal published a list of the 600+ companies it shares customer data with. It has taken the page offline, but the information has been saved. Rebecca Ricks (accessed 24 Apr 2018), "How PayPal shares your data," https://rebecca-ricks.com/paypal-data.

185 **Additionally, legislatures worldwide:** Mark Scott and Laurens Cerulus (31 Jan 2018), "Europe's new data protection rules export privacy standards worldwide," *Politico*, https://www.politico.eu/article/europe-data-protection-privacy-standards-gdpr -general-protection-data-regulation.

185 **Organizations are already doing things:** Clint Boulton (26 Jan 2017), "U.S. companies spending millions to satisfy Europe's GDPR," *CIO*, https://www.cio.com/article /3161920/privacy/article.html. Nick Ismail (2 May 2017), "Only 43% of organisations are preparing for GDPR," *Information Age*, http://www.information-age.com/43 -organisations-preparing-gdpr-123465995. Sarah Gordon (18 Jun 2017), "Businesses failing to prepare for EU rules on data protection," *Financial Times*, https://www.ft .com/content/28f4eff8-51bf-11e7-a1f2-db19572361bb.

185 **Fines can be as high as 4%:** EUGDPR.org (accessed 24 Apr 2018), "GDPR key changes," https://www.eugdpr.org/key-changes.html.

185 **The EU fined Google 2.4 billion euros:** Mark Scott (27 Jun 2017), "Google fined record $2.7 billion in E.U. antitrust ruling," *New York Times*, https://www.nytimes.com/2017 /06/27/technology/eu-google-fine.html. Aoife White and Mark Bergen (29 Aug 2017), "Google to comply with EU search demands to avoid more fines," *Bloomberg*, https:// www.bloomberg.com/news/articles/2017-08-29/google-faces-tuesday-deadline-as -clock-ticks-toward-new-eu-fines.

185 **Separately, the EU fined Facebook:** Hayley Tsukayama (18 May 2017), "Facebook will pay $122 million in fines to the E.U.," *Washington Post*, https://www.washingtonpost .com/news/the-switch/wp/2017/05/18/facebook-will-pay-122-million-in-fines-to -the-eu.

185 **Under the GDPR, the fine would:** Paul Roberts (2 Nov 2017), "Hilton was fined $700K for a data breach. Under GDPR it would be $420M," *Digital Guardian*, https:// digitalguardian.com/blog/hilton-was-fined-700k-data-breach-under-gdpr-it-would -be-420m.

186 **"The EU is already the world's":** Eireann Leverett, Richard Clayton, and Ross Anderson (6 Jun 2017), "Standardization and certification of the 'Internet of Things,'" *Institute for Consumer Policy*, https://www.conpolicy.de/en/news-detail/standardization -and-certification-of-the-internet-of-things.

186 **If European regulations force minimum:** In this way, software is similar to textbooks in the US market, where a few states effectively control what is available nationally because of their very onerous demands.

186 **In April 2018, Facebook announced:** Cyrus Farivar (4 Apr 2018), "CEO says Facebook will impose new privacy rules 'everywhere,'" *Ars Technica*, https://arstechnica .com/tech-policy/2018/04/ceo-says-facebook-will-impose-new-eu-privacy-rules -everywhere.

186 **Singapore has the Personal Data Protection Act:** Kennedy's Law LLP (20 Apr 2016), "Personal data privacy principles in Asia Pacific," http://www.kennedyslaw.com /dataprivacyapacguide2016.

186 **In 2017, India's Supreme Court:** Wire Staff (24 Aug 2017), "Right to privacy a fundamental right, says Supreme Court in unanimous verdict," *Wire*, https://thewire.in /170303/supreme-court-aadhaar-right-to-privacy.

187 **Singapore passed a new Cybersecurity Act:** Bryan Tan (9 Feb 2018), "Singapore finalises new Cybersecurity Act," *Out-Law*, https://www.out-law.com/en/articles /2018/february/singapore-finalises-new-cybersecurity-act.

187 **New Israeli security regulations:** Omer Tene (22 Mar 2017), "Israel enacts landmark data security notification regulations," *Privacy Tracker*, https://iapp.org/news /a/israel-enacts-landmark-data-security-notification-regulations.

187 **In 2016, New York fined Trump Hotels:** Steve Eder (24 Sep 2016), "Donald Trump's

hotel chain to pay penalty over data breaches," *New York Times*, https://www.nytimes
.com/2016/09/25/us/politics/trump-hotel-data.html.

187 **California investigated companies:** Adolfo Guzman-Lopez (2 Nov 2016), "California
attorney general warns tech companies about mining student data for profit," *Southern California Public Radio*, https://www.scpr.org/news/2016/11/02/65908/attorney
-general-warns-tech-companies-to-follow-ne.

187 **In 2017, Massachusetts sued Equifax:** Francine McKenna (15 Sep 2017), "Equifax
faces its biggest litigation threat from state attorneys general," *MarketWatch*, https://
www.marketwatch.com/story/equifax-faces-its-biggest-litigation-threat-from
-state-attorneys-general-2017-09-15/print.

187 **Missouri began investigating Google's:** Nitasha Tiku (14 Nov 2017), "State attorneys
general are Google's next headache," *Wired*, https://www.wired.com/story/state
-attorneys-general-are-googles-next-headache.

187 **Thirty-two state attorneys general:** Maria Armental (6 Sep 2017), "Lenovo reaches
$3.5 million settlement over preinstalled adware," *MarketWatch*, https://www
.marketwatch.com/story/lenovo-reaches-35-million-settlement-with-ftc-over
-preinstalled-adware-2017-09-05.

187 **Even the city of San Diego:** Brian Krebs (18 Mar 2018), "San Diego sues Experian over
ID theft service," *Krebs on Security*, https://krebsonsecurity.com/2018/03/san-diego
-sues-experian-over-id-theft-service.

187 **In 2019, these standards will also apply:** Michael Krimminger (25 Mar 2017), "New
York cybersecurity regulations for financial institutions enter into effect," *Harvard
Law School Forum on Corporate Governance and Financial Regulation*, https://corpgov
.law.harvard.edu/2017/03/25/new-york-cybersecurity-regulations-for-financial
-institutions-enter-into-effect.

187 **In 2017, California temporarily tabled:** Karl D. Belgum (21 Jun 2017), "Internet of
Things legislation in California is dead for this year, but it will be back," *Nixon Peabody*, http://web20.nixonpeabody.com/dataprivacy/Lists/Posts/Post.aspx?ID=1155.

187 **Ten other states debated legislation:** Eyragon Eidam and Jessica Mulholland (10
Apr 2017), "10 states take Internet privacy matters into their own hands," *Government Technology*, http://www.govtech.com/policy/10-States-Take-Internet-Privacy
-Matters-Into-Their-Own-Hands.html.

187 **"Teddy Bears and Toasters" bill:** California Legislative Information (accessed 24 Apr
2018), "SB-327 Information privacy: Connected devices," https://leginfo.legislature
.ca.gov/faces/billHistoryClient.xhtml?bill_id=201720180SB327.

188 **As this book went to press:** Alan L. Friel, Linda A. Goldstein, and Holly Al Melton
(31 Jan 2018), "AD-ttorneys@law—January 31, 2018," *Baker Hostetler*, https://www
.bakerlaw.com/alerts/ad-ttorneyslaw-january-31-2018.

188 **California's legislature is also considering:** Elizabeth Zima (23 Feb 2018), "California wants to govern bots and police user privacy on social media," *Government
Technology*, http://www.govtech.com/social/California-Wants-to-Govern-bots-and
-Police-User-Privacy-on-Social-Media.html.

188 **There are some things concerned consumers can do:** Deborah Gage (15 Sep 2017),
"Eight questions to ask before buying an internet-connected device," *Wall Street
Journal*, https://www.wsj.com/articles/eight-questions-to-ask-before-buying-an
-internet-connected-device-1505487931.

188 **There's plenty of good advice:** Here are two things to get you started: Electronic

Frontier Foundation (21 Oct 2014, last updated 21 Sep 2015), "Surveillance self-defense," https://ssd.eff.org. Motherboard Staff (15 Nov 2017), "The Motherboard guide to not getting hacked," *Vice Motherboard*, https://motherboard.vice.com/en_us/article/d3devm/motherboard-guide-to-not-getting-hacked-online-safety-guide.

189 **Two years previously, the Swedish Transport Agency:** Rick Falkvinge (21 Jul 2017), "Worst known governmental leak ever is slowly coming to light: Agency moved nation's secret data to 'the cloud,'" *Privacy News Online*, https://www.privateInternetaccess.com/blog/2017/07/swedish-transport-agency-worst-known-governmental-leak-ever-is-slowly-coming-to-light.

190 **Do you prefer Apple's iMessage:** For security, use Signal. If having Signal on your phone would be suspicious, use WhatsApp. Micah Lee (22 Jun 2016), "Battle of the secure messaging apps: How Signal beats WhatsApp," *Intercept*, https://theintercept.com/2016/06/22/battle-of-the-secure-messaging-apps-how-signal-beats-whatsapp.

190 **for example, Microsoft's ongoing battle:** Joe Uchill (23 Jun 2017), "DOJ applies to take Microsoft data warrant case to Supreme Court," *Hill*, http://thehill.com/policy/cybersecurity/339281-doj-applies-to-take-microsoft-data-warrant-case-to-supreme-court.

191 **Elsewhere I have argued that:** Bruce Schneier (2015), *Data and Goliath: The Hidden Battles to Collect Your Data and Control Your World*, W. W. Norton, https://books.google.com/books/?id=MwF-BAAAQBAJ.

11. WHERE POLICY CAN GO WRONG

193 **Luckily, the courts prevented:** Ian Urbina (23 Mar 2007), "Court rejects law limiting online pornography," *New York Times*, www.nytimes.com/2007/03/23/us/23porn.html.

193 **Not only does it not prevent:** Electronic Frontier Foundation (1 Mar 2013), "Unintended consequences: Fifteen years under the DMCA," https://www.eff.org/pages/unintended-consequences-fifteen-years-under-dmca.

193 **"The widespread use of robust":** Louis J. Freeh (9 Sep 1997), "The impact of encryption on public safety: Statement of the Director, Federal Bureau of Investigation, before the Permanent Select Committee on Intelligence, United States House of Representatives," https://fas.org/irp/congress/1997_hr/h970909f.htm.

193 **"As the gap between authority and":** Valerie Caproni (17 Feb 2011), "Statement before the House Judiciary Committee, Subcommittee on Crime, Terrorism, and Homeland Security," *Federal Bureau of Investigation*, https://archives.fbi.gov/archives/news/testimony/going-dark-lawful-electronic-surveillance-in-the-face-of-new-technologies.

193 **"We may not be able to identify":** James B. Comey (8 Jul 2015), "Going dark: Encryption, technology, and the balances between public safety and privacy," *Federal Bureau of Investigation*, https://www.fbi.gov/news/testimony/going-dark-encryption-technology-and-the-balances-between-public-safety-and-privacy.

194 **"But the advent of 'warrant-proof' encryption":** Rod J. Rosenstein (4 Oct 2017), "Deputy Attorney General Rod J. Rosenstein delivers remarks at the Cambridge Cyber Summit," *US Department of Justice*, https://www.justice.gov/opa/speech/deputy-attorney-general-rod-j-rosenstein-delivers-remarks-cambridge-cyber-summit.

194 **golden age of surveillance:** Peter Swire and Kenesa Ahmad are responsible for

that term. Peter Swire and Kenesa Ahmad (28 Nov 2011), "'Going dark' versus a 'golden age for surveillance,'" *Center for Democracy and Technology*, https://cdt.org /blog/%E2%80%98going-dark%E2%80%99-versus-a-%E2%80%98golden-age-for -surveillance%E2%80%99.

194 **The idea was called "key escrow":** Andi Wilson, Danielle Kehl, and Kevin Bankston (17 Jun 2015), "Doomed to repeat history? Lessons from the crypto wars of the 1990s," *New America Foundation*, https://www.newamerica.org/oti/doomed-to-repeat -history-lessons-from-the-crypto-wars-of-the-1990s.

194 **In the early 2000s, the FBI argued:** Federal Bureau of Investigation (3 Jun 1999), "Encryption: Impact on law enforcement," https://web.archive.org/web /20000815210233/https://www.fbi.gov/library/encrypt/en60399.pdf.

194 **A decade later, demands devolved:** Ellen Nakashima (16 Oct 2014), "FBI director: Tech companies should be required to make devices wiretap-friendly," *Washington Post*, https://www.washingtonpost.com/world/national-security/fbi-director-tech -companies-should-be-required-to-make-devices-wire-tap-friendly/2014/10/16 /93244408-555c-11e4-892e-602188e70e9c_story.html.

195 **Rosenstein has given this security-hostile proposal:** Rod J. Rosenstein (10 Oct 2017), "Deputy Attorney General Rod J. Rosenstein delivers remarks on encryption at the United States Naval Academy," *US Department of Justice*, https://www.justice.gov/opa /speech/deputy-attorney-general-rod-j-rosenstein-delivers-remarks-encryption -united-states-naval.

195 **UK policy makers are already implying:** Bhairav Acharya et al. (28 Jun 2017), "Deciphering the European encryption debate: United Kingdom," *New America*, https:// www.newamerica.org/oti/policy-papers/deciphering-european-encryption-debate -united-kingdom.

195 **In 2016, Croatia, France, Germany:** Amar Tooer (24 Aug 2016), "France and Germany want Europe to crack down on encryption," *Verge*, https://www.theverge.com /2016/8/24/12621834/france-germany-encryption-terorrism-eu-telegram. Catherine Stupp (22 Nov 2016), "Five member states want EU-wide laws on encryption," *Euractiv*, https://www.euractiv.com/section/social-europe-jobs/news/five-member -states-want-eu-wide-laws-on-encryption.

195 **Separately, the EU is considering legislation:** Samuel Gibbs (19 Jun 2017), "EU seeks to outlaw 'backdoors' in new data privacy proposals," *Guardian*, https://www .theguardian.com/technology/2017/jun/19/eu-outlaw-backdoors-new-data-privacy -proposals-uk-government-encrypted-communications-whatsapp.

195 **Australia is also trying to mandate access:** Rachel Baxendale (14 Jul 2017), "Laws could force companies to unlock encrypted messages of terrorists," *Australian*, http://www.theaustralian.com.au/national-affairs/laws-could-force-companies -to-unlock-encrypted-messages-of-terrorists/news-story/ed481d29c956dfac93610 61a60dcf590.

195 **In Brazil, courts temporarily shut down:** Vinod Sreeharsha (19 Jul 2016), "WhatsApp is briefly shut down in Brazil for a third time," *New York Times*, https://www.nytimes .com/2016/07/20/technology/whatsapp-is-briefly-shut-down-in-brazil-for-a-third -time.html.

195 **Egypt blocked the encrypted:** Mariella Moon (20 Dec 2016), "Egypt has blocked encrypted messaging app Signal," *Engadget*, https://www.engadget.com/2016/12/20 /egypt-blocks-signal.

195 **And both Russia:** Patrick Howell O'Neill (20 Jun 2016), "Russian bill requires encryption backdoors in all messenger apps," *Daily Dot*, https://www.dailydot.com/layer8/encryption-backdoor-russia-fsb. Adam Maida (18 Jul 2017), "Online and on all fronts: Russia's assault on freedom of expression," *Human Rights Watch*, https://www.hrw.org/report/2017/07/18/online-and-all-fronts/russias-assault-freedom-expression. Kenneth Rapoza (16 Oct 2017), "Russia fines cryptocurrency world's preferred messaging app, Telegram," *Forbes*, https://www.forbes.com/sites/kenrapoza/2017/10/16/russia-fines-cryptocurrency-worlds-preferred-messaging-app-telegram.

195 **and China:** Benjamin Haas (29 Jul 2017), "China blocks WhatsApp services as censors tighten grip on internet," *Guardian*, https://www.theguardian.com/technology/2017/jul/19/china-blocks-whatsapp-services-as-censors-tighten-grip-on-internet.

196 **If a company like Apple received:** Mallory Locklear (23 Oct 2017), "FBI tried and failed to unlock 7,000 encrypted devices," *Engadget*, https://www.engadget.com/2017/10/23/fbi-failed-unlock-7-000-encrypted-devices.

196 **"Any measure that weakens encryption":** Fred Upton et al. (20 Dec 2016), "Encryption working group year-end report," *House Judiciary Committee and House Energy and Commerce Committee Encryption Working Group, US House of Representatives*, https://judiciary.house.gov/wp-content/uploads/2016/12/20161220EWGFINALReport.pdf.

196 **"My personal view is that we should":** Steve Cannane (9 Nov 2017), "Cracking down on encryption could 'make it easier for hackers' to penetrate private services," *ABC News Australia*, http://www.abc.net.au/news/2017-11-10/former-mi5-chief-says-encryption-cut-could-lead-to-more-hacking/9136746.

196 **If Apple adds a backdoor:** Lily Hay Newman (21 Apr 2017), "Encrypted chat took over. Let's encrypt calls, too," *Wired*, https://www.wired.com/2017/04/encrypted-chat-took-now-encrypted-callings-turn.

197 **These controls ended when the Internet:** Whitfield Diffie and Susan Landau (1 Oct 2001), "The export of cryptography in the 20th century and the 21st," *Sun Microsystems*, https://pdfs.semanticscholar.org/1870/af818dd0075bb5e79764427a7c932fe3cfc6.pdf.

197 **In 2015, then–UK prime minister David Cameron:** British Broadcasting Corporation (12 Jan 2015), "David Cameron says new online data laws needed," *BBC News*, http://www.bbc.com/news/uk-politics-30778424. Andrew Griffin (12 Jan 2015), "WhatsApp and Snapchat could be banned under new surveillance plans," *Independent*, https://www.independent.co.uk/life-style/gadgets-and-tech/news/whatsapp-and-snapchat-could-be-banned-under-new-surveillance-plans-9973035.html.

197 **Current prime minister Theresa May:** Charles Riley (4 Jun 2017), "Theresa May: Internet must be regulated to prevent terrorism," *CNN*, http://money.cnn.com/2017/06/04/technology/social-media-terrorism-extremism-london/index.html.

198 **In 2016, I surveyed the market:** Bruce Schneier, Kathleen Seidel, and Saranya Vijayakumar (11 Feb 2016), "A worldwide survey of encryption products," *Publication 2016-2, Berkman Center for Internet & Society, Harvard University*, https://papers.ssrn.com/sol3/papers.cfm?abstract_id=2731160.

198 **Keeping those foreign products out:** Cory Doctorow (4 Jun 2017), "Theresa May wants to ban crypto: Here's what that would cost, and here's why it won't work anyway," *Boing Boing*, https://boingboing.net/2017/06/04/theresa-may-king-canute.html.

198 **In their attempts to demand backdoors:** Daniel Moore and Thomas Rid (Feb 2016), "Cryptopolitik and the Darknet," *Survival* 58, no. 1, https://www.tandfonline.com/doi /abs/10.1080/00396338.2016.1142085.

199 **"We believe that the greater public good":** Mike McConnell, Michael Chertoff, and William Lynn (28 Jul 2015), "Why the fear over ubiquitous data encryption is overblown," *Washington Post*, https://www.washingtonpost.com/opinions/the-need -for-ubiquitous-data-encryption/2015/07/28/3d145952-324e-11e5-8353-1215475949f4 _story.html.

200 **Anonymous speech is valuable:** Helen Nissenbaum (1 Sep 1998), "The meaning of anonymity in an information age," *Information Society* 15, http://www.cs.cornell.edu /~shmat/courses/cs5436/meaning-of-anonymity.pdf.

201 **The US government collected phone call metadata:** The NSA's bulk collection pro-gram ended in 2015. Now, the phone companies save the metadata, and the NSA is able to query the database on demand. This seems like a difference without a differ-ence. Charlie Savage (2 May 2017), "Reined-in NSA still collected 151 million phone records in '16," *New York Times*, https://www.nytimes.com/2017/05/02/us/politics/nsa -phone-records.html.

201 **Many local governments keep:** Catherine Crump et al. (17 Jul 2013), "You are being tracked: How license plate readers are being used to record Americans' move-ments," *American Civil Liberties Union*, https://www.aclu.org/files/assets/071613 -aclu-alprreport-opt-v05.pdf.

201 **Governments regularly demand access:** Fred H. Cate and James X. Dempsey, eds. (2017), *Bulk Collection: Systematic Government Access to Private-Sector Data*, Oxford University Press, http://www.oxfordscholarship.com/view/10.1093/oso /9780190685515.001.0001/oso-9780190685515.

201 **Making them a reality would require:** Jeanne Guillemin (1 Jul 2006), "Scientists and the history of biological weapons: A brief historical overview of the development of biological weapons in the twentieth century," *EMBO Reports* 7, http://www.ncbi.nlm .nih.gov/pmc/articles/PMC1490304.

202 **No amount of surveillance can stop:** Jim Harper (10 Nov 2009), "The search for answers in Fort Hood," *Cato at Liberty*, http://www.cato.org/blog/search-answers -fort-hood. Jim Harper (11 Nov 2009), "Fort Hood: Reaction, response, and rejoinder," *Cato at Liberty*, http://www.cato.org/blog/fort-hood-reaction-response-rejoinder.

202 **The failure to anticipate the Boston Marathon bombing:** Office of the Inspectors General for the Intelligence Community, Central Intelligence Agency, Department of Justice, and Department of Homeland Security (10 Apr 2014; unclassified summary released 6 Dec 2016), "Summary of information handling and sharing prior to the April 15, 2013 Boston Marathon bombings," https://www.dni.gov/index.php/who-we -are/organizations/ic-ig/ic-ig-news/1604.

203 **"active cyber defense":** Irving Lachow (22 Feb 2013), "Active cyber defense: A frame-work for policymakers," *Center for a New American Security*, https://www.cnas.org /publications/reports/active-cyber-defense-a-framework-for-policymakers.

203 **On the surface this might seem reasonable:** Patrick Lin lays out the various argu-ments well. Patrick Lin (26 Sep 2016), "Ethics of hacking back: Six arguments from armed conflict to zombies," *California Polytechnic State University, Ethics + Emerging Sciences Group*, http://ethics.calpoly.edu/hackingback.pdf.

203 **Vengeance is satisfying:** Josephine Wolff (17 Oct 2017), "Attack of the hack back," *Slate*, http://www.slate.com/articles/technology/future_tense/2017/10/hacking _back_the_worst_idea_in_cybersecurity_rises_again.html.

204 **Almost everybody agrees with this:** Josephine Wolff (14 Jul 2017), "When companies get hacked, should they be allowed to hack back?" *Atlantic*, https://www.theatlantic .com/business/archive/2017/07/hacking-back-active-defense/533679.

204 **Both the FBI and the Justice Department:** Jordan Robertson and Michael Riley (30 Dec 2013), "Would the U.S. really crack down on companies that hack back?" *Bloomberg*, https://www.bloomberg.com/news/2014-12-30/why-would-the-u-s -crack-down-on-companies-that-hack-back-.html.

204 **A 2017 bill legitimizing some:** Tom Graves (13 Oct 2017), "Rep. Tom Graves formally introduces active cyber defense bill," https://tomgraves.house.gov/news /documentsingle.aspx?DocumentID=398840.

204 **The main exception seems to be:** Stewart A. Baker (8 May 2013), "The attribution revolution: Raising the costs for hackers and their customers: Statement of Stewart A. Baker, Partner, Steptoe & Johnson LLP, before the Judiciary Committee's Subcommittee on Crime and Terrorism, United States Senate," https://www.judiciary.senate .gov/imo/media/doc/5-8-13BakerTestimony.pdf. Stewart A. Baker (11 Sep 2013), "Testimony of Stewart A. Baker before the Committee on Homeland Security and Governmental Affairs, United States Senate: The Department of Homeland Security at 10 Years: Examining Challenges and Addressing Emerging Threats," https://www.hsgac .senate.gov/hearings/the-department-of-homeland-security-at-10-years-examining -challenges-and-achievements-and-addressing-emerging-threats. Stewart A. Baker, Orin Kerr, and Eugene Volokh (2 Nov 2012), "The hackback debate," *Steptoe Cyberblog*, https://www.steptoecyberblog.com/2012/11/02/the-hackback-debate. Stewart A. Baker (22 Jul 2016), "The case for limited hackback rights," *Washington Post*, https:// www.washingtonpost.com/news/volokh-conspiracy/wp/2016/07/22/the-case-for -limited-hackback-rights.

205 **For example, what Mattel, Disney:** Charles Finocchiaro (18 Mar 2013), "Personal factory or catalyst for piracy? The hype, hysteria, and hard realities of consumer 3 -D printing," *Cardozo Arts and Entertainment Law Journal* 31, http://www.cardozoaelj .com/issues/archive/2012-13. Matthew Adam Susson (Apr 2013), "Watch the world 'burn': Copyright, micropatent and the emergence of 3D printing," *Chapman University School of Law*, http://papers.ssrn.com/sol3/papers.cfm?abstract_id=2253109.

206 **I worry that analogous laws:** Cory Doctorow (10 Jan 2012), "Lockdown: The coming war on general-purpose computing," *Boing Boing*, http://boingboing.net/2012/01/10 /lockdown.html. Cory Doctorow (23 Aug 2012), "The coming civil war over general purpose computing," *Boing Boing*, http://boingboing.net/2012/08/23/civilwar.html.

206 **With respect to radios, one solution:** Kristen Ann Woyach et al. (23–26 Sep 2008), "Crime and punishment for cognitive radios," *2008 46th Annual Allerton Conference on Communication, Control, and Computing*, http://ieeexplore.ieee.org/document/4797562.

12. TOWARDS A TRUSTED, RESILIENT, AND PEACEFUL INTERNET+

208 **On the Internet, the universe:** There's a lot to this trend that's beyond the scope of the book. Jean M. Twenge, W. Keith Campbell, and Nathan T. Carter (9 Sep 2014), "Declines in trust in others and confidence in institutions among American adults and late adolescents, 1972–2012," *Psychological Science* 25, no. 10, http://journals

.sagepub.com/doi/abs/10.1177/0956797614545133. David Halpern (12 Nov 2015), "Social trust is one of the most important measures that most people have never heard of—and it's moving," *Behavioural Insights Team*, http://www.behaviouralinsights.co .uk/uncategorized/social-trust-is-one-of-the-most-important-measures-that-most -people-have-never-heard-of-and-its-moving. Eric D. Gould and Alexander Hijzen (22 Aug 2016), "Growing apart, losing trust? The impact of inequality on social capital," *International Monetary Fund Working Paper* No. 16/176, https://www.imf.org /en/Publications/WP/Issues/2016/12/31/Growing-Apart-Losing-Trust-The-Impact -of-Inequality-on-Social-Capital-44197. Laura D'Olimpio (25 Oct 2016), "Fear, trust, and the social contract: What's lost in a society on permanent alert," *ABC News*, http://www.abc.net.au/news/2016-10-26/fear-trust--social-contract-society-on -permanent-alert/7959304.

208 **A 2017 survey illustrated that 70%:** Kenneth Olmstead (27 Sep 2017), "Most Americans think the government could be monitoring their phone calls and emails," *Pew Research Center*, http://www.pewresearch.org/fact-tank/2017/09/27/most -americans-think-the-government-could-be-monitoring-their-phone-calls-and -emails.

208 **"The success of the digital economy":** Thomas E. Donilon et al. (1 Dec 2016), "Report on securing and growing the digital economy," *Commission on Enhancing National Cybersecurity*, https://www.nist.gov/sites/default/files/documents/2016/12/02/cyber security-commission-report-final-post.pdf.

209 **In 2011, I published *Liars and Outliers*:** Bruce Schneier (2012), *Liars and Outliers: Enabling the Trust That Society Needs to Thrive*, Wiley, http://www.wiley.com/Wiley CDA/WileyTitle/productCd-1118143302.html.

209 **Surveillance capitalism is not sustainable:** Tim Hwang and Adi Kamdar (9 Oct 2013), "The theory of peak advertising and the future of the web," version 1, *Working Paper, Nesson Center for Internet Geophysics*, http://peakads.org/images/Peak _Ads.pdf.

210 **In particular, complex systems:** Charles Perrow (1999), *Normal Accidents: Living with High-Risk Technologies*, Princeton University Press, https://www.amazon.com /Normal-Accidents-Living-High-Risk-Technologies/dp/0691004129. Charles Perrow (1 Sep 1999), "Organizing to reduce the vulnerabilities of complexity," *Journal of Contingencies and Crisis Management* 7, no. 3, http://onlinelibrary.wiley.com/doi/10.1111 /1468-5973.00108/full.

211 **"Resilience is the capacity to cope with":** Aaron B. Wildavsky (1988), *Searching for Safety*, Transaction Publishers, https://books.google.com/books?id=rp6U8JsPlMoC.

211 **I have been talking about resilience:** Bruce Schneier (14 Nov 2001), "Resilient security and the Internet," *ICANN Community Meeting on Security and Stability of the Internet Naming and Address Allocation Systems, Los Angeles, California*, http://cyber .law.harvard.edu/icann/mdr2001/archive/pres/schneier.html. Black Hat (accessed 24 Apr 2018), "Speakers," *Black Hat Briefings '01, July 11–12 Las Vegas*, https://www .blackhat.com/html/bh-usa-01/bh-usa-01-speakers.html.

211 **"Good security systems are resilient":** Bruce Schneier (2006), *Beyond Fear: Thinking Sensibly about Security in an Uncertain World*, Springer, https://books.google.com/ books?id=btgLBwAAQBAJ&pg=PA120.

211 **In 2012, the World Economic Forum:** World Economic Forum (7 Jun 2012), "Risk and responsibility in a hyperconnected world: Pathways to global cyber resilience,"

https://www.weforum.org/reports/risk-and-responsibility-hyperconnected-world
-pathways-global-cyber-resilience.

211 **"The most resilient societies will likely be":** Gregory Treverton et al. (5 Jan 2017),
"Global trends: Paradox of progress," *NIC 2017-001, National Intelligence Council,*
https://www.dni.gov/files/documents/nic/GT-Full-Report.pdf.

213 **A 2017 report by the New York Cyber Task Force:** Jason Healey (28 Sep 2017), "Building a defensible cyberspace: Report of the New York Cyber Task Force," *Columbia
School of International and Public Affairs,* http://globalpolicy.columbia.edu/sites
/default/files/nyctf_2017-09-28_report.pdf.

213 **International laws regarding pollution:** Jason Healey and Hannah Pitts (1 Oct 2012),
"Applying international environmental legal norms to cyber statecraft," *I/S: A Journal
of Law and Policy for the Information Society* 8, no. 2, http://moritzlaw.osu.edu/students
/groups/is/files/2012/02/6.Healey.Pitts_.pdf.

213 **"Cyber peace is not the absence of attacks":** Scott J. Shackelford (1 Jan 2016),
*Managing Cyber Attacks in International Law, Business, and Relations: In Search of
Cyber Peace,* Cambridge University Press, https://books.google.com/books /?id
=_q2BAwAAQBAJ.

213 **"cyber peace must be grounded in":** Heather M. Roff (24 Feb 2016), "Cyber peace:
Cybersecurity through the lens of positive peace," *New America Foundation,* https://
static.newamerica.org/attachments/12554-cyber-peace/FOR%20PRINTING-Cyber
_Peace_Roff.2fbbbob16b69482e8b6312937607ad66.pdf.

CONCLUSION: BRING TECHNOLOGY AND POLICY TOGETHER

217 **"A technology that can give you everything":** Dan Geer (6 Aug 2007), "Measuring security," *USENIX Security Symposium,* http://geer.tinho.net/measuringsecurity
.tutorial.pdf.

218 **Yet when Deckard—Harrison Ford's character:** Economist Tim Harford recently
pointed this out. Tim Harford (8 Jul 2017), "What we get wrong about technology," *FT
Magazine,* http://timharford.com/2017/08/what-we-get-wrong-about-technology.

218 **We also tend to overestimate:** This "law" was coined by Stanford University computer scientist Roy Amara, who also directs the Institute for the Future. Matt Ridley
(12 Nov 2017), "Amara's law," *Matt Ridley Online,* http://www.rationaloptimist.com/
blog/amaras-law.

219 **This will lessen the relative advantages:** Bruce Schneier (Mar/Apr 2018), "Artificial
intelligence and the attack/defense balance," *IEEE Security & Privacy,* https://www
.schneier.com/essays/archives/2018/03/artificial_intellige.html.

220 **"Politics is the art of the possible":** Wikiquote (accessed 8 May 2018), "Otto von
Bismarck," https://en.wikiquote.org/wiki/Otto_von_Bismarck.

220 **"the lawyers and engineers whose arguments":** Nicholas Bohm, Ian Brown, and
Brian Gladman (31 Oct 2000), "Electronic commerce: Who carries the risk of fraud?"
Journal of Information, Law & Technology 2000, no. 3, http://www.ernest.net/writing
/FraudRiskAllocation.pdf.

221 **"I think much of the problem we face today":** Toomas Hendrik Ilves (31 Jan 2014),
"Rebooting trust? Freedom vs. security in cyberspace," *Office of the President, Republic of Estonia,* https://vp2006-2016.president.ee/en/official-duties/speeches/9796
-qrebooting-trust-freedom-vs-security-in-cyberspaceq.

222 **"Well the laws of Australia prevail":** James Titcomb (14 Jul 2017), "Malcolm Turnbull

says laws of Australia trump laws of mathematics as tech giants told to hand over encrypted messages," *Telegraph*, http://www.telegraph.co.uk/technology/2017/07/14 /malcolm-turnbull-says-laws-australia-trump-laws-mathematics.

222 **She's probably the best analyst:** Here, Sweeney describes research that led to the de-anonymization of medical data belonging to then–Massachusetts governor William Weld. Latanya Sweeney (8 Jan 2001), "Computational disclosure control: A primer on data privacy protection," http://groups.csail.mit.edu/mac/classes/6.805 /articles/privacy/sweeney-thesis-draft.pdf.

222 **She has also exposed bias in Internet algorithms:** Here's one paper: Latanya Sweeney (Jan 2013), "Discrimination in online ad delivery," *Communications of the Association of Computing Machinery* 56, no. 5, https://arxiv.org/abs/1301.6822.

222 **has made significant contributions to privacy technologies:** Latanya Sweeney (2002), "*k*-Anonymity: A model for protecting privacy," *International Journal on Uncertainty, Fuzziness and Knowledge-Based Systems* 10, no. 5, https://dataprivacylab .org/dataprivacy/projects/kanonymity/kanonymity.html.

223 **writing books and articles:** This is her latest book: Susan Landau (2017), *Listening In: Cybersecurity in an Insecure Age*, Yale University Press, https://books.google.com /books?id=QZ47DwAAQBAJ.

223 **testifying before Congress on the topic:** This is her latest testimony: Susan Landau (1 Mar 2016), "Testimony for House Judiciary Committee hearing on 'The encryption tightrope: Balancing Americans' security and privacy,'" https://judiciary.house.gov /wp-content/uploads/2016/02/Landau-Written-Testimony.pdf.

223 **He's probably best known:** Here's one paper: Ariel Feldman, J. Alex Halderman, and Edward W. Felten (13 Sep 2006), "Security analysis of the Diebold AccuVote-TS voting machine," *2007 USENIX/ACCURATE Electronic Voting Technology Workshop*, https:// citp.princeton.edu/research/voting.

223 **Through its Speech, Privacy, and Technology project:** American Civil Liberties Union (accessed 24 Apr 2018), "About the ACLU's Project on Speech, Privacy, and Technology," https://www.aclu.org/other/about-aclus-project-speech-privacy-and-technology.

224 **Many universities now offer:** A discussion of this trend, and a good list of programs, can be found here: Alan Davidson, Maria White, and Alex Fiorille (26 Feb 2018), "Building the future: Educating tomorrow's leaders in an era of rapid technological change," *New America/Freedman Consulting*.

224 **Internet Policy Research Initiative:** Internet Policy Research Initiative (accessed 24 Mar 2018), *Massachusetts Institute of Technology*, https://internetpolicy.mit.edu.

224 **Center on Privacy and Technology:** Georgetown Law (accessed 24 Apr 2018), "Center on Privacy & Technology," https://www.law.georgetown.edu/academics/centers -institutes/privacy-technology.

224 **Digital HKS program:** Digital HKS (accessed 24 Apr 2018), *Harvard Kennedy School*, https://projects.iq.harvard.edu/digitalhks/home.

224 **We need to create a viable career path:** NetGain is a consortium of large foundations that are trying to make this happen. Tom Freedman et al. (10 Feb 2016), "A pivotal moment: Developing a new generation of technologists for the public interest," *NetGain Partnership*, https://www.netgainpartnership.org/resources/2018/1/26 /a-pivotal-moment.

224 **A good model can be found:** Freedman Consulting (3 Mar 2006), "Here to there: Lessons from public interest law," unpublished memo.

224 **In the late 1960s, there were 92:** Robert L. Graham (1977), "Balancing the scales of justice: Financing public interest law in America," *Loyola University Chicago Law Journal* 8, no. 3, http://lawecommons.luc.edu/luclj/vol8/iss3/10.

224 **by 2000, there were over a thousand:** Laura Beth Nielsen and Catherine R. Albiston (1 Jan 2005), "The organization of public interest practice: 1975–2004," *North Carolina Law Review* 84, http://scholarship.law.berkeley.edu/facpubs/1618.

224 **Today, 20% of the graduating class:** Indeed, some consider this number to be embarrassingly low. Pete Davis (26 Oct 2017), "Our bicentennial crisis: A call to action for Harvard Law School's public interest mission," *Harvard Law Record*, http://hlrecord .org/wp-content/uploads/2017/10/OurBicentennialCrisis.pdf.

INDEX

ABOUT THE AUTHOR

Bruce Schneier is an internationally renowned security technologist, called a security guru by the *Economist*. He is the author of fourteen books—including the *New York Times* bestseller *Data and Goliath: The Hidden Battles to Collect Your Data and Control Your World*—as well as hundreds of articles, essays, and academic papers. His influential newsletter *Crypto-Gram* and blog *Schneier on Security* are read by more than 250,000 people. Schneier is a fellow at the Berkman Klein Center for Internet and Society at Harvard University; a lecturer in public policy at the Harvard Kennedy School; a board member of the Electronic Frontier Foundation, AccessNow, and the Tor Project; and an advisory board member of EPIC and VerifiedVoting.org. He is also a special advisor to IBM Security and the chief technology officer of IBM Resilient.